Everyman, I will go with thee,
and be thy guide

THE EVERYMAN
LIBRARY

*The Everyman Library was founded by J. M. Dent
in 1906. He chose the name Everyman because he wanted
to make available the best books ever written in every
field to the greatest number of people at the cheapest possible
price. He began with Boswell's 'Life of Johnson';
his one-thousandth title was Aristotle's 'Metaphysics',
by which time sales exceeded forty million.*

*Today Everyman paperbacks remain true to
J. M. Dent's aims and high standards, with a wide range
of titles at affordable prices in editions which address
the needs of today's readers. Each new text is reset to give
a clear, elegant page and to incorporate the latest thinking
and scholarship. Each book carries the pilgrim logo,
the character in 'Everyman', a medieval morality play,
a proud link between Everyman
past and present.*

Sophokles

THREE DRAMAS
OF OLD AGE

ELEKTRA, PHILOKTETES,
OIDIPOUS AT KOLONOS
WITH TRACKERS AND
OTHER SELECTED FRAGMENTS

Edited by
MICHAEL EWANS
University of Newcastle, Australia

Translated by
MICHAEL EWANS
GRAHAM LEY
GREGORY McCART

EVERYMAN
J. M. DENT · LONDON
CHARLES E. TUTTLE
VERMONT

This edition first published by Everyman Paperbacks in 2000

J. M. Dent
Orion Publishing Group
Orion House,
5 Upper St Martin's Lane, London WC2H 9EA
and
Tuttle Publishing
Airport Industrial Park
364 Innovation Drive
North Clarendon, VT 05759-9436, USA

Typeset in Sabon by SetSystems Limited, Saffron Walden, Essex
Printed in Great Britain by
The Guernsey Press Co. Ltd, Guernsey, C.I.

British Library Cataloguing-in-Publication Data
is available on request

ISBN 0 460 87742 9

CONTENTS

NOTES ON THE AUTHOR,
EDITOR AND TRANSLATORS

SOPHOKLES was born at Kolonos, a northern suburb of Athens, around 496 BC. At the age of sixteen he was selected to lead the dance, playing the lyre, at the celebrations for the Athenian victory over the Persian navy at Salamis, which ended Xerxes' hopes of conquering Greece. He won the prize with his first entry in the tragedy competition, at the age of twenty-eight. He had a distinguished public career at Athens; he was elected to serve two terms as a general, one as State Treasurer and one as Special State Commissioner. He was selected to compete at the annual Festival of Dionysos on approximately thirty occasions, and won the first prize eighteen times. He lived almost to the end of the twenty-four-year Peloponnesian War between Athens and Sparta; he died in 406 BC, at the age of ninety, leaving *Oidipous at Kolonos* to be produced posthumously by his grandson.

MICHAEL EWANS read Classics at Oxford and wrote his Cambridge PhD thesis on Aischylos. He was appointed in 1973 to a Lectureship in Classics at the University of Newcastle, Australia, and began teaching Drama when the discipline was introduced there in 1974. He became Associate Professor of Drama in 1982, was Head of the Department of Drama from 1982 to 1985, and is now Associate Professor of Drama and Music, with special responsibility for developing postgraduate studies. His publications include scholarly articles and programme notes on Greek tragedy and opera, his other main research field, and five books: *Janáček's Tragic Operas* (1977), *Wagner and Aeschylus* (1982), *Georg Büchner's 'Woyzeck'* (1989), and the Everyman Classics editions of *Aeschylus: 'Oresteia'*, and *Aeschylus: Suppliants and other Dramas*. He is also the editor of *Sophokles: Four Dramas of Maturity*. He has directed and supervised numerous productions of Greek tragedy, twentieth-century drama (especially expressionist plays) and opera.

GRAHAM LEY read Classics at Oxford and took his MPhil in Renaissance Historical Studies at the Warburg Institute in London. From 1977 he was Lecturer in Drama at the University of London, Goldsmiths' College, and was Australian Studies Fellow in Drama at the University of New South Wales in 1984. In 1986 he took up the post of Lecturer in Greek Literature in the University of Auckland, where he founded a training company, Sigma Theatre. From 1990 he became a text-writer and editor for Hutchinson Reference (Helicon), and was a supervisor for the faculties of English and Classics at Cambridge from 1994 to 1995. In 1995 he was appointed to a Lectureship in Drama at the University of Exeter. He has adapted and translated a number of Greek tragedies, directed in Auckland and Cambridge, and published many studies of ancient performance, including *A Short Introduction to the Ancient Greek Theater* (1991). He also writes on theatrical theory, in *From Mimesis to Interculturalism: Readings of Theatrical Theory Before and After Modernism* (1990) and, with Jane Milling, *Performance and Theory* (2000). He has been a consultant to professional productions of Greek tragedy, to the director John Barton, and to the Theatre Museum in London.

GREGORY MCCART studied English Literature and Classics at the University of Queensland, Australia. His involvement in the university drama society led him to a career training theatre practitioners and lecturing on Theatre Studies. He has been an actor and a playwright and has directed over forty university productions for the stage. He has translated, directed and performed ancient Greek drama and his commissioned translation of Euripides' *Medeia* was premiered by the Sydney Theatre Company in 1996. In recent years, he has explored the design, manufacture and use of the Greek tragic mask in performance and has conducted numerous workshops on the mask. He currently teaches at the University of Southern Queensland where, after serving as Head of Theatre Department and Associate Dean (Resources) in the Faculty of Arts for many years, he is currently Associate Professor, Director of the Performance Centre (www.usq.edu.au/performancecentre) and Chair of the University's Academic Board.

CHRONOLOGY OF SOPHOKLES' LIFE

Year	Age	Life
c. 496		Sophokles born at Kolonos, a northern suburb of Athens
490	6	
480	16	Leads the *choros* for the victory sacrifice at Salamis
468	28	Wins with his first entry in the tragedy competition

CHRONOLOGY OF HIS TIMES

Year	Age	Life
c.450–430	46–66	*Aias*
443/2	53	State Treasurer
441–39	55–7	General against Samos. Sails to fetch reinforcements from Chios and Lesbos
438	58	Wins the tragedy competition, probably with *Antigone*
438/7	59–60	General against the Samian dissidents at Anaia
431	65	second in tragic competition
430	66	?*Young Women of Trachis*
425	71	?*Oidipous the King*
421	75	Installs cult of Asklepios at his home

Year	Artistic & Historical Events
460–445	First Peloponnesian War
458	Aischylos, *Oresteia*
456/5	Aischylos dies at Gela in Sicily
455	Euripides wins tragedy competition for first time
449	Peace of Kallias ends hostilities with Persia
443	Ostracism of Thoukydides, son of Milesisas; Perikles becomes Athens' leading politician
441	Samian revolt from the Athenian Empire
439/8	Revolt on Samos put down by Perikles
438	Euripides second with four dramas including *Alkestis*, his first surviving drama
432	Athenian alliance with Kerkyra
431	Attika invaded by Peloponnesians. Start of the Peloponnesian War Aischylos' son Euphorion wins; Euripides is last with *Medeia*, his (lost) *Philoktetes*, and other dramas
430	First outbreak of the great plague at Athens
429	Euripides, *Hippolytos*, first edition (not performed) Death of Perikles
428	Euripides, *Hippolytos*; second version performed
425	Kleon becomes Athens' leading politician Aristophanes, *Acharnians* (his first surviving comedy)
424	Aristophanes, *Knights*
422	Death of Kleon Aristophanes, *Wasps*
421	Peace of Nikias between Athens and Sparta Aristophanes, *Peace*
420	Athens/Argos alliance

Year	Age	Life
413	83	*Elektra?* Serves as magistrate (Special State Commissioner)
409	87	*Philoktetes*
406	90	dies
401		*Oidipous at Kolonos* produced posthumously

Year	Artistic & Historical Events
416	Athenians sack Melos
415	Euripides, *Women of Troy* Athenian expedition to Sicily
c. 414	Euripides, *Iphigeneia among the Taurians*
414	Aristophanes, *Birds* Sparta resumes hostilities against Athens
413	Athenian defeat by Syracuse
412	Euripides, *Helene* (January) Aristophanes, *Lysistrata*
411	(March) Aristophanes, *Thesmophoriazousai* (May) Right-wing coup at Athens; government of the 'Four Hundred' (August) 'Four Hundred' expelled and replaced by moderate oligarchy of 'The Five Thousand'
410	Restoration of full democracy at Athens
408	Euripides, *Orestes*
408/7	Euripides leaves Athens for the court of Archelaos in Makedonia
406	Euripides dies leaving *Bakchai* and *Iphigeneia at Aulis* unperformed
405	Aristophanes, *Frogs* Final defeat of Athens at Aigispotamoi
404	Surrender of Athens and installation of Spartan-backed junta, 'The Thirty'.
403	Restoration of democracy and general amnesty

INTRODUCTION

The Fall of Athens

The Peloponnesian War, which began in 431 BC, apparently concluded with the 'Peace of Nikias' (422/1), which was welcomed by both sides: the Athenians as a consequence of their recent defeats at Delion and Amphipolis, and the Spartans because of a number of factors, especially the Athenian capture of 292 soldiers from the Spartan aristocracy who had become isolated on the island of Sphakteria in 425, and were still held hostage at Athens.[1] However, the peace was rapidly subverted, after the alliance between Athens and democratic Argos in 420, which seriously alarmed Sparta; and hostilities were covertly resumed, although technically the treaty remained in force.

During the next decade the balance of power tipped decisively against the Athenians: partly because of their disastrous decision to open up a second front, with a massive expedition to Sikilia which set sail in 415 and was completely annihilated by the Syrakousans in 413; partly by the Spartans' success in setting up an armed fortification at Dekeleia, twelve kilometres from Athens, also in 413; and finally by the involvement of the Persians in the war after 411, which led, together with Spartan naval action in Ionian Greece, to a series of revolts by island members of the Athenian Empire.[2]

The stress of these events caused increased tensions inside Athens. In the aftermath of the news of the defeat of the Sikilian expedition, the democracy established an emergency body of ten Special Commissioners to advise on the situation.[3] Sophokles, at the age of eighty-three, commanded enough support to be elected as a member of this body. However, anti-democratic conservatives felt that this was an inadequate measure, and they

[1] Thoukydides, *Histories* 5.14ff.
[2] The most important was that of the Milesians; Thoukydides 8.17.
[3] Thoukydides 8.1; Aristotle, *Athenian Constitution* 29.2.

staged a coup in 411,[4] which concentrated power in the hands of 400 individuals; they presented themselves as 'a more sensible form of government', and claimed that by moving to the right Athens might be able to secure Persian support.[5] The Special Commissioners apparently found favour with the junta; they were retained as members of a group of thirty entrusted with redrafting the Athenian constitution.

However, the Athenian navy, stationed in Samos, would not tolerate the change of government, and moderates among the Four Hundred attempted to cling to power by declaring themselves willing to make theirs truly a government of 'the Five Thousand'. This figure had been a paper fiction which the Four Hundred had inserted into their new constitution, to give it a quasi-democratic appearance;[6] it was designed to reflect the number of cavalry and bronze-armoured *hoplites*,[7] and to exclude the lower classes. However, this concession by the moderates did not prevent the government of the Four Hundred from being overthrown by the democrats after only four months; it could not survive the loss of Euboia and the threat of invasion by a Spartan fleet.

After the fall of the Four Hundred, plans were made for a government which genuinely was of the Five Thousand. Thoukydides – himself a member of the *hoplite* class – praised this as the best government Athens had in his lifetime;[8] but it would appear that a constitution was never formally drawn up or implemented, and over the next few months Athens reverted imperceptibly to democracy. This democracy was overthrown by the Spartans in 404, after their decisive victory at Aigispotamoi (one year after Sophokles' death). They installed a vicious right-wing régime, the Thirty, who began with show trials, and then instigated mass murder of all their political opponents;[9] internal peace was only restored when they were deposed in 403.

---

[4] Narratives in Thoukydides 8.45–97 and Aristotle, *Athenian Constitution* 29–33.

[5] Thoukydides 8.53, 3.

[6] Thoukydides 8.66, 89.

[7] All italicized Greek terms are defined in the Glossary.

[8] Thoukydides 8.97; cf. Aristotle, *Athenian Constitution* 33.2.

[9] Xenophon, *Hellenika* 2.3–4; Plato, *Letter* 7. The victims of the Thirty included Sokrates as well as all citizens with known democratic views.

This turbulent sequence of events, which led to the destruction of Athens as the fifth century had known it, was caused by an increasingly deteriorating political and social situation. After the death of Perikles, Athens had become excessively democratic, in the eyes of those who regarded themselves as *agathoi* by virtue of the traditional excellences of birth, wealth and their military ability as cavalry or *hoplites*. Winning this war did not depend primarily on the military skills of the *agathoi*, since Athens now depended for survival upon its navy, and the navy was manned by the lower classes; and inside the *polis* their traditional authority was no longer automatically accepted, in an assembly that valued persuasive rhetoric whatever its source.[10]

To counter these threats to their position, many *agathoi* turned to the sophists, who taught the art of speaking persuasively, and other skills which could lead to success in a newly hostile political environment. They also developed the traditional definition of *arete* in a new and sinister direction. Greek ideals of excellence had always given priority to the *agathos* himself and his *oikos*, and very few Athenians saw anything wrong with the desire to increase one's possessions at the expense of others, in the late fifth century ordinary men would still define *arete* as the ability to succeed in helping your *philoi* and harming your enemies.[11] However, in our sources for this period we repeatedly encounter ruthlessly amoral men who went considerably beyond this. They believed that 'might is right' and that absolutely any course of action is to be commended, provided that it succeeds in achieving your aim. What is expedient, is good.

There was also an increased feeling, as the war developed, that sudden change could happen at any time, and there was little point in believing in gods or oracles.[12] To many, *tychê* –

[10] An anonymous right-wing pamphleteer, known to scholars (misleadingly, since his prose style and many of his ideas are immature) as 'the Old Oligarch', brings these implications out starkly at [Pseudo-Xenophon] *Athenian Constitution* 1ff.

[11] E.g. Plato, *Meno* 71e; further citations at Kells 1973, 8; cf. Blundell 1989, *passim*.

[12] Cf. especially Thoukydides 2.52–3 – quoted and discussed at Ewans 1999. xxff., since these ideas are fundamental to the four surviving dramas from Sophokles' maturity.

the *daimôn* of fortune, of pure blind chance – seemed to rule the world.[13] With both human and divine sanctions in question, it was unclear whether there was any external basis for morality. 'What action is wrong, if it does not seem so to those who do it?' said Makareus in Euripides' *Aiolos*, justifying consensual sex with his sister Kanake.[14] Many claimed that there was no such thing as moral responsibility; love, for example, is an overwhelming force which cannot be resisted, and therefore absolves those under its influence from blame for their actions.[15]

These trends caused concern to every major writer of the period, whether their medium was tragedy, comedy, history or philosophy. Thoukydides singled out the discussions at Athens on how to deal with the revolt of Mytilene, and the abortive negotiations before the sack of Melos, and composed their essence into remarkable set-piece debates which expose, with chilling objectivity, the ruthlessness of Athenian *Realpolitik*. Plato in two separate dialogues re-created debates in which Sokrates attempted (with only partial success) to tackle head-on two unrepentant exponents of the doctrines that 'might is right' and 'justice is [effectively only] the interest of the stronger'.[16] Aristophanes repeatedly pillories the new amorality – in particular through the portrait of Kleon as Paphlagonian in *Knights*, the victory of the Unjust Argument in *Clouds*, and the character of Philokleon ('Kleon-lover') in *Wasps*.

The tragic playwrights also responded to these unpleasant aspects of the *Zeitgeist*. The later critic Kephisodoros compiled a rogues' gallery of 'objectionable quotations'; from Euripides, as well as Makareus' justification of incest, it included Hippolytos' repudiation of his sworn oath: 'it was my tongue that swore, and not my mind.'[17] Sophokles contributed *Elektra* 61:

[13] Cf. esp. Euripides, *Hekabe* 488ff., *Andromache* 458ff. Thoukydides, chronicling the significant military and political actions of the period, stresses frequently throughout his *Histories* the incidence of the unexpected, and the ways in which chance occurrences disrupted human expectation.

[14] Aristophanes, *Clouds* 1371 and ancient commentary *ad loc.*

[15] Gorgias, *Defence of Helene passim*; cf. Euripides, *Medeia* 530–31; *Hippolytos* 443.

[16] Plato, *Gorgias* (Kallikles) and *Republic* (Thrasymachos). Thrasymachos was a sophist from Kalkedon, and it is probable that Kallikles was a real historical figure, aligned with the Thirty Tyrants.

[17] *Hippolytos* 612, ridiculed by Aristophanes at *Thesmophoriazousai* 275

'For me, no spoken word is wrong, as long as it brings gain.'[18] Both playwrights created situations in which their characters could shock the audience by challenging the traditional belief in *miasma*. In *Orestes* (408 BC) Euripides' Helene feels no reason why she should not come near Orestes and Elektra, who have murdered her sister, their mother Klytaimestra (71ff.); over the next two years, Sophokles was to create a drama in which Oidipous argues that his ignorance of what he was doing absolves him from responsibility for incest and parricide (*Oidipous at Kolonos* 264ff., 975ff.).

Sophokles and Euripides were fiercely critical of the new, expedient amorality. The brutal speech and behaviour of Menelaos in *Andromache*[19] may primarily be a reflection of Spartan crimes against humanity in the early years of the Peloponnesian War – but the sentiments he utters were also beginning to be heard at Athens. The total self-interest and hypocrisy displayed by Odysseus, Agamemnon and Polymestor in *Hekabe* (c. 425), are matched in the shocking ending by Hekabe's own revenge. Like Sophokles' Elektra at line 1465, she becomes unexpectedly 'the stronger', and joins the three principal male characters in defining justice as whatever suits her own ends. And Euripides' critique of brutality becomes more overt in two subsequent dramas. The Athenians voted *Women of Troy*, which was performed three months after the sack of Melos, into third (and last) place, probably because the utter brutality and ruthlessness, with which the Greek chieftains treat the women and children who survived the sack of Troy, reflected all too closely on their own behaviour.

In *Orestes*, the last tragedy he created at Athens before departing into self-imposed exile in Makedonia, Euripides drastically reinflected the events after the murder of Klytaimestra to create a panoramic picture of a democratic mob, totally at the mercy of its demagogues, and a variety of ruthless aristocrats,

and at the climax of *Frogs* (1471). Iason's rejection of his marriage-vows in *Medeia* is no less discreditable.

[18] Athenaios, *Deipnosophistai* 122b–c, 582d4. A full Sophokles collection should also include Odysseus' remarks at *Phil* 107–18 (below, p.52), and two fragments from lost dramas: 'gain is sweet, even if achieved through lies', and 'do as all wise men do; praise Justice, but cling to gain' (frags. 833 and 28; Lloyd-Jones 1996, 367 and 23). See further Kells 1973, 6–7.

[19] 410ff., 440, 520.

both young and old, prepared to murder their kin in order to survive. It is hard to decide whose behaviour is more immoral between Orestes, Elektra and Pylades on the one side and Menelaos, Helene and Tyndareus on the other. The drama moves through a sequence of shocking scenes to an extraordinary climax: Orestes, having attempted to murder Helene, holds a dagger to the throat of her daughter Hermione on the roof of the *skene* while Menelaos and his men, finding the doors barred against them, threaten to set fire to the palace.

Sophokles did not evolve in his eighties towards a serene, detached contemplation of life.[20] I believe that the sack of Melos caused him to adopt as critical a response to the political and social behaviour of his fellow-Athenians as Thoukydides and Euripides. In all three of the dramas that survive from Sophokles' old age a towering central figure, suffering under the weight of past misdeeds, becomes enmeshed in a web of deceit. But there are few other similarities. *Elektra* is a devastating exposé of the new amorality, which Orestes and the Old Man practise from the outset; it consumes Elektra in her final blood-thirsty quest for revenge. Sophokles must have begun to write the text of *Philoktetes* soon after the coup and counter-coup of 411. In this drama Odysseus attempts to impose the philosophy of ruthless self-interest, lies and deceit on Neoptolemos, who stands in this drama for traditional *arete*; Neoptolemos' integrity eventually defeats Odysseus, and threatens to thwart the plans even of the gods. In *Oidipous at Kolonos* Oidipous gains the power to conquer both the hypocritical and vicious Kreon and the self-serving Polyneikes, reaffirming in an extraordinary way the traditional ideal of helping his friends and harming his enemies, as he consigns the remains of the Theban royal family to self-destruction and confers great benefits for the future on Athens.[21] A drama of transcendent hope for Athens when the text was completed in 406, *Oidipous at Kolonos* must have evoked bitterly ironic reactions when Sophokles' grandson presented it posthumously to the enfeebled democracy which was

[20] *Pace* esp. Grene 1967, an attempt to compare his last works with those of Shakespeare and Ibsen.
[21] There is the unpleasant side-effect that his curses will also destroy his beloved daughter Antigone (below, p. 50).

restored after defeat in the war and the ravages of the Thirty Tyrants.[22]

The New Tragedy

Aischylos' surviving tragedies, and the first four extant dramas of Sophokles, are all shaped to a similar pattern: the action gradually moves towards a climax which becomes more and more deeply expected as the drama unfolds; in Greek terms, a *moira* takes shape.[23] There is one great moment of revelation when (for example) Oidipous realizes who he is and what he has done in *Oidipous the King*, or when Herakles near the end of *Young Women of Trachis* realizes that his manner of death fulfils oracles that were given to him long ago. This moment does not inflict on the audience the shock of surprise; they are released from suspense, and the preceding action all makes sense, since it has now reached its inevitable culmination.

This pattern of action was not suited for creating dramas that responded to the events, and the Athenian perception of events, after around 420 BC. There was now little faith in divine patterns of causation; unexpected, chance reversals of fortune could suddenly, sometimes violently, alter the direction in which action appeared to be moving, and raise wholly new possibilities. Both Sophokles and Euripides accepted the challenge of devising a new kind of tragedy which reflected this new world. Some of the dramas that they created between 420 and 406 are theatrical experiments of startling boldness: for example, Euripides' *Women of Troy*, which is virtually without a plot or a coherent sequence of action, and inhabits a timeless no-man's land almost prophetic of Samuel Beckett's world; or his *Orestes*, where almost every successive scene provides a new and totally unexpected twist of events. In this drama the passions and hatreds of the characters drive the action so far away from the legendary course of events after the death of Klytaimestra that Apollo is needed to appear on the *mechane* and reimpose the traditional sequence 'by means of a solution so inadequate and

[22] Cf. further p. li below; also McCart, below, p. 270, on Choros 2.

[23] Ewans 1996b provides a discussion of this process, with reference to Aristotle on tragedy and to Shakespeare's *Macbeth* and *Hamlet* as well as to Sophokles. (On Aischylos, cf. Ewans 1995, xxviiff.)

so unreal by contrast with the created reality of the play that it is doomed into insignificance.'[24] Much the same might be said of *Philoktetes*, which Sophokles had created in the previous year; the action reaches a satisfying conclusion when Neoptolemos suddenly and unexpectedly resolves to take Philoktetes back to his home; so once again a (demi-)god on the *mechane* needs to intervene to reimpose the 'correct' outcome required by the tradition, in which Philoktetes went to Troy and was instrumental in its sack.[25]

In this period Sophokles and Euripides applied the 'reversals of fortune' and 'recognitions', which Aristotle was later to regard as central to 'complex tragedy', to new ends.[26] In earlier tragedy there was normally only one person or oracular truth to be recognized, and only one (or at most two) reversals of fortune, usually at the climax of the drama. For example, in *Aias* there are two reversals of fortune: Aias' death, and his reintegration when the funeral cortège is finally able to form and depart; and one truth is recognized: Aias must remain in his tent for this one day, or die. But in these later dramas reversal becomes central, and the fortunes of the central figure rise and fall throughout the drama. After the first scene *Elektra* entirely revolves around the heroine's reactions to successive intrusions of good news and bad. Klytaimestra's dream portends the return of Orestes (Scene 2); Orestes is reported dead (Scene 3); offerings have been laid at Agamemnon's grave, which indicate that Orestes is alive and back in Argos (Scene 4); Orestes is visibly dead – here is the urn that contains his ashes (Scene 5); Orestes is in fact alive, and here (also Scene 5). Similar reversals afflict Philoktetes throughout his drama (will these Greeks give him his homecoming, or not?) and Oidipous at Kolonos (will he be able to win the help of Athens, and repel the attempts by Kreon and Polyneikes to enlist him for their own selfish ends?).

In all three late Sophoklean dramas a satisfactory ending is reached – but not by the direct, cumulative method that Sophokles and Euripides had inherited from Aischylos. Sophokles in one surviving drama, and Euripides in nine, found it necessary

[24] Arrowsmith 1958, 110.
[25] Below, p. xl.
[26] Aristotle, *Poetics* 50a33–5, 52a12ff. For a detailed analysis of Euripides' 'tragedies of mixed reversal' see Burnett 1971.

for a god to intervene on the *mechane*, so the position to which the human characters' behaviour had brought the action could be reconciled with a traditional outcome to the legend. And in all their dramas after 420, the audience is deliberately not given precise expectations. There is nothing in the earlier phases of the action to correspond, for example, with the prophecy of Kalchas which predicts the death of Agamemnon at Klytaimestra's hands in Aischylos' *Agamemnon* (148ff.), Aphrodite's clear declaration of her intent at the beginning of Euripides' *Hippolytos* (42ff.), or the full and terrifying prophecy by Teiresias which tells the audience exactly what the outcome will be in *Oidipous the King* (449ff.).

Euripides in his later work either dispenses entirely with initial information about the likely course of the action, or places such speculation in the mouth of a character whose knowledge is limited;[27] Sophokles follows a similar strategy. In *Elektra* the oracle given to Orestes merely tells him how to go about his revenge, if he wishes to succeed; the contrast with Aischylos' *Libation Bearers* is acute.[28] So when the climax is reached, it is very far from certain whether the revenge will be accomplished.[29] In fact it is, but Sophokles then shocked his Athenian audience outrageously at the end. In both Aischylos and Euripides the Furies pursued Orestes, calling for vengeance for his murdered mother. In Sophokles' brave new world, Orestes and Elektra are left alone, untroubled by gods or goddesses from Olympos or from the underworld, to live happily ever after – if they can.[30]

Oidipous at Kolonos might seem at first sight to belong to a more traditional format, since Oidipous in his address to the Furies at 84ff. informs the audience of a prophecy by Apollo that he would here find his final resting-place, and be called to his death by thunder and lightning. And the expectations set up by this speech are totally fulfilled by the action from Scene 5 to

---

[27] E.g. *Andromache, Elektra, Iphigeneia among the Taurians, Orestes*. The exception that proves the rule is *Bakchai*, which deliberately reverts to the earlier, authoritative opening for its almost Aischylean story of a powerful god and his terrible revenge.

[28] Below, p. 184.

[29] As the Old Man points out (1326ff.), Elektra has imperilled the entire project by her protracted song and dance of joy after she recognized Orestes.

[30] Below, p. 219.

the end. But this appearance is misleading. By choosing to dramatize a local legend that Oidipous was buried in a sacred grove in his own *deme* of Kolonos, Sophokles gave himself the freedom to invent his own version of the events after Oidipous' discovery of who he is and what he has done, accepting or rejecting whatever he liked both from his own earlier *Antigone* and from other stories, including those dramatized in Euripides' Theban dramas. As a result, nothing that happens between Scene 1 and Scene 5 is predictable or expected;[31] Sophokles does exactly what he wants with his situation and his characters, between setting up Oidipous' arrival near the grove of the Furies, and sounding the *bronteion* to signify that the gods are calling him to die within it.[32]

These new kinds of stories were accompanied by innovative dramatic forms. Both Sophokles and Euripides experimented with new ways of using song and dance in tragedy. *Elektra* is remarkable for the extended *kommos* between Elektra and the Women, which performs the function of a Choros 1. Similar lyric dialogues had followed the first entry of the *choros* before;[33] but there had been nothing to equal this in length and complexity. Sophokles went on to compose a similar though shorter *kommos* for the entry of the *choros* in *Philoktetes*, and an extended *kommos* with Philoktetes as Choros 5. The long Choros 1 *kommos* in *Oidipous at Kolonos* uses *antilabe* as well; see below.

Another advanced technique is the splitting of a choral ode, so the *strophe* is danced some considerable time before the corresponding (and correspondingly choreographed) *anti-strophe*, and separated from it by spoken dialogue. This device is used in *Philoktetes* to subdivide the long scene between Neoptolemos and Philoktetes (391ff. and 507ff.), and in *Oidi-*

---

[31] Some critics have been considerably unsettled by this. Waldock (1951, 218–28) claimed that Sophokles had to improvise to 'fill out the middle' between Oidipous' arrival at Kolonos and his apotheosis; Tanner (1966) speculates that inconsistencies between scenes demonstrate that Sophokles composed a first draft in 407, and added some of the middle scenes (parts of the confrontation with Kreon, and the whole Polyneikes scene) after the execution of the Arginou-sai generals in 406.

[32] Below, pp. xlvff.

[33] E.g. in Euripides' *Elektra, Hekabe, Women of Troy*.

pous at Kolonos to punctuate the extremely violent sequence where Kreon abducts Antigone (832ff. and 875ff.).[34]

The honour of having created the most drastic surviving experiment must go to Euripides, for the sensational appearance in *Orestes* (1368ff.), in place of a messenger-speech, of a Phrygian slave, who enters by climbing down the *skene* façade, gibbering free-form lyrics that are only half intelligible; but Sophokles' experiments were also radical. Perhaps the most remarkable use of lyrics in these three tragedies is Choros 4 of *Elektra*, where Sophokles imports into lyrics the device of *antilabe*, dividing some lines between four singers to express the close-bonded agony with which Elektra and the Women of Argos respond to the 'death of Orestes'. The same technique is used in *Oidipous at Kolonos*, both in Choros 1 and at the centre of Scene 2 (510ff.), where the Elders probe Oidipous about his parricide and incest; there is also a complex interaction between Antigone, Ismene and the Elders in the Finale.[35]

These late dramas are also notable for their use of the playing space, and in particular for the relationship between action in the *orchêstra* and the *skene* façade.[36] In all three of the tragedies collected in this volume the action begins with a sequence in which characters arriving from one of the *parodoi* quickly establish a close interaction with the place represented by the façade, and describe it in detail: the 'house of many deaths' at Mykenai; Philoktetes' cave; and the grove of the Furies at Kolonos. It has been disputed whether the Athenians represented such locations with scenery. There has been an occasional fashion for the minimalist position, which claims that the *skene* remained unaltered between dramas and the Athenian play-

---

[34] The fragment from *Eurypylos* (frag. 3 below) shows the reverse of this process, with a messenger-speech divided into two by a *kommos* between the *choros* and the mother of the young man whose death the messenger is narrating, to show the intensity of her reaction to her suffering.

[35] Note esp. the B stanzas (1724ff.), where the singers are altered between the two stanzas, while the metric patterning and division remain totally parallel.

[36] Newcomers to Greek tragedy are recommended to Ley 1991 for a concise but comprehensive account of the performance space. Several significant aspects of Greek tragedy are also discussed in the introductions to previous volumes in this series: the playing space and style of performance in Ewans 1995, xviiiff.; the origins of tragedy and its role in society in Ewans 1996a, xvff.; and Sophokles' dramatic methods in Ewans 1999, xxivff.

wrights required the audience to use their imagination to 'create' the place where the action was set.[37] However, the three contributors to this volume are convinced that these locations were represented in *skenographia*, painted panels affixed to the façade of the *skene* for the duration of a drama.[38] In each of these three tragedies the newcomers are confronted with a locale that is wholly unknown to them;[39] and in each case they need to enter into a relationship with the locale to ensure the success of their enterprise. In the first two dramas this involves deceiving the inhabitant(s) of the place represented by the *skene*, and in *Oidipous at Kolonos* Oidipous must pass from an improper to a proper relationship with the goddesses inside the grove. In all three dramas the importance of the location represented by the *skene* is established by the interaction with it in the first scene; the primary focus is then transferred to the actors in the *orchêstra*, and this relative neglect of the *skene* during a large part of the action prepares by contrast for a decisive entry into it at a climax later on in the drama.[40]

These three tragedies all demand a consummate performance from the lead actor in the title role, and the range of emotion is so great that the protagonist must be able to sing and dance. Each of the title figures is also marked out completely from the other characters by appearance: Elektra is beaten and bruised, in mourning and dressed like a slave; Philoktetes wears rags or animal skins after ten years alone on an island, and limps with a foul sore on his foot; Oidipous enters blind, in rags, bearing a beggar's wallet for food scraps. By contrast every other charac-

[37] Cf. esp. Arnott 1962 and Brown 1984b. The affinity in other respects between Greek tragedy and the equally rich open-air verse drama of the Elizabethans is misleading. Shakespeare's spectators needed to use their imaginations to fill the Globe because his action sometimes took place in locations that could not conceivably be represented by Elizabethan scenic artistry; also because those locations changed frequently. The Athenians in the fifth century were very proud of their innovations in the visual arts, and normally the action of one tragedy was confined to a single location; so for them scene-painting was both practicable and desirable.

[38] On *skenographia* in the fifth century see Ley 1989.

[39] Except for the Old Man in *El*, who introduces Orestes (and Pylades) to the house of Pelops.

[40] See our Notes below on the ending of *El* Scene 5, *Phil* Scene 2 and *OKol* Scene 6.

ter in the three dramas, except Antigone, is well-dressed and clean.[41]

In all three dramas – perhaps especially in *Elektra* – the emotional range required of the principal actor is quite extraordinary, and his or her intense sufferings – mental and emotional in the cases of Elektra and Oidipous, but literal and physical as well for Philoktetes – become the principal focus of attention in scene after scene. The reactions of these title figures to the changes in their fortunes, as the drama unfolds, constitute the throughline of these tragedies; they will therefore be the main preoccupation of any director, since she or he must work as closely as possible with a gifted and highly trained actor in the title role for any hope of success. It is therefore unfortunate that many scholars have preferred to focus rather on physical properties.[42] There are of course moments where props are important, just as there are climaxes at which Sophokles used the special effects available in his theatre;[43] but a Greek tragedy was primarily a performance involving up to three masked actors and a *choros* inside a circular playing space, and their interaction – what they do, and when they do it – needs to be the primary focus of study.

Elektra

Agamemnon's three daughters Chrysothemis, Laodike and Iphianassa appear in Homer.[44] A seventh-century lyric poet, Xanthos, was the first to use the name Elektra, which means 'the unbedded woman' (i.e. one who remained a *parthenos* beyond the normal age for marriage), and identify her with Laodike.[45] The sixth-century Sikilian choral poet Stesichoros

---

[41] It is irresistible to mark out Elektra's defiance of the régime by costuming both Chrysothemis and Klytaimestra as richly as possible.

[42] Cf. e.g. the Chicago conference on *El*, where no fewer than two papers and one production concept were devoted to the urn (Dunn 1996).

[43] See below, pp. 199 and 210ff., 244ff., 260–1 on the altar and urn in *El*, Philoktetes' bow, and the two benches in *OKol*; p. 218 on the *ekkyklêma* in *El*; p. 253 on the *mechane* in *Phil*; and p. 281 on the *bronteion* in *OKol*.

[44] *Iliad* 9.145. The story of the sacrifice at Aulis of an additional, eldest sister – Iphigeneia – first appeared in Stasinos' poem *Kypria*, written in the eighth century.

[45] Aelian, *Varia Historia* 4.26.

created a substantial poem called *Oresteia*, which was indebted to Xanthos' work;[46] this in turn was undoubtedly studied and used by Aischylos when he created the *Oresteia* for performance in 458. Since Elektra is a character in Aischylos' trilogy, it is probable that Stesichoros took up Xanthos' idea and included her in his version of the story.

The central drama of Aischylos' *Oresteia, Libation Bearers*, dramatizes Orestes' return, and his revenge killing of Aigisthos and Klytaimestra. Euripides was confident that most of his audience would know it, doubtless because it had been recently revived, when he mocked Aischylos' recognition scene in his own *Elektra*.[47] It is evident that Sophokles also created his drama in the knowledge of Aischylos', and could expect some of his audience to be aware of the ways in which he has accepted unchanged, creatively modified or deliberately deviated from the Aischylean version.[48]

Libation Bearers dramatizes Orestes' gathering of the powers, both human and divine, that made it possible for him to achieve his revenge. The drama focuses on his dilemma, and even includes at the climax a scene – never attempted in any subsequent treatment of this story, ancient or modern – in which mother confronts son in front of the spectators and pleads for mercy. The god Apollo has commanded Aischylos' Orestes to kill his mother, and has warned of the most horrific penalties from his father's Furies if he does not do this deed (269ff.); but against that Klytaimestra raises the threat of a mother's avenging Furies (924). Faced with the choice of two equally appalling consequences if he does or does not do a deed commanded by the gods, Orestes chooses to do it: 'you killed, and it was wrong; now suffer wrong' (930).[49]

Aischylos' Elektra lives 'like a slave' (135); none the less, she prays that she may be a better woman than her mother, and achieve the Greek female ideal of *sophrosyne*: self-control, and reverence (140–41). After the recognition scene with Orestes,

---

[46] Athenaios, *Deipnosophistai* 513a.

[47] Euripides, *Elektra* 520ff.

[48] This can of course be taken too far. Several critics have written as if the Sophoklean audience had *Libation Bearers* almost constantly in their minds; cf. e.g. Jebb 1894, xlii. *Contra* Stevens 1978, 112.

[49] Translation from Ewans 1995, 84.

and an extended lyric *kommos* in which brother and sister invoke the power of their dead father to help them with their vengeance, Orestes assigns to Elektra the passive part of supervising what goes on inside the palace (579), while he, with Pylades, intrigues to gain admission; her speaking part ends here.[50]

Sophokles' main divergences from Aischylos should now be obvious. Like Euripides in his *Elektra*,[51] Sophokles focuses throughout on the sufferings of the humiliated, endlessly waiting daughter; also like Euripides, Sophokles removes the divine pressure for – and eventual condonation of – matricide which Aischylos dramatized in the *Oresteia*; the behaviour of his Orestes and Elektra is viewed less than favourably. His Elektra has conspicuously lost the *sophrosyne* of Aischylos' character;[52] and she confronts Klytaimestra in a bitter *agôn*, to thrash out the rights and wrongs of her mother's murder of her father. She takes over the Libation-Bearers' role in getting Klytaimestra's offerings turned against her (by Chrysothemis, who does not appear in Aischylos); and she takes over their subsequent role in luring Aigisthos to his death.[53] She has also become the Nurse who in Aischylos raised Orestes, while his mother neglected him.[54] There is one more new element, totally absent from Aischylos but present in Euripides' treatment of the legend: Elektra's sexual frustration. In Euripides she is jealous of her more sexually attractive mother; in Sophokles she has an implacable anger against Klytaimestra for taking Aigisthos into what had been her father's bed (272ff.).

All these innovations have a significant place in Sophokles' design; but that design is a subject of acute controversy. Most interpreters read *Elektra* as a drama in which Sophokles expected his audience to approve of the 'heroic constancy' of Elektra,[55] and to be gratified by the triumph of Orestes and Elektra. Jebb wrote of 'a deed of unalloyed merit, which brings the troubles of the house to an end', and more recent commen-

---

[50] However, I argue in Ewans 1995, 177–8 and 188 that Elektra should be present as a silent figure in Scenes 3 and 7.

[51] Euripides probably created his *Elektra* before Sophokles (below, p. 181).

[52] Below, Notes on Choros 1 and Scene 2. Cf. esp. 307ff.

[53] *Libation Bearers* Scene 5; *El* Finale.

[54] *Libation Bearers* 749ff.; *El* 1143ff.

[55] Jebb 1894, xxii.

tators have elaborated on this reading.⁵⁶ However, it seems to me to be quite impossible, in the light of what actually happens in the Finale;⁵⁷ it also interprets *Elektra* without any reference to its cultural context.⁵⁸

Sophokles unambiguously aligned his Orestes with the new, ruthless amorality in his opening speech.⁵⁹ Elektra lectures Klytaimestra on the deserts that revenge-killers incur (580–83); it apparently does not occur to her that 'this is an awkward principle for a person intent on murder'.⁶⁰ Orestes picks up her theme at the end of the drama, when he delivers to the audience a complacent little lecture on the desirability of summary execution (1505–8).⁶¹

Clearly Elektra's remark about the danger of revenge-killing could well be applied to Elektra and Orestes themselves, as well as to Klytaimestra and Aigisthos. But at the end of the drama it is not applied to them. In this version of the legend, and this version alone, Elektra is freed for evermore by the murders (1508–10), and there is no hint that his mother's Furies will pursue Orestes.⁶² Having become 'the stronger', Elektra and

---

⁵⁶ Jebb 1894, xl. Cf. e.g. Bowra 1944, 260: 'a new light shines for men. Justice and order are restored, and even in the welter of vengeance and hatred rises a new force of love'; also Whitman 1951, 171. This reading has been aggressively (but no more convincingly) revived by Gardiner 1987, 164ff. and March 1996.

⁵⁷ See Notes below, pp. 215ff.

⁵⁸ The alternative interpretation of *El* which I develop in this volume would not have been possible without the pioneering work of Sheppard (1918, 1927) and Kells (1973).

⁵⁹ Above, pp. xviiff. A failure adequately to distinguish the new amorality from traditional *arete* undermines the critique of Kells by Stevens 1978.

⁶⁰ Gellie 1972, 110; cf. Segal 1966, 537.

⁶¹ Capital punishment without trial was regarded as a characteristic of anti-democratic tyrannies and oligarchies (Kells 1973, 12). Athenian democrats suffered exactly this fate at the hands of the Thirty Tyrants, after their final defeat in the war (Aristotle, *Constitution of Athens* 35; cf. Plato, *Letter* 7). Segal (1966, 534) rightly compares Orestes' preference for instant 'justice' to Kleon's deeply disturbing position on the fate of the Mytileneans (Thoukydides, *Histories* 3.38) – one which the Athenian *demos*, fortunately for the Mytileneans, rejected.

⁶² 1508–10; cf. Waldock 1951, 190–91. *Contra* Winnington-Ingram 1980, 226–8; also, less subtly, the many critics who insist that we are to imagine the Furies as gathering to pursue Orestes, as they do in Aischylos. But almost the entire point of using previously known stories was the impact that could be

Orestes stand at the end among the most unpleasant represen-
tatives of the 'new amorality'. Ruthless and remorseless, they
have quite literally got away with murder.[63]

The extremism of their position has been demonstrated far
earlier in the drama, by the reactions of both the Women of
Argos and Chrysothemis to Elektra's behaviour. Elektra is an
outsider, deprived of the privileges of her rank for her defiance.
She is treated like a slave, and accordingly suffers poverty,
hardship and physical violence (1192ff.). But when she is faced
with the Women's opposition to her decision to defy the rulers
and suffer, Elektra is forced to admit that her behaviour is self-
destructive;[64] and Sophokles created the character of her sister
Chrysothemis to bring out the fact that Elektra did not make
the only possible choice. Critics who romantically admire Elektra's 'heroic defiance' have repeatedly condemned Chrysothemis
for cowardice and muddled thinking.[65] This destroys their
chances of interpreting Sophokles' tragedy, which was created
in a city and by a dramatist whose morality placed a realistic,
non-Romantic focus on a person's own best interests.

Late fifth-century Athenians valued prudence and expediency
far above self-sacrifice. They were well aware of the choices that
need to be made when living under an oligarchy, a tyranny, or
an imperialist regime, and the consequences that can be suffered
by real people living in such societies.[66] So Chrysothemis'

made by deviating in particular respects from earlier visions. The Furies
appeared to Orestes at the end of Aischylos' *Libation Bearers* (1048ff.), and
their appearance is imminent at the end of Euripides, *Elektra* (1342ff.). So the
absence of the Furies in *El* is arguably even more striking and significant than
the absence of Herakles' apotheosis at the end of *YWT* (cf. Ley's Notes in
Ewans 1999, 264).

[63] As Seale notes (1982, 82 n. 43), the remorselessness of Elektra and Orestes
'does not underline the justice of their cause but rather points to their moral
bankruptcy'. *Contra* e.g. March 1996, 78–81.

[64] See commentary below on Choros 1 and Scene 1, pp. 229–30ff.

[65] For relatively recent examples cf. Gardiner 1987, 164 and Blundell 1989,
157–8; 'Chrysothemis fails . . . to do what she admits is just. She produces no
argument to explain this lapse beyond the "necessity" of physical convenience
(339ff.).' Those who lived, for example, in Eastern Europe during the hegemony
of the USSR would have no difficulty in telling Blundell just how real is the
necessity which she apostrophizes so lightly.

[66] Cf. Adkins 1960, 195–240.

position in Scene 2 would have been perceived as sound.[67] Later, in Scene 4, Chrysothemis is absolutely right about the facts: Orestes did indeed leave the offerings that she has found; she is also morally right, when she argues (992ff.) against a suicidal attempt by the sisters to kill Aigisthos.[68] Elektra's scorn for her sister's belief is based on a faith in words which the audience knows to be misplaced; and her plan for vengeance is totally idealistic and impractical, and is rightly rebuffed by Chrysothemis. So there is a hideous irony to the entire scene;[69] although Chrysothemis is right, there is no further place for her in Sophokles' drama.[70] Elektra, who is wrong, wins out in the end, while Chrysothemis' rightness and practical wisdom have become 'wrong', in the sickening world of the Finale.

The linchpin around which *Elektra* revolves is the end of Scene 1. Orestes is about to depart when he is interrupted by an outcry, which he rightly suspects to be from Elektra. But the Old Man turns on him, reaffirms in 82ff. the idea of the *kairos*, the right moment for action (which Orestes himself had put forward at 75–6), and overrides Orestes' instinctive desire to stay. 'So they go. Had they only waited, Electra might have learnt the truth at once, and have been spared at least the agony of hearing the grim messenger's unseemly eloquence, which bids her think her brother, whom she loves, is dead.'[71]

[67] See further below, pp. 190ff.

[68] Readers should be warned that this view, that Chrysothemis is right, is 'an absurd conclusion' (Winnington-Ingram 1980, 246) to most modern classical scholars.

[69] Gellie partly caught this (1972, 118): 'Elektra . . . is magisterial, realistic and wrong; Chrysothemis is made to sound romantic and naïve, and she is right.' But he credits Elektra with much more realism, and debits far more naïveté from Chrysothemis, than we could find when rehearsing the text.

[70] Von Hofmannsthal sensed this imbalance, and introduced into his '*Elektra: Tragedy after Sophokles*' a third appearance of Chrysothemis, to crystallize the contrast between the two sisters after the murders (Ewans 1984, 149–51).

[71] Sheppard 1927, 5. Aischylos' Orestes actually waited two minutes to see if the approaching woman who looks like his sister really is Elektra (*Libation Bearers* 10–21); so his Elektra recognizes Orestes early in the drama, and is fully involved in the plan and the deception. Euripides' tactic in his *Elektra* was very similar, so Sophokles' deviation from the traditional sequence is very significant (cf. Wilamowitz 1917, 168–9). As Seale notes (1982, 80), 'distance is created out of virtual contact' (cf. also Reinhardt 1979, 139). Perhaps therefore in performance the Sophoklean Orestes should hesitate, and leave with a mime of reluctance to emphasize the point.

Elektra triumphs at the end. But she has already been corroded by years of physical and emotional abuse and seemingly endless waiting.[72] So the effect on her of Orestes' deception in Scenes 1, 3 and 5 is so great that she becomes an example of a figure who is tragic because she 'loses in the winning'.[73] In performance, the central feature of *Elektra* is the sequence of emotional depths and heights which the title character suffers.[74] The Old Man, who insists in Scene 1 that right now is the *kairos* for going to pour libations, will manage to choose his *kairos* precisely 'right' once again, when he enters in Scene 3 and delivers his all-too-credible account of 'Orestes' death', just after Klytaimestra's prayer to Apollo; by doing this, he wounds Elektra irretrievably. His success in both scenes assists in the fulfilment of the vengeance; but it will destroy Elektra, who receives her good news too late, and after she has already been convinced that it can never come. Ruthless self-interest and treachery do not always help your *philoi*, especially when combined with haste.

The action of the drama subjects Elektra to a sequence of alternately believing that Orestes' return is imminent, and that he is dead. When she is finally reunited with him, she tells Orestes that 'you've wounded me in ways I cannot understand' (1315); and she is so deluded that she believes the Old Man to be her father returned (1361). After that her madness becomes even greater, and she becomes a dementedly ruthless and insatiable avenger. Elektra's triumph is marred by her savagery as Klytaimestra is being murdered ('if you can, strike twice as hard', 1415), by her hideous toying with Aigisthos, and by her demand that he be denied two basic rights: a last speech and decent burial. Meanwhile the whole revenge is overshadowed by the telling points that Aigisthos makes in the last exchanges

---

[72] Cf. Segal 1966, 505ff. and Gellie 1972, 122ff.

[73] Smith 1973, 10.

[74] I cannot accept the view of Reinhardt (1979, 140) and Vickers (1973, 569–70) (cf. also Stevens 1978, 115) that this tragedy is diminished because the audience is aware from the outset that Elektra's deliverance from suffering is at hand. This is precisely the challenge of Sophokles' strategy; he deliberately privileges the spectators in Scene 1, so they can observe the subsequent effects on Elektra of the conspirators' choice not to stay. *El* is a quite different kind of *tragoidia* from, say, *Ant* – but in its own way it is just as tragic.

with Orestes, and the self-righteous complacency of Orestes' final words; and above all by the absence of the Furies.[75]

This story of revenge powerfully evokes the ruthless political assassinations, also committed under the cloak of 'justice', which had increasingly disfigured Greek life as the Peloponnesian War went on.[76] *Elektra* reinflects the Orestes myth to create a searing indictment of the new 'amoralists', as tough in its own way as Euripides' more blatant but equally trenchant *Orestes*. It is also a remarkable study in psychopathology: Elektra's personality is destroyed before the spectators' eyes by her extreme devotion to her father's memory.[77]

Elektra is another tragedy, like *Young Women of Trachis*, in which the normal three-way opposition of the performing space is 'skewed'. The left *parodos*, leading to downtown Argos, is used only by the Women of Argos when they enter and leave, and by Aigisthos near the end. This drama is primarily a dialogue between the female-dominated interior of the *skene* and a succession of male entries from the right *parodos*, which represents the road from Agamemnon's grave and, further, from Orestes' place of exile.[78]

The *skene* represents the palace at Mykenai. Given the horror inside which is evoked in the opening description (10), Sophokles might well have commissioned for *Elektra*, as we did for our production, scenic panels that presented a less prepossessing, more sinister façade than the standard *skenographia* for a neutral palace exterior.[79] But this drama does not show the obsession with the *skene/orchêstra* boundary, and with control

[75] See Notes below on Scene 5 and the Finale. The dark tone of the last scenes is underscored by the use of imagery and the perversion of rituals throughout the drama, on which see Segal 1966 and 1981, and Seaford 1985.

[76] Cf. Thoukydides' analysis at *Histories* 3.82ff.

[77] In the light of other major tragedies in which the central figure goes mad (e.g. *King Lear*, *Woyzeck*, *Kát'a Kabanová*) I cannot agree with Waldock (1951, 188) that 'there can be no tragedy in a work of fiction, if the character concerned does not feel it.' Elektra's progressive deterioration is precisely the source of this drama's tragic stature.

[78] Cf. Ewans 1999, lx–lxi on *YWT*. Chrysothemis, a female, does of course re-enter for Scene 4 from the right *parodos*; but she enters bringing news of the offerings which two male youths have left on Agamemnon's grave.

[79] Euripides' choice of a peasant's hut for the setting for his *Elektra* was an even more radical reorientation from the noble façade of the house of Atreus, which Aischylos had presented in the *Oresteia*.

or domination of the threshold, which is evident in Aischylos' dramatization of the same story.[80] Crossing the boundary between darkness and light is important at Elektra's first appearance, and becomes so again towards the climax of the drama, when the Old Man – after gaining admission by his narrative of 'Orestes' death' – guards the threshold against anyone coming from inside to overhear, and then hurries Orestes and Pylades inside for the murder. The role of guardian is then reversed, when Elektra reappears to guard against Aigisthos' return, and on his arrival ushers him in a sinister way towards the threshold, where he encounters the *ekkyklêma* bearing the shrouded body of his wife.[81] Similarly, the action twice focuses around the altar of Apollo, when first Klytaimestra in Scene 3, and then Elektra at the end of Scene 5, pray to the god. But elsewhere, this is a drama that requires the use of the whole *orchêstra*, and repeatedly returns to the contrast between focus at the centre and positions nearer to the periphery, which was the most significant single aspect of the Athenian performance space.[82]

Elektra is focused around its protagonist, who speaks or sings almost exactly 39 per cent of the lines. This intransigent, passionate heroine dominates the drama, more even than Sophokles' other great, suffering, isolated title figures (Aias, Antigone, Philoktetes). A production will fail unless Chrysothemis and Klytaimestra are sensitively and well portrayed; but no performance of *Elektra* can succeed unless director and principal actress create a credible throughline for Elektra, from the devastated grief of Choros 1 to the dementia and savagery of the Finale, and invest every phase of her emotional journey with intensity and total credibility.[83]

[80] Taplin 1977, 299–300; Ewans 1995, 126–7 and ff.; cf. Rehm 1992, 98.

[81] 1458ff. This moment has been briefly prefigured, when Elektra pretends to act as usher to Orestes and Pylades at 1323ff.

[82] Cf. Notes below, esp. on Scenes 2, 3 and 4 – the three confrontational *agones* in the centre of the drama.

[83] I owe much to the Australian professional actress and dancer Alida Vanin, who performed the title role in my own 1998 production, and gave me direct understanding of what this extraordinary role requires for credible realization in the theatre.

Philoktetes

Sophokles created this tragedy less than two years after he had played a central and difficult role during the coup and counter-coup of 411, which had affected him both as a Special Commissioner, forced to approve the installation of a regime that he found repulsive, and as a resident in the *deme* of Kolonos, which the Four Hundred chose as their rallying place.[84] Once again the subject-matter is chosen in a way that maximizes audience uncertainty and suspense; just as the sequence of good news and bad to which Elektra is subjected between Scene 1 and the recognition of Orestes is totally unpredictable, so too here almost anything can happen – and several remarkable incidents do! – between the arrival of Odysseus and Neoptolemos on Philoktetes' island, and the departure of all three commanders to win the Trojan War.[85]

Philoktetes is the most overtly political and ethical of Sophokles' suriviving dramas;[86] its relevance to the Athenian context is even more direct than that of *Antigone*. By making Lemnos a desert island, Sophokles creates a laboratory experiment in which the three principal characters represent three different models of *arete*, removed from their Athenian context and set in an *eremia*.[87] The *skene* façade represents Philoktetes' cave, so the action takes place between the right *parodos*, leading directly to the savage *eremia* of the rest of the island, and the left *parodos* leading to the Greek ship. Philoktetes is the only character who enters from the right; in this way his cave is established as a temporary living-space which is poised between *eremia* and civilization. Philoktetes enters from the deserted space in which he has lived alone, and he departs at the end with Neoptolemos to the harbour and therefore back to civilization. As in the Athenian assembly, there are no women present; Odysseus and Neoptolemos play out their attempt to

[84] Sophokles and the 400; Aristotle, *Rhetoric* 19a25ff. Kolonos; Thoukydides 8.67.

[85] Cf. Seale 1982, 30. This deliberate uncertainty about possible events in the middle of the drama is taken even further in *OKol*; below, pp. xlvff.

[86] Kitto 1956; cf. esp. 108–9 on Scene 1.

[87] For discussion of the importance of *eremia* in *Phil*, and of Sophokles' innovations in contrast to the previous versions of this story by Aischylos and Euripides, see Ley's Notes below, pp. 220ff.

deceive Philoktetes with only the *choros* of Sailors as accomplices; they might be taken to represent the attitudes of ordinary, decent but not particularly perceptive Athenian citizens.[88] Odysseus and Neoptolemos represent contrasting types which the Athenian audience would, by this stage of the war and of their political decline, have found immediately recognizable. Neoptolemos' principal role in legend, as the bloodthirsty conqueror who murdered King Priam at an altar, is banished from the drama;[89] from the outset *Philoktetes* stresses his ancestry as the son of Achilleus, and his nobility as king of Skyros.[90] He is also an *ephebos*, making the transition from boy to young warrior.[91] He therefore stands for traditional, inherited ideals of *arete*. He wants to play his proper role as the junior *agathos*, and respect as much as possible the authority of Odysseus and the Atreidai; but he finds this increasingly difficult because it involves deceit and lies, not open combat (79, 86ff.).[92]

Sophokles' Odysseus is a ruthless schemer, for whom any means are acceptable as long as they serve his ends.[93] By the end of Scene 1 Odysseus has been firmly established – like Orestes at a comparable point in *Elektra* – as a representative of the new amorality, willing without hesitation to lie and cheat if it will help to achieve his ends.[94] Neoptolemos reluctantly

---

[88] On the characterization of the Sailors see Gardiner 1987, 19–20, 46–9.

[89] Except for some ominous words from Herakles at the end (1440ff.). Winnington-Ingram (1980, 302–3) rightly compares the way in which hints at Antigone's future death are injected into the final scene of *OKol*.

[90] 3–4, 138ff. Neoptolemos' noble father is contrasted with both Odysseus and the sons of Atreus throughout the drama; references at Kitto 1956, 114.

[91] Cf. e.g. 79–80, 95–6. Vidal-Naquet 1981, ch. 7.

[92] Cf. Blundell 1989, 189–90.

[93] 55ff., 100ff. This characterization of Odysseus, which is not Homeric, was already so developed thirty or forty years before *Phil* that the Sailors and Tekmessa in *Ai* (where Odysseus actually plays a noble and gentle role) expect the worst from him (*Ai* 189, 952–73.). Cf. also Euripides, *Hekabe*. Myths involving Odysseus, and using the rumour that he was the bastard son of the trickster king Sisyphos, not the true descendant of the royal house of Ithaka (cf. e.g. *Phil* 417, 1312), were useful when Sophokles or Euripides wished to portray amoral expediency. On the evolution of Odysseus' character from Homer onwards, cf. Stanford 1968.

[94] NB in this scene 109, 111. As Segal notes (1995, 102) in later scenes Odysseus interprets the gods' will as being coextensive with his own (989ff., 1293–4). Cf. the revolutionaries and counter-revolutionaries described in Thoukydides, *Histories* 3.82.

agrees (120), well aware that by doing so he may incur shame; and avoiding shame was the single most important motivation of the traditional *agathos*, in Sophokles' time no less than in the Homeric age.

The rest of the action revolves around Neoptolemos' sequence of oscillations; his mental anguish as he attempts to suppress his aristocratic heritage and adopt the 'new values' of expediency and ruthlessness reaches a climax in 895ff.; and the attempt breaks down in the Finale, where he refuses to deceive any further, and consents to take Philoktetes back to his homeland, as he had asked.

The protagonist, of course, was anything but a common figure, in Athens or elsewhere. Sophokles' radical decision to depopulate prehistoric Lemnos enables him to create an extra-ordinary Philoktetes.[95] In his isolation and his pain Philoktetes has become a savage, living in a primitive condition, and unable to care hygienically for his incurable wound.[96] His betrayal by the Greek chieftains has made him cynical about a world in which rogues flourish and honest men die (446ff.);[97] his physical misery, though originally due to violation of a goddess's sanc-tuary (192ff.), is also an indictment of the brutality of the Atreidai who abandoned him on Lemnos.[98] Philoktetes is not the 'noble savage' of the eighteenth-century Enlightenment – unlike Robinson Crusoe, he has replicated none of the trappings of civilization on his island, even after ten years; but he fulfils a similar role in this drama. Isolation and excruciating pain have not diminished Philoktetes' immense *arete* (symbolized in the theatre by the great bow of Herakles, which he alone can

[95] It is a particularly daring rewrite of mythology, since Lemnos was the site for a notorious incident, the massacre of their menfolk by the women of Lemnos (alluded to as the worst of all crimes by the *choros* in Aischylos' *Libation Bearers*, 631ff.).

[96] Sophokles establishes these facts very early, when Neoptolemos approaches the mouth of Philoktetes' cave and describes its contents to Odysseus (31ff.).

[97] This was precisely the malady of contemporary Athens, as diagnosed by both Thoukydides (*Histories* 6.15) and Aristophanes (*Frogs* 686–737). It is fascinating that Sophokles created such a jaundiced view of his city in a drama composed during the rule of the 'Five Thousand', which in the view of both Thoukydides (then in exile) and Aristotle (one hundred years later) was the best government Athens ever had (above, n.8). Living in Athens at the time, Sophokles was clearly less sanguine.

[98] Kitto 1956, 110–11.

wield);[99] they have sharpened it to an uncompromising ideal, and his hatred for those who have wronged him takes absolute priority.[100] When he sings Choros 5 with the Sailors, Philoktetes is revealed as having been almost driven mad by the length of his suffering; he would rather die than help his enemies. By this point in the drama the audience has been encouraged to admire even this extreme breach of their morality, which always ultimately placed one's own interests first.[101] As Ley argues acutely below,[102] Philoktetes in several ways resembles one who is dead; and death was the most extreme negation of self-interest in a society that believed in an afterlife populated only by shadows.

This scene is followed by the first part of the Finale, in which the two great opposing values of the late fifth century – what is expedient, and what is just – come into overt opposition. Neoptolemos now wrests control from Odysseus, who has attempted throughout to direct the action of the drama; Philoktetes wields his bow, almost kills Odysseus, and banishes him from the scene for the rest of the drama; then Neoptolemos deploys Helenos' prophecy in full, placing intense pressure on Philoktetes to come to Troy.[103]

Philoktetes now faces a dilemma which is almost insoluble in Greek ethics: he is required by his new *philos*, Neoptolemos, to help his enemies (1350ff.; 1386).[104] His living death on Lemnos, his suffering and his obduracy make one outcome inevitable. He still refuses to go; and in the remainder of the action neither Neoptolemos nor Herakles blames Philoktetes for this; indeed, Neoptolemos accepts that Philoktetes' position is 'reasonable' (1373). So Neoptolemos agrees to take him home; the outcome is as the audience have been led to hope and expect. Neoptolemos displays his *arete*, casts off the baleful influence of the

[99] Although Philoktetes carries it from his first appearance at 219, Sophokles deliberately does not draw attention to this prop until 654. From there on it plays an increasingly important role.

[100] Blundell 1989, esp. 217–19.

[101] Kitto 1956, 126; Winnington-Ingram 1980, 293–4. There is a clear parallel with the effect on the audience of *Ant* Scene 5; cf. Ley's Notes below, pp. 249ff.

[102] p. 225.

[103] On the theatricalist dimensions of *Phil* cf. Ley, below, pp. 225ff.; on Odysseus' precipitate departure at 1304, cf. Seale 1982, 43.

[104] Winnington-Ingram 1980, 295–6.

amoral Odysseus, and undertakes to help his friend (1401ff.). Philoktetes, the victim of the Atreidai, and Neoptolemos, whom they have tried to use as a pawn, leave them to their thoroughly deserved fate of being unable to sack Troy.

Sophokles has at this point created an 'impossible' situation, very much like, though perhaps not quite as extreme as, that which Euripides was to devise the next year in *Orestes*. The human action has, through a sequence of surprising but plausible developments, reached a point totally opposed to the ending demanded by the myth.[105] And, like Euripides, he sends in a god on the *mechane* to provide the element of persuasion that no human being (not even Neoptolemos) could achieve; by showing Philoktetes that it is truly in his interest to go to Troy, Herakles restores the ending the audience expected, from post-Homeric epic and from previous theatrical treatments of the myth. Philoktetes obeys Herakles; he takes his bow, goes willingly to Troy, and together with Neoptolemos becomes instrumental in its sack. The wound will be cured, and in the last moments of the drama the island which has been so hostile to Philoktetes' existence for ten years becomes benign.[106]

This resolution raises fascinating ironies. The honest behaviour of Neoptolemos, after he escapes from his reluctant consent to go along with Odysseus' scheme of deception, may well have been admirable for the majority of Sophokles' Athenian audience (and hopefully will still seem so for modern spectators as well); but it is not necessarily what the gods want;[107] indeed, their final solution vindicates Odysseus' ends (if not his means)! Naturally, therefore, scholars have been divided on the implications. For Kitto the 'second ending' imposed by Herakles is wholly detached from that of the main action; the god dissolves Philoktetes' refusal, and redirects his new bond of *philia* with Neoptolemos to Troy, without invalidating Philoktetes' earlier

---

[105] On *Orestes* see above, p. xxi. For similar distances between the realities of the point just reached by the previous human action and the pronouncement delivered by the god from the *mechane* cf. also Euripides *Andromache*, *Elektra* and *Iphigeneia among the Taurians*.

[106] 1452ff.; Segal 1995, 115.

[107] Winnington-Ingram 1980, 299. 'Philoctetes must go to Troy as a free agent, yet it is, apparently, what the gods – and not merely the Greeks – have done to him that makes this virtually impossible. Can the gods have it both ways? Of course they can: they are gods. They send Heracles.'

decision.[108] By contrast, for Segal the ending reasserts *eusebeia*, piety or reverence for the gods, which Philoktetes conspicuously lacked both in his violation of the precinct of the island-goddess Chryse, and in his cynical view of the gods earlier in the drama (442–6). Hence the prophetic warning at 1140ff., and Herakles' closing emphasis on 'the imperishable piety'.[109]

It is certainly true in Sophokles' tragedy that the gods sent Odysseus to Lemnos, as Philoktetes says at 1035ff.; and Neoptolemos views Philoktetes' afflictions as part of a divine plan at 191ff. But it is also true, as the Sailors sing at 168ff., that Philoktetes' ten years of suffering on Lemnos are a strong example of the excess of suffering which the gods' contrivances inflict on mortals. Given our knowledge of the despair and cynicism that were endemic at Athens during the later years of the war, it is difficult to see how Sophokles could have asserted the wisdom of divine providence in a drama performed at Athens in 409 without being laughed out of the theatre.

The prophecy that underlies the action of *Philoktetes* is one of those 'if-clauses', familiar to viewers of Sophokles from his earlier dramas.[110] If Herakles in *Young Women of Trachis* completes the sack of Eurytos' city, he will after that have release from his toils; if Laios in *Oidipous the King* has a son, he will kill his father and marry his mother. If Troy is to fall, Philoktetes must be persuaded to go there with his bow.[111] None of Sophokles' other divine predictions invites us to speculate on the purposes or motivation of the gods;[112] Herakles' prediction in *Philoktetes* is no exception. The fall of Troy is a 'given' of the legend – one of those facts of mythology that is

[108] Kitto 1956, 137; cf. Winnington-Ingram 1980, 302–3 and Seale 1982, 46.

[109] Segal 1995, esp. 116; he makes much of Philoktetes' violation of Chryse's precinct, which for him is very far from the accident it was e.g. for Grene (1957, 191). For Philoktetes' attack on the gods at 442–6 cf. e.g. Euripides, *Women of Troy* 469ff.

[110] Cf. Ley's Notes below, pp. 228 (n.25) and 239–40.

[111] Far too much has been made of the fluctuations in the view of this oracle during the course of the drama. It is quite natural that Odysseus, for example, should prefer to assume that taking Philoktetes to Troy by force will be no less effective. Cf. Gill 1980, 140.

[112] The exception, Kalchas' prophecy in *Ai*, proves the rule; in that drama, exceptionally, the goddess Athena has already appeared to the spectators, and made them realize why she is so angry with Aias that it is unsafe for him to leave his tent for twenty-four hours.

too big to be altered for the purposes of any one particular new work of art; and in his few words after Herakles has spoken, Philoktetes simply accepts his *moira*, a release from his sufferings which will lead to glory.[113] Far from proving divine providence, Herakles only asserts about the gods that they are angered by those who fail to pay them *time* – an idea that is fundamental to Greek life and literature from the opening scene of the *Iliad* onwards, and which doubtless many of Sophokles' Athenian audience still believed, or wanted to believe.[114]

Pity and human sympathy were the 'wild cards' in ancient Greek values. The *agathos* was under no obligation to feel emotion on behalf of, or to help, anyone who was not a member of his *oikos*; this is, for example, why the unexpected pity that Achilleus feels for his enemy King Priam during their confrontation in his hut is the climactic moment which resolves the action of the *Iliad*.[115] In *Philoktetes*, Neoptolemos' emotional state, as he watches Philoktetes' suffering, becomes crucial. The Sailors have enough imagination to pity Philoktetes' plight even before they see him (168ff.); for them, pity is relatively easy, as for them it has no consequences (cf. 317–18). When Neoptolemos pities Philoktetes, however, he establishes a binding *philos*-relationship between two *agathoi* with Philoktetes, and resolves to act on it, rather than on his allegiance to the rest of the Greek army (NB 1252ff.). Sophokles studies the development of Neoptolemos' pity, which gradually overtakes the task of deception imposed by Odysseus, with great care; note especially the pivotal altercation with the Sailors at 507ff., and the establishment of the mutual friendship when Philoktetes makes plain that he regards Neoptolemos as worthy to handle the bow (654ff.). Then Philoktetes suffers a devastating attack of pain in Scene 3;[116] as it abates, Neoptolemos pledges that he will stay with him.

---

[113] 1447 and 1464ff. Winnington-Ingram 1980, 298 and 301. Cf. Robinson 1969, 55.

[114] '[Herakles confirms] that the gods are just only with respect to rectificatory justice . . . Philoctetes' faith in divine justice is therefore confirmed only to a very limited degree, and certainly not in the way he most desires' (Blundell 1989, 222–3). In this, *Phil* is very close to *Ant*.

[115] 24.507ff.

[116] It is so protracted that modern actors (and audiences) may at first wince at the number of inarticulate cries, e.g. in 745ff. The ancient Greeks had no

Philoktetes is physically disgusting; but Neoptolemos is willing to tolerate close proximity to his foul stench. During Choros 4, while Sleep relieves Philoktetes' suffering, Neoptolemos is obliged to confront something less palatable: his own self-disgust at having to engage in a deception that is foreign to his nature.[117] When in the next scene he attempts to persuade Philoktetes to go to Troy, this feeling reasserts itself violently, before he even starts; from 895 onwards Neoptolemos agonizes over his dilemma, embarrassed and ashamed as he attempts to uphold the new 'morality' of obeying those stronger than you, and pursuing your own best interests (921–6). After this, Philoktetes' searing denunciation of Neoptolemos is enough for him to make explicit that he has long felt 'an overwhelming pity'. As yet, it does not lead to action; and Odysseus' immediate entry, as the personification of 'the stronger' and of political necessity (994), leads to a scene that ends with Neoptolemos apparently acquiescing in Odysseus' wishes. However, the very act of letting the Sailors stay is a typical Sophoklean blend of practical necessity (he needs the *choros* to sing a *kommos* with Philoktetes, and then they must remain until the end of the drama) with psychological insight; it implies that Neoptolemos is not able simply to leave Philoktetes on the island.

However, in that scene Philoktetes has accurately and devastatingly denounced Odysseus as having corrupted Neoptolemos, whom he regards as his own equal in *arete* (1004ff.); and this leads after his *kommos* to the deeply expected, if on the surface surprising, first part of the Finale: Odysseus' authority from Scene 1 is reversed, and he has to chase after Neoptolemos – both literally and psychologically – without success. Neoptolemos now reasserts the excellence of traditional *arete* over the modern 'morality' of ruthless self-interest, sophistry and deceit; and this is the core of the drama. Philoktetes' subsequent intransigence, which precipitates Herakles' intervention, is then necessary because Sophokles wants to show how far Neoptolemos' *philia* for Philoktetes, established at full strength at

anaesthetics to relieve the pain of those afflicted with severe wounds; and after twenty years of virtually continuous warfare most of Sophokles' audience would, I imagine, have encountered wounded men whose sufferings were as acute as Philoktetes'.

[117] 842; Kitto 1956, 120.

1381ff., extends. It emerges after 1400 that Neoptolemos will honour his commitment to doing what is 'right' at all costs (cf. 1246, 1251). Even though Neoptolemos knows that it goes against Helenos' prophecy, and is not in Philoktetes' best interests (1329ff.), he will take Philoktetes home.

Oidipous at Kolonos

At the end of Oidipous the King, Oidipous seeks to be expelled from Thebes as soon as possible and die outside, on Mount Kithairon, where all his troubles began.[118] This is the right conclusion to Sophokles' first Oidipous tragedy, in which Oidipous feels all the indelible *miasma* of one who has killed his father and married his mother.

However, in Sophokles' native *deme* of Kolonos – an outlying village, less than three kilometres from the acropolis of Athens – there was a cult of Oidipous as a local *heros*. And in the last years of his life Sophokles clearly realized that a new tragedy could be constructed around this legend. It begins with a third example of the new technique that he had developed in *Elektra* and *Philoktetes*, the arrival of strangers at a place that is terrible and awe-inspiring, and their gradual engagement with the inhabitants of that place.[119] *Oidipous at Kolonos* takes this technique to a new level of complexity; although the grove of the Furies is the most awe-inspiring of the places represented by the *skene* in these three dramas, Oidipous and Antigone actually go into it, and re-emerge during Choros 1.[120] At the end, the gods summon Oidipous into the grove, and Sophokles once again deploys theatrical machinery to startle his audience; the *bronteion* here complements the *ekkyklêma* at the climax of *Elektra* and the *mechane* in *Philoktetes*. Then, in a scene that is truly marvellous theatre, the blind old man, who was totally dependent on Antigone to be his eyes at the opening of the drama, walks unaided into the sacred grove of the Eumenides.

[118] *OKing* 1433–4, 1451–4.
[119] Of course, Sophokles may have used this procedure in other, lost dramas as well.
[120] Cf. McCart's reconstruction of the action below, p. 259, for the ways in which Oidipous establishes his harmony with the place to which he has come. Winnington-Ingram has an appendix (1980, 339–40) which demonstrates the frequency of words establishing locality in the opening phases of the drama.

In the middle of the drama, after Oidipous has been made to leave the sacred grove, the extreme back centre of the playing area is forbidden territory, and the drama focuses around Oidipous, who takes up a seated position at the centre.[121] Here Sophokles could create a new version of the Theban saga, dovetailing to whatever extent he saw fit with his own account of previous events in *Oidipous the King*, and foreshadowing, if he so desired, his account of the attack of the Seven against Thebes in *Antigone*.[122] Apart from the basic data of this cycle of myth – that Oidipous had in ignorance killed his father and married his mother, and that Polyneikes and Eteokles killed each other in single combat – almost anything could be invented to fill the middle of this drama.

For one critic, that is almost exactly what Sophokles did; the central scenes are simply filling in, a 'distraction' between an impressive beginning and a sublime end.[123] However, recognizing that *Oidipous at Kolonos* does not possess the taut construction and rigorous sequential development of *Oidipous the King* does not in any way denigrate its dramatic structure.[124] We should not expect such methods in the new tragedy; they suited neither the realities of the times, nor Sophokles' response to those realities as already established in *Elektra* and *Philoktetes*.[125] Surprise, suspense and uncertainty fill Scenes 2–5; but there is a throughline to the action, and it is totally connected to the opening and closing sequences. Oidipous arrives at Kolonos, as he stresses in the opening lines, in an utterly wretched condition: a blind beggar, dependent on handouts and on the aid of a *parthenos* who is vulnerable by virtue of her

[121] For the position of the seat cf. McCart's Notes below, pp. 260–1. Obviously, however, Oidipous does not remain static throughout from midway through Choros 1 to Choros 5; *ibid.* pp. 260n.24.

[122] So, for example, he makes at 87ff. an addition to Apollo's prophecy to Oidipous at Delphi (first version at *OKing* 787ff.), foreshadowing what will happen in *OKol*.

[123] Waldock 1951, 218–20.

[124] To defend this drama, commentators have sometimes resorted to mysticism, trying to confer on *OKol* the wrong kind of profundity – e.g. by dubious analogies with music; Winnington-Ingram 1980, 249, claims to detect five 'movements' in *OKol*; and Linforth 1951, 189, writes about its 'sonata form'(!).

[125] Much of the power of Euripides' *Bakchai* lies in the deliberate reversion, for a particular kind of story, to techniques and structural procedures that had not been seen in the theatre of Dionysos for at least twenty years.

youth and her gender.[126] During Scenes 2 to 5, Oidipous
gradually gains in authority, until he possesses sufficient *thymos*
to be fully capable of helping his friends and harming his
enemies; then he is powerful enough to become a *heros*, and so
then he is summoned by the gods.[127] Like the Furies in whose
grove he goes to his death, Oidipous will become a *chthonian*
power, able to protect the inhabitants of the place where he
died.[128]

More specifically, he will be able to protect his new friends
the Athenians against invasion by the Thebans. Sophokles wrote
Oidipous at Kolonos when the Spartans and their allies –
including the Thebans – had already occupied fortified forward
positions in Attika, and were likely to assault Athens itself
within a few years or at worst months. It may well have seemed
to many that the gods had deserted Athens; but perhaps they
had not, and the resting-place of a *heros* might protect the
Athenians against their enemies, whose greatest legendary king,
Oidipous, was once bound to Athens by firm bonds of reciprocity. In Oidipous' last speech and in the Finale, Sophokles
expresses his faith in the mysteries of the hero-cult of Oidipous
and the moral strength of Athens (1522ff.). Together, these may
protect Kolonos and Athens from devastation:

> That way you'll live in Athens unmolested by
> the Thebans. Many cities treat others
> who wish to live in peace with wanton violence.
> The gods take note, after some time perhaps,
> when any man spurns them and turns to madness. (1533ff.)[129]

---

[126] Kreon not only points this out (745ff.), but proves his point by abducting
Antigone (821ff.).

[127] Cf. Burian 1974, 408 and 412.

[128] Jebb 1900, xxix–xxx. Oidipous' power to protect those living near
Kolonos was still a reality for the orator Aristeides, writing, c. AD170. Theseus,
Orestes, Aias and Eurystheus were among other figures from the earliest period
in Greece who were believed to have this power. Recently deceased men could
also become the subjects of such a cult; Sophokles himself had received and
given hospitality to Asklepios – in the form of his sacred serpent – when the god
first arrived in Athens; for this Sophokles was worshipped after his death under
the cult title Dexion ('the receiver').

[129] Cf. Theseus' last words, at 1764ff. The Thebans did in fact show mercy
after the surrender of Athens, and sheltered Athenian refugees during the régime
of the Thirty Tyrants (Ploutarchos, *Lysandros* 27).

The emphasis that is laid throughout the drama on the virtues of the Athenians goes much further than jingoism – though some patriotic fervour might well be forgiven in a tragedy written twenty-five years into a war that was about to destroy everything the dramatist and his prospective audience had lived for.[130] The Scout sets out the distinctive excellence of the Kolonians (and by extension of all Athenians) as early as 61–3; their reverence for the gods is exemplified not so much in mythology 'but by the way we live'.[131] This emphasis on deeds rather than words is central to the portrait of Theseus;[132] it is also present in the celebrated (and beautiful) hymn to Athens and Attika in its Choros 2. The central attributes of Athens, praised in the final stanza, are its horses and its ships; between them, these enshrine the military power, that had made Athens the greatest city in Greece.

The character of Theseus is accordingly designed to stand in diametric contrast with the two Thebans who visit Oidipous.[133] Kreon and Polyneikes exemplify in two different ways the 'wanton violence' and spurning of the gods which Oidipous denounces in his final speech. Kreon is an old opportunist, a considerably more depraved portrait of the new amorality and ruthless self-interest than the Odysseus of *Philoktetes* (whose cynicism and *Realpolitik* at least have an air of freshness and vigour). Polyneikes is a young representative of the same amorality, prepared to resort to even the most sophistic arguments (e.g. 1298–9, 1335–6) to cover his moral viciousness. Despite what Polyneikes says (1299), in this version of the story the conflict between the sons is caused not by Oidipous' curses but by their own selfish dispute over their inheritance. Such internal

[130] Athenian patriotism also wears its heart on its sleeve in several dramas of Euripides, especially *Suppliant Women*. There too the city's excellence is stressed by dramatizing its willingness to receive suppliants regardless of the potential consequences.

[131] The same emphasis on action is also present in Thoukydides' analyses of the Athenian character (*Histories* 1.70, 2.43). It is richly ironic that while the deeds on which the Athenians prided themselves have faded into history, words created in ancient Athens and by Athenians have been preserved, studied and valued for two and a half millennia.

[132] Cf. e.g. his immediate reaction to the abduction of Antigone and Ismene at 891ff.; also 1016–17, 1148–9.

[133] On Theseus' role and characterization cf. Blundell 1989, 248–53.

conflict in an *oikos* leads, in the vision expressed by this drama, inexorably to self-destruction. Oidipous therefore makes much of the contrast between his daughters, who have abandoned their chances of marriage (the normal goal of a Greek *parthenos*) to look after him in his old age, and his sons, who have chosen instead to fight for his inheritance.[134] By contrast, the goodwill that Oidipous displays throughout his supplication for refuge in Kolonos, and the goodwill that Theseus shows him in return, are rewarded by reciprocal benefits between them, which will far outlast their lifetimes.

In the *Oresteia* Aischylos had bequeathed a very similar vision to his fellow-Athenians, in Athena's advice to her future citizens at *Eumenides* 681ff., and in the final concord between the Furies and the Athenians. When Sophokles chose Oidipous' assimilation into a grove of the Furies as the subject of this drama, he invoked the precedent of the *Oresteia*; and his vision was sharpened (by contrast to Aischylos' trilogy, which was created before a strong and confident Athenian audience) by the imminent presence of the besieging enemy.

How could Oidipous, who had violated two of the strongest taboos of his own society (and of most other human cultures), achieve the authority and the power to become a *heros*? In *Oidipous the King* his responsibility for his two crimes remains absolute, despite the fact that he did them in ignorance; that is why he blinded himself, and sought to be expelled from the city. Nor should we expect anything else, since Greek ethics up until this period did not recognize intentions as relevant to responsibility for actions.[135]

However, there is evidence that in the last years of the century absolute responsibility became one of many aspects of Greek culture which the sophists subjected to questioning.[136] And the Oidipous of this new drama mounts a passionate defence of himself, pleading that he is essentially innocent – and almost

[134] This is achieved partly by symmetrical construction; the issue is raised both when the daughters occupy the focus immediately after the opening (Scene 2) and when one of the sons is present, in the scene immediately before the conclusion (Scene 5). Sophokles even draws upon his friend Herodotos' research into reversed gender roles in Aigyptian society to reinforce Oidipous' point (337ff.; Herodotos, *Histories* 2.35).

[135] Adkins 1960, ch. 5, esp. p. 98 on *OKing*.

[136] Above, p. xviii[x].

that he is now free of *miasma*[137] at 270ff. and 960ff. But Sophokles does not present this new vision of Oidipous' 'innocence' uncritically.

Oidipous gradually becomes stronger as the drama unfolds; and as he becomes stronger he becomes increasingly powerful – grim, passionate, and an instrument of *dike*;[138] better able to help his friends and harm his enemies, and also able to prophesy the future with ever-increasing clarity.[139] But Sophokles casts a shadow over his ending. Once again, as in Scene 1, a technique essayed on a small scale at the end of *Elektra* (Aigisthos' warning about the fate of the Pelopidai) and *Philoktetes* (Herakles' warning against impiety in the sack of Troy) is put to much more extensive use in *Oidipous at Kolonos*. Antigone is reticent for most of the drama, and by being so she supports her father's view that young women should not speak much (1115 16). However, she intervenes passionately (1181ff.) when Oidipous refuses to grant Polyneikes an audience. Much earlier, Oidipous had made an almost sophistic claim that he would have been right to retaliate against his father even if he had known whom he was attacking.[140] In direct counter to this – as she makes quite explicit at 1195ff., to support her central case that 'the result of bitter anger is more bitterness' – Antigone offers something equally extraordinary in fifth-century ethics: a plea for reconciliation.[141] She gets her wish, and Polyneikes is heard; but this gives her no joy. Oidipous takes his revenge, and devastates Polyneikes; and her parting from her brother is a scene of heartbreaking pathos (1414ff.). At the end of the drama she resolves to go back to Thebes. Sophokles deliberately foreshadows in the final minutes the now inevitable impending fate of Antigone, who will die – according to the story told in one of his own most famous earlier works – because she attempts to bury Polyneikes' body against Kreon's express decree (cf. 1405–13).

[137] But note 1132ff., where Oidipous draws back from wishing to touch Theseus in gratitude for rescuing his daughters.

[138] Winnington-Ingram 1980, 255.

[139] Notice how his vision becomes increasingly clear from 91ff. to 607ff. to his first open prophecy at 787ff., and finally to the devastating prophecy which destroys Polyneikes' hopes at 1370ff.

[140] 271–3. Cf. Blundell 1989, 227–8.

[141] Cf. Winnington-Ingram 262 n. 41, and 263.

Antigone embodies in *Oidipous at Kolonos* a feeling that is central to Sophokles' last three extant dramas – pity. Conspicuous precisely by its absence from his hate-filled *Elektra*, it was this emotion that gave Neoptolemos the courage to break out from Odysseus' sophistries, and do right by Philoktetes. Now Oidipous' daughter urges pity on him in vain – and is destroyed. Oidipous' love for his daughters is as great as his hatred of his sons; indeed, the almost unprecedentedly violent action at the centre of the drama, when Kreon's guards abduct Antigone, is designed to show how much he is alone, and helpless, without her. But at the end of the tragedy his hatred for his sons involves and consumes his most faithful and beloved daughter. Harming one's enemies, when done with devastating effect to sons who were once by definition *philoi*, may involve harming one's dearest remaining *philoi* as well.

These aspects of *Oidipous at Kolonos* are in my view designed to evoke the internal situation at Athens. After 411 the polarization between the left and the right increased; and in 406 the democrats acted with great savagery, when they secured the death penalty for the generals who had been unable to rescue sailors from the sea after the naval disaster at Arginousai in 406.[142] It is clear from Aristophanes' response in *Frogs*, performed in January 405, that this action crystallized a need for mutual tolerance and reconciliation, which had hardly been felt in Athens before 411, but which became more and more desirable as internal politics became increasingly polarized. Aristophanes used the *parabasis* at the centre of *Frogs* to plead for reconciliation.[143] His appeal to his fellow Athenians was so passionate, and so important, that *Frogs* was revived in January 404; but in vain. Soon afterwards Athens surrendered to Sparta, and the Thirty Tyrants whom the Spartans installed committed even greater excesses against the democrats.

In *Oidipous at Kolonos*, created at least a year earlier than *Frogs*, Sophokles' Antigone pleads that even a justified anger may well deserve to be tempered with pity. Perhaps he too perceived the trend among his fellow-countrymen towards internal strife and self-destruction before it had reached its appalling culmination; perhaps he even rewrote the last phases of the text

---

[142] Xenophon, *Hellenika* 1.7.
[143] *Frogs* 675ff.

after the Arginousai trial, in the very last months of his life, to emphasize Antigone's plea for pity, and her subsequent fate.[144]

Unfortunately for the Athenians, neither Sophokles' vision of transcendent hope for a *polis* that can show goodwill, nor his warning against the implacable pursuit of hatred, were exhibited to them in time. The playwright's grandson was only able to bring *Oidipous at Kolonos* to performance in 401 BC, when after great bloodshed the restored but muted democracy had reached a precarious reconciliation with the surviving members of the Thirty Tyrants and their supporters, then in exile at Eleusis. Sophokles' posthumous legacy must have troubled its first spectators; both his faith and his warning came to them too late.

Trackers

Satyr-drama was performed at the Festival of Dionysos from very early in the fifth century. Many scholars believe that it was added to the festival because of the complaints about tragedy preserved in the expression 'nothing to do with Dionysos', which later became proverbial. However, it is far more likely that each competing dramatist had to provide both tragedies and a *satyr-drama* from the first competition onwards; tragedy and *satyr-drama* go naturally together, since they are both direct developments out of the celebration of Dionysos. In myth, in iconography and in cult, Dionysos' followers include satyrs as well as his human worshippers, *bakchantes*. Satyr *choros* members wear a bearded, slightly balding mask, with pointed ears and a snub nose; they are naked except for a furry loin-cloth, from which a phallos protrudes at the front and a horselike tail from the rear. They invariably accompany their father, Silenos;[145] his features are similar, and he wears a body-suit of

---

[144] To this limited extent my view concurs with Tanner's otherwise over-ingenious speculation (1966) that there were two drafts of *OKol*.

It is possible that Sophokles did not finish the script, and that the text was completed after his death, e.g. by his son Iophon, who was then beginning his own career as a tragic dramatist. But there are no clear signs of this in the text.

[145] The satyrs of Athenian tragedy are an amalgamation of Attic or Ionic 'silenoi' with Dorian 'satyroi' from the Peloponnese. Seaford 1984, 6.

white hair.[146] Like the god whom they follow and serve, the satyrs are contradictory in character: amoral hedonists (especially in the pursuit of sex and wine), they can also be incarnations of superhuman wisdom.

Apart from small fragments, we possess one complete *satyr-drama* (*Kyklops* by Euripides), about one hundred lines each from Aischylos' *Fishermen* and *Ambassadors to the Isthmian Games*, and the first 400 lines of *Trackers*.[147] These dramas use techniques that we would associate with farce and burlesque to tell stories, based on Dionysiac ritual, in which the *thiasos* of satyric worshippers of Dionysos comes into conflict with other, more normal gods and goddesses, heroes and heroines who have to survive their mockery, abuse, deception and (if female) the threat of sexual harassment.[148] Typically, the satyrs find themselves temporarily freed from the service of Dionysos, either voluntarily (Aischylos, *Ambassadors*), or under compulsion (Euripides, *Kyklops*); it is not clear from the fragment of *Trackers* why Silenos and his sons are free to enter Apollo's service to try to find his cows. Their natural curiosity is stimulated by an encounter with some marvellous new discovery; Danaë's chest in *Fishermen*; Hephaistos' 'new toys' in *Ambassadors*; and Hermes' strange new invention, the lyre, whose sound drives them crazy in *Trackers*. In *Fishermen* and *Trackers* they are confronted by a woman or nymph who emerges miraculously from under the sea or the earth (Danaë, Kyllene); in both these dramas, and in the lost *Amymone* by Aischylos, they harass or threaten to harass this female; a god rescues her from them. In *Fishermen* they find themselves temporarily caring for a heroic male infant (Perseus); it is possible that in the lost second half of *Trackers* they similarly nurtured Hermes.

All this is grounded in aspects of Dionysiac ritual;[149] the surviving drama and fragments all take a fairly straightforward story from myth – in *Trackers*, the story of the invention of the lyre from the Homeric *Hymn to Hermes* – and inject the satyrs

---

[146] The physical appearance of performers in *satyr-drama* is known from a late fifth- early fourth-century vase depicting an acting company, the 'Pronomos vase'. Illustration e.g. in Green and Handley 1995, plate 5.

[147] The two fragments of Aischylos are translated in Ewans 1996, 117ff.

[148] Cf. Seaford 1984, 33ff.

[149] Cf. Seaford 1984, 40–44.

into it, creating situations where their farcical, burlesque and amoral behaviour clashes with the more elevated world of gods, goddesses and heroes. These characters try to speak the language of tragedy: Danaë in *Fishermen*, Odysseus in *Kyklops*, Kyllene and above all Apollo in *Trackers* attempt a heroic tone. However, their role as characters in a *satyr-drama* soon punctures their rhetoric, and their speech descends into bathos. Danaë becomes a sulky teenager (*Fishermen* 781ff.), Odysseus turns coward (*Kyklops* 271ff.), Kyllene abuses the satyrs like a fishwife (*Trackers* 381ff.): and Apollo's 'noble rage and grief'[150] soon become mere petulance.

'Without the satyr-play we cannot know enough about the way in which the Greek spirit coped with catastrophe. The residue of a few tragedies might give us the illusion of something resolutely high-minded but it is a distortion . . .'[151] It has been hard for many modern critics, nurtured on a firm division between high and low culture, to imagine the inclusive, wide-ranging tastes of the Athenian theatre, where poets had to satisfy at once the demands of peasant and philosopher, craftsman and priest; no surprise therefore to find that *Kyklops* is among Euripides' least admired surviving dramas (though Shelley knew better), and *Trackers* was regarded even by one of the archaeologists who discovered it as 'slight enough'.[152]

Like Athenian tragedy, *satyr-drama* can only be effective in the theatre. A powerful scene like *Trackers* 92ff., where groups of satyrs hunt, lying doglike upon the ground to search for the cattle, then retreat in fear as they hear the terrifying sound of the lyre, was designed for open-air performance before a vast and diverse audience; it means little if read in a study, without any effort to imagine the text in performance. *Trackers* has twice been put into rhyming English verse and conjecturally completed: once by Lancelyn Green, in a translation that now seems dated but captures much of the energy of the original; and more recently by Tony Harrison, whose *Trackers of Oxyrhynchus* includes a robust translation and ingenious restoration of Sophokles' drama; as his play develops the satyrs become a critique of the privileged modern theatre and its disjunction

---

[150] Lancelyn Green 1957, 57.
[151] Harrison 1991, xi.
[152] Hunt, quoted at Harrison 1991, xvii.

from an inclusive vision of life.[153] I have not created a third modern restoration; this volume prints an accurate blank verse translation confined to the fragments that survive of Sophokles' original script.

Other Fragments

The 'Fragments' of Sophokles are portions of lost dramas preserved either in quotations in the work of other ancient authors or in papyri recovered (usually in a poor state of preservation) from the sands of Egypt. Sophokles is known to have written over 120 tragedies and at least twenty *satyr-dramas*; although there are more than 1100 'fragments' many of these consist of a single word or a single line.[154]

The later writers who quoted from Sophokles had no sense of the performance idiom and dramatic style of his dramas; their interest was either in words and/or Greek usage that they found exotic or in quotations that illustrated particular ideas – usually moral ideas – or that made unusual comparisons. So, for example, anthologists have preserved for us two short discourses on wealth (frags. 2 and 4), one on seafaring (frag. 7), and one on the power of the goddess Aphrodite (frag. 23). We are more fortunate, perhaps, when the subject of a fragment chimes in with themes we recognize from the surviving dramas, as with fragments 15 and 22 on the mutability inherent in the human condition, or with Prokne's meditation on the fate of women,

---

[153] In the London version, this becomes very apparent at the end, where the satyrs become the impoverished homeless on London's South Bank, excluded from the elite cultural centres of the Royal Festival Hall and National Theatre. The irony of this finale is at Harrison's own expense, since his own drama played inside the National Theatre to an audience of those wealthy enough to afford its seat prices.

[154] In this book I have translated only fragments of seven or more consecutive lines, since small extracts in translation induce nothing but frustration. Two authors (Kiso 1984, Sutton 1984) have attempted to reconstruct the plots and subject-matter of Sophokles' lost tragedies; in the case of almost every drama we know nothing about which version of the myth Sophokles used, so both their books are highly speculative. (For an edition of all fragments of one line or more with English translation see Lloyd-Jones 1996; for a balanced discussion of the fragments and what we can tell from them cf. Radt 1983.)

which puts into explicit words the kinds of oppression suffered in surviving dramas by Antigone and Deinaneira.[155]

Only the papyrus fragments add anything to our knowledge of Sophokles as a dramatist; but these are of some value. The fragment from *Eurypylos* (frag. 3), dramatizing an episode from the Trojan War, shows Sophokles interrupting a messenger-speech, an account of the death of Astyoche's son, with a vivid short *kommos* and subsequent dialogue between the bereaved mother and the women of the *choros*; and the fragments from *Niobe* give us the bare bones of an extraordinary action sequence, in which Artemis is pursuing and killing Niobe's daughters inside the *skene*, and one of them is first heard crying out, and then seen running for her life. Scholars who still believe that Greek tragedy was primarily verbal, with little action, should take this fragment together with Aias' suicide and the abduction of Antigone in *Oidipous at Kolonos*, and change their views.

Apart from the first half of *Trackers*, we have substantial fragments from only one *satyr-drama* by Sophokles: *Inachos* (frags. 25, 26). Again the action appears to have been intensely dramatic: Inachos' narrative of his daughter's transformation into a cow was followed by two appearances of Hermes, first invisible (wearing the cap of invisibility) and terrifying the satyrs, and later as a visible presence, arguing with Inachos. Together with *Trackers*, these fragments (and frag. 27 from *Oineus*) demonstrate that Sophokles wrote vigorous and entertaining *satyr-drama*.

MICHAEL EWANS

---

[155] Cf. also Euripides, *Medeia* 230ff. It is a great pity that the surviving fragments from the intensely powerful story of Tereus and Prokne do not give us any idea of how Sophokles dramatized this myth.

NOTE ON THE TRANSLATION AND NOTES

Translation

The contributors to this book were all initially trained as scholars of the Greek language, but we teach, and direct productions, in Departments of Drama or Performance Studies. We have translated these dramas for performance; our scripts have been modified in workshop or rehearsal to make them fully actable. We also attempt to render the meaning(s) of the text into English as closely and accurately as possible.

The style of our translations varies, to reflect the way in which Sophokles adapted his own Greek style to reflect the very different subject-matter of the three dramas. As translators we have tried to be alert to what we find in each tragedy, rather than imposing some kind of uniform English style on Sophokles.

The attribution of speeches, and all stage directions in any translation from Greek tragedy, are modern. The directions in this edition are for the Greek theatre shape, and based on the experience gained in our workshops and productions. Modern directors who need to modify these directions to suit a differently shaped performance space must still be aware of Sophokles' own practice and the reasons for it. Only those directions that we regard as certain are printed in the text; further suggestions will be found in the Notes.

Characters enter either actor right – from the countryside/abroad – actor left – from the downtown district of the place in which the action is located – or through the single set of double doors in the centre of the *skene* façade.[1] A character entering down a *parodos* is in the sight of some of the actors and audience, on the opposite side from where he is making his

---

[1] We draw readers' attention to the fact that this series follows normal theatrical practice, and gives stage directions from the viewpoint of the actor, since a recent book on Athenian staging (Wiles 1997) gives all directions from the spectator's viewpoint.

entry, long before he steps into the *orchêstra*. Presumably the convention was that the actor was in character from the moment he became visible to any of the audience, but engaged in interaction with the players already there only after he stepped into the *orchêstra*. Accordingly in these texts the direction *Enter X* is positioned at the moment where X enters the *orchêstra*, not when the actor fist comes into sight of some of the audience.

The text is divided into Scenes (predominantly consisting of spoken dialogue) and Choroses (passages which are, usually, sung and danced by the *choros* alone). These are numbered in separate consecutive series for each drama. Sometimes a choral ode is too short to interrupt the development of a scene as a whole (e.g. *Philoktetes* Choros 2); these are numbered as new odes, but the number is placed in parentheses, and the scene is not ended when they begin.

Alternation between Choroses and Scenes is the basic structural feature of Greek tragedy; we have therefore not obscured it by importing the later technical terms found in the twelfth, probably interpolated, chapter of Aristotle's *Poetics*.[2]

Notes

The Notes in this book are framed around the units of Greek dramatic structure: Scenes and Choroses. They are designed to help readers towards an understanding of how, as the original production unfolded through time, each individual drama made its effect on the audience. We believe that modern theatre companies and students can only render these dramas into contemporary theatrical terms by understanding how they used their original performance space and its conventions; and we have found that insights gained through study can only be tested and augmented through workshop or production in a replica of the original performance space.

Because we adopt a common approach, we have been able to cross-reference similarities and parallels between Sophokles' dramatic techniques in different dramas. However, a uniform methodology does not imply that we are in monolithic agree-

---

[2] 'Prologos', 'parodos', 'stasimon', 'epeisodion' and 'exodos'; *Poetics* 52b14–27. We also do not accept the over-ingenious theory of Act-dividing and non-Act-dividing odes with which Taplin (1977, 49ff.) sought to replace this terminology.

ment on all aspects of his stagecraft; we therefore also note some specific points on which our views differ.

Positions in the *orchêstra* are described in the Notes by a combination of letters: F = front (nearest to the Priest of Dionysos at the centre of the front row of spectators); B = back (nearest to the *skene*); L = (actor) left; R = (actor) right; C = centre; E = extreme (i.e. at the perimeter).[3]

Lyric and Spoken Verse

The interplay between lyric, sung verse and spoken verse in the Greek text is marked in this edition by double-indenting all verses that were sung in the original performances.

Strophic responsion in lyrics is denoted by numbering the first *strophe* (A1) and its matching *antistrophe* (A2); if there is a concluding *epode* that is marked (A3). The second pair in a system is marked (B1), (B2) – and so on.

Choral dialogue was almost certainly divided between different members of the group. Accordingly we prefix lines spoken by 'the *choros*' with e.g. 1 Sailor, 1 Elder; directors will choose who is to speak each line as they develop their interpretation of each scene.

Transliteration, Glossaries

In this edition, following the practice of an ever-increasing number of classical scholars, proper names are transliterated directly from the Greek original, and the traditional Latinized spellings (e.g. Oedipus for Oidipous) are not employed. *Upsilon* is transliterated by *y*, not *u*; and *chi* by *ch*, not *kh*.

Two Glossaries are provided, one of all the Greek names that occur in the text, and the other of all the Greek words italicized in the Introduction and Notes.

Line Numbering

The three tragedies are translated from the corrected second edition of the Oxford Classical Text edited by H. Lloyd-Jones and N. G. Wilson. For uniformity in referencing, all modern scholars use the line numbering of one of the early editions of Sophokles. However there has been much research, particularly in the last fifty years, on the nature of Greek lyric verse; this has

---

[3] There is further discussion of this notation, with a diagram, in Ley and Ewans 1985.

led to revisions of the line structure. Our translations follow the Oxford text's presentation; accordingly in lyric sections there are sometimes more, sometimes less than ten lines of English verse between the line-markers.

Where there is reason to believe that a line or lines are missing from the Greek text, we add our suggested text for performance in square brackets. Where lines have been interpolated into Sophokles' Greek text, we omit them from the translation, and draw attention to this by supplying a line number for the line immediately preceding and that immediately following the omission (cf. e.g. *El* 427ff).

Abbreviations
In the footnotes we abbreviate the titles of Sophokles' seven surviving tragedies: *Ai (Aias), Ant (Antigone), YWT (Young Women of Trachis), OKing (Oidipous the King), El (Elektra), Phil (Philoktetes)* and *OKol (Oidipous at Kolonos).*

ELEKTRA

Translated by Michael Ewans

THE ACTORS AND THEIR ROLES

OLD MAN	Actor 3
ORESTES	Actor 2
PYLADES	Silent Face
ELEKTRA	Actor 1
WOMEN OF ARGOS	Choros
CHRYSOTHEMIS	Actor 2
KLYTAIMESTRA	Actor 2
MAIDSERVANT	Silent Face
AIGISTHOS	Actor 3

The skene *represents the palace at Mykenai*
Preset an altar of Apollo, front centre

SCENE I

(*Enter* OLD MAN, ORESTES *and* PYLADES *right*)

OLD MAN: Son of the great commander, Agamemnon,
who sacked Troy; here they are now –
the places that you always longed to see!
This is the ancient plain of Argos which you dreamed about,
the grove of Io, gadfly-persecuted child of Inachos;
down there, Orestes, lies the city's central meeting-place,
named for Apollo, wolf-god; on the left
stands Hera's famous temple. Where we've come,
know you are looking at Mykenai rich in gold.
This is the house of many deaths – the home of Pelops'
    family.   10
I took you from the hands of close kin, from your sister
long ago, when your father was murdered here;
I carried you away, I saved you, and I brought
you up so you can now avenge his death.

So now, Orestes – and you, dearest friend,
Pylades – we must quickly make our plan.
The bright light of the sun's rays is awakening
for us the birds' first morning-songs,
and the black night of stars has disappeared.
So now, before some man comes out,   20
we must decide together; it's no longer
the right time to shrink back, but to act.

ORESTES: Dearest of all man-servants, you have now become
most valuable to us, giving me such clear advice.
A horse of noble birth, even when old,
does not lose courage as the moment of pure terror comes,
but sticks his ears up straight; just so do you
encourage us to act, and follow right behind.
I'll show you what I think; pay keen
attention to my words, and if in anything   30
I do not hit the target, pull me back in line.

When I went to the oracle at Delphi
to learn how I should exact
the vengeance on my father's murderers,
Apollo gives me roughly what I'll tell you now:
that I myself, without other armed men, should execute
them, using stealth and trickery to aid my just, avenging
     hand.
Since we have heard this oracle,
you must, as soon as you can find a chance,
get in this house, discover everything   40
so you can tell us how things stand.
You won't be recognized. You have been long away,
blossomed to ripe old age; they won't suspect you.
Use this story: you're a friend, you've come
from Phanoteus the Phokian lord – he is
their greatest, closest friend abroad.
Tell them – adding some padding to this sketch –
that Orestes is dead – a fatal accident;
during the Games at Delphi he was thrown
out of his chariot. Establish this as truth.   50
Meanwhile, as the god ordered, I will go out to
my father's grave, crown it with liquid offerings
and give him locks of hair. Then we'll come back,
first picking up the bronze urn, which
you know we've hidden in some bushes.
We shall deceive them with our words, and bring
a story they'll enjoy; we'll tell them that my body
is destroyed – already burned and turned to ashes.
What harm can it do me, if in words I am dead –
when in deed I am saved, and bring myself to glory?   60
For me, no spoken word is wrong, as long as it brings gain.

Before now I have often seen how clever men
can falsely be reported dead; and then, when they
come home again, rich honours fall on them.
I boast that just so, from this story that I'm dead,
I'll live, and shine out like a star against my enemies.

Land of my fathers, gods who live here, welcome me
and make my journey turn out well –
and you, house of my fathers; I come back
with Justice, spurred by the gods to cleanse you.   70
Do not send me away without success; receive
me as lord of your wealth, to bring good order to these halls.

That's what I have to say. Now you, old friend,
must go, and keep close watch upon your task.
We will depart. It is the right time – and Timing
is the most powerful overlord of everything men do.
ELEKTRA: (*inside the* skene) Oh! I hate my life!
OLD MAN: Hey! I thought I heard one of the servant girls
moan softly to herself inside the doors.
ORESTES: Might it not be Elektra who is suffering? Do
you   80
think we should stay, and listen to her cries of grief?
OLD MAN: Certainly not! We must do nothing else before we
try
to execute Apollo's orders; start from his command
and pour libations to your father; that, I say, will bring
us victory, and mastery in all we do.

[*Exeunt* OLD MAN, PYLADES *and* ORESTES, *right*]

CHOROS I

(*Enter* ELEKTRA *from the* skene)

ELEKTRA: Oh sacred Sunlight,
            Air as boundless as the Earth,
            you've heard my many songs of grief,
            seen many direct blows
            make blood flow from my breasts   90

when the dark gloom of night has gone;
My hateful bed here in this ghastly house
knows that my all-night festivals
are songs of grief for my ill-fated
father, whom the murderous War-god would
not grant the gift of death at Troy;
my mother and her bedmate Aigisthos
felled him like loggers, cleaving
his head open with a bloodstained axe.
And no one hears laments for this, father,   100
from any other woman except me,
although you died so shamefully and horribly.
But I won't stop my tears
and cries of grief for you
as long as I still see the radiant swirl
of stars, and light of day –
like the poor nightingale who killed her child,
weeping outside my father's doors
so everyone can hear.
Oh house of Haides and Persephone,   110
Hermes, and powerful Curse,
and solemn Furies, daughters of the gods,
who look upon those who have died unjustly,
and have had their wives seduced,
come, help, avenge
my father's death,
and send me back my brother.
By myself I can no longer keep
my heavy grief from overwhelming me.   120

(*Enter* WOMEN OF ARGOS, *left*)

WOMEN (AI):   Elektra, daughter of
the worst of mothers,
why do you always shriek aloud
insatiable grief for Agamemnon
godlessly destroyed so long ago
by your deceitful mother's tricks;
her wicked hand betrayed him. If it's right to say,
I wish the man who planned all this was dead.

ELEKTRA: Daughters of noble parents,
           you have come to console me.   130
           I understand what you are saying, it does not
           escape me; but I do not want to let this go,
           stop mourning for my pitiable father.
           You are my dearest friends, we have shared
           every kind of joy; but please, allow me to
           be crazed by grief.

WOMEN (A2):   All right – but groans and prayers will never
           resurrect your father from the stagnant
           pond of Haides where we all must go.
           At first your feelings were appropriate – but now   140
           by constant lamentation you destroy yourself
           in hopeless pain which cannot cure your sufferings.
           Why d'you reach out for the intolerable?

ELEKTRA: Only a fool forgets
           parents who have died wretchedly.
           The grieving nightingale lives in my mind,
           the bird of utter desolation, Zeus' messenger,
           always crying out for Itys, Itys.
           All-suffering Niobe, I worship you;   150
           frozen to stone,
           you weep for evermore.

WOMEN (B1):   Look, girl, you aren't
           the only one this grief
           has come upon; why is it worse
           for you than for your other siblings?
           Chrysothemis still lives, and Iphianassa,
           and the noble man good Fortune
           sheltered in boyhood from this pain;   160
           this famous land of Mykenai will one day
           welcome him when he comes home,
           his steps endorsed by Zeus – Orestes!

ELEKTRA: Yes – the man I wait for, never-resting, childless,
           miserable, husbandless; I waste away,
           drenched in my tears, fated
           for never-ending grief! – while he forgets

both what he's suffered and what he's been told.
I get his messages – but they are lies!   170
He says he longs to come – but never thinks
it's worth his while to actually appear.

WOMEN (B2):   Take courage, girl, take courage.
        Zeus is still great in heaven; he looks down
        on everything, and has great power.
        Yield your excessive anger up to him; do not
        forget your enemies, nor hate them overmuch.
        Time is a kindly god.
        The son of Agamemnon lives in   180
        Krisa, grazing-place beside the sea.
        He won't forget; nor will his father, now
        a god, a king in Haides' halls.

ELEKTRA: What about me? Most of my life has gone,
        and left me without hope; I can't hold out.
        I waste away; I have no children,
        no man is my friend and fights for me.
        I'm like a worthless foreign slave,
        housemaid in my father's rooms, wearing   190
        these shabby clothes, waiting in hope
        there'll be some leftovers for me to eat.

WOMEN (C1):   When he came home we heard
        a piteous cry from his ancestral
        banquet-couch, as the bronze double-
        headed axe struck him straight down.
        Cunning devised his death, and Lust killed him;
        their deed of horror gave birth to a shape
        of horror, whether gods or men
        caused this.   200

ELEKTRA: That was by far the worst
        of all days in my life;
        oh Night, oh fearful anguish
        of that feast of horror.
        Their hands were joined together,
        and my father saw his shameful death;
        they took away my life,

betrayed it and destroyed me.
I pray that Zeus, the great Olympian,
may punish them with equal suffering   210
so they may not do that
and enjoy luxury.

WOMEN (C2):   Take care; do not say more.
Do you not realize why you
are suffering? You're falling into great
humiliation by your own free choice!
You've brought a lot of your misfortune
on yourself; your bad temper always
breeds new conflicts. Tolerate this!
You can't fight against our overlords.   220

ELEKTRA: The horror of my situation has forced me
to behave horribly. I know I'm almost crazy;
but while I am surrounded by this horror,
I will act destructively
as long as I still live.
Dear sisters, who could ever
say words which might heal me,
who could understand my needs?
Leave, leave me, good advisers.
My problems are incurable,   230
I will not ever stop my suffering;
my cries and groans are infinite.

WOMEN (C3):   I care for you, and I'll speak like
a loyal mother; do not breed
disaster from disaster.

ELEKTRA: Has Nature set a limit for such suffering? Tell me,
how could it ever be right to forget the dead?
What man or woman started life believing that?
I never want such people's praise;
if any goodness stays with me,   240
may I enjoy it not at all, if I neglect
my father, pinning back the wings
of piercing cries of grief.
If he, poor wretch, lies dead

– just earth and nothingness –
and they do not pay back
the penalty of death for death,
mankind will lose all reverence
and respect for what is right.   250

SCENE 2

1 WOMAN: Dear girl, I came here because I care
for you, and not just for myself. If I say anything
unfair, I yield to you; we're always on your side.
ELEKTRA: Women, I am ashamed if I appear to you
to be too angry, with all these laments.
But I am forced to do this, so please
pardon me. How could a princess from
a noble family not act like this, when I see all
my father's sufferings grow greater every day
and night, and not die down?   260
The mother who gave birth to me has now
become my greatest enemy: I have to live
in this house with my father's
murderers; I'm under their command, and they
decide if I am to be fed or starve.
What sort of days d'you think I have?
I watch Aigisthos sitting grandly on
my father's throne; I'm forced to see him wear
Agamemnon's clothes, and pour libations at
the hearth, exactly where he slaughtered him.   270
And then I see this last and worst outrage:
my father's murderer together in my father's bed
with my revolting mother – if I have to call
that woman mother who makes love to him.
She's so depraved she lives with a man stained
by crime, not fearing an avenging Fury!
It is as if she gloated over what they did;
she celebrates the day on which
they used deceit to kill my father.
Each month she thanks the gods for her security,   280
with choral dances and with sacrifice of sheep.
I watch all this inside, alone in utter misery;

I cry, I pour out tears and bitter groans
because of her disgusting festival
in honour of my father's death; and I am not
allowed to cry enough to satisfy my heart.
That woman, who's supposed to be of noble birth,
says things like this, reproaching me for feeling sad:
'You loathsome creature, are you the only
girl whose father's died? Does no one else   290
suffer such grief? Just go to Haides; may the gods
down there bind you to your laments for evermore.'
That shows her arrogance – except when someone says
Orestes is about to come; then she goes crazy, comes
right up to me and screams: 'You caused all this!
You did it, when you stole Orestes
from my hands and smuggled him away!
You'll pay the penalty that you deserve.'
Those are the kind of words she screeches; by her side,
urging her on with this abuse, there stands her famous   300
bridegroom – utter coward, piece of scum – Aigisthos,
who only fights when there's a woman at his side.
I wait and wait for Orestes to come
and stop this; it's destroying me.
Because he's always going to do something – but does not –
he has dashed my open and my secret hopes.
My friends, in such a situation it's impossible
to be modest and reverent; when times are bad
there is tremendous pressure to act badly too.

1 WOMAN: Tell me; is Aigisthos nearby while you   310
tell us all this, or has he gone away?

ELEKTRA: He is not here. Do not believe I'd dare to come
outdoors if he was near. Right now he's out of town.

1 WOMAN: If that is so, I certainly could dare
to speak with you some more.

ELEKTRA: He is away. Ask me; what do you want to know?

1 WOMAN: I will. Tell me about your brother;
is he coming? Is he going to? I want to know.

ELEKTRA: He says he will – but does not do what he has
said.

1 WOMAN: A man might hesitate, facing so great a deed.   320

ELEKTRA: I did not save his life by hesitating.

1 WOMAN: Be confident. He is of noble birth, so he will help
     his friends.
ELEKTRA: I do believe it; otherwise, I would be dead by
     now.

(*Enter* CHRYSOTHEMIS *from the* skene, *carrying a bowl of
offerings*)

1 WOMAN: Don't say another word. I see your sister –
     child of the same father (and mother) –
     Chrysothemis emerging from the house;
     she's carrying the offerings we place on graves.
CHRYSOTHEMIS: My sister! You have come outdoors;
     what are you going on about again?
     D'you still not want to learn   330
     not to indulge your heart with empty words?
     I know this much about myself, that I
     am grieved by what is happening here; if I could only
     get the strength, I'd show just what I think of them.
     Things are so bad that I must trim my sails,
     and not seem to be doing something, when I can't
     hurt them. I wish you could behave like me.
     I know that what I say is wrong; the judgement
     you have made is right. But if I want to live
     in freedom, I must do all the rulers say.   340
ELEKTRA: It's terrible to see you, daughter of a noble man,
     have totally forgotten him, and do your mother's will.
     All these reproaches aimed at me
     are learned from her; nothing you say's your own.
     Take your choice; either 'behave badly' like me,
     or 'be a good girl' – and forget your dearest kin.
     You said just now that you – if you could only find
     the strength – would show how much you hate them.
     I'm trying to avenge my father – you don't help;
     indeed, you want to turn me from my path.   350
     Is that not cowardly, as well as wrong?
     Show me – or rather, learn from me; what would
     I gain, if I stopped grieving for my father?
     I am alive. My life is bad, I know – but it's enough.
     And I annoy them – so, I'm giving something to
     my father, if there's any pleasure down among the dead.

You say you hate them – but it's all just words;
your actions show you're with your father's murderers.
I could not ever – even if someone gave me
the gifts in which you take such great delight –   360
be subject to their will. Go on, sit at a table heaped
with riches, live an overflowing life of luxury.
The only food I need is not to harm
myself; I do not want your privileges.
Nor would you, if you were wise. You've got the chance
to be called daughter of the greatest of all fathers –
but you choose to be your mother's. Everyone will see that
    you
are wrong, a traitor to your father and your living relatives.
1 WOMAN: Please, by the gods, don't be so angry!
There's value in what both of you have said,   370
if either was prepared to learn.
CHRYSOTHEMIS: By now I've pretty much got used to how
she speaks to me. I would have said nothing – but I
have heard that something terrible is going to happen
to her, which will stop her long-drawn-out laments.
ELEKTRA: Tell me this awful thing. If it's worse
than how I am right now, I'll have to agree.
CHRYSOTHEMIS: I'll tell you everything I know.
If you do not give up these loud laments, they'll send
you where you will not ever see sunlight again;   380
buried alive, you will sing your hymns of grief
somewhere away from here. So think about
how you behave, and don't blame me, if later on
you suffer; now's a good time to be sensible.
ELEKTRA: They've really planned to do this to me?
CHRYSOTHEMIS: Yes, as soon as Aigisthos gets home.
ELEKTRA: Then let him come, quick as he can.
CHRYSOTHEMIS: My poor, unhappy sister, what d'you
    want?
ELEKTRA: Him to come back, if that's what he intends.
CHRYSOTHEMIS: So you can suffer? Are you mad?   390
ELEKTRA: So I can get as far as possible away from you.
CHRYSOTHEMIS: Do you not care about your present life?
ELEKTRA: Oh yes, it's wonderful! It's beautiful!
CHRYSOTHEMIS: Well, it could be, if you'd learn some sense.
ELEKTRA: Don't try to teach me I must neglect my relatives.

CHRYSOTHEMIS: No; but we have to yield to those in power.
ELEKTRA: Flatter them all you like; I can't behave like that.
CHRYSOTHEMIS: It's right not to let foolishness destroy you.
ELEKTRA: If I must be destroyed, it will be helping to avenge
   my father.
CHRYSOTHEMIS: I know my father will forgive me.   400
ELEKTRA: Only a worthless person could praise what you
   say.
CHRYSOTHEMIS: You will not listen to me and agree?
ELEKTRA: Certainly not. I'd never want to be that stupid.
CHRYSOTHEMIS: Then I will go where I was sent.
ELEKTRA: Where are you going? Who are these offerings for?
CHRYSOTHEMIS: My mother's sending me to pour libations
   at my father's grave.
ELEKTRA: What! Her greatest enemy?
CHRYSOTHEMIS: The man she killed herself – that's what you
   mean.
ELEKTRA: Who persuaded her; why does she want to?
CHRYSOTHEMIS: I think it was because of a nightmare.   410
ELEKTRA: Gods of my fathers, come and help me now!
CHRYSOTHEMIS: Her terror gives you confidence?
ELEKTRA: Tell me her dream before I speak to you.
CHRYSOTHEMIS: I don't know all of it, only a little.
ELEKTRA: Tell me anyway. Often little words
  have ruined people – or have rescued them.
CHRYSOTHEMIS: The story is that in her dream our father
  – yours and mine – came back to life, and once again
  had sex with her, then took the royal sceptre
  which he carried once, but Aigisthos now holds,   420
  and planted it beside the hearth. A new branch
  sprang, and blossomed out so mightily,
  it overshadowed all the land of Mykenai.
  I heard the story from a servant who'd been there,
  when Klytaimestra told the Sun her dream.
  I don't know any more, except
  she's sending me because this made her scared.   427
ELEKTRA: No! My dearest sister, don't put any of   431
  these offerings upon his grave. It would be
  an outrage, if you take our father gifts, and pour
  libations from that woman who hates him;
  scatter them to the winds, or hide them in a deep

hole underground, so none of them will ever
reach our father where he sleeps. When she's dead
they can be souvenirs for her down there.

She must be the wickedest of women, if
she dares to make you give the man   440
she killed these hateful offerings.
Ask yourself if he'll gladly take her gifts,
the dead man in that grave, whom she
killed ruthlessly, with hatred, then cut off
his hands and feet, and wiped the blood
from herself on his head. D'you really think
these offerings can free her from the murder?
It's impossible. Throw them away; instead,
cut off the end strands from your hair
and mine. I'm nothing, it's a tiny offering   450
– but all I have. Give him this suppliant lock –
and my belt too, not rich in ornaments.
Fall on your knees, and beg him to come up
to favour us, and help against our enemies;
pray that his son Orestes is alive to seize
the upper hand, crushing our enemies beneath his foot,
so for the rest of time we can give gifts
and offerings from hands with greater wealth.
Yes, I'm sure, I'm sure he had something to do
with sending her these terrifying dreams!   460
Sister, do this to help yourself, and me, and him,
the dearest to us both of all who ever lived,
our father who now lives in Haides' halls.
1 WOMAN: Her words show reverence; dear friend,
if you are wise, you will do this.
CHRYSOTHEMIS: Yes, I will. When something's right there is
no place for argument; it simply must be done.
But while I try, my friends,
I beg you by the gods, don't say a word.
If Mother hears about it, I know I   470
will suffer terribly for what I'm trying to do.

[*Exit* CHRYSOTHEMIS, *right*]

CHOROS 2

WOMEN (A1):   Unless I am a crazy prophetess
          with no true insight,
          Justice will come here,
          bringing just triumphs in her hands;
          my child, she will pursue them soon.
          I'm filled with confidence,
          since I've just heard   480
          the sweet breath of that dream.
          They will not forget – that
          great king among the Greeks who was
          your father, and the ancient double-sided axe
          which slew him – shameful outrage!

WOMEN (A2):   The bronze-shod Fury will come here,
          the beast with many feet and hands,   490
          lurking in fearful ambushes.
          They tried to consummate a bloodstained marriage
          – gross impiety! They are not truly wed, not true in bed.
          So I am sure we never, never could
          have seen this monstrous dream come near
          that pair of murderers without portending harm.
          Mankind should not believe that there is truth
          in terrifying nightmares and in oracles
          if this dream does not bring   500
          the outcome we desire.

WOMEN (A3):   Pelops, once long ago
          you cheated in a chariot race;
          when you came here, you brought
          destruction to this land.
          Since Myrtilos was laid
          to rest in the sea's depths
          – tossed headlong from his gilded   510
          chariot, a monstrous crime –
          never since then have suffering
          and crime departed
          from this house.

SCENE 3

(Enter KLYTAIMESTRA from the skene, followed by a
MAIDSERVANT carrying a bowl of fruit)

KLYTAIMESTRA: So! You have escaped, you're roving round
    outside again!
  Aigisthos is not here – and he has always kept you from
  disgracing your own family, a woman out of doors.
  Right now he is away, and you don't care at all
  about how I feel; you have told so many people   520
  that I'm arrogant, I have no right to rule,
  and I do violence to you and yours.
  That is not true! I speak sharply to you because
  I always hear sharp words from you.
  Your father – there is nothing else. That's your excuse –
  the fact that I killed him. Yes, I myself. I
  know it well; I won't deny the truth.
  Justice took him, not I alone; you should
  have been on her side, if you'd any sense.
  This father, whom you always grieve for, was   530
  the only Greek ruthless enough to sacrifice
  your sister to the gods; he had not suffered any pain
  when he created her like mine when I gave birth.
  Come; explain this to me. For whose sake
  did he sacrifice her? For the Greeks?
  They had no right to put my child to death.
  Did he kill her to help his brother Menelaos?
  She was mine – so I was bound to punish him.
  His brother had two children, and they should
  have died instead of her, since their father   540
  – and especially their mother – caused the Trojan War.
  Did Haides feel a special lust to feast
  upon my children more than hers?
  Or did your all-destructive father lose his love
  for my children, but still love Menelaos'?
  Does that not show he was a reckless, worthless man?
  I think he was, even if you do not agree; and if
  the girl who died could speak, she'd say so too.
  My conscience is at ease with what
  I've done; if you think I'm wrong, make sure   550

your own opinion's right before you criticize.
ELEKTRA: At any rate you can't say now that I abused
you first, and only then heard you reproach me;
if you'll allow me, I would like to set the record
straight about my father and my sister.
KLYTAIMESTRA: Most certainly; if you always began with
    words
like these, you would not have to fear reproach.
ELEKTRA: Then I will speak. You say you killed my father.
Could there be a worse admission, whether he
deserved to die or not? I will say that you   560
did not kill him with Justice; that worthless man
you live with now pressed and seduced you into it.
Ask Artemis, goddess of hunting, whom she punished
when she sent a calm to keep the ships at Aulis.
Better – I'll tell you, since she can't be a witness.
The story I was told is that my father once, relaxing in
a sacred grove of hers, disturbed by his footfall
a dappled, antlered stag, and when he killed it
boasted, letting slip some foolish words.
Angered by this, the virgin goddess made   570
the Greeks stay there, until my father sacrificed
his daughter as her compensation for the animal.
That's why my sister died; the army had
no other way to go home or to sail to Troy.
He was compelled; he fought against it many times,
then most reluctantly he sacrificed her – not just for his
    brother.
However – to anticipate what you'll say – even if
he'd done this to help Menelaos, was it right
for you to kill him for it? By what law?
Watch out; if you lay down such laws you may   580
create both suffering and repentance for yourself.
If we all kill each other in revenge, you know
you'd be the first to die, if you get your deserts.
Take care you don't use an invalid plea.

If you can be so kind, please tell me why
you are now doing the most shameful act of all,
sleeping with the bloodstained man who once
helped you to end my father's life, and having

children with him, while you cast aside your former
offspring, though we're royal, and legitimate.   590
How can I approve? Or will you say that you
are also doing this in vengeance for your daughter?
If you do, you'll shame yourself. It would be an outrage
if you're married for her sake to enemies.
No! No one can reproach you, since you keep
on finding different ways of saying we
badmouth our mother. But I think you are
our slavemistress more than our mother.
I live in misery; you and
your lover always make me suffer.   600
You very nearly killed your son –
and Orestes lives wretchedly, in exile.
You often say I brought him up
to take vengeance on you. And know this well:
I would, if I'd been strong enough. Your heralds can
denounce me to the world as vicious,
far too free of tongue, or shameless;
but if I am like that, no one can say I've not
inherited my mother's character.

I WOMAN: [My Queen, I see her words have left]
you breathing fury; I no longer see   610
you thinking carefully whether you're right.

KLYTAIMESTRA: Why should I have to think, confronted by
    this one,
who says such violent things about her mother;
she's a full-grown woman! Don't you think
she could do anything and feel no shame?

ELEKTRA: No! Understand this well; I do feel shame,
even if you can't see it. I know I am
behaving crazily, and I demean myself.
I cannot help it; your hostility, and what
you've done, force me against my will;   620
shameful acts teach others they must act the same.

KLYTAIMESTRA: You little bitch, how dare you tell me what I
    do and say makes you go on too much!

ELEKTRA: The words all come from you, not me. You've done
the deed; and deeds find their own words.

KLYTAIMESTRA: By Artemis, you won't escape from
    punishment

for this defiance, when Aigisthos comes back home.

ELEKTRA: Look here! You told me I could speak my mind;
but now you've lost your temper; you can't listen.

KLYTAIMESTRA: At least I let you get it off your chest;   630
won't you let me make offerings in peace?

ELEKTRA: I will. Please do; make all your offerings. You'll
have no cause to blame me; I won't say a thing.

KLYTAIMESTRA: Come, servant, lift these offerings
of fruit, so I can raise my prayers to the god,
to free me from these dreams.
Phoibos, protector of the house, please hear
this prayer although it's secretive. I am not speaking
among friends – nor is it right to unfold all I want
into the light when she's near me;   640
she's hostile, and will use her busy tongue
to spread malicious rumours through the town.
Hear my secret thoughts, concealed in what I'll say.
The images I saw last night in those
elusive dreams – Apollo, god of light, if they
mean good to me, grant that they be fulfilled;
but if they don't, send them back to my enemies.
If someone's planning to deprive me of
my wealth by treachery, prevent them;
may I always live unharmed, and rule   650
this house and hold this royal sceptre,
living with the friends I live with now,
enjoying my prosperity with them
and with those of my children who do not hate me.
Lord Apollo, hear this prayer with favour,
give us everything the way we ask for it.
Although my other needs are all unspoken,
I expect you, as a god, to know them;
you are Zeus' son, and should see everything.

(*Enter* OLD MAN, *right*)

OLD MAN: Ladies of Argos, can you tell me if   660
this is the house of lord Aigisthos?

I WOMAN: Stranger, it is; you have guessed well.

OLD MAN: And would I also rightly guess this lady
is his wife? She looks as if she's royal.

1 WOMAN: Most certainly; the Queen stands here before you.

OLD MAN: Greetings, my lady. I bring words of joy from one
who is a friend of you and Aigisthos.

KLYTAIMESTRA: I welcome what you've said. Tell me
at once who sent you here.

OLD MAN: Phanoteus the Phokian; and my message is
important.   670

KLYTAIMESTRA: What message? Stranger, tell me. You've
come from a man
we like; I'm sure we'll like your news as well.

OLD MAN: In three words, Orestes is dead!

ELEKTRA: I'm desolate, destroyed this day.

KLYTAIMESTRA: What? Stranger, what? Ignore that girl.

OLD MAN: I told you, and I tell you once again: Orestes has
died.

ELEKTRA: I'm utterly destroyed; I'm nothing any more.

KLYTAIMESTRA: Mind your own business! Stranger, now,
tell me the truth; how did he die?

OLD MAN: That's why they sent me; I will tell you
everything.   680
He went to compete in the Games at Delphi,
the most famous contest among Greeks.
When he heard the umpire heralding
the first event, the footrace, he stood out
and took his place – glowing with health, admired by all.
His finish did full justice to his body;
he came first, and took the prize.
To tell you much in a few words,
I've never heard of any success such as his.
Know this one thing: in all the contests which   690
the stewards held, he carried off the spoils of victory 692
and acclamation of the audience; each time he was
proclaimed – a man from Argos, Orestes, the son
of Agamemnon, who once led a famous panhellenic force.
Remarkable! – but when one of the gods
causes injury, even a strong man can't escape.
A few days later, when the swift-horsed
chariot race was to be held at dawn,
he entered, one of many charioteers.   700
One was Achaian, one from Sparta, two
masters of yoked chariots were Libyan;

then came Orestes, fifth, and driving with
horses from Thessaly. The sixth was from Aitolia,
with chestnut mares, the seventh from Magnesia;
the eighth, an Ainian by birth, had white horses;
the ninth man came from Athens, city built by gods;
and there was a Boiotian, in tenth place.

They took positions where the games officials
had assigned them by a lottery; their chariots stood   710
until the trumpet-call. Then they were off – shouting
out to the horses all at once, as their
hands shook the reins; the rattling chariots filled
the whole racecourse with sound, and dust
leaped up. They were all mixed together;
no one spared the whip, all trying to outstrip
each other's chariots and snorting horses.
The foam from all the horses' breath
fell on the drivers' backs and round their wheels.
Orestes always went close by the turning-pillar,   720
grazing it with his axle, while he let his right trace-horse
run free, and reined in tight the left that pressed near it.
For some time everyone stood upright in the chariots;
but then the horses of the man from Ainia ignored
the bit, pulled him off course, and wheeled around
as they were finishing the sixth lap, just about to start
the seventh; they collided head-on with the Barkian.
This accident then caused man after man to smash
and collide with each other, till the plain of Krisa
was entirely covered in wrecked chariots.   730

The clever charioteer from Athens swerved into
the outer lane, holding his horses back a moment
so he missed the surge of riders in confusion
at the centre. Orestes, in the inner lane, was holding
back; he put his trust in the last lap.
But when he saw only one man was left,
he made a shrill cry echo through the ears of his
swift horses, and sped in pursuit. Soon those two
rode side by side; each man in turn
got just ahead of his competitor.   740
Now, poor Orestes had completed many laps

in safety, and had kept his chariot upright;
but suddenly, rounding the turning-post,
he accidentally let his left rein slacken, and
his chariot hit the post. The axle-holder smashed,
and he was hurled over the rim, then caught
up in the reins; as he fell on the ground,
his horses bolted to the middle of the track.
When the crowd saw he'd fallen from his chariot,
they screamed in grief for this young man,   750
who'd done so well and now suffered this fate,
first hurled onto the ground, then with his legs
up in the air, until the other charioteers, who only just
managed to get his horses back under control,
released the wretched, bloodstained corpse,
so mutilated that no friend would recognize him.
He was cremated straight away; some Phokians
have been sent here to bring that mighty
body, now reduced to pitiable ashes in a tiny urn,
so he can have a burial in native soil.   760
That is what happened – painful even
spoken; to all who saw it for ourselves,
the worst disaster I have ever seen.
1 WOMAN: Oh! Oh! So now it seems all of our ancient
royal house has been destroyed, down to the roots.
KLYTAIMESTRA: Oh Zeus, what should I say? Is this good
    news – or something
terrible which has brought gain? It's horrible, if I
save my life through my own sufferings.
OLD MAN: Lady, why does my news upset you so?
KLYTAIMESTRA: Being a mother's strange; you cannot hate   770
your children, even when you suffer at their hands.
OLD MAN: So it would seem I've come in vain.
KLYTAIMESTRA: No! Not in vain! How could you tell this
    tale in vain?
If you have come here bringing certain proof
that he is dead, who was the fruit of my own soul,
but tore himself from my breast and my nurture, lived
in exile among strangers; after he had left this land,
he never saw me any more, but charged me with
his father's murder, threatened me with terrible revenge,
so neither night nor day would sweet sleep give   780

protection to me, but each moment I was safe
simply postponed the death I always knew would come.
And now! Today I am released from fear of him –
and from this woman too; she's been the greater harm,
sharing my house, a vampire always sucking out
the pure blood of my life. Now I am sure
we'll pass our days in peace, free from her threats.

ELEKTRA: I'm finished. Orestes, I must truly grieve
for you, since you are dead, and your
mother just gloats. Is that what's right for me?   790

KLYTAIMESTRA: Perhaps not. *He's* right just the way he is.

ELEKTRA: Listen to that, avenging goddess of the newly
dead!

KLYTAIMESTRA: She heard our needs, and did exactly right.

ELEKTRA: Insult us! Luck is on your side – just now.

KLYTAIMESTRA: So you and your Orestes won't stop me?

ELEKTRA: We have been stopped – no question now of
stopping you.

KLYTAIMESTRA: Stranger, you are a friend worthy of great
rewards
if you have stopped this woman's constant, vicious tongue.

OLD MAN: Should I then take my leave, if everything's all
right?

KLYTAIMESTRA: Certainly not; you would not then receive
what's due   800
from me, due to the friend who sent you
Please come inside – and let this one cry here
about her sufferings and her brother's.

[*Exeunt* KLYTAIMESTRA, OLD MAN, *and* MAIDSERVANT *into
the* skene]

ELEKTRA: D'you really think she was in pain, in agony,
dissolved in tears, grieving to break her heart –
that devastated woman who'd just lost her son?
No! She went in laughing. I am desperate;
dearest Orestes, your death has destroyed me.
You have torn out from my heart
the slender hope I still possessed, that you   810
would come back here alive some time,
and take revenge for us. Where can I go?

I am alone, bereft of you and of
my father. Must I now become a slave again
to the two people I hate most of all,
my father's murderers? Is that what's right for me?
No! Never for the rest of Time will I
live there with them. I will collapse
beside this door, and waste away alone.
If that displeases anyone inside, he can   820
kill me. That would be a favour –
it is torture to survive. I've no desire for life.

CHOROS 3

1 WOMAN (A1): Where are the thunderbolts of Zeus,
              and blazing Sun-god, if they see
              and happily conceal all this?
ELEKTRA: Ah! Ah! Aiai!
1 WOMAN: Child, why do you cry?
ELEKTRA: Oh!
        1 WOMAN: Restrain yourself.
              ELEKTRA: You will destroy me –
                  1 WOMAN: How?   830
ELEKTRA: – if you tell me to rest my hopes
          on those whom we know certainly
          have gone to Haides, you'll be trampling
          on me as I melt away.
1 WOMAN (A2): I will! I know Amphiaraos
          was put underground, trapped by a gold-bribed
          woman's snare, and now beneath the earth –
ELEKTRA: Ah! Ah! Aaah!   840
1 WOMAN: – he is a king, fully alive.
ELEKTRA: Oh!
        1 WOMAN: Yes, 'oh'; his murderous wife
              ELEKTRA: was killed.
                  1 WOMAN: Yes.
ELEKTRA: I know; his son came back to take revenge
          for that poor king. I now have no one;
          him I had is vanished, snatched away.

1 WOMAN (B1):   This must be torture for you.
ELEKTRA: Yes, I know; I know, and suffer;   850
    all my life is filled with surging waves
    and circling moons of terror and of hatred.
1 WOMAN: We have seen all that.
ELEKTRA: Don't any longer give me
    false hopes, now –
                1 WOMAN: now that?
ELEKTRA: – all hope has gone of any help
    from my great, noble brother.
1 WOMAN (B2):   It's natural that human beings die.   860
ELEKTRA: But is it natural to be tangled up
    like that poor man, under the horses'
    flashing hooves, and lacerated by the reins?
1 WOMAN: It's unbelievable and horrible.
ELEKTRA: Yes, it is! He's buried
    in a foreign land –
                1 WOMAN: Oh! Oh!
ELEKTRA: – without my hands; I haven't given him
    a grave or funeral laments.   870

SCENE 4

(*Enter* CHRYSOTHEMIS *right, running with her skirt lifted
above her knees*)

CHRYSOTHEMIS: My dearest sister, I've rushed back pursued
    by joy, abandoning all modesty to reach you fast.
    I bring you blessings, and the end of all
    those sufferings you've grieved about.
ELEKTRA: Where could you find relief from all
    my sufferings, for which no cure can now be found?
CHRYSOTHEMIS: Orestes is among us. Understand what I
    tell you; he can be seen, he's just as real as me!
ELEKTRA: Have you gone mad, poor girl? Making a mockery
    of your misfortunes and of mine?   880
CHRYSOTHEMIS: No! By our ancestral hearth, I do not speak
    to hurt you; he has come back for us both.
ELEKTRA: Poor girl! Who on earth told
    this tale in which you trust so much?

CHRYSOTHEMIS: I saw clear signs myself; I did not take
this story on trust from somebody else.

ELEKTRA: What proof did you see? What made you
warm your heart with false fires?

CHRYSOTHEMIS: Listen to me; let me tell you, then choose
whether to call me sensible or crazy. 890

ELEKTRA: Tell me then, if the story gives you joy.

CHRYSOTHEMIS: I'll tell you everything I saw.
When I came to my father's ancient tomb,
I saw new streams of milk flow from the top
of his grave-mound; and all around
it was adorned with flowers of every kind.
I was excited and afraid; I looked around
in case someone had come up near to me.
But when I saw that all was quiet, I began
to creep back to the tomb; and hanging from 900
the very edge I saw a new-cut lock of hair.
The sight astonished me – but suddenly my heart
was struck with a familiar vision; I just knew this was
a token from Orestes, dearest of all men to me.
I touched it, but kept reverently silent; and
at once my eyes were filled with tears of joy.
I'm still sure that this offering
could come from nobody but him.
Who else would have the right to place it there,
except for me and you? I know I did not do it; 910
nor did you. How could you? They don't let you leave
this house unpunished, even to revere the gods.
Our mother never wants to do such things
– and we'd have known about it if she had.
These offerings are from Orestes.
Take courage, dearest sister; the same daimon
does not stay with people all the time.
Ours has been hateful up till now; perhaps this day
will be the start of a new, joyful life.

ELEKTRA: All through I have felt pity for your foolishness. 920

CHRYSOTHEMIS: What's wrong? My news does not please
you?

ELEKTRA: You're out of touch; you are deceived.

CHRYSOTHEMIS: How could I not be sure of things I've
clearly seen?

ELEKTRA: You wretched girl, he's dead. He'll never
save you now; don't look to him for anything.

CHRYSOTHEMIS: Yes, I am wretched; where did you hear
this?

ELEKTRA: From one who was there when he died

CHRYSOTHEMIS: Where is the man? I find this very strange.

ELEKTRA: Inside the house, our mother's welcome guest.

CHRYSOTHEMIS: Then truly I am wretched! Who on
earth   930
put all those offerings upon our father's grave?

ELEKTRA: I think most probably that someone left
them there as a memorial to Orestes.

CHRYSOTHEMIS: This is such agony! I hurried here
with joy to bring my news, not knowing
how we've been destroyed; we have
new torments added to the old.

ELEKTRA: You're right; but if I can persuade you,
you'll be free of all this weight of suffering.

CHRYSOTHEMIS: What? Shall I bring the dead to life
again?   940

ELEKTRA: Not what I said. I am not quite that mad.

CHRYSOTHEMIS: Will I be able to do what you want?

ELEKTRA: Get tough, do what I tell you.

CHRYSOTHEMIS: If I can help, I won't push you away.

ELEKTRA: Remember, all success needs work.

CHRYSOTHEMIS: I know; I will do anything for which I'm
strong enough.

ELEKTRA: Then listen; this is how I plan
to end it all. We both know that we are
bereft of friends. Haides has taken them,
snatched them from us; we two are left alone.   950
As long as news came that our brother
was alive and flourishing, I still had hopes
that he would come back to avenge his father;
now he's dead, I look to you.
I want you not to shrink from killing
with your sister's help your father's murderer –
Aigisthos. I no longer need to hide my plan from you.
How can you just do nothing? Does any hope
remain? You have good cause to grieve:
they have deprived you of your father's wealth,   960

and made you wait so long; you're growing
old, unmarried and without enjoying sex.
Don't hope you'll ever get a husband;
Aigisthos is not such a fool
as to let any child of yours or mine
be born – an obvious threat to him.
But if you are persuaded by my plan,
first you will win rewards for piety
from your dead father and your brother down below;
then you'll regain your birthright, and be called   970
a free woman forever; you will win a worthy man,
since everyone admires great deeds.
Do you not see how much fame you
will bring us both, if I persuade you?
Who, of all our citizens and immigrants,
will not hail us on sight with praise like this?
'Friends, look at these two sisters,
who have saved their father's house.
They risked their lives, and brought death down
upon its well-protected enemies.   980
We must all love and worship them,
and celebrate them both with banquets for
their manly courage at each city festival.'
I tell you, that's what everyone will say about us;
we'll be famous both alive and dead.
My sister, please work with our father
and our brother, and release us both
from sufferings; remember that to live a life of shame
is shameful for a woman who's of noble birth.
I WOMAN: In such a venture, both people need   990
Foresight to be an ally on their side.
CHRYSOTHEMIS: Yes, exactly; if she'd thought
before she spoke, she would have kept
her caution, which she has now lost!
Where were your senses, when you armed yourself
with all that courage and enlisted me to help?
Do you not realize? You are a woman, not a man;
your hands have far less strength than theirs.
Some daimon gives them greater fortune every day,
while ours just flows away and dwindles into
      nothingness.   1000

Who could plan to bring down a man like him, expecting
she'll escape her own destruction quite unscathed?
We're suffering enough – watch out; we'll suffer
even worse, if any of them hears these words.
It's not exactly going to help us to escape, if we
acquire great fame, while being tortured till we die.   1006
No! I beg you, don't destroy us both   1009
completely, and exterminate this family;   1010
restrain your rage. I promise I will hide
what you have said; it's secret, and will do no harm –
but you must learn sense now, late though it is.
You have no power; obey the ones who do.

1 WOMAN: Listen to her. Careful foresight and true sense
are the most precious gifts people can have.

ELEKTRA: You've said nothing I did not expect; I knew
how gladly you would throw away what I proposed.
So my hand by itself must do
this work; I will not let it go undone.   1020

CHRYSOTHEMIS: Wow!
If only you'd been this strong when they killed
our father; you could have done anything.

ELEKTRA: My character was strong; I just lacked sense.

CHRYSOTHEMIS: Try always to be just as sensible as then.

ELEKTRA: That sounds as if you won't help me.

CHRYSOTHEMIS: Yes; if we try, we'll probably be hurt.

ELEKTRA: I envy you your good sense, hate your cowardice.

CHRYSOTHEMIS: I'll still be here for you, when you see I am
right.

ELEKTRA: That will not ever happen.

CHRYSOTHEMIS: The rest of Time is long enough for judging
that.   1030

ELEKTRA: Get out of here! You are no use to me.

CHRYSOTHEMIS: I could be; you don't want to learn.

ELEKTRA: Go back and tell your Mummy all of this.

CHRYSOTHEMIS: I never could hate you like that.

ELEKTRA: At least accept that you are hurting me.

CHRYSOTHEMIS: I am not hurting you; I'm trying to help.

ELEKTRA: So you think I should follow your idea of right?

CHRYSOTHEMIS: When you are sane, I'll let you be my guide
again.

ELEKTRA: It's terrible to use such clever words – and be so wrong.
CHRYSOTHEMIS: That is precisely your problem.   1040
ELEKTRA: What? You don't think I'm right?
CHRYSOTHEMIS: Perhaps – but sometimes even being right can harm.
ELEKTRA: I could not ever live like you.
CHRYSOTHEMIS: If you do this, some day you will praise me.
ELEKTRA: I'll do it anyway; you have not moved me.
CHRYSOTHEMIS: Truly? You won't change your plan?
ELEKTRA: No! I hate all plans which are not right.
CHRYSOTHEMIS: You don't see any sense in what I say.
ELEKTRA: I made my mind up long ago; this is not new.   1049
CHRYSOTHEMIS: Enough! If you believe you're thinking straight,   1055
   go on; when you have fallen into suffering,
   you'll praise what I have said.

[*Exit* CHRYSOTHEMIS *into the* skene]

CHOROS 4

WOMEN (A1):   The birds up in the sky are wise;
         they nurture both their parents
         and the young ones who give joy; so why   1060
         do we not do the same?
         By Zeus' thunderbolts,
         and Law enthroned on high,
         they will be punished soon!
         Voice that can reach the dead,
         send down this pitiable cry
         to Agamemnon; speak
         of shame too great for dance –

WOMEN (A2):   his house diseased,   1070
         his daughters quarrelling
         so badly it can't be resolved
         in loving harmony;
         this poor child's now alone,
         betrayed, tossed by the storm,

always grieving her father's death,
as wretched as
the plaintive nightingale.
She doesn't care if she is killed;
she's ready to no longer see the light,
if she can kill the double Fury.   1080
Who else could be so loyal to her noble father?

WOMEN (B1):   No woman from a great house could
desire to be a disgraced nobody,
shaming her family.
So you have chosen a life full
of glory – and of everlasting tears;
you have not given arms to what you don't
believe is right. You won't be hailed as wise,
but called the very best of children.

WOMEN (B2):   I want to see you raised up far above   1090
your enemies in power and wealth, as much
as you now lie beneath their hand;
I have seen you suffer
terribly, but you
have won first prize
for piety to Zeus, because you've given
honour to the greatest laws of all.

SCENE 5

(*Enter* ORESTES *and* PYLADES, *who carries an urn, right*)

ORESTES: Women, have we been directed right, and are we
travelling straight to where we want?
1 WOMAN: What are you looking for? Why are you
here?   1100
ORESTES: I have been asking all the way for where Aigisthos
lives.
1 WOMAN: They guided you correctly; you are there.
ORESTES: Could one of you go in and tell them that two men
have come whom they'll be glad to see?

1 WOMAN: She should, if you want the nearest relative to
   herald you.

ORESTES: Then go, woman, and tell the people inside that
   some men from Phokis want to see Aigisthos.

ELEKTRA: Oh no! Don't tell me you have brought clear
   evidence to prove the rumour that we heard?

ORESTES: I don't know what you've heard; old Strophios   1110
   has ordered me to bring some news about Orestes.

ELEKTRA: What news? Fear's creeping into me.

ORESTES: We've come bringing some few remains of him in
   this small urn. As you can see, he's dead.

ELEKTRA: I am destroyed. That's it, now all too clear; my
   grief is here before my eyes – and small enough to touch.

ORESTES: If you have cause to weep about Orestes' fate,
   know that this urn contains his body.

ELEKTRA: Stranger, by the gods, if he's inside the urn
   please let me hold it in my hands;   1120
   I want to weep and share my sorrow with
   these ashes for myself and my whole family.

ORESTES: Bring it, and give it to her; whoever
   she may be, she does not ask in hatred.
   She's a friend, or a blood-relative.

ELEKTRA: Oh last memorial of Orestes, dearest
   of all men to me! I sent you out with such
   great hopes – and this is how I take you back.
   Now I embrace you in my hands – and you are nothing;
   when I sent you out, you were a radiant boy.   1130
   I wish that I had left this life,
   before I sent you to a foreign land, with these
   two hands abducting you and saving you from death;
   I wish you'd died that very day, so I could give
   you your due place in our ancestral tomb.
   Instead you fell in agony away from home,
   an exile in another place, far from your sister.
   So, I'm suffering; with my loving hands
   I could not wash your body as I should have, or pick up
   the miserable remains after the raging fire.   1140
   You suffered also; foreign hands attended you
   and brought you back, a tiny weight inside a tiny urn.
   I'm desperate with grief; the upbringing I once
   gave you was useless – that sweet, loving work

I often did for you. I know your mother
never loved you more than I.
I was the sister whom you always called for, since
no nurse looked after you; I did.
Now everything has vanished in one day
with your death. You have gone like   1150
a hurricane, and taken everything. My father has departed:
I am dead, because of you; death's taken you;
our enemies are laughing. That mother who is not
a mother will go mad with joy – whom you so often sent
me secret words about, to say you'd come yourself
to take revenge. A daimon of ill fortune stole
all this from you and me, when he sent you
to me like this; not your most precious flesh, but
just a piece of dust, the useless shadow of a man.
    Oh!   1160
    This wretched body!
    Oh! The dreadful
    path you trod, my dearest, has destroyed me;
my own brother, you've destroyed me.
So you must take me with you in this little box,
nothing to nothing; I will live below
with you for ever. When you were alive
I shared in everything with you; so now I want
to die, and not wait to be buried after you.
Death is the one release from pain and suffering.   1170

1 WOMAN: Elektra, be more practical! Your father was a
    mortal;
Orestes was mortal too. Don't grieve so much;
all of us must suffer this.

ORESTES: Oh god, what shall I say? I'm lost
for words. I have no power of speech.

ELEKTRA: Why are you hurting? Why do you say that?

ORESTES: Are you the famous, beautiful Elektra?

ELEKTRA: Yes; but I have lost my looks.

ORESTES: Poor woman, you have suffered terribly.

ELEKTRA: Stranger, you surely do not grieve for me?   1180

ORESTES: Look at this body, wasted by godless abuse!

ELEKTRA: You really are concerned about my suffering.

ORESTES: They have neglected you – ill-fated, and unmarried.

ELEKTRA: Stranger, why d'you look at me so sadly?

ORESTES: I did not realize the depth of my misfortune.
ELEKTRA: What has been said to make you feel like that?
ORESTES: I see you etched by many sufferings.
ELEKTRA: You only see a little of my misery.
ORESTES: What worse could there be than what I can see?
ELEKTRA: I have to live with them – the murderers.   1190
ORESTES: Whose murderers? Where does all this pain come
    from?
ELEKTRA: My father's murderers; I'm forced to be their slave.
ORESTES: Who forces you to that necessity?
ELEKTRA: My so-called mother; but she doesn't act like one!
ORESTES: What does she do? Beat you? Humiliate you all the
    time?
ELEKTRA: She beats, humiliates and torments me.
ORESTES: Is there no one to help you, and prevent her?
ELEKTRA: No. You've brought in ashes my one hope of help.
ORESTES: Poor woman, as I look I pity you.
ELEKTRA: Then you're the only person who has ever pitied
    me.   1200
ORESTES: Perhaps I am the only person hurt by what you suffer.
ELEKTRA: You aren't a distant relative of mine?
ORESTES: I would tell you, if we can trust these women.
ELEKTRA: Yes, we can; they are my loyal friends.
ORESTES: To learn the whole truth, you must first let go that
    urn.
ELEKTRA: Stranger, I beg you, don't make me.
ORESTES: Trust me, and you will not be wrong.
ELEKTRA: No! Please! I beg you. It is dear to me; don't take it.
ORESTES: I will not let you keep it.
         ELEKTRA: Orestes, we're
    both lost in misery, if I can't bury you!   1210
ORESTES: Be careful what you say; you are not right to grieve.
ELEKTRA: What? Not right to grieve for my dead brother?
ORESTES: You must not speak like that of him.
ELEKTRA: The dead man now rejects me too?
ORESTES: No one rejects you; this urn's not for you.
ELEKTRA: Yes, if Orestes' body is now in my hands.
ORESTES: It's not Orestes' body – just a story, so they think it
    is.
ELEKTRA: Where is that poor boy buried?
ORESTES: Nowhere; living people do not need a grave.

ELEKTRA: What do you mean?
     ORESTES: I am not telling lies.   1220
ELEKTRA: He is alive?
     ORESTES: If I'm alive.
ELEKTRA: Then you are he?
     ORESTES: Here is our father's
signet-ring; look, and make sure I tell the truth.
ELEKTRA: Oh day of joy!
     ORESTES: Yes, it is.
ELEKTRA: Orestes, are you here?
     ORESTES: Yes, I am.
ELEKTRA: I am embracing you.
     ORESTES: Now and forever.
ELEKTRA: Dearest friends, women of Argos,
  look! This is Orestes, 'dead' by trickery –
  and now by trickery he has come back to life.
1 WOMAN: Dear girl, we see; and in my happiness   1230
  at your good fortune tears creep from my eyes.

ELEKTRA (A1):   My child reborn!
    Child of my dear, dear father,
    you've come back;
  you're here, you've found and seen your loved ones.
ORESTES: Yes, I'm here; but wait – be quiet.
ELEKTRA: Why?
ORESTES: Silence is best; someone might hear us from inside.
ELEKTRA: By Artemis, invincible,
    I'll never deign to fear   1240
    that useless pack of women
    in the house!
ORESTES: Watch out! The War-god can make even women
  fierce; you should know that from experience.
ELEKTRA: No! No!
    It can't be clouded over, cannot be undone,
    and cannot be forgotten; the first crime
    which caused our sufferings.   1250
ORESTES: I know that too; but we can talk about
  it when there's lots of time to spare.

ELEKTRA (A2):   For me the whole of Time would be
    all right, always, to speak

of this with Justice at my side.
I only just restrained myself from shouting out aloud.
ORESTES: Restraint is good; stay like that.
ELEKTRA: What must I do?
ORESTES: It's not the right time; do not try to speak at length.
ELEKTRA: But who could give enough   1260
        to make me celebrate
        your homecoming in silence?
        I have seen you – beyond my dreams,
        beyond my hopes.
ORESTES: You only saw me, when the gods told me
        that I must come [and take revenge].
ELEKTRA: This is an even greater
        joy than what you said before, if the
        god sent you back home to us;
        it really is a daimonic event.   1270
ORESTES: I do not want to hold you back from joy, but I'm
        afraid you will be overcome by your delight.

ELEKTRA (A3): No – it's been so long
        before you thought it right to make
        this dearest of all journeys to appear to me,
        so please – because you see me full of suffering –
ORESTES: What must I do?
                ELEKTRA: Do not deprive me
of the joy of touching your dear face.
ORESTES: Just let somebody try to stop you!
ELEKTRA: I can?
                ORESTES: Of course.   1280
ELEKTRA: Dear one, I heard
        some news I never thought I'd hear.
        But still, I kept my anger muted,
        did not cry out in my misery.
        Now I have you! You have come back; yours is
        the dearest face to me; no suffering
        could ever make me forget you.

ORESTES: Don't bother now with words we do not need;
        don't tell me just how bad our mother is,
        nor that Aigisthos pours out all of my inheritance –   1290
        either just wasting it, or spending it on useless bribery;

the time you take would make us lose the moment for our
    deed.
Just tell me what I need right now; where must
we come from? Or, where should we hide,
so our return will stop our enemies from gloating?
And make sure Mother does not see through you because
your face is radiant now we have come back.
Weep, as if that disaster which we lied about
was true; when we've succeeded, then
we will have freedom to rejoice and laugh.   1300
ELEKTRA: Dearest brother, if that's what you want
I'll want it too; I have received
this joy from you, not by myself.
And I could never take great pleasure
if it hurt you at all. That would not serve
the god who is now on our side.
You must know how things stand in there.
I've heard Aigisthos is not now at home;
our mother is. Don't fear that she might see
my face all radiant with joy.   1310
The hate of many years has melted into me,
and now I've seen you, I will never stop
my tears of joy. How could I stop?
I've seen you come back here first dead and then alive;
you've wounded me in ways I cannot understand.
So if my father came back here alive, I would not think
that was a monstrous phantom; I'd believe I saw him.
You've come so far to save me; guide me
as you will. If I'd been left alone
I would have either gloriously saved myself   1320
or gone in glory to my death.
ORESTES: Be quiet. I hear someone at the door;
    they're coming out.
              ELEKTRA: Strangers, come in –
especially because you've brought some things no one
in there could possibly resist – but which they won't enjoy.

(*Enter* OLD MAN *from the* skene)

OLD MAN: You idiots! Are you quite mad,
    do you no longer care for life,

or have you never had a brain at all?
You are not just beside, but right inside
the greatest danger – but you do not seem to know!   1330
If I had not been keeping guard behind
this door for a long time, they would have known
what you are up to long before
you got inside; but I took care of that.
You must stop all this talk
and endless cries of joy at once,
and go inside. Delay would now be wrong;
the moment's at its height for you to make an end.
ORESTES: How will I find them, when I go inside?
OLD MAN: Just right! I've made sure nobody will know
   you.   1340
ORESTES: You have told them I am dead?
OLD MAN: Know that in there you live in Haides.
ORESTES: Do they rejoice at that? What do they say?
OLD MAN: I'd better tell you when it's over. Just now
   everything
is good – including what is not so good for them.
ELEKTRA: Brother, who is this? By the gods, tell me.
ORESTES: Do you not know?
          ELEKTRA: I've no idea.
ORESTES: Remember you once gave me to somebody.
ELEKTRA: Who? What do you mean?
          ORESTES: Thanks to your foresight,
he took me in secret to the plains of Phokis.   1356
ELEKTRA: This is the man – the only man, out of them all,
   whom I found true when our father was being killed?
ORESTES: Yes. Do not ask more questions – there's no need.
ELEKTRA: Oh dearest light! Oh only saviour of the house
of Agamemnon, how did you come? Are you the man
who saved me and Orestes from our sufferings?
You have the dearest hands, and sweetest, faithful
feet – how have you been here for so long,
unrecognized? Your radiance did not shine
on me; your words destroyed me, though you planned   1360
what I desire! Welcome, Father! For I seem to see my
   father;
welcome! Know that of all men I've hated you
and loved you most in just one day.

OLD MAN: Enough, I think. The words we need to speak –
a lot of days and nights will circle round,
Elektra, and make these things clear to you.
Now I tell you two at the ready that this is
the moment for the deed. Klytaimestra's alone;
there is no man inside, and if you stay your hand,
remember we must fight with them – and many   1370
others too, who're cleverer than them.
ORESTES: Pylades, it seems our deed has no more use
for big speeches; let's go inside as fast
as possible, first honouring the places where
my father's gods live, just outside the doors.

> [*Exeunt* ORESTES, PYLADES, OLD MAN *into the* skene]

ELEKTRA: Lord Apollo, listen favourably to them
– and to me as well; I've often stood
before you earnestly, with all the offerings I had.
Apollo, wolf-god, all I have now is my prayer.
I beg you, I bow down before you, and I pray.   1380
Be on our side and help us in our plan;
show every human being that the gods
reward impiety with punishment.

> [*Exit* ELEKTRA *into the* skene]

CHOROS 5

WOMEN (A1):   Look! The war-god's on the move,
breathing blood
of bitter strife.
They've just gone in the house,
the hounds who punish wicked deeds.
They cannot be escaped;
my dream won't have
to hover longer in the air.   1390

WOMEN (A2):   The champion of the gods below
creeps on stealthy feet into

his father's halls to win their ancient wealth,
by bringing keen-edged death;
Hermes the son of Maia
hid their trickery in darkness, and leads
him to the goal; there is no more delay.

FINALE

(*Enter* ELEKTRA *from the* skene)

ELEKTRA (AI):   My dearest friends, at any moment now
the men will finish it; be quiet!
1 WOMAN: How? What are they doing?
    ELEKTRA: She is readying   1400
the urn for burial, and they stand over her.
1 WOMAN: Why have you come outside?
    ELEKTRA: To guard
so Aigisthos can't get inside unseen.
KLYTAIMESTRA: (*inside the* skene) Aiai! This house! There are
no friends in here; it's full of murderers.
ELEKTRA: A cry from inside! Did you hear it, friends?
1 WOMAN: I heard an awful cry;
  it's horrible. I shudder.
KLYTAIMESTRA: Help! Aigisthos, where on earth are you?
ELEKTRA: See! Another cry!
    KLYTAIMESTRA: My son, my son;   1410
pity your mother.
    ELEKTRA: You did not show
him pity, or his father!
1 WOMAN: Wretched city! Wretched family! Now the fate
which has been yours each day is dead! Is dead!
KLYTAIMESTRA: Ah! They've struck me!
    ELEKTRA: If you can, strike twice as hard!
KLYTAIMESTRA: Ah!
    ELEKTRA: Get Aigisthos, too!
1 WOMAN: Now curses are fulfilled, and corpses
  come to life. Men who died long ago
  are draining blood in recompense   1420
  from their own murderers.

(*Enter* ORESTES, *with a bloodstained sword, and* PYLADES
from the skene)

I WOMAN (A2):   And here they are! His bloody hand drips
    with the war-god's sacrifice; but I can't blame them.
ELEKTRA: Orestes, how are you?
              ORESTES: Everything in there
is fine, if Apollo's prophecy was fine.
ELEKTRA: That wretched woman's dead?
            ORESTES: You need not fear;
your mother's arrogance will never hurt you any more.
ELEKTRA: [This is
the supreme moment of my joy.
ORESTES: You have what you desired.]
I WOMAN: Stop; I see Aigisthos
    in full view.
ORESTES: [On his way here?]
ELEKTRA: Go back inside!
            ORESTES: You're sure   1430
he's coming?
           ELEKTRA: Yes, we'll get him! He
is on his way back from the suburbs, full of joy.
I WOMAN: Go back inside, quick as you can;
you've done well so far; once again –
ORESTES: Relax; we will succeed.
           ELEKTRA: Hurry!
ORESTES: I am off!

          [*Exeunt* ORESTES *and* PYLADES *into the* skene]

        ELEKTRA: Then I must handle things out here.
I WOMAN: It would be best
    to slip some gentle words
    into his ear, so he may rush   1440
    into the hidden trap of Justice.

[*Enter* AIGISTHOS, *left*]

AIGISTHOS: Does anyone know where the Phokian strangers
    are,
    whom people say have told us that

Orestes lost his life in a wrecked chariot?
You – I pick you; yes, you – the woman who till now
was always impudent. I imagine you would be
especially concerned, and so most likely know the truth.

ELEKTRA: I know; how could I not? Or else I would
be ignorant about the fate of one most dear to me.

AIGISTHOS: Where are they then? Tell me.   1450

ELEKTRA: Inside; they've found a gracious hostess.

AIGISTHOS: And did they really say that he is dead?

ELEKTRA: No; they've shown evidence, not just mere
words.

AIGISTHOS: It would be possible for me to see this too?

ELEKTRA: Of course – but it is not a pleasant sight.

AIGISTHOS: It's very strange for you to try to please me.

ELEKTRA: You may take pleasure, if this truly pleases you.

AIGISTHOS: I order you to open up the doors and show
so all the Mykenaians and Argives can see;
if anyone once fed on empty hopes raised by   1460
this man, let him now see the corpse,
accept my bridle, and not have to feel the force
of my chastisement before breathing sense.

ELEKTRA: I for one have learned my part completely; now at
last
I have gained wisdom – serving my superiors.

(ELEKTRA *opens the doors of the* skene; *enter* ORESTES *and*
PYLADES *on the* ekkyklêma, *with the completely shrouded
corpse of* KLYTAIMESTRA)

AIGISTHOS: Zeus, I see a miracle – something which chanced
because
the gods were angry; if that thought is impious, I take it
back.
Remove the covering from the eyes, so that
this kinsman may receive my elegy.

ORESTES: Take it yourself; it is not mine, but yours   1470
to see and speak with kindness to this corpse.

AIGISTHOS: That's good advice, and I will follow it. Woman,
if my wife is in the house, call her.

ORESTES: She is near you; don't look elsewhere.

(AIGISTHOS *opens the shroud*)

AIGISTHOS: What do I see?
              ORESTES: Whom do you fear? Whom can't you
     recognize?
AIGISTHOS: Who are these men into whose trap
     I've fallen wretchedly?
              ORESTES: Can't you see you
     are still alive, but playing word-games with the dead?
AIGISTHOS: Now I understand. The man who's speaking
     can't be anyone except Orestes.   1480
ORESTES: Since you're so good a prophet, why so long
     deceived?
AIGISTHOS: I'm finished. But let me
     say just a few words
              ELEKTRA: No! By the gods, brother,
     don't let him speak again, and spin out words at length.   1484
     Kill him as quickly as you can, and when he's dead   1487
     give him the kind of burial a man like him deserves,
     out of our sight. That is the only way
     to free me from my years of suffering.   1490
ORESTES: Get in there quickly; now there is no trial
     of words – just the struggle for your life.
AIGISTHOS: Why take me inside? Why, if this deed's so
     glorious, d'you need the dark to do it? Kill me now!
ORESTES: Don't give me orders! Go to where you killed
     my father; you will die in that same place.
AIGISTHOS: Must this house see all the sufferings
     of Pelops' children, now and evermore?
ORESTES: Yours at least; that I can prophesy.
AIGISTHOS: Not something which your father could do
     well!   1500
ORESTES: You're full of clever answers, but our road grows
     long.
     Get in!
              AIGISTHOS: Lead the way.
              ORESTES: You must go first.
AIGISTHOS: Afraid I will escape you?
              ORESTES: No, just so you don't
     die easily. I must make sure your death is bitter.
     That's the penalty which everyone should get at once,

who wants to go beyond what's sanctioned by the law;
capital punishment! Then we'd have fewer criminals.

[*Exeunt* AIGISTHOS, ORESTES *and* PYLADES *into the* skene]

1 WOMAN: Elektra, you have suffered much,
          and only just regained your liberty;
          this violence has made you free for evermore.   1510

(ATTENDANTS *withdraw the* ekkyklêma *with the corpse of*
KLYTAIMESTRA)

[*Exeunt* WOMEN, *left*]

[*Exit* ELEKTRA *into the* skene]

PHILOKTETES

Translated by Graham Ley

THE ACTORS AND THEIR ROLES

ODYSSEUS   Actor 3
NEOPTOLEMOS   Actor 2
LOOKOUT   Silent Face, later Actor 3 when
                  disguised as the Merchant
GREEK SAILORS   Choros
PHILOKTETES   Actor 1
TWO SAILORS   Silent Faces
HERAKLES   Actor 3

The skene *façade represents a cave*

SCENE I

(*Enter* ODYSSEUS *and* NEOPTOLEMOS, *with the* LOOKOUT, *left*)

ODYSSEUS: Here we are, on the shoreline of Lemnos, surrounded
by the sea, on an uninhabited, desert island.
Neoptolemos, you are still young, but you are the son
of Achilleus, strongest of the Greeks. It was here,
a long time ago, I marooned the son of Poias from Malis –
I was ordered to do it by the commanders –
a man whose foot was festering with a devouring ulcer.
We had our reasons: it was impossible for us to put
our hands to libation or sacrifice as we chose, because
he filled the whole of the camp with his wild curses,   10
shouting and shrieking. But what is the point of talking
about this? We should not get involved in a discussion now.
If he learns that I am here, then the trick by which
I expect to take him without any delay will be wasted.
Now your job in what remains to be done is to serve me.
Look around here for a cave with two entrances,
of a kind that in cold weather offers a choice of places
to sit in the sun, while in the summer a breeze
wafting through the tunnel brings sleep with it.
A little bit below, on the left-hand side, you might   20
see a spring of fresh water, if it has not dried up.
Approach the place, and signal to me silently
whether he is still living there, or has moved elsewhere.
Then, as for the rest of the plan, you can listen,

I shall talk, and we'll both share in the action.

NEOPTOLEMOS: Lord Odysseus, I shall not have to go far to get this done,

because I think I can see a cave like the one you described.

ODYSSEUS: Above you, or below you? I cannot pick it out.

NEOPTOLEMOS: This one, up here, and so far no sound of footsteps.

ODYSSEUS: Be careful. Look and see. He may be sleeping inside.   30

NEOPTOLEMOS: I see an empty shelter, with no human being in sight.

ODYSSEUS: And nothing to make a home, to make a life in there?

NEOPTOLEMOS: Yes. A bed of leaves, as if someone sleeps here.

ODYSSEUS: But the rest is bare. Nothing there except a cave?

NEOPTOLEMOS: Yes, a cup hacked out from wood, something contrived by a very poor craftsman, and with it this kindling here.

ODYSSEUS: Clear indications. That's him, and his store of things.

NEOPTOLEMOS: Ah! Ugh! There are some rags here as well, drying

out, heavily plastered in pus from a sore.

ODYSSEUS: That's certain, then. The man lives here, in this spot,   40

and he won't be far away. How could someone cursed

for years with a diseased leg range very far?

He has either come out to look for food,

or he knows of some soothing herb somewhere.

Send the man you have with you to keep a lookout,

so he does not come on us by surprise: he would rather

take me than the rest of the Argives together.

(NEOPTOLEMOS *gestures to the* LOOKOUT, *and he exits left*)

NEOPTOLEMOS: He is on his way, and the track will be watched.

Now tell me the second part of the plan, if you feel like it.

ODYSSEUS: Son of Achilleus, what you have come to do calls on   50

your nobility: not just physical proof of nobility,
but if you are told something unexpected, something you
have not heard before, do your duty. You are here to serve.
NEOPTOLEMOS: What are your orders?
                    ODYSSEUS: You must deceive
the mind of Philoktetes with a story you will tell him.
When you are asked who you are and where from,
you say 'the son of Achilleus'. No deception there.
Your story: you are sailing home, leaving the fleet:
and the Achaian expedition, in hatred, in great hatred.
Why? Because after they had moved you with prayers   60
to leave home, as their only means of taking Ilion,
when you arrived they refused to give you
the armour of Achilleus when you claimed it by right.
Instead, they gave it to Odysseus. You can add
as much extreme abuse as you like against me.
You will not upset me with that; but if you do not
carry this through, all the Argives will suffer.
If his bow and its arrows are not taken from him,
it is beyond your power to sack the land of Dardanos.
In your dealings with him, you can count on his trust.   70
There will be no danger. Not so with me. Learn why.
You have sailed without being bound by an oath,
under no compulsion, and not in the first fleet
but I cannot deny any of these things.
So if he recognizes me while he still has his bow,
I am a dead man; being in my company will kill you too.
What we must contrive is a trick, and you must
become a thief, and steal his invincible weapons.
I know, my boy, that you were not born with the nature
to tell lies like this, or be cunning, or do wrong.   80
But to lay hands on victory is to hold a sweet possession:
make yourself do it. A reputation for justice can come later.
For now, give yourself to shamelessness and to me
for the short space of one day, and then, for the rest
of time, hear yourself called the most pious of all men.
NEOPTOLEMOS: For myself, when I hear an argument that
        distresses me,
son of Laertes, I find it repugnant to put it into action.
It is not in my nature to succeed by underhand means;
not in my nature nor, as they say, in that of my father.

But I am prepared to take the man away by force,   90
instead of by deceit; if he is fighting from one good leg
he cannot get the better of two men like us.
I may have been sent to work with you, but
I refuse to be called treacherous. I should rather, lord,
act well and not succeed than act badly and win.

ODYSSEUS: You are the son of a noble father. When I was
    young,
I was slow to speak, and let my arms do the work.
But now, putting experience to the test, I see
that words not actions take the lead amongst men.

NEOPTOLEMOS: Have you other orders for me, apart from
    telling lies?   100

ODYSSEUS: I am instructing you to take Philoktetes by a
    trick.

NEOPTOLEMOS: Why should we take him by a trick, rather
    than by persuasion?

ODYSSEUS: He will not be persuaded, and you won't take
    him by force.

NEOPTOLEMOS: Are his strength and his determination that
    terrible?

ODYSSEUS: His arrows are inescapable, and they deal out
    death.

NEOPTOLEMOS: So much so that no one would dare to
    confront him?

ODYSSEUS: No. Not unless he is taken by trickery, as I say.

NEOPTOLEMOS: Do you not think it is shameful to tell lies?

ODYSSEUS: No, not if telling lies brings you security.

NEOPTOLEMOS: So how does one find the face to mouth
    them?   110

ODYSSEUS: You don't hold back, if you stand to gain.

NEOPTOLEMOS: What do I stand to gain if he comes to Troy?

ODYSSEUS: That bow will capture Troy, and that bow alone.

NEOPTOLEMOS: So I am not going to sack the city, as you
    said?

ODYSSEUS: Not you without it, nor it without you.

NEOPTOLEMOS: If that is how it is, then the hunt must go on.

ODYSSEUS: There are two prizes for you to win, if you do so.

NEOPTOLEMOS: What are those? I shall not refuse, if I know.

ODYSSEUS: A reputation for wisdom and for bravery, both at
    once.

NEOPTOLEMOS: Let it happen. I'll do it, and discount any
   sense of shame.   120
ODYSSEUS: So do you remember the advice that I gave to
   you?
NEOPTOLEMOS: I do, clearly, now that I've agreed, once and
   for all.
ODYSSEUS: Stay here then, and keep waiting for him to come.
   I shall go away, so that I am not spotted with you,
   and I shall send the lookout back to the ship.
   If I think you two are dawdling, taking
   too much time, I'll send that same man back
   here again, but in disguise, with the look and attitude
   of a merchant-captain, to conceal his own identity.
   You, my boy, must then pick up whatever might help
   you   130
   as he is talking his way through some contrived story.
   I am off to the ship, leaving all this up to you:
   may Hermes, the trickster, be our guide and companion,
   with Victory and Athene Polias, who is my constant saviour.

                                              [*Exit* ODYSSEUS, *left*]

                              CHOROS I

[*Enter* SAILORS, *left*)

SAILORS (A1):   As a stranger in a strange land, what should I
      conceal,
      master, or what should I say to a suspicious man?
      Tell me.
      A skill above all other skills
      and a judgement that excels rest in
      the ruler who has a divine sceptre from Zeus.   140
      This total, primeval power has
      descended to you, my son. So tell me,
      how should I serve you?
NEOPTOLEMOS: Perhaps you would like to look at the place
      where he rests, here on the margins. For now,
      look around without fear; he is out wandering,
      has left his lair. But he is awesome, and when he

returns come to me when I beckon you,
and try to serve me as the occasion demands.

SAILORS (A2):   You mention a duty that has long concerned
        me, lord,   150
to keep a careful eye, above all, on what is best for you.
But now
tell me where he lives, what kind of
shelter he uses as his home? Now is
the right time for me to know:
he may surprise me, appearing suddenly from
        somewhere.
Where is he? Where is his home? If he is about,
is he at home, or outside?

NEOPTOLEMOS: You see it here: his house, with two doors,
        a resting-place of rock.   160
I SAILOR: Then where has he gone, the poor man?
NEOPTOLEMOS: It is clear to me that he is ploughing his way
        along somewhere near to this spot in search of food.
For the word is that this is how he provides
himself with food, by hunting continually
with his feathered arrows, in constant pain,
with no healer
of his suffering coming forward to him.

SAILORS (B1):   I pity him, that
with none to care for him,   170
without a companion's face to gaze on,
always alone, in misery,
he suffers this savage sickness,
at a loss for every
necessity as it arises. How does he ever endure his
        misery?
Oh, the gods contrive,
and the human race is wretched,
when what life brings is excessive.

SAILORS (B2):   This man is perhaps no lower   180
        than those of the most noble families,
        but he has none of the means of life,

and lies in isolation, alone
with wild, spotted or fur-covered
beasts, pitiable in his pain and
his hunger combined, enduring incurable, uncared-for
   misery,
Garrulous Echo
in the distance answers
his bitter cries.   190

NEOPTOLEMOS: None of this is amazing to me.
The assaults of that suffering came upon
him, if my thinking is right, from a
divine source, from savage-minded Chryse.
His continuing affliction, without carers,
must be due to some god's intention,
that he should not aim his divine
and invincible weapons against Troy
before this time had come, at which,
they say, it is destined to fall to them.   200

1 SAILOR (C1):   Be quiet, my boy!
        NEOPTOLEMOS: What is it?
           SAILOR: There was a noise,
one that might come from a man who is worn out.
It came either from here, or from over there.
I can hear it now, and it is just like
the voice of a man who has to force
his way along . . . I am certain!
The painful cry, in the distance,
of a man in pain, an unmistakable sound.

1 SAILOR (C2):   But take, my son . . .
        NEOPTOLEMOS: Take what?
           1 SAILOR: – take thought again.   210
The man has been away, but now he is back,
not returning from the fields like a shepherd
accompanied by the music of a reed-pipe,
but his cry carries to us from a distance,
and it is that of a man who cannot avoid
stumbling, or who sees an anchorage which
has no ship as its guest. It is a terrible cry.

SCENE 2

(*Enter* PHILOKTETES, *right*)

PHILOKTETES: Hey there, strangers!
  Who are you? You have used your oars to row in here,   220
  and put into a land without harbour or inhabitants.
  What country are you from? Can I guess?
  What race of men? Your clothing looks like that
  of Greece, of all places the dearest to me.
  But I want to hear you speak. Don't hesitate
  from fear of me, scared of the savage I have become,
  but have pity on a wretched and a lonely man,
  a loveless outcast, as you can see, who has been wronged.
  Speak up, if you have come here as friends.
  Oh, do answer me! It is unfair for you   230
  to deny that to me, or for me to deny it to you.

NEOPTOLEMOS: Stranger, know this thing first, that we
  are Greeks. That is, after all, what you want to know.

PHILOKTETES: Oh, darling language! Ah, what it means just
  to hear the greeting of a man like this after so long!
  What brought you to land here, my son? Something you
  needed? What motive? Which of the winds was my best
    friend?
  Let me hear the whole story, so I know who you are.

NEOPTOLEMOS: I am by birth from the sea-washed island
  of Skyros. I am sailing home. I am called   240
  son of Achilleus, Neoptolemos. Now you know all.

PHILOKTETES: Oh, son of a father most dear to me, from a
    dear country, child nurtured by old Lykomedes! What is
    your purpose in landing here? Where have you sailed
    from?

NEOPTOLEMOS: Since you ask, I hold my present course from
    Ilion.

PHILOKTETES: What did you say? How is that? I know you
    did not sail with us in the beginning of the expedition
    against Ilion.

NEOPTOLEMOS: Do I take it you played a part in that
    struggle?

PHILOKTETES: My boy. Do you not know the man you are
    looking at?

NEOPTOLEMOS: How can I know someone I have never seen
  before?   250

PHILOKTETES: Have you not heard my name, then? No
  rumour at all of what
 was done to me? Of my sufferings? They have destroyed
  me.

NEOPTOLEMOS: Be quite certain: I know nothing of what you
  are asking me.

PHILOKTETES: What an utterly defeated man I am, how
  hateful to the gods,
 if no report of how things are with me has reached
 my home, or any part at all of the land of Greece.
 Those who made me an outcast, in their impiety,
 keep quiet and laugh at me, while my sickness
 continues to bloom and increases in strength.
 Oh, my boy, who has Achilleus for your father,   260
 I who stand here am that man of whom perhaps you
 have heard, who is master of the weapons of Herakles,
 Philoktetes the son of Poias, whom the two
 generals and the lord of the Kephallenians
 shamefully marooned as an outcast, while I was
 wasting away with a savage sickness, struck
 by the fierce bite of a killer snake.
 Those men, my boy, put me ashore here in that
 state, and left me alone, after sailing here
 with the expedition from the island of Chryse.   270
 After their rough crossing they were glad to see
 me sleeping on the shore, in the arch of a cave.
 They deserted me and were gone, leaving a few rags,
 suited to a man down on his luck, and some little
 sustenance – and may they have the same themselves!
 I slept. But what kind of awakening do you
 think I had, my son, when they had gone?
 Can you imagine how much I cried, and groaned in misery?
 How I saw that the ships, which I led on the expedition,
 had disappeared, that there was not a man in the place,   280
 no one who could help me, no one who might lend
 a hand when I was racked by sickness. As I looked
 around I found nothing except pain by my side,
 and of that there was a plentiful supply, my son.

So, as it was, time went on from one day to the next,
and alone, in this humble shelter, I was forced
to act as my own servant. This bow here procured
what I needed to eat; I shot the doves
in flight; then I would haul myself
wretchedly towards whatever the arrow, speeding   290
from the string, had struck, dragging this painful foot,
and would reach it. If it was water I needed to get,
or perhaps, when the frost lay on the ground in winter,
if I had to break up some wood, I crept out miserably
and found a way to get it done. Then there was no fire:
but by rubbing two stones together I would just manage
to strike out the hidden spark, which still keeps me alive.
For with a shelter as somewhere to live and a fire in it
I am provided with everything except an end to this disease.

Come, my son, now you must learn about the island.   300
It is not one that a sailor approaches willingly.
There is not a single harbour, nor is there a location
to which one can sail for profitable trade, or find welcome.
This is not a place to which careful men plot their course.
So let us say someone is forced to land here, and this
might happen many times in the full length of a lifetime.
When these men do come here, my son, they say that
they pity me, and because they feel compassion
they donate some portion of food, or some clothing.
But not one of them, when I bring the subject up, is
     willing   310
to rescue me and take me home. My condition is wretched,
a living death, in its tenth year now, from hunger
and hardship, while I nourish this gluttonous sickness.
The sons of Atreus and 'heroic' Odysseus
did this to me, boy; and may the Olympian gods
grant that they suffer in retribution, just as much as me.

I SAILOR: I too find myself drawn to pity you, son of Poias,
     just like those who have come here before.

NEOPTOLEMOS: And for my part I shall bear witness to what
     you
     have said. I know it is true, since I myself have   320
     suffered wrong from the Atreidai and heroic Odysseus.

PHILOKTETES: So do you too have some charge to make against those

villains, the Atreidai, a wrong that stirs you to anger?

NEOPTOLEMOS: I hope I have the chance to satisfy my anger
with my hands, to make Mykenai and Sparta come
to realize that Skyros is the mother of brave men.

PHILOKTETES: That is good to hear, my son. You have come here,

in great anger, with a charge against them; what is it?

NEOPTOLEMOS: Son of Poias, I shall tell you, although I find it hard,

the injuries I suffered from them when I came to Troy.   330
When it was the allotted time for Achilleus to die . . .

PHILOKTETES: Ah, no! Do not tell me any more, until I know
about this first. Has the son of Peleus died?

NEOPTOLEMOS: He is dead, but at the hands of a god, not a man,

shot, as men say, and brought down by Phoibos.

PHILOKTETES: Then both are noble, both the killer and the slain.

I cannot be sure, my boy, whether I should
question you about your suffering, or mourn him.

NEOPTOLEMOS: I should think your own sorrows should be enough

for you, poor man, without mourning for those near to you.   340

PHILOKTETES: What you've said is right. So take up your story of what

happened to you again, the nature of their violent insult.

NEOPTOLEMOS: They came for me in a ship with a decorated prow,

excellent Odysseus and the man who brought up my father,
and they said – what may be true or just a lie –
that it was ordained that, after the death of my
father, none but I should take the citadel of Troy.
That is how they put it to me, my friend, and they
did not intend that I should delay for long. I set sail
hurriedly, largely because of my longing to look at   350
the dead man before he was buried; for I had never seen him.
And then there was, in addition, that story – attractive,
if it was true – that by going to Troy I might take the citadel.

It was now the second day out on my voyage,
and I was coming in to land at bitter Sigeion,
helped in by breeze and oar; and as soon as I came ashore,
the whole army encircled me with greetings, swearing that
it was the dead Achilleus they were looking at, alive again.
So there he lay. I felt dismal; but when I had
wept over him, I did not leave it long before   360
I went to the Atreidai in friendship, naturally,
and asked for my father's armour and his other possessions.
The reply they gave to me was utterly disgraceful:
'Seed of Achilleus, you may take everything
your father owned except his armour;
another man is master of that, the son of Laertes.'
The tears started in my eyes, and I leaped up on
the spot in a violent rage, giving voice to my grief:
'This is criminal! Have you dared to give my armour
to another man instead of me, and without asking me?'   370
There was another voice – of Odysseus, who was near us:
'Yes, my boy, and the award that they made was just.
I was right there; I secured his body and his armour.'
Then my anger flared, and I struck out with
every kind of abuse, leaving nothing out of the reckoning,
if that man was going to deprive me of my armour.
It came to the point where, although he was not angry,
he was stung by what he had heard, and so he answered me:
'You were not here as we were, but elsewhere, and that was
     wrong.
You have a bold tongue, and you use it. My response?   380
You'll never sail to Skyros with this armour.'
That was what I heard, and, thoroughly insulted,
I am sailing back home, without what is mine,
thanks to the worst of a bad breed, Odysseus.   384
That is the whole story. And may he who hates   389
the Atreidai be as dear to the gods as he is to me.   390

(CHOROS 2: PART I)

SAILORS (A1):   All-nurturing Earth, mountain goddess,
                mother of Zeus himself,
            who rules over great, gold-bearing Paktolos,

there as well, lady mother, I called upon you,
when all the violent insults of the Atreidai
moved in array against this man,
when they treacherously handed his father's armour –
oh, you who ride blissfully on the backs   400
of bull-killing lions – to the son of Laertes,
in its awesome splendour.

PHILOKTETES: It seems as if, friends, you have sailed here
to me bringing a secure pledge of grief with you,
and the song that you sing to me allows me to recognize
that this is the work of the Atreidai and of Odysseus.
I know him well: he'd lend his tongue
to any underhand scheme, or anything criminal, if he
had hopes to bring some injustice to completion.
None of this amazes me. But if the greater Aias was   410
there, could he see this going on and hold himself back?
NEOPTOLEMOS: My friend, he was no longer living. Had he
    been alive,
I could not possibly have been robbed of the armour.
PHILOKTETES: What did you say? Is he, too, dead and gone?
NEOPTOLEMOS: You should think of him as no longer in the
    light of day.
PHILOKTETES: Oh, that is hard to bear. But the son of
    Tydeus,
and the son of Sisyphos, sold on to Laertes,
they won't die: the mistake was to let them have a life.
NEOPTOLEMOS: That is true. You're right; as things stand
they are alive and flourishing in the Argive camp.   420
PHILOKTETES: Ah! And then . . . that dear, good old friend of
    mine,
Nestor from Pylos, is he dead? He was often
a defence against their mischief, with his sound advice.
NEOPTOLEMOS: I am afraid his fortunes are low, since his son
Antilochos, who was at his side, is dead and gone.
PHILOKTETES: Ah, no, those two whom you have mentioned
    are just
the men I should least have wished to hear are dead.
No, no, no. What is there to look for, when men
like these have died, but Odysseus lives on,
who by rights should be listed as dead instead of them?   430

NEOPTOLEMOS: The man is a clever wrestler, but even clever
   plans,
Philoktetes, often come up against obstructions.
PHILOKTETES: Now, by the gods, tell me this: where was
   Patroklos
at your time of crisis, who was your father's dearest friend?
NEOPTOLEMOS: He, too, had died. I shall tell you this, as
the shortest summary; war never willingly takes
an evil man, but ever and always takes the good.
PHILOKTETES: I will bear witness with you there. And in that
   respect,
and only that, I shall ask what has happened to a man
who was worthless, but sharp-tongued and clever.   440
NEOPTOLEMOS: Who else but Odysseus would fit that
   description?
PHILOKTETES: No, I was not speaking of him. But there was
   one Thersites,
who would never choose to speak and be done, despite
disapproval from all. Do you know if he is still living?
NEOPTOLEMOS: I did not see him myself, but I gathered that
he was.
PHILOKTETES: Most probably, since nothing bad has ever
   passed on.
Instead, the divine powers take very great care of it,
and for some reason take pleasure in turning back
from Haides anyone crafty or criminal, while they
dispatch there all the just and good.   450
How should I make sense of this, or praise it? When I
scrutinize what they do, I conclude the gods are bad.
NEOPTOLEMOS: For my part, Philoktetes, son of an Oitaian
   father,
from now on I shall beware of Ilion
and the Atreidai, and watch them from a distance.
When the worse man is stronger than the better man,
the good cause is in decline, the worthless man in power,
and I shall never find affection for men like these.
But, for the future, rocky Skyros will suffice
for me, and make me content to be at home.   460

Now I'm on my way to my ship. Goodbye to you,
son of Poias, and farewell. And may the gods

bring you relief from your sickness, as you wish.
But we must be going, so that we can set sail
as soon as heaven allows us to make our voyage.
PHILOKTETES: Are you leaving already, my son?
                    NEOPTOLEMOS: Yes, we need to watch
for the right moment to sail; on the spot, not guessing.
PHILOKTETES: In the name of your father, of your mother,
    my son,
in the name of anything you hold most dear at home,
I come to you as a suppliant; do not leave me alone   470
like this, deserted, in the miserable circumstances you
can see, living in the dreadful way you have heard about.
Spare me an afterthought. I know only too well
that a cargo such as myself is quite repugnant.
But do not be squeamish. The nobly born are enemies
to what is shameful, and gain glory from what is good.
If you fail to take me, it will be an ugly reproach;
but if you do it, my boy, you will have the finest reward
if I come back alive to the land of Oita; a good name.
Come, it is the work of less than one whole day.   480
Bring yourself to do it; take me, stow me wherever
you like, in the hold, at the prow, in the stern, wherever
I shall bring least discomfort to those I am with.
Nod in agreement, by Zeus the god of suppliants, my son,
be persuaded! I fall to my knees in front of you, even though
I am a weak, wretched, lame man. I beg you, do not
leave me like this, cut off completely from the paths of men.
Either take me safely back with you to your own home,
or back to the farms and villages of Chalkodon in Euboia:
from there it will not be a long journey for me to Oita,   490
and to the highlands of Trachis and to the beautiful,
flowing Spercheios, and you may show me to my own dear
    father.
It is a long time now since I was first afraid that he
might be gone from me. Many is the time I sent off a
    message
to him by those who came here, begging and praying
that he would sail here in his own ship and rescue me.
Perhaps he is dead. Or perhaps – as is, I think,
most likely – the messengers thought my affairs of small
account, and hurried their ships on a course for home.

But now I have you as a messenger and an escort   500
combined, be my saviour, take pity on me, seeing
that all human life is hazardous, and there is a constant
risk whether things will turn out well, or turn out badly.   503

(CHOROS 2: PART 2)

SAILORS (A2):   My lord, pity him. He has told   507
          of a struggle of unbearable hardship,
          which I pray none of those dear to me will face.
          If, my lord, you hate the Atreidai bitterly,   510
          then turning the harm done
          by them into a great
          gain for him, I should take this man
          on your ship with its fine equipment
          swiftly to where he longs to be, to his home,
          and escape the anger of the gods.

NEOPTOLEMOS: Take care. You may feel kindly now, on the
          sidelines. But
when you have had your fill of proximity to his disease,   520
then you may not find yourself urging the same argument.
I SAILOR: I reject that! I shall never give you the opportunity
          to feel justified in levelling that accusation at me.
NEOPTOLEMOS: Then it would certainly be shameful if I
          fell short of you in my efforts to meet the needs of a
          stranger.
So, if that is decided, let us sail, and he must come
quickly; our ship shall carry him, and not refuse.
Just let the gods see us safely away from this
land, and send us wherever we may wish to sail.
PHILOKTETES: Oh, dearest of all days to me, most welcome
          of men!   530
Kind sailors, how can I clearly show to you by
anything I do how firmly you have made me your friend?
Let us go, my boy, with a proper farewell to that
home inside there that is no home, so you can learn
what I survived on, and how strong-hearted I was.
In fact, it is my belief that no one else would
have stood the sight you'll see, but I lived through it.

I had no choice in learning as I went to put up with
   hardship.

I SAILOR: Wait a moment, we must stay here. There are two
   men –

one is a sailor from your ship, the other I don't know –   540
coming here together. See what they say, and then go in.

(*Enter* LOOKOUT, *disguised as a* MERCHANT, *with another
sailor, left*)

'MERCHANT':   Son of Achilleus, I asked this member of your
   crew,
who was standing guard at your ship with two others,
if he could tell me where you happened to be.
I had not expected that we should be meeting like this,
but chance had it that I anchored on the same shore.
I am a merchant-captain, and I'm sailing home
with a small crew from Ilion to Peparethos,
famous for its vines, and when I heard that all
the sailors I saw came from your ship's complement,   550
I thought I shouldn't continue on my voyage without
speaking to you, since chance finds us in the same place.
It may be that you know nothing of your own situation,
what the recent decisions are that the Argives have
made about you, which are not just decisions, but
are now actions in progress, not a form of inaction.

NEOPTOLEMOS: My friend, your considerate attitude is a
   favour to me,
and it would be despicable if I did not remain grateful.
Tell me about the activity you have mentioned, and then I
shall know what new schemes of the Argives you have in
   mind.   560

'MERCHANT':   They have left to pursue you, in a squadron;
Phoinix, the old man, and the sons of Theseus.

NEOPTOLEMOS: Do they intend to bring me back by
   persuasion or force?

'MERCHANT':   I don't know. I heard of it, and here I am to
   tell you.

NEOPTOLEMOS: Is it to win favour with the Atreidai that
   Phoinix
and those sailing with him are in such a hurry?

'MERCHANT':   It's all in progress, not waiting to happen. Be
    sure of that.
NEOPTOLEMOS: So why was it that Odysseus was not ready
    to sail
    and bring this message himself? Was he frightened of
    something?
'MERCHANT':   He and the son of Tydeus were setting out
    after   570
    another man, just as I myself was putting to sea.
NEOPTOLEMOS: Who was this, then, that Odysseus was
    sailing after?
'MERCHANT':   Well, there was a . . . but first tell me who this
    man is. And when you say his name, don't speak loudly.
NEOPTOLEMOS: The man you see, friend, is the famous
    Philoktetes.
'MERCHANT':   Don't ask me any more for now, but set sail
    from this country as quickly as you can, and get away.
PHILOKTETES: What is he saying, my boy? Why is the sailor
    trading dark secrets with you? What is this about?
NEOPTOLEMOS: I don't understand what he is saying. But
    whatever he has   580
    to say, he must say it openly: to you, to me, and to these
    men.
'MERCHANT':   Seed of Achilleus, do not denounce me to the
    army
    for saying what I should not. I have done things for them,
    and do well from them in return, as much as a poor man
    may.
NEOPTOLEMOS: I am their enemy, and this man is my
    greatest
    friend, since he hates the Atreidai as I do.
    You came to me in a friendly spirit; so you must not
    conceal from me anything of what you have heard.
'MERCHANT':   Watch what you are doing, my son.
                    NEOPTOLEMOS: I have been.
'MERCHANT':   I hold you responsible for this.
                    NEOPTOLEMOS: Do so, and talk.   590
'MERCHANT':   I shall. Those that I said, the son of Tydeus
    and heroic Odysseus, are sailing after
    this man here. They have taken an oath: to bring him
    back by persuasion, or by force.

Odysseus made that declaration, and all the Achaians
heard him say it clearly. He was much more assertive
about his ability to carry it through than the other man.

NEOPTOLEMOS: There must be some purpose in this. What
    made the Atreidai
  turn their thoughts keenly to this man, after so long a
    time?
  It is a very long time indeed since they cast him away.   600
  They must have wanted something badly. Did the gods
    compel
  them as retribution, in the way they reward wrong-doing?

'MERCHANT':   I shall take you through all of this, since you
    may
  not have heard it. There was a noble prophet,
  a son of Priam, and the name he had was
  Helenos. Odysseus captured him at night, by treachery,
  all by himself; Odysseus, who should be ashamed
  to hear the insults levelled at him. He tied his arms,
  and led him into the middle of the Achaians, a fine catch.
  Well, Helenos pronounced a whole range of prophecies,
    and   610
  some about the citadel of Troy, how they would never
  sack it unless they persuaded this man here to go with
  them and brought him from this island on which he is living.
  And when the son of Luertes heard the prophet
  saying this, he immediately made a promise, that he
  would bring this man and display him to the Achaians.
  He thought he would probably find him willing to be taken,
  but if he refused, he would take him anyway. If he failed,
  then he offered his own head to anyone who wanted it.
  You have heard the whole story, my son. I should   620
  advise you, and anyone you care for, not to delay.

PHILOKTETES: Oh, this is bad for me. So that appalling man
  has sworn that he will persuade me to go to the Achaians?
  I shall be as soon persuaded, when I am dead,
  to come up again into the light, as his father did.

'MERCHANT':   I don't know about that. But I must away now
  to my ship. May a god help you both, for the best.

[*Exit* 'MERCHANT', *with the* SAILOR, *left*]

PHILOKTETES: Isn't that astounding, my boy? That the son
of Laertes hoped, with the aid of soft talk, to lead me
from his ship and display me in the midst of the Argives? 630
No! I would sooner listen to that snake, which made
me lame like this, and is the thing I hate most.
But there is nothing that man wouldn't say, nothing
he would not do. And now I know he will be coming.
But we must go, my son, so that a wide stretch
of sea separates us from the ship of Odysseus.
Come on; making haste when the time is right leads
to sleep and to rest, once the labour is over.

NEOPTOLEMOS: So when the present head-wind begins to
slacken, that
is when we shall sail. At present, it is against us. 640

PHILOKTETES: It is always fair sailing, when you are escaping
trouble.

NEOPTOLEMOS: I know. But the wind's against them too.

PHILOKTETES: There is no such thing as an opposing wind
for pirates,
when there is a chance to steal, or snatch things by force.

NEOPTOLEMOS: If that is how you feel, let's go. You must
collect
from in there whatever you need or most want to take.

PHILOKTETES: There are some things I need, though I have
few enough.

NEOPTOLEMOS: What is there that I do not already have on
the ship?

PHILOKTETES: I have the leaves of a herb there, my most
reliable remedy
for soothing the wound, and easing it down from a crisis. 650

NEOPTOLEMOS: Fetch it out here, then. What else are you
keen to take?

PHILOKTETES: Any of these arrows which may have slipped
out, and been
overlooked. I do not want to leave them for someone else.

NEOPTOLEMOS: Is that the famous bow that you are holding
now?

PHILOKTETES: This, the one I am holding in my hands, and
no other.

NEOPTOLEMOS: Is it possible for me to have a closer look at
it?

For me to handle it and salute it like a god?

PHILOKTETES: For you it is, my son. This, or anything else I
    have,
will not be refused you, if it can do you any good.

NEOPTOLEMOS: I long to touch it. But it is this kind of
    longing: 660
if it is lawful, I should like to, if not, let it be.

PHILOKTETES: Those are pious words, and, yes, it is lawful,
    my son:
you alone have granted me the liberty to look on
the light of the sun, to see the land of Oita,
to see my old father, to see my friends. I was
under the heel of my enemies, and you have restored me.
Do not hesitate: you shall be able to hold it,
and to hand it back, and to boast as well that your
excellence allowed you that touch, alone of living men.
For it came to me through what I myself did for another. 670

NEOPTOLEMOS: I cannot regret meeting you, and having you
    as a friend.
Whoever knows how to return one favour for another has
to be a friend who is worth more than any possession.
Do, please, go in.

PHILOKTETES: And I shall take you with me,
because this sickness of mine would dearly love your help.

[*Exeunt* PHILOKTETES *and* NEOPTOLEMOS *into the* skene]

CHOROS 3

SAILORS (AI):   I have heard the story, but was not there to
    see,
        how the man who once
        approached the bed of Zeus
        was taken and bound to the rim
        of a wheel in Haides
        by the almighty son of Kronos.
        But I have not heard of any other, nor have I seen
            one,   680
        encountering a fate worse than this man.
        He had not wronged or robbed anyone,

but lived in harmony with other men,
and was destroyed, as he did not deserve.
It is this that amazes me,
how, oh how, when he listened in solitude
to the beat of the waves around him, how
could he keep hold like this
of a life that was full of tears?   690

SAILORS (A2):   He was there on his own, heard no
          approaching footstep,
had no neighbour
with whom to share his suffering,
who might echo his loud lament
at the bloodthirsty disease
which was eating his flesh.
No one who might stem the hot flow of blood
bubbling from the wound in his poisoned foot,
if a spasm took him, with gentle
herbs gathered from the grassy ground.   700
He would creep about, from one place
to another, limping along,
like a child without a kindly nurse,
in search of the sustenance
he needed, whenever the soul-
destroying curse of his wound relented;

SAILORS (B1):   not picking for food crops sown in the holy
          earth, nor
anything else that we men who work the soil enjoy;
but whatever he chanced to hit with the   710
feathered arrows of his bow, that was food for his belly.
A grim life it was.
Without the pleasure of poured wine for the length of
          ten years,
he looked around to see where he could find standing
          water,
and made his way yet again towards it.

SAILORS (B2):   But now, after that misery, he will attain
          happiness

and greatness, because he has met the son of noble
    ancestors,   720
who will take him back across the sea
in his ship, after a mass of months, to the home of the
    Malian
nymphs, his own land,
to the banks of Spercheios, where, as a god, the man of
    the
brazen shield was drawn to the gods, resplendent in
    divine fire,
up and above the mountainside of Oita.

SCENE 3

(*Enter* NEOPTOLEMOS *and* PHILOKTETES *from the* skene)

NEOPTOLEMOS: Come along, if you want to. Why so silent
    like this?   730
Why have you stopped, struck dumb? Is there a reason?
PHILOKTETES: Ah, ah, ah!
NEOPTOLEMOS: What is it?
    PHILOKTETES: Nothing to worry you. Go on, my son.
NEOPTOLEMOS: Is the sickness coming on you? Are you in
    some pain?
PHILOKTETES: No, no, not I. I have felt an easing of it lately.
    Oh, gods!
    NEOPTOLEMOS: Why do you groan, and call upon the
    gods?
PHILOKTETES: That they might be my saviours, and come to
    me gently.
    Ah, ah, ah!
NEOPTOLEMOS: What is happening to you? Must you stay
    silent like this,   740
and not speak? Clearly there is something badly wrong with
    you.
PHILOKTETES: I am lost, son, and shall not have the strength
    to hide
my sufferings from you, aah! It is going right through me,
    right through
me! Ah, the miserable creature that I am.

I am lost, son. I am being eaten, son. Aah, oh,
aah, aah, aah, oh, oh, aah, aah, oh, aah, aah!
By the gods, if you have one to hand, son, by your
hands, a sword, strike at the end of my foot, the heel!
Scythe it off, as quickly as you can! Don't stop to think of
    my life.
Do it, my boy!   750
NEOPTOLEMOS: But this is new, and so sudden. What is it
    that
has brought on this fit of groaning, and shrieking?
PHILOKTETES: Don't you know, son?
        NEOPTOLEMOS: What is it?
            PHILOKTETES: Don't you, boy?
                NEOPTOLEMOS: No. What?
    I don't know.
                PHILOKTETES: How can you not know? Aah,
    aah, aah!
NEOPTOLEMOS: This sickness is a terrible burden for you to
    carry.
PHILOKTETES: Terrible, and unspeakable. But have pity for
    me.
NEOPTOLEMOS: What shall I do?
            PHILOKTETES: Don't be frightened. Don't
    betray me.
It comes back to me, this sickness, after a time, when
    perhaps
it has had enough of wandering.
            NEOPTOLEMOS: Your life is wretched,
    wretched in all manner of suffering, manifestly so.   760
Do you want me to lend you an arm, and support you?
PHILOKTETES: No, no, not that. But you can take this bow
    from
me, as you asked me just now, until the bout
of the sickness that is with me now has eased.
Keep it safe, and guard it. Sleep takes over
usually, you see, when the worst of it has passed;
there is no end to it before then. But you must allow me
to sleep without disturbing me. If in the time I am sleeping
those men do get here, I forbid you by the gods,   770
voluntarily or not, by any means at all, to give
it up to them. If you do, you will be the cause

of my death and of your own, and I am your suppliant.
NEOPTOLEMOS: Take heart; I shall take care. It won't be
    given to
anyone but you or me. Hand it to me, and we will prosper.
PHILOKTETES: There you are; take it, boy. Make a prayer to
    divine Jealousy,
that these weapons do not bring you hardship, in the way
they did to me, and to him who owned them before me.
NEOPTOLEMOS: Oh gods, grant this to us both. And grant a
    following
wind for an easy voyage, to whatever destination god   780
decrees to be just, and to which our journey tends.
PHILOKTETES: Ah, oh, ah, aah!
I am afraid, boy, that your prayer may be unfulfilled.
I can see the blood oozing and dripping again from
the depths of the ulcer, and I expect a new attack.
Oh, no, oh!
Aah, oh, my foot, what agony do you have in store?
It creeps up on me,
coming closer and closer now. Oh, my misery!
You know it all; do not turn your backs on me.
Aah, oh!   790
Odysseus, I wish you could feel
the pain piercing right through your chest. Oh, aah!
Aah, again, again! You two generals, I wish that   793
you might nurse this disease for as long as I have.   795
Oh, oh!
Oh, death, death, I have called on you again and again
like this, day after day: why can't you come to me?
Oh my son, noble boy, take me up and burn me in
this volcano here, which is invoked as the Lemnian,   800
as you are noble. That is the obligation I accepted,
in return for the gift of these weapons, which are now
in your safe-keeping. I did it for the son of Zeus.
What do you say to that, boy?
What do you say? Why are you silent? Where are you, son?
NEOPTOLEMOS: I am caught in grief, deep grief, for your
    pain.
PHILOKTETES: You should be strong, my son. Bear up. This
    crisis
comes on me sharply, but it is quickly over and gone.

But I do beg you, do not leave me on my own.

NEOPTOLEMOS: Take heart; we shall stay.

PHILOKTETES: You'll stay?

NEOPTOLEMOS: Be sure of it. 810

PHILOKTETES: It would be insulting to put you to the oath,
my boy.

NEOPTOLEMOS: No need; it is not lawful for me to go
without you.

PHILOKTETES: Give me your hand on it; a pledge.

NEOPTOLEMOS: Here: of staying.

PHILOKTETES: Now take me there, there . . .

NEOPTOLEMOS: Where do you mean?

PHILOKTETES: Up . . .

NEOPTOLEMOS: Your mind is wandering again. Why are you
staring at the sky?

PHILOKTETES: Let me go, let me.

NEOPTOLEMOS: Go where?

PHILOKTETES: Just let me, at last.

NEOPTOLEMOS: No, I shall not let you.

PHILOKTETES: You'll kill me, if you
touch me.

NEOPTOLEMOS: There, I'm letting go, since you're coming to
your senses.

PHILOKTETES: Oh earth, take me as I am now, a man close
to death!

I can't keep on my feet; this sickness won't let me. 820

NEOPTOLEMOS: It looks to me as if he will be asleep not long
from now. There, you can see his head is drooping.
The whole of his body is drenched in sweat,
and a black stream of blood has broken out
from his foot. My friends, we should leave him
to rest in peace, and let him fall asleep.

CHOROS 4

SAILORS (A1): Sleep, you know no pain or suffering; oh,
Sleep,
come to us in a gentle breath, bringing happiness,
happiness, lord, and keep before his eyes 830
the radiance that is stretched over them now.

Come, come to me, Healer!
My son, see where you are now,
and where you may go,
where your thinking
may lead. You see how it is.
Why are we waiting to act?
Opportunity, which considers everything,
often and again wins an outright victory in a moment.

NEOPTOLEMOS: Yes, he cannot hear anything we say. But I
    can see that
holding the bow as a prize is pointless, if we sail without
    him.   840
For the crown is his, and god has told us to bring him
    with us.
Shame and disgrace together to boast of work
    unfinished, and of lies.

SAILORS (A2).   But god will look to that, my son.
When you answer me the next time, let your
voice speak the words ever so softly, my son.
The unsleeping sleep of the sick
is always sharp-sighted.
I urge you to consider,
with the utmost care,
how you can achieve   850
that purpose secretly;
you know what I mean.
If you keep up this attitude to him,
any fool could see the future is fraught.

SAILORS (A3):   The wind is favourable, my son, favourable;
the man has his eyes closed, so with no help at hand,
stretched out in the dark of night –
a sound sleep fears nothing –
he has no command of his hands, of his feet, of
    anything,   860
but is like a man who rests with Haides.
Come, see that what you say
suits the occasion. The only thought

I can capture, my boy, is that
security is the best course of action.

SCENE 4

NEOPTOLEMOS: I order you to be quiet, and keep your wits
about you.
The man is opening his eyes, and lifting up his head.
PHILOKTETES: Oh sunlight that follows sleep, and the
vigilance
of these strangers, for which I never dared to hope.
I should never have boasted to myself of this, my boy,
that you would have tolerated and pitied my sufferings,   870
have stayed by my side and brought help to me.
The Atreidai were not so tolerant, those brave
generals; they did not put up with me patiently like this.
But your nature is noble from noble ancestors,
my boy, that is the reason. You have taken all this
easily, the shouting, the stench, all overwhelming.
It looks as though I now have a breathing space,
son, when I can forget this sickness for a while.
So lift me up, do it yourself, set me on my feet,
son, so when I have finally recovered from my
exhaustion   880
we can set out towards the ship, and not delay the voyage.
NEOPTOLEMOS: I am delighted, against all my fears, to see
you still
alive, breathing, looking about you, free from pain.
In the critical state you were in just now, all
the symptoms seemed to indicate you were a dead man.
Now, lift yourself up. Or, if you would prefer it,
these men here will carry you. No one will be reluctant
to put in the effort, since we both know what we want to do.
PHILOKTETES: Thank you, my boy, but lift me yourself, a
good idea.
Don't involve these others; they don't need to be   890
oppressed by the bad smell. It will be hard enough
for them to live with me on board the ship.
NEOPTOLEMOS: As you wish. But stand up yourself, and hold
on to me.

PHILOKTETES: Don't worry. I am used to getting up. I'll manage.

NEOPTOLEMOS: Ah, no. What comes next? What should I do now?

PHILOKTETES: What is the matter, my boy? What is distracting you?

NEOPTOLEMOS: How can I express what is so hard to say? It's hopeless.

PHILOKTETES: Hopeless, for you? Why hopeless? Don't say that, my son.

NEOPTOLEMOS: But that is the sorry state I find myself in now.

PHILOKTETES: Don't say that my disease has struck you as being so   900
disgusting that you are now unwilling to take me on board?

NEOPTOLEMOS: Everything is disgusting, when a man deserts his own
nature, and does what he should never contemplate.

PHILOKTETES: But you are not doing, not saying, anything at all
against your father's nature in helping a good man.

NEOPTOLEMOS: The prospect of shame; that's distressed me from the start.

PHILOKTETES: Shame? Not in your actions. But your words are worrying.

NEOPTOLEMOS: Oh Zeus, what shall I do? Be a coward twice over,
concealing what I should reveal, and using words of shame?

PHILOKTETES: This man here, if my judgement is not warped,   910
is going to betray me, leave me behind and sail away.

NEOPTOLEMOS: I am not leaving you behind. What has distressed me from
the start is that I am sending you on a painful voyage.

PHILOKTETES: What on earth are you saying, my son? I don't understand.

NEOPTOLEMOS: I shall conceal nothing from you: you must sail to Troy,
to join the Achaians and the army of the Atreidai.

PHILOKTETES: No! What did you say?

NEOPTOLEMOS: First find out, then
protest.

PHILOKTETES: Find out what? What do you intend to do to
me?

NEOPTOLEMOS: To save you, first, from this misery, and then
to

go on and ravage the plains of Troy with you.   920

PHILOKTETES: Do you really intend to do this?

NEOPTOLEMOS: Necessity is
the rule in this, and you must listen without anger.

PHILOKTETES: My case is hopeless, I am lost, betrayed. Why
have you

done this to me, stranger? Give me back my bow, right now.

NEOPTOLEMOS: That I cannot do. I must listen to those in
authority: that is right, and is in my best interest.

PHILOKTETES: No fire, no creature of terror could have done
what you

have done to me, deceived me as you have. You are a
loathsome

artifice of consummate evil. Can you look at me without
shame?

I was your suppliant, I turned to you; you are corrupt.   930
By taking my bow, you've deprived me of my livelihood.
Give it back, I beg, back to me, I implore you, son.
By the gods of your fathers, don't take my life away from
me.

Oh, my case is hopeless. Now he won't even speak to me;
so he looks away, because he will never give them back.

Oh harbours and headlands, wild mountain beasts
with whom I share this place, oh precipitous cliffs,
I weep aloud to you, because I have no one else
to tell about this, and you are used to hearing me:
see what the son of Achilleus has done to me!   940
He swore he would bring me home, and is taking me to
Troy.

He put his right hand in mine, but he has stolen and
kept the sacred bow I had from Herakles, son of Zeus,
my bow, and intends to display it to the Argives,
as if he were bringing back a strong man by force,
not noticing he is killing a corpse, a shadow cast

by smoke, no more than a ghost. He would not have
taken me when I was fit, nor even as I am, without lies.
Now I have been deceived, my luck is out. What should I
    do?
But give it back! Even now, be your own true self again.   950
What do you say? Silence. My luck has gone. I'm nothing.

I have a hollow rock, with two openings; I shall go
back into it again, disarmed, with no way to feed myself.
I shall wither away to nothing, all alone in this chamber of
    mine.
I shall not be killing any birds in flight, any animal
on the mountainside with these weapons: I will die
in misery, and be the feast for what was once my food;
creatures I hunted once will hunt me down.
My blood will be forfeit for the blood I have shed,
deceived as I am by a man who seemed to know no evil.   960
May you die – but not yet; not before I know if you
will really change your mind. If not, then may you die foully.
1 SAILOR: What shall we do? The decision is yours, my lord;
to sail, or listen to this man, and take his side.
NEOPTOLEMOS: A terrible pity has come over me for this
    man. This
is no recent feeling. I've felt this way for a long time.
PHILOKTETES: By the gods, indulge that pity, my boy Don't
    leave
yourself open to men's insults by deceiving me.
NEOPTOLEMOS: Oh, what shall I do? I wish I had never left
Skyros. All of this is too much for me to bear.   970
PHILOKTETES: You're not a bad man. But you've been taught
    by bad men,
and came here to play a shameful part. Now leave it to
    others
better suited to it, and sail away; but leave me my weapons.
NEOPTOLEMOS: What shall we do, men?

(*Enter* ODYSSEUS, *with two* SAILORS, *left*)

        ODYSSEUS: Not a bad man? You're the worst!
What are you doing? Get back, and leave the bow with me.

PHILOKTETES: Ah, no, who is this man? Is it Odysseus I
    hear?

ODYSSEUS: Odysseus. You're right. That's me. You're
    looking at him.

PHILOKTETES: Oh, I'm lost, I've been utterly betrayed. It was
    he that trapped me, and robbed me of my weapons.

ODYSSEUS: I, and no other. You're right. I acknowledge
    that.   980

PHILOKTETES: Give the bow back to me, my boy, give it
    back.

                    ODYSSEUS: But that's
something he'll never do, even if he wanted to. As for you,
you must come with it now, or they'll use force on you.

PHILOKTETES: You are the most despicable and ruthless
    criminal!
They will take me by force?

                    ODYSSEUS: If you don't come willingly.

PHILOKTETES: Oh land of Lemnos, and the all-powerful
    flame
kindled by Hephaistos, is it acceptable to you
that Odysseus will drag me forcibly away?

ODYSSEUS: To correct you, it is Zeus, Zeus who rules this
    land,
Zeus whose will this is; I am merely his servant.   990

PHILOKTETES: You are hateful. What kind of specious
    argument is this?
If the gods are your pretext, you make the gods into liars.

ODYSSEUS: Not so, but truth-tellers. We must start on our
    journey.

PHILOKTETES: I say no.

                    ODYSSEUS: But I say yes. Give in. You must.

PHILOKTETES: What am I to do? My father obviously
    engendered
me to be just a slave, and not to be a free man.

ODYSSEUS: No, but to be the equal of the best, with whom
    you are destined to take Troy and level it by force.

PHILOKTETES: Never, not even if I must suffer all kinds of
    torment,
just as long as I have this steep slope beneath my feet.   1000

ODYSSEUS: What are you up to?

                    PHILOKTETES: I shall leap off this ledge

right now, and bloody this head of mine on the rocks below.

ODYSSEUS: Take hold of him, the two of you! Don't let him
   do it!

(*The two* SAILORS *pinion* PHILOKTETES)

PHILOKTETES: Oh, my hands! You are both caught in the
   same trap, by
   him. This is the penalty you pay for missing your dear bow.
   You have never had a healthy thought or the mind of a
   free man, and now you've crept up on me again, hunted me
   out,
   using this boy as a screen, who was unknown to me,
   far above you in worth, but an equal of mine,
   who knew no better than to carry out his orders.   1010
   And now it is quite clear he is taking it all badly,
   upset at his own mistakes, and what has been done to me.
   But your evil soul peeps out from the shadows,
   as always; he had no talent for it, nor any inclination,
   but you schooled him thoroughly in the sophistry of evil.
   And now your intention is to bind me and take me
   away from this coastline, on which you deposited me,
   deserted, friendless, banished, a corpse among the living.
   Oh!
   Death to you! How many times have I prayed for that.
   But the gods grant me nothing that would please me,   1020
   and so you smile and live, while I grieve for
   the fact that I am still living in such misery,
   an object of derision to you and to the joint
   commanders, the Atreidai, whom you serve in this.
   Yet you were brought under the yoke yourself by deceit
   and compulsion, and then sailed with them, while I
   sailed willingly (abject man!), joining with seven ships,
   to be cast away dishonestly – by them, you say; but they
   blame you.
   So now, why are you taking me? Why ship me out? To what
   end?
   I am nothing, and I have been dead to you for a long
   time   1030
   You, whom the gods despise; why am I not lame or
   foul-smelling to you? If I sail with you, how can

you burn sacrifices to the gods? Keep pouring libations? 1033
I hope you come to a bad end. And you will come to a bad
    end   1035
for the harm you have done to me, if the gods care for
    justice.
And I know that they do, because you would never
have sailed on this mission after me, a man of no worth,
unless some divine good had urged you on.

Land of my fathers, and the gods who watch over men, 1040
bring vengeance, bring it even if vengeance comes late,
down on all of them, if you have any pity for me.
My life is pitiable, but if I could see these men
destroyed, I would believe I had escaped from my sickness.

1 SAILOR: An embittered man, this stranger, and that was an
embittered speech, Odysseus, not submission to his troubles.

ODYSSEUS: If I had the time available, I could find many
    points to
answer what he has said; I have just one at my disposal now.
l am the person that circumstances demand of me.
When an examination is made of men who are just and
    good,   1050
you would not find anyone who would be more righteous.
Yet I was born with the desire to win in every engagement,
with you as the exception: to you, I'm willing to give way.
Let him go, and don't lay hands on him again.
Let him stay here. We have no great need of you,
providing that we have these weapons. After all, we
have Teukros with us, who exercises this skill,
and me myself, and I think I could handle it
no worse than you, and point it as well at the target.
So, what need of you? You're welcome to beat about on
    Lemnos.   1060
We ourselves are going. And may your prized possession
soon bring honour to me, which was to be yours by right.

PHILOKTETES: Oh, what shall I do? It's hopeless. Let you
    flaunt
yourself in front of the Argives with my weapons?

ODYSSEUS: Don't bother to answer me, because I am on my
    way.

PHILOKTETES: Seed of Achilleus, shall I hear no further word

from you as well? Will you leave me in the same way?
ODYSSEUS: You, get moving. Don't look at him, for all your noble
impulses, or you may destroy all the luck we are having.
PHILOKTETES: And you, friends – will you desert me too, and   1070
leave me on my own? Have you no pity for me?
I SAILOR: This boy is the commander of our ship. Whatever
he has to say to you, that will be what we say.
NEOPTOLEMOS: I shall be told that I was full of pity for
him; nevertheless, stay here, if he wants it, for the
length of time it takes the sailors to prepare the ship
for sailing, and for us to offer a prayer to the gods.
And in that space of time perhaps he may choose to
think better of us. So the two of us must make a move,
and you must be quick to move when we give the call.   1080

[*Exeunt* ODYSSEUS *and* NEOPTOLEMOS, *left*]

CHOROS 5

PHILOKTETES (AI):   Oh cave of hollow rock,
            hot and icy by turn, I
            was never meant to leave
            you, but instead you will
            witness the death of a wretched man.

(*He cries aloud*)

            Oh shelter filled
            full of the pain I suffer,
            what will keep me alive from day to day?
            How shall I ever find   1090
            a hope of food, disabled as I am?
            The doves will fly away
            above me on the whistling wind:
            I have no way of catching them.
I SAILOR: This bitter existence is what you chose for
                yourself,
            not some stroke of bad luck or compulsion.

When you could have thought of a better god,
you chose to approve one who was worse.   1100

PHILOKTETES (A2):   Hard, hard is my life, and ruined by
          exhaustion. Now
I must live on here
with no one to comfort
me, and then die,

(*He cries*)

no longer bringing home food,
no longer with my flighted
weapons in my powerful hands.   1110
I was unsuspecting,
undermined by lies from a crafty mind.
I wish I could see him,
the man who devised this, stuck with my suffering
for the same length of time.
I SAILOR: This is the fate decreed for you by the gods; no
          trickery
from my hand has held you down. Aim any harsh
curse you make at other men's fortunes.   1120
For it matters to me that you should not reject my
          friendship.

PHILOKTETES (B1):   Ah, he is sitting somewhere
on a beach by the sea
laughing at me, balancing my
means to eat in his hands,
which no one ever held before.
Oh my dear bow, torn
from my hands by violence,
if you can think you must feel pity   1130
when you see that the unhappy man
who had you from Herakles
will not be using you ever again,
that you have changed owners, and
will be bent by the hands of a schemer.
You'll see shameful deceit,
and the hateful creature himself,

who devised an infinity of evil to
follow his shameful treatment of me.

I SAILOR: It is right for a man to voice his sense of
    justice,   1140
but once he has spoken not to
thrust out an envious, verbal sting.
He was appointed, one from many,
and under the other's instruction,
acting for his friends, he helped the common cause.

PHILOKTETES (B2):   Birds I hunted, tribes of
bright-eyed beast, found in the
mountains of this land,
do not start in flight from shelter
any more; I do not have in my hands   1150
the help I had before, my arrows,
and my life is now disastrous.
This lame man can no longer
frighten you; go your way
just as you choose; now it is fine
to glut your maws in bloody revenge just as you
will, on my living flesh.
I shall soon be leaving life behind;
for how shall I find food?
Who can feed on the wind,   1160
when he has no control any more
over anything the life-giving earth supplies?

I SAILOR: By the gods, if you have any respect for a friend,
come closer to one who approaches you in all goodwill.
Take time to reflect, and think carefully: it is in
your power to escape from this killing disease.
It is pitiful to feed it on your flesh, nor
can whoever lives with it learn how to bear the infinite
    grief.

PHILOKTETES (C1):   Again, again you have
brought to mind the old pain, yet you   1170
are the best of those who have been here.
Why destroy me? What have you done to me?

I SAILOR: What do you mean by that?

                    PHILOKTETES: If you hoped

to take me away to the land of Troy that I detest.

1 SAILOR: That is what I think is best.

PHILOKTETES: Go away and leave me now.

1 SAILOR: That is the command I have been longing
to hear, and am most keen to carry out.
Let's go, let's go
and take up our posts in the ship!   1180

PHILOKTETES: No, by Zeus the god of curses,
don't go, I beg of you!

    1 SAILOR: Keep calm.

PHILOKTETES: Oh my friends,
by the gods, stay!

    1 SAILOR: Why are you calling to us?

PHILOKTETES: Oh, god,
oh, the power that rules me! I am lost in misery.
Oh, my foot, my foot, what shall I
do with you in the time ahead of me?
Oh, my friends, come back to me.   1190

1 SAILOR: But what shall we do? Has your
attitude changed from what you revealed before?

PHILOKTETES: Retribution should not fall
on a man who is mad from storms
of pain, who is out of his mind when he speaks.

1 SAILOR: Take a step forward, now, you poor man: those
are our orders.

PHILOKTETES: Never, never, know that for certain,
not even if the fiery lord of the lightning
sets me blazing with the flame of his thunderbolt.
Let Ilion go hang, and all of those   1200
besieging it, who were cruel enough to
shun this limb, this foot.
Oh my friends, at least concede me one prayer.

1 SAILOR: What is it you mean?

PHILOKTETES: Send me a sword,
if you can find one, or an axe, or any weapon.

1 SAILOR: What would you do with a weapon of violence?

PHILOKTETES: I shall cut off my head, and my limbs, with
my own hand.
My mind is on blood and death now.

1 SAILOR: What is this?

    PHILOKTETES: I am seeking my father.   1210

1 SAILOR: Where?
                    PHILOKTETES: In Haides.
He is not in the light of day, not now.
Oh, my city, city of my fathers,
if only this suffering
man might look on you,
who left your sacred streams
and went with the Danaans, my enemies,
to be their defender. Now I am nothing.   1217

[*Exit* PHILOKTETES *into the* skene]

FINALE

(*Enter* NEOPTOLEMOS *and* ODYSSEUS, *left*)

ODYSSEUS: Are you not going to tell me why you are
   retracing   1222
your steps like this along the path, in such a hurry?
NEOPTOLEMOS: I am going to set right what I did wrong
   before.
ODYSSEUS: That's a remarkable statement; what did you do
   wrong?
NEOPTOLEMOS: I was obedient to you and to the whole
   army.
ODYSSEUS: What did you do that you feel was disreputable?
NEOPTOLEMOS: I caught a man by a deceitful trick, and that
   is shameful.
ODYSSEUS: Who do you mean? Ah, no. You're planning to
   be subversive.
NEOPTOLEMOS: No, not subversive; but the son of Poias is
   going to . . .   1230
ODYSSEUS: What do you intend to do? This makes me
   apprehensive.
NEOPTOLEMOS: I took this bow from him, and back to him
   again . . .
ODYSSEUS: Oh Zeus, what are you going to say? No. Not
   give it back?
NEOPTOLEMOS: I have it because I took it shamefully and
   unjustly.

ODYSSEUS: By the gods, you must be saying this just to
     provoke me.

NEOPTOLEMOS: If it is provocative to tell you the truth.

ODYSSEUS: What are you saying, son of Achilleus? What
     kind of talk is this?

NEOPTOLEMOS: Do you want me to repeat it two and three
     times over?

ODYSSEUS: I should rather not have heard it at all in the first
     place.

NEOPTOLEMOS: Well, now you can be certain you have heard
     everything.   1240

ODYSSEUS: There is some body that will prevent you from
     doing this.

NEOPTOLEMOS: What's that? Who is the man who will try to
     prevent me?

ODYSSEUS: The whole force of the Achaians, and amongst
     them myself.

NEOPTOLEMOS: You're a clever man, but what you're saying
     isn't clever.

ODYSSEUS: Neither what you say, nor what you're doing, is
     clever.

NEOPTOLEMOS: But if it is right, then that is better than
     clever.

ODYSSEUS: And how can it be right, to give straight back
     again
  what you have taken by my advice?

                    NEOPTOLEMOS: I have made
  a mistake, a shameful one, and I shall try to retrieve it.

ODYSSEUS: But have you no fear of the Achaian army in
     doing this?   1250

NEOPTOLEMOS: If right is on my side, your army does not
     frighten me.

ODYSSEUS: [I may have to make sure you do sense that]
     fear.

NEOPTOLEMOS: I am not going to give in to violence from
     you.

ODYSSEUS: So shall we fight with you, rather than with the
     Trojans?

NEOPTOLEMOS: Let that be the future.

ODYSSEUS: Do you see that my right
  hand is on my sword-hilt?

NEOPTOLEMOS: Yes, but you'll see me
doing the same thing as you, and quickly, too.
ODYSSEUS: All right. I shall let you go. But I'm going to report
this to the whole army, and they will punish you.

[*Exit* ODYSSEUS, *left*]

NEOPTOLEMOS: That shows discretion. And if you keep to that
resolve, perhaps you might steer clear of trouble.   1260
But you, oh son of Poias, Philoktetes, I am calling to you!
Come outside, and leave the shelter of that cavern.
PHILOKTETES: What is this noise? Shouting in front of my cave? Again?
Why are you calling me out? What do you want, friends?

(*Enter* PHILOKTETES *from the* skene)

Oh, no. This is a bad business. Have you come here
to make matters worse? They are bad enough already.
NEOPTOLEMOS: Take heart, and hear what I have come here
to tell you.
PHILOKTETES: That makes me frightened. Last time you started with
fair words, and I did badly from it, when I believed you.
NEOPTOLEMOS: So there is no possibility of making a change
for the better?   1270
PHILOKTETES: That was how you were talking when you were engaged
in stealing my bow; overtly trustworthy, and secretly a
disaster.
NEOPTOLEMOS: That is not how it is now. I want to hear
from you,
whether you are firmly decided on staying here obstinately,
or on sailing with us.
PHILOKTETES: Stop, don't bother to go on.
NEOPTOLEMOS: So that is your decision.
PHILOKTETES: And more so than I can say.

NEOPTOLEMOS: Well, I should have preferred you to have
    been persuaded
by what I said. But if what I say does not serve the
purpose, then no more.
                        PHILOKTETES: Anything you'll say will
    be pointless.   1280
You will never make my attitude to you a friendly one,
after you tricked me and deprived me of the means
I have to live. And then you came here to give me
advice, you hateful child of the best of fathers.
Death come to all of you, first of all the Atreidai,
then the son of Laertes, and then you.
                        NEOPTOLEMOS: No more curses.
Now take your weapons from these hands of mine.
PHILOKTETES: What did you say? Am I being tricked for the
    second time?
NEOPTOLEMOS: No. I swear by the holy majesty of highest
    Zeus.
PHILOKTETES: The dearest words I could hear, if what you
    say is true.   1290
NEOPTOLEMOS: They will be matched plainly by actions.
    Hold out your
right hand, and take command of your own weapons.

(*Enter* ODYSSEUS, *left*)

ODYSSEUS: But I forbid it, with the gods as my witnesses,
    on behalf of the Atreidai and the whole army.
PHILOKTETES: Son, whose voice was that I heard? Was it
    Odysseus?
                        ODYSSEUS: That's right. You see him
here, and he will take you away to the plains of Troy by
force, whether the son of Achilleus approves, or whether
he does not.
PHILOKTETES: But all the worse for you, if this shaft flies
    straight.
NEOPTOLEMOS: Ah, no, by the gods, don't do it, don't
    shoot!   1300
PHILOKTETES: Let me go, by the gods, free my arm, my dear
    boy!

NEOPTOLEMOS: I shall not free it.

          PHILOKTETES: Oh, why prevent me
from killing my hated enemy with my own weapons?

NEOPTOLEMOS: But this would not be to my credit, nor to
    yours.

                              [*Exit* ODYSSEUS, *left*]

PHILOKTETES: So, there you are. At least you can see that the
    army's
leaders, the lying heralds of the Achaians, are cowards
when it comes to fighting, but bold enough with words.

NEOPTOLEMOS: Well, then. You have the bow, and no
    reason to
be angry with me, or to blame me for anything.

PHILOKTETES: I agree with that. You've showed your true
    nature,   1310
my son, which is that of your parentage. Your father was
not Sisyphos, but Achilleus, who held the highest
reputation amongst the living, and now holds it with the
    dead.

NEOPTOLEMOS: To hear you speaking well of my father and
    of myself
gives me pleasure. But listen to what I most want
from you. Men have no choice but to take whatever
is given to them by the gods in the way of fortune.
But those who wrap themselves in misery by their own
    choice,
as is the case with you, have no right to receive
any sympathy or any pity from anyone at all.   1320
You have become savage, and you accept no advice,
should someone who is well-disposed to you offer it,
but hate the man, regarding him as an outright enemy.
Yet I will speak; I call on Zeus the god of oaths.
Listen and take note, and write a copy in your mind.
The pain of this sickness that you have comes from god.
You approached the guardian snake of Chryse, which
stealthily protects the roofless precinct which is her home.
And you must know that you will never experience the end
of this oppressive disease – not as long as the sun rises
    here   1330

where it does now, and sinks over there, where it does –
until you come of your own free will to the plains of Troy,
where you will find the sons of Asklepios amongst us,
and will be relieved of this affliction, winning fame for
sacking the citadel of Troy with these weapons, and with my
    aid.
I shall tell you how I know that this will be the case.
We have a man with us, a captive from Troy,
Helenos, a noble prophet, who plainly declares that
this is destined to happen; and, in addition to all of this,
that in the course of the current summer the whole city   1340
of Troy is bound to be taken. He insists that his life
should be forfeit, if he is found to have prophesied falsely.
Now that you know all of this, come with us, willingly.
The additional gain is a fine one, to be picked out
as the best of the Greeks; but first, to be placed in
healing hands, and then to take Troy, a city that
has caused so much grief, and win the highest renown.
PHILOKTETES: Oh hateful life, why do you keep me lingering
    up here
in the light of day, instead of packing me off down to
    Haides?
Oh, no, what shall I do? How can I distrust   1350
his words, when they come as friendly advice to me?
Should I give in, then? But if I do it, how can
a wretch like me be seen in public? Who will speak to me?
Oh my eyes, that take in everything around me, how
will you bear the sight of me keeping company with
the sons of Atreus, the men who destroyed me?
Or with the son of Laertes, that utter villain?
It is not the pain of what has happened that has its
teeth in me, but the thought of what is still to come
from them, which I foresee. For once the will has
    become   1360
a mother of evil, a criminal upbringing follows.
And you surprise me; I cannot understand you.
By rights, you should never go back to Troy yourself,
and should keep me from there. These men have violently
insulted you, by stealing your father's gift. So are you then
going to go and fight for them, and compel me to do so?
Surely not, my son. But do what you swore to me you

would do, and put me on my way home. Then stay in
  Skyros,
and leave them, as bad men, to come to a bad end.
If you do this, you will win double thanks from me,   1370
and double from your father; and by not helping bad men,
you will not risk gaining a similar reputation yourself.
NEOPTOLEMOS: What you say is reasonable. Nevertheless, I
  want you
to have faith in the gods and in the words of a man
who is your friend, and to sail away from this land.
PHILOKTETES: What? To the plains of Troy, and to the son
  of Atreus,
whom I hate so much? And with this dreadful foot?
NEOPTOLEMOS: No, but to those who can bring you relief
  from
the pain of this festering ulcer and cure you completely.
PHILOKTETES: That is terrible advice. Do you realize what
  you are saying?   1380
NEOPTOLEMOS: What I see as coming to fruition for both of
  us in the best way.
PHILOKTETES: But have you no shame in saying this in the
  hearing of the gods?
NEOPTOLEMOS: How could anyone be ashamed of helping
  his friends?
PHILOKTETES: Is this for the benefit of the Atreidai, or for my
  benefit?
NEOPTOLEMOS: For you. I am your friend. And so I speak as
  a friend, too.
PHILOKTETES: How can that be? You want to hand me over
  to my enemies.
NEOPTOLEMOS: My good man, suffering has made you
  obstinate. Learn not to be.
PHILOKTETES: You will destroy me, I know you will, with
  these words.
NEOPTOLEMOS: Not I. But I'm convinced you do not
  understand.
PHILOKTETES: Don't I know that the Atreidai marooned
  me?   1390
NEOPTOLEMOS: They did that. But you should see if they will
  rescue you.

PHILOKTETES: Never, if I must look on Troy of my own free
   will.
NEOPTOLEMOS: What can we do, then, if we cannot bring you
   to believe in anything that I am saying to you?
   It has come to the time when I must stop talking,
   and you must go on living as you have done, without cure.
PHILOKTETES: Leave me to the sufferings that I must endure.
   But carry out that promise, my son, that you made
   to me with your right hand in mine, and send me home,
   and don't permit any delay, or remind me ever again   1400
   of Troy. I have heard enough wild talk of that.
NEOPTOLEMOS: If that is your decision, let's go.
                PHILOKTETES: Oh, words nobly spoken!
NEOPTOLEMOS: Lean against me as you go.
                PHILOKTETES: As much as I can.
NEOPTOLEMOS: How shall I defend myself to the Achaians?
                PHILOKTETES: Don't give it a thought.
NEOPTOLEMOS: If they put my country to the sword? What
   then?
                PHILOKTETES: I shall be there ...
NEOPTOLEMOS: And what can you do to help?
                PHILOKTETES: with the arrows of
   Herakles –
NEOPTOLEMOS: Meaning?
                PHILOKTETES: I'll keep them away.   1406
NEOPTOLEMOS: Kiss the ground farewell, and walk.   1408

(HERAKLES *appears on the* mechane)

HERAKLES: Not yet, before you have heard
            what I have to say, son of Poias.   1410
            Yes, you are looking on the face of Herakles,
            and it is his voice you are hearing.
            For your sake I have left the
            heavens where I live,
            and come to tell you the plans of Zeus,
            detaining you from this journey.
            You must listen to what I say.

   And first of all I must tell you of my own fortune,
   how I undertook and completed so many labours and have

gained fame in immortality, as you can see for yourselves.   1420
You must be clear that the same reward is ordained for you,
that these labours of yours will result in renown.
In the first place you will go with your companion here to
the citadel of Troy, and there be released from this grim
    disease.
You will be chosen from the whole armed force for your
    courage,
and with these weapons of mine you will deprive Paris of his
life, the man who is most responsible for this calamity.
And you will sack Troy, and send back to your own halls
the spoils of war – for you will receive the prize of arms
    from
the army – back to your father Poias and to mountainous
    Oita.   1430
From the spoils that you do receive from the army there,
dedicate some as a remembrance of my bow at the site
of my pyre. This same advice I give to you as well, son
of Achilleus. For without this man you do not have the
    strength
to capture the plains of Troy, nor does he without you.
You should be like lions in a pride protecting each other,
he watching for you, and you for him. I myself shall
send Asklepios to Ilion, to bring an end to your sickness,
since it is fated to be taken for a second time by
my weapons. But take great care, when you come to
    sack   1440
the land, to show reverence in matters concerning the gods,
for father Zeus considers everything else to come second
to that. Reverence for the gods does not perish with
    mortals,
but whether they are living or dead, it does not pass away.

PHILOKTETES: Oh, the sound of that voice I desired most,
        and your appearance after so long!
        You have spoken: I shall not disobey.
NEOPTOLEMOS: And I assent to that myself.
HERAKLES: Do not delay now in taking action.
        The time is right, and   1450
        presses, the wind blows you forwards.

(HERAKLES *is withdrawn from sight*)

PHILOKTETES: Come now, I'll call on this land as I go.
    Farewell, cavern that kept watch over me,
    Nymphs of the streams and the meadows,
    deep, booming sea around the headland,
    where my head was often moistened by
    the blast of the south wind as I sheltered inside,
    and Mount Hermaion sent a resounding
    echo of my own voice back to me,
    as the pain hurled its storms upon me.   1460
    But now, you springs and fount of Lykios,
    I am leaving you, leaving you at last,
    as I never once dared to believe.
    Farewell, plain of Lemnos, circled by the sea,
    send me on a fair voyage, a contented man,
    to where Fate in its might conveys me,
    with the will of my friends and the all-conquering
    god, who has brought all this to fruition.

SAILORS: We should go, all of us together, after
    offering a prayer to the Nymphs of the sea   1470
    to bring us safely back on our return journey.

     [*Exeunt* PHILOKTETES, NEOPTOLEMOS, SAILORS, *left*]

OIDIPOUS AT KOLONOS

Translated by Gregory McCart

THE ACTORS AND THEIR ROLES

OIDIPOUS	Actor 1
ANTIGONE	Actor 2
SCOUT	Actor 3
ELDERS OF KOLONOS	Choros
ISMENE (Scene 2 and Finale)	Actor 3
ISMENE (Scenes 4, 5 and 6)	Silent Face
THESEUS (Scenes 2, 4 and 6)	Actor 3
THESEUS (Scene 3)	Actor 2
THESEUS (Finale)	Actor 1
KREON	Actor 3
POLYNEIKES	Actor 3
ATTENDANT AS MESSENGER	Actor 1

The skene *represents a grove at Kolonos, near Athens*

Preset a statue of the horseman, Kolonos, extreme back centre
Preset a stone bench or rock at the entrance to the skene, *and*
another just behind the centre of the orchêstra

SCENE I

(*Enter* OIDIPOUS *and* ANTIGONE, *right*)

OIDIPOUS: Antigone, child of a blind old man, which
place have we reached? Whose city?
Who will give the wanderer Oidipous
today some scanty handout?
I don't ask for much and I get even
less, but it is enough for me.
My experience and my length of days
teach me to be content, and my own nobility.
But now, Antigone, do you see somewhere
to sit – a public resting-place or holy grove?   10
Set me down there until we find out
where we are. We come as strangers
to listen, learn and do what we are told.
ANTIGONE: Poor Oidipous, dear father, there are towers I see
far ahead which crown a city.
This place here, quite clearly, is holy. It is overgrown
with laurel and olive trees and vines. Flocks of
nightingales sing cheerfully in there.
Now bend your knees. Sit on this rock, rough though it is.
You've come a long way for an old man.   20
OIDIPOUS: Yes, sit me down and look after the blind fellow.
ANTIGONE: No need to teach me what I've learned over time.

(ANTIGONE *seats* OIDIPOUS *in the* skene *entrance*)

OIDIPOUS: Are you able to tell me where we've come to?
ANTIGONE: Well, I know Athens but I don't know this area.
OIDIPOUS: Everyone we've met has said the same thing.
ANTIGONE: Shall I go and find out about the district?
OIDIPOUS: Yes, Antigone – if there's anybody living here.
ANTIGONE: Somebody does. I don't have to do
  anything. I can see this man near us.
OIDIPOUS: Is he coming towards us in this direction?   30
ANTIGONE: He's just about here. If you want to
  welcome him, speak up. Here he is.

(*Enter the* SCOUT, *left*)

OIDIPOUS: Sir, I hear from my daughter, who sees for us
    both,
  that you've come – properly – to look us over
  and to tell us what we are puzzled –
SCOUT: Now before you ask more, move away
  from where you're sitting. It's unlawful to go where you are.
OIDIPOUS: What is the place? Which god possesses it?
SCOUT: You can't touch it. You can't be there. The terrifying
  goddess-daughters of Earth and Darkness own it.   40
OIDIPOUS: What is their holy name which I should invoke?
SCOUT: The Eumenides who see everything. That's what
  the people round here call them. In other places, other
    names.
OIDIPOUS: Then may they kindly accept me as a suppliant.
  I will never leave this resting-place.
SCOUT: What's this mean?
OIDIPOUS: This sign draws my life together.
SCOUT: It's not for me to dare move you without approval
  from the town – until I report what I am doing.
OIDIPOUS: Come on, sir, don't treat me shabbily – homeless
  as I am – and don't refuse to tell me what I beg.   50
SCOUT: I won't treat you shabbily. Speak up.
OIDIPOUS: What then is this place we've wandered into?
SCOUT: You listen and you'll learn what I know.
  This is a sacred site, possessed by
  great Poseidon and Prometheus, the Titan

god of fire. You've stumbled into a place
called the Bronze Threshold of the land,
which protects Athens. The people round here
boast of this horseman, Kolonos, as their
founder, and the common name that they   60
all bear is the same as his. These
beliefs are not acclaimed so much in stories,
you should realize, sir, but by the way we live.

OIDIPOUS: So there are people living here?

SCOUT: Certainly. Named after this very god.

OIDIPOUS: Is there a ruler or do the people debate matters?

SCOUT: There is a ruler – the king down in the city.

OIDIPOUS: And who's this man whose strength and word
    hold sway?

SCOUT: Theseus he's called, the son of Aigeus.

OIDIPOUS: Will someone take a message to him from us?   70

SCOUT: What for? Just a message? Or to get something for
    you?

OIDIPOUS: To give a little service and get a great reward.

SCOUT: How can a man who can't see help anyone?

OIDIPOUS: What I have to say will be clear enough.

SCOUT: All right sir, but don't you play tricks now. You
    seem to be well born, despite your misfortunes.
    Stay where I saw you. I'll go to the
    local villagers, not the townspeople, and
    tell them about you. They'll decide for you
    whether you stay or go back again.   80

[*Exit the* SCOUT, *left*]

OIDIPOUS: Antigone, has the stranger left us?

ANTIGONE: He's gone. You can say what you like
    in peace and quiet, father. There's only me here.

OIDIPOUS: Oh fierce-eyed goddesses, since the first place
    I found rest now in this country is your sanctuary,
    do not be hard-hearted towards me or Apollo.
    When he predicted my many disasters,
    he told me they would stop eventually
    when I reached a final resting-place, where
    I would find a welcome from the holy gods.   90
    There I'd round the last bend in my life of pain,

bringing rewards to those receiving me
and ruin to those who shunned me, who exiled me.
He spoke to me of signs of these things happening –
a storm and thunder and the lightning flash of Zeus.
I know for sure that it was your trusty omen
which led me along the path into this grove;
or else I'd never have come upon your sanctuary
first in my wanderings – I who, like you,
drink no wine, would not have sat here on   100
this sacred stone that's felt no axe. So grant me,
goddesses, according to Apollo's
prophecy an end, a final turning.
Please may I not appear too undeserving
because I've been subjected to the world's worst hardships.
Come, children of the ancient Dark, sweet children.
Come, you who bear the name of mighty Pallas,
that most honoured city, Athens, have pity
on this wretched shadow of a man,
poor Oidipous. I am not what I was once.   110
ANTIGONE: Quiet. People are on their way, older
   people – to check where you are sitting.
OIDIPOUS: I will be quiet and you must hide me out
   of the way, off the path, inside the grove,
   until I learn what they're talking about.
   Knowing this, we can go ahead with caution.

[*Exit* OIDIPOUS, *led by* ANTIGONE, *into the* skene, *centre*]

(*Enter the* ELDERS, *left*)

CHOROS I

ELDERS (AI):   Look out! Where is he? Where's he now?
   Where's he gone from here, this reckless,
   this most reckless man?   120
   Look for him; call to him;
   listen for him – everywhere!
   Some wanderer,
   some old wanderer who can't
   be from here – or else he'd never

set foot off-limits in the grove
of the goddesses of fury.
We tremble to name them;
we pass by in silence,   130
without sound, without whisper,
moving our lips in still, silent
prayer. Now someone's come,
they say, showing no reverence.
I'm searching for him everywhere
but I cannot find
the place where he hides from me.

(*Enter* OIDIPOUS *and* ANTIGONE *from the* skene, *centre*)

OIDIPOUS: Here is that man. I see by sound,
     as they say of the blind.
I ELDER: Oh!   140
     Terrible to see, terrible to hear.
OIDIPOUS: Do not, I beg you, treat me as a criminal.
I ELDER: Zeus, protector, who on earth is this old man?
OIDIPOUS: Not one, for sure, whose life's been fortunate
     or happy, oh dear guardians of this place.
     I'm proof; or I'd not have crept here
     by another's eyes,
     a grown man led by a little girl.

I ELDER (A2):   Ah, have you been sightless   150
     since you were born? You've had a long
     and unhappy life, it seems.
     But you'll not pass these curses
     on to me. You're out of bounds,
     out of bounds. You must not
     trespass on the grassy bank
     where silence rules, where libations
     of water mixed with
     honey are poured;   160
     then you poor creature – take care –
     move away from there, come on. Let a
     decent space keep you apart from it.
     Do you hear, you stricken wanderer?
     If you've got something

    to say to us, come on, come on away,
    to where it is right
    to talk. Don't speak till then.

OIDIPOUS: Daughter, what do you think?   170
ANTIGONE: You must do what the people expect, father.
    Yield where you must and obey.
OIDIPOUS: Hold me then.
ANTIGONE: I've got you.
OIDIPOUS: Oh friends, don't wrong me now. I trust you. I
    am moving away.

(ANTIGONE *leads* OIDIPOUS *onto the* orchêstra)

I ELDER (B1):   No one will make you leave these seats here,
    sir, if you don't want to.
OIDIPOUS: Further still?
I ELDER: Come forward still.
OIDIPOUS: Still more?
I ELDER: Lead him forward,   180
    young lady. You can see.
ANTIGONE: Come on, come here, on
    your blind way, father, to where I'm leading you.
OIDIPOUS: [Zeus, help me.
ANTIGONE: Come this way, father, this way.
    Let me guide you on your path.
OIDIPOUS: I don't know where my steps take me.]
I ELDER: Courage. You are a stranger up against strangers
    but be patient. Hate
    what the city hates; pay
    due respect to what it loves.
OIDIPOUS: Take me then, my girl,
    to where it is right to set foot
    so that we can talk, and we can listen   190
    and not fight against what's necessary.

I ELDER (B2):   There. Don't step beyond that slab of rock.
OIDIPOUS: This far?
I ELDER: It's enough, do you hear?
OIDIPOUS: Can I sit down?
I ELDER: To your side; crouch down there

on the edge of the stone.
ANTIGONE: That's my task, father. Take one quiet step
after the other. .
OIDIPOUS: Oh dear me.
ANTIGONE: Lean your old body   200
on my helping hand.
OIDIPOUS: My sorrows confuse me.

(ANTIGONE *seats* OIDIPOUS *just behind centre* orchêstra)

I ELDER: Be patient. Relax now.
Tell me; who were your parents?
Who set you on your painful way? What
might I learn of your homeland?

OIDIPOUS (B3):   Sirs, I have no home. But don't, please . . .
I ELDER: Don't what, old man?
OIDIPOUS: Don't, don't insist on who I   210
am; don't question me to find out more.
I ELDER: Why not?
OIDIPOUS: My origins are dreadful.
I ELDER: Tell me.
OIDIPOUS: Oh no. My child, what should I tell them?
I ELDER: Who fathered you?
Tell us about him, stranger
OIDIPOUS: Oh, what will happen to me, my child?
I ELDER: You're at the point, so speak.
OIDIPOUS: Then I'll tell you, since I can't avoid it.
I ELDER: It's a long wait. Hurry up.
OIDIPOUS: Do you know of a son of Laios?
I ELDER: Oh! Oh!   220
OIDIPOUS: . . . of the race of Labdakos . . .
I ELDER: Oh Zeus!
OIDIPOUS: . . . miserable Oidipous?
I ELDER: You are this man?
OIDIPOUS: Don't let what I say frighten you.
I ELDER: Oh!
OIDIPOUS: Luckless Oidipous!
I ELDER: Oh!
OIDIPOUS: Now what's to come, my daughter?
I ELDER: Go away, far away from here.

OIDIPOUS: Then how will you fulfil what you have
          promised?
I ELDER: There's no impending price to pay for someone
          who's already paid the price.   230
          Deceit piled up against deceit
          brings pain, not gain; that's
          the outcome. Go on – off that seat! Get out of here!
          Back off and clear out from my land.
          Don't lay any more
          demands on my city.

ANTIGONE: Sirs, have respect.
          And though you've not put up
          with this old man, my
          father – because you've heard   240
          stories of his unintended actions –
          at least, I beg you, sirs,
          take pity on an unhappy girl, and on what
          for my father's sake I pray.
          I pray – not blindly but looking eye
          to eye, as would someone of
          your own blood – that you respect
          this victim. On you, as on a god,
          we depend in our troubles. So come, and grant
          an unexpected kindness.
          I implore you by all that's near and dear to you –   250
          children, marriage, wealth, god.
          Look closely and you'll see that no single
          mortal can escape
          when god leads him on.

SCENE 2

I ELDER: Be sure we pity you, child of Oidipous,
          and the situation that you're in.
          But we're frightened of the gods and we can't
          say more than we've said already to you.
OIDIPOUS: Then what is the point when honoured
          reputation and renown amount to nothing?
          What if they say of Athens she is most god-fearing and   260

alone will keep the desperate stranger safe,
indeed, alone is able to do so?
Is this the way it is for me? You made me
leave where I was sitting and then you drive me out.
Simply because you fear my name – not
my person, not my actions. And you ought to know
I didn't initiate so much as suffer what was done.
Must I tell you what my mother and father actually did?
Because this is why you're frightened of me. I know that
well enough. And yet how can I be depraved by nature   270
when I merely fought back after I was injured? Even if I'd
    known
what I was doing, how could that make me depraved?
In ignorance, I went on . . . to where I went on to.
And those who caused my injuries wanted me dead.

Now, sirs, I beg you before god,
since you made me leave the grove, keep me safe.
You fear the gods so don't, on any account,
make light of them. Be firm in your belief
that they see when mortals do what's right,
and when they do what's wrong. The unholy   280
have never yet found an escape.
With your gods' help, do not cloud Athens' bright
prospects by bowing to unholy works.
But since you pledged to keep me safe – a beggar –
continue to look after me. Don't look on my
disfigurement as robbing me of worth.
I've come devout, with reverence, to the
advantage of these citizens. And when
your leader comes – whoever he might be –
then you will hear and understand. Meanwhile   290
don't treat me unjustly in any way.
1 ELDER: All these arguments of yours, old man,
are certainly disturbing. You've not
spoken lightly. But I am content
to leave all this to our ruler to decide.
OIDIPOUS: And where is he who governs this land?
1 ELDER: In the ancestral city. The scout
who sent me here has gone to bring him.
OIDIPOUS: Do you think he'll have any respect or thought

for a blind man that he'd come here himself?   300
1 ELDER: Certainly, when he learns your name.
OIDIPOUS: And who is there to tell him that?
1 ELDER: The journey's long. Travellers' stories tend
   to get around. He'll hear of it
   and rest assured will come. Your name's been noised
   abroad, old man. So even if he's resting,
   he'll be here quickly once he's heard of you.
OIDIPOUS: Well, may he come with good fortune for his city
   and for me. Which good man is not his own best friend?
ANTIGONE: Oh Zeus, what can I say, what can I think,
      father?   310
OIDIPOUS: What is it, my child Antigone?
ANTIGONE: I see a woman
   coming towards us, riding a horse
   of Aitnaian stock. She wears a Thessalian-style hat
   on her head to keep the sun off her face.
   What do I say?
   Is it? Or isn't it? Am I thinking straight?
   Yes? No? I can't think what to say.

(*Enter* ISMENE, *right, on a horse led by a servant*)

   Dear girl,
   it is no one else. She's smiling
   as she comes towards me, showing me,   320
   for sure, that it is no one other than dear Ismene.
OIDIPOUS: What are you saying?
ANTIGONE: I see your girl, my
   sister. You'll know her by her voice right now.
ISMENE: My father and my sister – the two people
   I'm so glad to greet. It's been hard
   to find you. It's hard now I see you.

(ISMENE *begins to dismount*)

OIDIPOUS: Oh child, you've come.
ISMENE: Father, you look so awful.
OIDIPOUS: You're here, my child?
ISMENE: Yes, with some effort on my part.
OIDIPOUS: Hold me, dear girl.

(ISMENE *embraces* OIDIPOUS *and* ANTIGONE)

ISMENE: I hug you both.
OIDIPOUS: My own flesh and blood.
ISMENE: Such a terrible life to lead.   330
OIDIPOUS: Antigone's and mine?
ISMENE: And mine too – all three of us.
OIDIPOUS: Why have you come, Ismene?
ISMENE: Out of care for you, father.
OIDIPOUS: You wanted to see me?
ISMENE: And tell you something personally –
with the only servant I can trust.
OIDIPOUS: Where are the boys, your brothers, when needed?
ISMENE: They are where they are. They're in a desperate
situation now.
OIDIPOUS: Oh, the way they are, the way they live –
it's how they carry on in Aigypt.
There the men stay inside the house
sitting at the loom while their wives   340
are forever outside gathering basic foodstuffs.
My daughters, they should bear the brunt of this
but no, they do the housekeeping like girls,
and it's you not they who shoulder all my
miseries. This one, from the time
she stopped needing a child's care and grew in strength,
has always wandered with me, deprived,
an old man's guide, forever roaming
barefoot, hungry, living in the wild,
worn out by the constant rains, the burning   350
heat. She carries on and disregards the comforts of
a home to give her father what he needs.
And you, Ismene, you came to me before
without the Thebans knowing and brought news
of what the oracles said about me. You set yourself
a trusty spy for me when I was driven out of Thebes.
But now what have you come to tell your father,
Ismene? What's made you leave your home?
You have not come empty-handed, I am sure
of that. You've not brought dreadful news, have you?   360
ISMENE: I let pass, father, what I went through
looking for you, finding out where you

were staying. I don't want to suffer a second
time by repeating it all again.
I've come to tell you about the desperate
situation that your two sons are in.
At first they were happy to let Kreon
have the throne to avoid polluting the city.
They were made watchful by stories of the long line
of disasters that's gripped your harrowed family.   370
Now from some god and from wrong-headed passion,
a bitter dispute's seized them – their agony has tripled.
Each wants power and absolute rule.
The hot-headed younger of the two, Eteokles, has despoiled
his elder brother, Polyneikes, of the throne
and expelled him from the country.
According to our latest information, he
has fled to the Argive valley. There
he's recently married and made friends and allies.
Any time now, he will seize the plain of Thebes   380
with glory – or achieve lasting fame in death.
This is not mere talk, father. It's bitter
fact. It's quite beyond me how the gods
will ever show compassion for your pain.

OIDIPOUS: Did you really hope the gods would one
day care for me? That I might be saved?

ISMENE: Oh yes, father, I do; yes, on the present oracles.

OIDIPOUS: What sort of oracles? What's predicted, child?

ISMENE: The Thebans will seek you, because alive
or dead, you will bring them prosperity.   390

OIDIPOUS: Who could do well from somebody like me?

ISMENE: The word is that their power will be from you.

OIDIPOUS: So when I don't exist, am I then a man?

ISMENE: The gods worked for your ruin, but now restore
you.

OIDIPOUS: Ruined young, restored when old – that's nothing
much.

ISMENE: Kreon is on his way here now for this very reason,
you can be sure; and he won't be long.

OIDIPOUS: What will he want to do, daughter? Explain to
me.

ISMENE: Set you near Thebes in his control. You'll
see the land, but not set foot on it.   400

OIDIPOUS: What's the point of me staying on the border?
ISMENE: It's a serious matter for them if your grave's not
   honoured.
OIDIPOUS: We do not need a god to teach us this.
ISMENE: And so they want you staying near their land
   but you would have no control over your life.
OIDIPOUS: And will they cover me with Theban soil?
ISMENE: No; spilling the blood of your kin forbids it.
OIDIPOUS: No? In that case, they'll not control me – ever!
ISMENE: This will one day oppress Thebes.
OIDIPOUS: Under what conditions, Ismene?   410
ISMENE: Through your anger when they take a stand near
   your tomb.
OIDIPOUS: Tell me, who told you all this?
ISMENE: The envoys from the altar at Delphi.
OIDIPOUS: Apollo truly says all this of me?
ISMENE: That's what they say – the ones who come to
   Thebes.
OIDIPOUS: Has either of my sons heard of this news?
ISMENE: Both have been told – they know it well enough.
OIDIPOUS: The wretches heard this, did they, and they still
   preferred to rule than want me back?
ISMENE: To hear this hurts me. All the same, I bear it.   420
OIDIPOUS: Then let the gods not tame this strife that's been
   ordained for them! Let it rest with me to end
   the conflict they are starting now, as
   they raise the spear against each other. That
   way the one who clings on to the sceptre and
   the throne would go and the other who's been ousted
   would not come back! They didn't stop me or
   prevent me being driven out from home, humiliated –
   their own father! They had me sent away
   and publicly proclaimed a banished man.   430

Perhaps you'd say the city gave me what
I wanted at that time and this was fair.
Not so. For on that day, the very moment
when my passion blazed, when even to
be stoned to death was most welcome to me,
no one came forward to fulfil my craving.
Eventually when all the pain had mellowed,

I saw my passion had outrun, had punished
more than due, the errors of my past.
Then after all that time the city   440
forced me from the land. Those sons of mine,
who could have done so much to help their father,
would not. And for want of a mere word from them,
I've always wandered – poor, outcast, exiled.
My girls, to the extent nature allows,
have given me the means to stay alive,
safe travel, and the support of family;
while those two chose the throne before their father,
to wield power and lord it over earth.
They must not get hold of me for their ally.   450
No joy in ruling Thebes will ever come
their way. I know this; I have heard
her oracle, and I know of the previous
prophecies Apollo has fulfilled for me.

So let them send Kreon out searching for
me – and anybody else with power in Thebes.
So if, my friends, you – together with these
sacred guardian goddesses – give me
strength, you will create a powerful saviour for
your city, to my enemies' destruction.   460
I ELDER: You deserve our pity, Oidipous –
you and your daughters. And since in this plea of yours
you claim to be this country's saviour,
I'd like to advise you of your situation.
OIDIPOUS: Friends, you are my hosts; I'll do anything now.
I ELDER: Make yourself clean now before these goddesses.
When you first came, you trespassed in their grove.
OIDIPOUS: How will I do this? Teach me, sir.
I ELDER: First fetch holy water from the running
spring. Cleanse your hands to carry it.   470
OIDIPOUS: And when I have this fresh water, then what?
I ELDER: There are bowls there made by a master-craftsman.
Crown the rims and both handles.
OIDIPOUS: With cuttings or with bits of wool? How?
I ELDER: Use the newly shorn wool from a lamb.
OIDIPOUS: Good. Then how must I complete the rite?
I ELDER: For the libation, stand and face the east.

OIDIPOUS: And do I pour it from the pitchers you described?
1 ELDER: Three times, three pourings; the last one entirely –
OIDIPOUS: – filled with what? Tell me.   480
1 ELDER: – with water and honey. Don't add wine to it.
OIDIPOUS: And when the shady ground has taken it in?
1 ELDER: Take twigs – three sets of nine – and with both hands
lay down these olive sprays. Then say the prayer.
OIDIPOUS: This is what I want to hear – it's important.
1 ELDER: You, or some other in your place, ask those
we call the Kind Ones to undertake, from their gracious
hearts, to be saviours to their suppliant.
Pray silently, don't speak out loud.
Then withdraw and don't turn back. After   490
you've done this I'd be glad to stand by you.
But otherwise, stranger, I'd have some fears for you.
OIDIPOUS: Girls, do you hear these people?
ANTIGONE: We heard them. Tell us what we have to do.
OIDIPOUS: There's no way I can do it, for I lack
the strength and sight – two disabilities.
One of you go and do what must be done.
I'm sure a single soul, if well-intentioned,
can pay honour on behalf of many.
But get it done quickly. And don't leave me   500
alone. I barely have the strength to crawl
along left to myself. I need a guide.
ISMENE: Then I will do it. I need to know
the place where I can find the garland.
1 ELDER: On the far side of this grove, lady. If
you need something, there is a guardian there to tell you.
ISMENE: I should get moving then. Antigone,
stay here and mind our father. If parents need
something done for them, best forget the cost.

[*Exit* ISMENE, *right, followed by the* SERVANT]

ELDERS (A1):   It's awful, sir, to stir up memories of pain   510
long lain to rest but still I'd like to ask . . .
OIDIPOUS: Ask what?
ELDERS: . . . about the dreadful grief – it seems
unbearable – that you have lived through.

OIDIPOUS: Do not shamelessly, as hosts,
        lay bare the things I've suffered.
ELDERS: Stories about you never stop.
        I want to hear the right one.
OIDIPOUS: Oh!
ELDERS: Please, I beg you.
OIDIPOUS: Ah!
ELDERS: Come on. I've done what you wanted.   520

OIDIPOUS (A2):   I've borne the worst disasters, sirs, borne
        them
        readily, God knows;
        though none of them my choice.
ELDERS: How's that?
OIDIPOUS: Thebes entangled me, knowing nothing,
        in a cursed marriage.
ELDERS: I hear the scandal was that
        you took your mother to bed.
OIDIPOUS: To hear this is like a death,
        sirs. And these two girls of mine . . .   530
ELDERS: Yes?
OIDIPOUS: My children, both accursed.
ELDERS: Oh Zeus.
OIDIPOUS: They sprang from my own mother's womb.

ELDERS (B1):   They are your children and?
OIDIPOUS: . . . sisters to their father.
ELDERS: Oh.
OIDIPOUS: Yes. Back they come,
        the countless sorrows.
ELDERS: You've suffered.
OIDIPOUS: I can't forget I've suffered.
ELDERS: It was your doing.
OIDIPOUS: It was not my doing.
ELDERS: What then?
OIDIPOUS: I was given
        a reward, a boon I wished I'd never   540
        won for the heartache it caused.

ELDERS (B2):   Poor man, there's more. Didn't you kill . . .
OIDIPOUS: Now what? What do you want to know?

ELDERS: . . . your father?
OIDIPOUS: Oh, a second time
    you've struck, pain on pain.
ELDERS: You did kill him?
OIDIPOUS: I killed him, yes. But for me it was . . .
ELDERS: Was what?
OIDIPOUS: . . . was somehow right.
ELDERS: How so?
OIDIPOUS: I'll tell you;
    trapped by a stroke of fate, I killed, I murdered.
    But I was clean before the law. I came to do it in
    innocence.

(*Enter* THESEUS, *left, with* ATTENDANTS

I ELDER: Here's our leader, Theseus, the son
    of Aigeus. He's left where he was because of your
    message.   550
THESEUS: For years now I have heard from many about
    the bloody mutilation of your eyes,
    and so I recognized you, son of Laïos. Now
    I've come here and seen you, I am even more assured:
    your clothes, your desperate features are proof
    to me of who you are. Pity prompts me
    to ask, poor Oidipous: what's your supplication
    to me and to my city? What is it
    you and the unhappy girl beside you want?
    Tell me. You'd need to speak of an horrific act   560
    indeed to make me turn away from you.
    I well recall my own youth spent in exile.
    Like you, I – more than any man on earth –
    struggled with perils to my life.
    Therefore, I'll not decline to help an exile
    as you are now to survive. For I
    well know that I am mortal, and have no
    more share in what tomorrow brings than you.
OIDIPOUS: Theseus, in few words your generosity
    has allowed me to answer briefly.   570
    You are right in saying who I am, and
    who my father was, and where I've come from.
    So there is nothing left for me except

to say what I need and that's the end of it.

THESEUS: Then tell me what it is so that I know.

OIDIPOUS: I've come to give you something. My poor body
is my gift – not one worth much to look at
but of far greater advantage than good looks.

THESEUS: What advantage do you think you've brought?

OIDIPOUS: In time you'll know, but not, I think, right
now.   580

THESEUS: When will the benefit you bring be revealed?

OIDIPOUS: When I am dead and you have buried me.

THESEUS: You ask for the last things in life, but either you
forget or you don't care what comes between now and
then.

OIDIPOUS: Here is where I'll get all that.

THESEUS: This favour you ask is a small one.

OIDIPOUS: You watch; it's not slight, no. This means conflict.

THESEUS: With regard to your sons or you – what do you
mean?

OIDIPOUS: They will make me go back to Thebes.

THESEUS: Well, if you want to . . . it's not good to be in
exile.   590

OIDIPOUS: When I did want to, they wouldn't let me.

THESEUS: That's foolish. There's no place for anger in your
situation.

OIDIPOUS: When you've heard me speak, advise me; not till
then.

THESEUS: Then tell me. You can't blame me if I'm
uninformed.

OIDIPOUS: I've suffered, Theseus, disaster on disaster.

THESEUS: You mean your family's past circumstances?

OIDIPOUS: No, no. That's common gossip among Greeks.

THESEUS: What pain do you carry that other mortals don't?

OIDIPOUS: This is how it stands for me. I've been banished
from my own country by my own sons. And I can't ever   600
go back there because I killed my father.

THESEUS: Why would they send for you if you can't live
there?

OIDIPOUS: The word of god will drive them on.

THESEUS: What's been predicted that has frightened them?

OIDIPOUS: That they'll be struck down in this land.

THESEUS: But how could their bitterness affect me?

OIDIPOUS: Oh most dear son of Aigeus, only
the gods themselves never grow old and die.
Almighty Time obliterates all else.
The earth decays. The body's strength decays.   610
Faith dies and faithlessness instead grows strong.
The winds of change forever blow among
the company of friends and alliances of cities.
For some, it's now, for others, later on,
when friendship sours before it sweetens again.
So Thebes might now spend happy days
with you, but endless Time in constant cycles
breeds an endless stream of days and nights.
Then, for little reason, they will sever
your present friendly embraces with the spear.   620
At that time, my sleeping, hidden corpse,
cold in the earth, will drink their boiling blood,
while Zeus is Zeus and Apollo true.
But it's not good to speak of what should be secret.
Let me finish where I started. Keep
the promise that you made. You'll never say
you took a useless Oidipous into
your land, as long as the gods don't play me false.
ELDERS: My lord, this man said before he'd fulfil
these and similar promises for our country.   630
THESEUS: Who is there who would reject goodwill from such
a man? He is our ally, first and foremost,
and deserves to share our hearth at any time.
What's more, he's come a suppliant to the gods –
and to reward this land and me in no small way.
I respect this. I'll never reject
his favour. I'll set him up within the city.
If our guest is pleased to stay here, I will have
you protect him or else he can come with me.
What pleases you, Oidipous? I leave the choice   640
to you. I will agree with your decision.
OIDIPOUS: O Zeus, grant every good to men like this.
THESEUS: What do you want? To come to my palace?
OIDIPOUS: If I thought it right . . . But here's the place.
THESEUS: What will you do here? I'll not interfere.
OIDIPOUS: It's here I'll master those who banished me.
THESEUS: It's well worth your while, you say, to stay here?

OIDIPOUS: If you do for me what you have promised.

THESEUS: Take courage; trust me. I'll not abandon you.

OIDIPOUS: I'll not bind you by oath as if you were
    untrustworthy.   650

THESEUS: You'd achieve no more than my word gives.

OIDIPOUS: What will you do then?

THESEUS: What especially do you fear?

OIDIPOUS: Men will come.

THESEUS: These will take care of them.

OIDIPOUS: Watch out when you leave me . . .

THESEUS: No need to tell me what I have to do.

OIDIPOUS: I'm frightened, I admit.

THESEUS: Well, I'm not frightened.

OIDIPOUS: You don't know their threats . . .

THESEUS: I know no man
  will drive you out of here against my will.   657
  What if they've dared to boast that they will take   661
  you off? I know that's quite a sea for them
  to cross, and one that simply can't be crossed.
  I urge you to take heart, if – my resolve
  apart – it is Apollo who's sent you.
  I also know, when I'm not here, my name
  will guarantee your safety and protection.

[*Exit* THESEUS, *left, with* ATTENDANTS]

CHOROS 2

ELDERS (A1):   Sir, you have come to the land
    of the horse, to the best of the
    pastures, the white soil of Kolonos.   670
    Nightingales often come
    here and sing their bright songs
    in the flourishing grove,
    with its wine-coloured ivy
    and abundant fruit – the god's special
    place, protected from the sun and
    the winter winds. There Dionysos sports
    always with his revellers,
    the divine nymphs who nursed him.   680

ELDERS (A2):   Every day, beautiful sprays
              of narcissus – the crown of the
              mighty goddesses of old –
              bloom afresh in the heavenly
              dew, with the golden crocus.
              Non-stop springs never
              let the meandering Kephissos
              river run dry. It
              spreads over the wide
              flatlands, renewing them   690
              daily with fresh water. The Muses
              and Aphrodite, riding with
              golden reins, love to dance there.

ELDERS (B1):   Something I have never heard
              to flourish in Asia or
              Pelops' great Dorian isle
              is a plant undestroyable by man,
              ever renewing itself,
              striking fear to our enemies'
              heart for it thrives only here: 700
              it's the nourishing grey olive
              tree. Young or old, no one will
              lay a violent hand on it
              for Zeus, the tree's guardian,
              watches it always,
              and the bright eyes of Athena.

ELDERS (B2):   What should I praise most in our
              mother-city? I sing of her
              gift from the deity – her
              proudest boast: it's her horses, horse-   710
              breeding and wonderful sea.
              Lord Poseidon, you enthroned her in
              this glory. Kronos' son,
              who first brought forth the bit to control
              the horse on these roads, then
              the oar, easy-to-row, as it
              flies on the sea past the land.
              It's a marvel! It leaps in pursuit
              of the train of sea-nymphs.

SCENE 3

ANTIGONE: You've sung your country's praises mightily.   720
Now put your glowing words into action.
OIDIPOUS: What's happening now, my girl?
ANTIGONE: It's Kreon, father.
He's come. He's here with his guards.
OIDIPOUS: Most dear friends, now show that your
promise of my safety was genuine.
I ELDER: Be brave. Our promise holds. I might be old,
but there's no way our country's strength has aged.

(*Enter* KREON, *right, with* GUARDS)

KREON: People of Kolonos. Noble residents.
Your eyes, I see, reflect some
sudden fear at my entrance. Don't shrink   730
away from me and don't start cursing me.
I've not come wanting action – I'm an old
man. And I understand this city is
as strong as any in all Greece – that's clear.
Old as I am, however, I've been sent
to persuade Oidipous to return to Thebes.
It's not a private mission. It is one
that's urged by the whole city. I am kin.
No one's wept more for his calamities.
And so, long-suffering Oidipous, you've heard   740
me. Now come home. Everyone in Thebes
is calling you, and rightly so – I more than most.   742
And more than most, I share your pain, old man.   744
I see you as you are: a sorry figure, exiled,
always wandering, relying on
one little girl, and no means of support.
How I regret I did not know she's fallen
into such a state of degradation,
tending to you and your condition in   750
beggary. She's of an age, not married,
yet she's ripe for snatching by the first comer.
Is this too savage a reproach to cast
at you, at me, our household? I'm sorry.
You cannot conceal what is an obvious shame. So now

let me persuade you, Oidipous;
give way, before our father's gods, and come back to
your city and your father's home. Thank Athens,
for she is worthy. Thebes, however,
your own mother-city, surely deserves more.   760
OIDIPOUS: You'd dare anything. You ply your tricksy
arguments that make a mockery of truth.
Why try this? You want to trap me again
so that I'd suffer far worse than I have?
When I was burdened with self-inflicted cares
I would have leaped for joy at banishment.
I wanted it but you would not grant it.
Then when I'd had my fill of anger,
when living at home was sweet, yes then
you cast me out! You banished me! You didn't   770
show much of this loving kinship then!
Now, once more, when you see this city and
its people are kindly disposed to me,
you try to tear me away with your soft, cruel words.
Where's the joy in friendship that's not wanted?
If you begged someone to do you a good turn,
and he would not help you – he gave nothing –
then when you had all you wanted, he made an offer,
that favour wouldn't be a favour.
Surely you'd find no genuine pleasure in this?   780
However this is what you offer me –
wonderful promises and terrible consequences.
I'll tell them all. I'll show your baseness – why
you've come to seize me; not to take me home,
but to the border so that Thebes will stay
unharmed, delivered from Athens itself.
Well, you'll not have it. What you'll have is my
eternal vengeance rooted in your soil.
As for my sons, their part in my bequest
is simply this: sufficient land to die in.   790
Don't I know better about Thebes than you?
By far! I listen to the wisest –
Apollo and his father, Zeus himself.
Oh, it's a lying tongue that's brought you here,
a tongue as sharp as steel. Well, lie on! You will do
much more to harm yourself than help yourself.

I can't persuade you, I know that. Go! Let
us live here. Even as we are, we don't
live badly. Just as long as we're content.

KREON: Who do you think has run out of luck, more
likely,   800
through this argument – me or yourself?

OIDIPOUS: I get most satisfaction from you failing
to convince me or these people here.

KREON: You misery, won't you ever show at last some
growth
in wisdom? Your life's a disgrace to old age.

OIDIPOUS: You have a slippery tongue! I don't know of any
upright man who can argue any case at all.

KREON: They're two different things; to gabble and talk sense.

OIDIPOUS: As if you speak so little and so well.

KREON: Not to a mind like yours, I'm sure I don't.   810

OIDIPOUS: Go away. I'll speak for these as well; don't
set a guard here where I'm going to stay.

KREON: These are my witnesses, not you, that you fling
such abuse at friends. If ever I take you –

OIDIPOUS: Take me forcefully with these defenders here?

KREON: Even if I don't, you will still come to grief.

OIDIPOUS: What can you do to back your threat?

KREON: I've just now sent to have one of your two
daughters abducted. And I'll have this one soon.

OIDIPOUS: Ah!

KREON: Soon you'll have more to groan about.   820

OIDIPOUS: You've got Ismene?

KREON: And this one before long.

OIDIPOUS: Friends, what will you do? Will you desert me?
Drive this impious man out of your land!

I ELDER: Away, sir! Move off! Now! What you intend
to do is wrong. And what you've done is wrong.

KREON: Guards, now's your chance to take this girl away.
If she won't go freely, drag her off!

ANTIGONE: No! Where can I get away? Where's
help from heaven or earth?

I ELDER: What are you doing, Kreon?

KREON: I will not touch this man, but she is mine.   830

OIDIPOUS: Leaders of Kolonos . . .

I ELDER: You're doing wrong, stranger.

KREON: No, I do right.

1 ELDER: How is it right?

KREON: I take what's mine.

OIDIPOUS (AT):   Oh Athens!

ELDERS: What are you doing, sir? Won't you let go?
     You're on the brink of testing arms.

KREON: Keep away.

ELDERS: No, not while you're intent on this.

KREON: You'll be at war with Thebes if you hurt me.

OIDIPOUS: Didn't I say this?

ELDERS: Let the girl
     go now.

KREON: Don't command what you can't
          enforce.

ELDERS: I tell you, release her.

KREON: And I tell you: be on your way!   840

ELDERS: Come forward, neighbours, come, come here!
     Our city Athens is under siege!
     Come forward, here, to me.

ANTIGONE: I'm being dragged away! Oh help, friends!

OIDIPOUS: Child, where are you?

ANTIGONE: I'm being forced away from you.

OIDIPOUS: Stretch out your hands, my girl.

ANTIGONE: I'm not strong enough.

KREON: You! Get her out!

OIDIPOUS: Oh my agony, agony!

(ANTIGONE *is dragged off by the* GUARDS, *right*)

KREON: No more wandering with your daughters propping
     you up. You want a victory over your own
     city and her friends? Well, it's Thebes' wish that I,   850
     ruler as I am, now act this way.
     Have your victory! You'll learn, I'm sure, in time
     you do yourself no favours carrying on
     like this – or as you did before. You've spurned friends,
     always indulging your self-destructive rage.

1 ELDER: Stay there, sir.

KREON: I warn you, don't touch me.

1 ELDER: I will not let you go while those two girls are gone.
KREON: Then you will soon give Thebes an even greater
   surety –
   it won't be them alone I'll seize.
1 ELDER: So what will you do?
KREON: I'll take this one as well.   860
ELDERS: You threaten to do this?
KREON: I'll do it. Now!
   While Theseus can't stop me.
OIDIPOUS: The voice of shame! You'll dare lay hands on me?
KREON: Keep quiet!
OIDIPOUS: May these goddesses now
   give me breath enough to make this curse.
   You coward, you've forced her away –
   my poor eyes since my own sight had gone.
   I pray the sun-god who sees everything one day
   gives you and all your family an old
   age every bit as wretched as is mine.   870
KREON: You see, you people of Kolonos?
OIDIPOUS: They see you and me. They understand I'm hurt
   by what you do, and fight you off with words.
KREON: I'll not control my temper. I might be alone and
   slowed by age, but I'll take him.

OIDIPOUS (A2):   Oh, the agony!
ELDER: You come with such arrogance,
         Kreon, if
   you think that you'll manage this.
KREON: Oh, I think I will.
ELDER: Not while I stay here.
KREON: When the cause is just, the weak beats the strong.   880
OIDIPOUS: Do you hear what he says?
ELDER: He won't manage it,
      Zeus knows.
KREON: Zeus knows, yes – you don't.
ELDER: What insolence!
KREON: Insolence? Well, you'll have to put up
         with it!
ELDER: Everybody! Leaders!
      Come quickly, come! Kreon's men
      are getting away over the border.

(*Enter* THESEUS, *left, with* ATTENDANTS)

THESEUS: What was that shouting? What's happened? What
    panic
has stopped my sacrifice to Poseidon, patron-god of
    Kolonos?
Speak up, I want to know it all.
I haven't rushed here for the pleasure of the walk.   890
OIDIPOUS: My friend, I recognize your voice. I've just
    suffered terribly from this man here.
THESEUS: Suffered what? Who caused the trouble? Tell me.
OIDIPOUS: Kreon! You see him here. He's come and snatched
    both of the children who still belong to me.
THESEUS: What are you saying?
OIDIPOUS: You've heard my troubles.
THESEUS: One of you servants there, go quickly to
the altars. Make the people – all of them –
leave off the sacrifice and hurry out
on foot or on their horses. And keep the reins loose!   900
Go to where the branches of the roads join up.
The girls won't pass. I'd be a laughing stock
to this man if I'm over-powered.
Go, as I command, and hurry up!

                    [*Exit an* ATTENDANT, *left*]

          If I
felt the anger that this man deserves
I'd not have let him safe out of my grasp.
But as it is he will be bound by those
same laws he brought here – and by no others.
You will not leave this place until you bring
those girls and set them before me in my sight.   910
You've acted most unworthily to me,
your family and your own country as well.
This city you're in practises what's right,
does everything according to the law. But you
ignore her authority, burst in, and take
what you desire. You forced your way in.
You've judged me and my city worth nothing –
empty of men or perhaps full of slaves.

It wasn't Thebes who taught you to do wrong.
She hates to nurture men outside the law.   920
She'd not approve you if she heard you had
despoiled what's mine and – yes! – the gods', in seizing
helpless suppliants by force.
If I set foot in your country, I'd not
grab this, take that, even for the most
legitimate reasons without the ruler's leave,
whoever he might be. I'd understand
my place as guest and how I must behave.
But you disgrace a city that does not
deserve it. And it's your own! Advancing time's   930
made you older and empty-headed.
So what I said before, I now repeat.
Have someone bring both girls immediately
if you do not want to be forced against
your will to stay in this country. I am telling
you this and I mean what I tell you.

I ELDER: You see where you've got to? Coming from Thebes
you'd seem just, but you're found doing wrong.

KREON: It's not because I say Athens is devoid
of men or counsel, as you say, son of   940
Aigeus, that I acted in this way.
I thought no one would ever care so much
for my kin to nurture them against my will.
And I was sure that they'd not harbour any
father-killer – a polluted man – a man
found joined in a most unholy marriage.
I knew this because of the Areopagos –
their land's seat of wise counsel – which won't
allow such wanderers to live in Athens.
I trusted in this when I seized my prey.   950
And I would not have done even that, if he
had not bitterly cursed me and my family.
I was hurt, and rightly I retaliated.   953
Now you will do whatever you wish. Although   956
I speak the truth, I've no support. That makes
me weak. Even so, old as I am, I will
try fighting back if I'm attacked.

OIDIPOUS: Shameless arrogance! What do you think   960
you insult now – my old age or your own?

The list of murder, marriage, accidents
you rattle off so readily I unfortunately had
to bear against my will. But it suited the gods.
Perhaps they've always had a grudge against our household.
But you'd not find a thing to blame me for –
on my own – that led me to commit
those wrongs against my family and myself.
Tell me: if it was foretold to my father
through oracles he'd die by his son's hand   970
then how could you rightly blame me for this?
My father had not even engendered me.
My mother was not pregnant. I did not exist!
And if – born to misery as I was –
I fought against my father and killed him,
I didn't realize what I did then or to whom.
How can you blame me for doing something
    unintentionally?
As for my mother's marriage – your sister's! –
do you feel no shame in forcing me, you wretch,
to speak of it? For I will! I'll not be silent   980
when you raise this – against all decency.
She bore me, yes, bore me – to my eventual distress.
I didn't know. She didn't. She bore me
and to her shame then gave birth to my children.
One thing I know: you're keen to slander me
and her as well, but I was loath to marry
her. And I am loath to talk of it.
But I won't be condemned because I married
thus or killed my father – which you always
throw up in my face in bitter reproach.   990
Answer me this one question I put to you:
if someone tried to kill you – and you were innocent –
here on the spot, would you ask if he was
your father or immediately fight back?
You'd fight back, I expect, if you loved
life, not look around to see what's right.
I walked into these misfortunes trapped
by the gods. And I believe my father,
were he still alive, would not deny me.
But you're not innocent. You say whatever   1000
you like whether you should or shouldn't say it,

maligning me in front of everybody.
How you flatter Theseus to his face
and praise the style of Athens' government!
You praise so much that you forget this point:
if any country knows how to pay homage
to the gods, it's Athens who's pre-eminent.
Yet you tried to steal me away, an old man, and a suppliant;
to abduct me. You captured my daughters.
That's why I now invoke these goddesses.   1010
I call on them. I enjoin them come to help
me and defend me so that you will learn
the kind of men who guard this city here.

ELDERS: My lord, he's a good man; his suffering
has been overwhelming. He deserves our help.

THESEUS: Enough talk. The perpetrators hurry off.
We're the victims and we stand around.

KREON: What do you want of me? I have no power.

THESEUS: You lead the way there. You'll have me   1019
and me alone for company. I know you   1028
weren't alone without support, coming with
such insolence on this daring expedition now.   1030
There's someone you trusted in this affair.
I'll have to look to it so Athens
is not made weaker than a single man   1033
On your way. If the girls are held somewhere round
    here   1020
near us, then you will point them out to me.
Even if your men escape with them, that's not a worry.
Others are rushing here; they'll put a stop
to prayers of thanks for any escape from us.
Go on ahead. The situation is reversed, you can be sure,   1025
and fortune's had the hunter caught. There's nothing
gained by trickery that will endure for long.   1027
Do you understand any of this? Or has what I've just
    said   1034
now seem as useless to you as when you planned all this?

KREON: You can say no wrong to me in your own land.
I'll know what to do when I am home

THESEUS: Threaten all you like now. On your way! Oidipous,
stay here. Don't worry. I promise you that,
so long as I don't die first, I'll not stop   1040

until I place your children in your care again.
OIDIPOUS: Bless you, Theseus. You are a noble man, fair and
considerate to us.

[*Exit* THESEUS, *right, with* KREON]

CHOROS 3

ELDERS (A1): I wish I was where our
    enemies turn quickly,
    clash armour and join
    in battle; the shore of Apollo
    or the torch-lit beach
    where the holy goddesses tend rites of the dead   1050
    for mortals – whose tongue
    receives the golden key from
    the priests of Eumolpos.
    I think it's there that Theseus,
    spoiling for a fight, soon makes
    the two unmarried sisters free as well
    inside the borders of our land.

ELDERS (A2): Or maybe the enemy's fled west
    of the snowy peaks   1060
    out from the pastures of Oia,
    fleeing on his horses
    and flying chariots.
    He will be caught! Fearsome is our ally, Ares,
    fearsome is the might of Theseus.
    Steel bits flash in the sun;
    horsemen career along with
    reins dropped low. They   1070
    worship Athena, goddess of the horse.
    and the sea god who binds the earth,
    Rhea's precious son.

ELDERS (B1): Do they fight or wait? Somehow
    my heart courts this
    hope: the quick deliverance
    of the two poor victims, victimized

even at the hands of their kin.
Zeus seals this thing, seals it today.
I can foresee a victory.   1080
I wish I were a dove, swifter than a storm,
to fly to the high clouds
and hover there –
a view above the battle.

ELDERS (B2):   Ruler of the gods, all-seeing
Zeus, may you grant
that this land's protectors,
through victorious strength, achieve
the ambush that brings success –
and your holy child, Pallas Athena, too.   1090
Also the hunter, Apollo,
and his sister who pursues the spotted
deer in flight – I entreat you both
to come as helpers
to this country and its people.

SCENE 4

1 ELDER: My homeless friend, you can't call this lookout
a poor prophet. For I see the girls
escorted on their way back here.
OIDIPOUS: Where? What's that? How?

(*Enter* ANTIGONE, ISMENE *and* THESEUS, *right*)

ANTIGONE: Father! Father!
If only some god would let you lay eyes on this   1100
exceptional man who's brought us back to you.
OIDIPOUS: My child, are you both here?
ANTIGONE: The hands of Theseus and his trusty
men have made us safe.
OIDIPOUS: Come here to your father, children. Let me
embrace
you both. I had not hoped you'd ever return.
ANTIGONE: You'll get what you ask for and what we want.

OIDIPOUS: Where then are you?
ANTIGONE: We're coming to you.
OIDIPOUS: My dear young daughters.
ANTIGONE: All our love is yours.
OIDIPOUS: The crutches of my life ...
ANTIGONE: Pitiful ones for a pitiful man.
OIDIPOUS: I hold those I love most. If I died now,   1110
I'd not regret it with these beside me.
Press close to me, my girls, one on each side.
Graft yourselves on my old trunk and rest
from the loneliness of our separation. It's over.
Tell me quickly what happened. For
girls your age, it's best to be brief.
ANTIGONE: This is the man who saved us. You should listen
    to him, father,
since he did it. So my role will be small.
OIDIPOUS: Please sir, don't be amazed, if I talk on
and on – for now my girls are back against my hopes.   1120
I know that this delight, this joy they give me,
is brought about by no one else but you.
You were the one to rescue them, none else.
And may the gods grant you my deepest wish –
for you and for your land – because alone
among you of all humanity I found true righteousness,
humaneness and an honesty.
I know this and I pay my thanks with these words;
I have what I have through you and none else.
Lord, give me your right hand that I may grasp   1130
it; and if it's permitted, let me kiss your cheek.
But what am I saying? How could a wretch like me
want you to touch him? Every taint of wickedness
lives in me. I can't touch you.
I won't allow you. Only those who've suffered
what I have can share my misery.
I thank you where you stand. For what remains,
deal with me fairly as you've done today.
THESEUS: The fact that you have talked so long, delighted
in your children, or that you preferred   1140
to talk with them than me does not surprise me;
indeed it doesn't offend me at all.
I am not keen to make my mark in life

through tales so much as through the things I do.
And here's the proof: I did not mislead
you with my promise, honoured sir. I'm here with both your
     rescued
daughters. They are untouched by those threats.
What's the point in idle boasting how the fight
was won? You'll know from talking with your daughters.

But there is something I've just heard on my   1150
way back. I'd like your opinion. The message
was short, but worth our wonder all the same.
One shouldn't ignore the slightest incident.

OIDIPOUS: What is it, Theseus? Tell me.
I've no idea what's puzzling you.
THESEUS: They tell me some man claims to be your relative
     though not your countryman. Somehow he has
     prostrated himself at Poseidon's altar
     where I was sacrificing before hurrying here.
OIDIPOUS: Where from? What's he a suppliant for?   1160
THESEUS: I don't know, except this; they say he wants a brief
     word with you, which is not much to ask.
OIDIPOUS: About what? Sitting at that altar is no frivolous
     claim.
THESEUS: They say he asks merely to come and speak with
     you and then to have safe passage back.
OIDIPOUS: But who can he be making this supplication?
THESEUS: Well, consider if there's a relative
     in Argos who would want this of you.
OIDIPOUS: My friend, stop right there.
THESEUS: What's the matter?
OIDIPOUS: Do not ask me –
THESEUS: Ask what? Tell me.   1170

OIDIPOUS: From what you've said, I know this suppliant.
THESEUS: Who is he? Am I supposed to object to him?
OIDIPOUS: My son, my hated son. Theseus, I couldn't bear to
     listen to him – him of all men!
THESEUS: Why not? Can't you just listen? You don't have to
     do
  what he wants. Is hearing him so painful?

OIDIPOUS: His voice, Theseus, is repulsive to me, his father.
Don't make me give in on this, please.
THESEUS: But wait. Doesn't his suppliance make you?
Respect for the god must be observed. 1180
ANTIGONE: Father, listen, though I'm young to offer advice.
Let this man here put his mind to rest
and please the god as he would wish.
Yield to us and let our brother come.
Rest assured, if what he says is out
of place, you won't be forced to change your mind.
What harm is there listening to words? Whatever plots
are hatched, you know, are often revealed in talk.
You gave him life. Even if he committed
the most atrocious things against you, 1190
to do the same to him in return is not right.
Have respect for him. Other people have bad children
and a sharp temper as well. But once chastised,
they grow up charmed by those who love them.
Think of the past not of the present. Look
at what you suffered for your parents.
See what's happened and you'll realize, I'm sure,
that the result of bitter anger is more bitterness.
You have reliable evidence for this;
you yourself do not have eyes to see with. 1200
Give in to us. It's not good that those
who want fair play should have to keep on begging, or
someone receives favours but doesn't know how to repay
them.
OIDIPOUS: Child, what pleases you burdens me but you've
convinced me. Let what you want done be done.
On one condition, Theseus: when he comes here, then
don't ever let him take control of my life.
THESEUS: I do not need to hear your wishes more
than once, old man. I will not boast – but know
you're safe as long as some god keeps me safe. 1210

[*Exit* THESEUS, *left*]

CHOROS 4

ELDERS (A1):   Whoever desires a bigger share
in life and ignores the middle
way persists, it seems
to me, in being foolish.
Long life
too often
means you're nearer to grief. You
won't find happiness
when someone gets more
than their due. Our unavoidable companion   1220
appears – without love, without
dance, without song
– death at last and
destiny in Haides.

ELDERS (A2):   Not to be born, for sure,
is best. But if you see the light
the next best thing is to
go back as fast as you can.
For once the heady, thoughtless
days of youth pass by   1230
what is there but sorrow
and strife? No end of trouble;
murders, factions, quarrels, wars
and malice. And despised old age
at last falls due – impotent, unsociable,
unloved. All the worst
miseries become your partners in life.

ELDERS (A3):   This man suffers from it – and me too.
It's like some northern cape battered   1240
by winds and storms and winter waves.
Dreadful curses, like the waves, break
savagely on him and never let up –
from the setting of the sun
to its rising,
from its midday rays
and from the gloomy mountains in the North.

SCENE 5

ANTIGONE: I think our visitor is here.
He's by himself, father. And tears   1250
are streaming from his eyes as he makes his way.
OIDIPOUS: And who is it?
ANTIGONE: The person we first thought.
The one who's come is Polyneikes.

(*Enter* POLYNEIKES, *left*)

POLYNEIKES: Oh, what will I do? Weep first for my
   misfortunes, sisters,
or for those of my father, this old man
I see? I've found him here – an outcast in
a foreign land, in company with you.
And dressed like this! Vile dirt all over him,
a dirt that's lived with him a long time;
his ribs wasted; no eyes in his head;   1260
his hair dishevelled and wind-blown; and
in keeping with all this, it seems, is
the food he carries for his poor stomach.
I am a scoundrel for learning this so late.
In regard to your care I'm proven the worst of men –
I witness to this fact – no need to ask someone else.
But there is Mercy, she who shares the throne
with Zeus and all he does. Let her
be with you, father. Mistakes can be
corrected and never more repeated.   1270
Why are you silent?
Say something, father. Do not turn away from me.
No answer at all? Will you send me off in silence,
in disdain, not tell me why you're angry?
You, his daughters, my own sisters, please
– our father's mouth is closed to me, shut tight
against me – persuade him to open it,
not shame me, a suppliant to Poseidon.
Don't let him send me away with no word in reply.
ANTIGONE: Speak up, my poor brother. Say what you've
   come for.   1280
Words often have the power to please,

or to annoy or to arouse pity.
They've also prompted a reply from those who would be
    silent.
POLYNEIKES: Then I will speak out. I'll take your lead; it's
    good.
First of all I call the god himself
my ally, from whose shrine your ruler
Theseus raised me and granted me freedom
to come here safely and to talk and to listen.
I will expect to receive this right
from you people and from my sisters and from my
    father.   1290
I want to tell you, father, why I've come.
I was driven out of Thebes as a fugitive
because, as the elder brother, I expected
to take my place on your mighty throne.
It was your younger son, Eteokles,
who banished me from Thebes – not after victory
in debate or physical combat.
No; he seduced the city. Indeed I hold
your family curse responsible.   1299
When I went to the Dorians in Argos   1301
I married into Adrastos' family. I made
sworn allies of Apians acknowledged
as leaders and decorated in battle
so that I'd form a seven-unit force of spearmen
against Thebes. There I'd die justified
or else banish those who caused all this.
So. Why have I happened to come here now?
I turn to you, father, in supplication
on my behalf and that of my comrades,   1310
who at this very moment have been staked
around Thebes – seven commanders, seven cohorts.
There's the lancer Ampiaraos who
excels in augury as well as war;
Tydeus is next, the Aitolian, Oineos'
son; and third, Eteoklos of Argos;
the fourth, Hippomedon, sent by his father
Talaos; the fifth, Kapaneus, boasts he'll level
Thebes, set fire to it and destroy it;

the sixth, Parthenopaios, is an Arkadian keen to
    fight,   1320
named after his mother who stayed unwed
so long – trustworthy son of Atalanta.
Then I, your son, or if not yours, son of
a terrible destiny, and yours at least in name,
I lead the fearless Argives against Thebes.
Together we beg you earnestly, father,
for your sake and for your daughters' sakes, abandon
your deep-seated anger towards me.
I'm going to take vengeance on my brother
who's banished me and robbed me of my home.   1330
If there's any truth in oracles
the side you choose, they say, will be the victor.
By Thebes our home and by our family's gods,
I beg you now to relent, give in. I'm poor
and I'm homeless. Yes, like you, homeless.
You and I, we depend on others for
a place to live. We've inherited the same misfortune.
Eteokles rules in Thebes to my disgrace.
He laughs at us both for the same reason while living in
    luxury.
You stand by me, father, back my plan   1340
and with little time and effort, I will scatter him to the
    winds.
And so I will set you in your own house,
me in mine and force him out of home.
I can boast of this if you agree
to it. Without you, I cannot survive.
I ELDER: Answer him properly, Oidipous, for his
sake who sent him. Then send him back.
OIDIPOUS: If this man, my friends of Kolonos, had not
been sent to me by none other than
Theseus, who deems it right that he   1350
should hear my words, he'd never know my voice.
That was a blessing for him, but now he'll hear things that
for certain will not make his life the happier.
You vermin! When you had the power and
the throne in Thebes, which now your brother has,
you were the one who drove out your own father.
You outlawed me and made me wear these rags.

And now you see it, you weep, when you have stumbled
into this same turmoil of misfortunes I'm in.
But there's no cause for grief. I put up with it   1360
and I remember, while I live, that you've destroyed me.
Through banishment, you have forced me to live
in this hardship. You made me a wanderer
begging others for my daily needs.
If I'd not fathered these two girls, my nurses,
I'd have died as far as you were concerned.
Now they keep me alive. They care for me.
They're men, not women, sharing my suffering.
You and your brother – you are not my sons.
The daimon watches you – more so than up   1370
to now, if troops of yours are marching on
the city of Thebes. One thing is sure: you'll never
tear her down. Before you do, you'll fall
defiled with blood, together with your brother.
I've sent such curses out to you before
but now I call them back to give me support.
You'll both learn to respect those who gave you life,
and not to dishonour them because I who fathered
you am blind. My daughters didn't act like this.
My curses crush your supplication and   1380
your claim to the throne, if Right, honoured of old,
still sits with the ancient laws of Zeus.
Go! I spit you out! I am not your father!
You worst of men! And take with you these curses
I call down. You'll never conquer Thebes
through civil war. You'll never return to the valley
of Argos. You will die at the hand of your brother
and in turn kill him who banished you.
I pray for this, and call the pitch-black fathering
Dark to take you away so that you'll never have a place to
   live.   1390
I call these goddesses. I call the god of war
who planted in you both such dire hate.
Now you've heard this, on your way, and take
this message to the Thebans and to
those trusting troops of yours; these are the gifts
that Oidipous bestows upon his sons.

1 ELDER: Polyneikes, I do not sympathize with you

coming this way. Now go back, quickly.
POLYNEIKES: So much for this journey, for my failure,
for my companions. What an end to the road   1400
I set out on from Argos. What can I do?
It is not possible for me to tell
my comrades, or to turn them back again.
I must say nothing as I meet this doom.
Daughters of my father, my sisters, you
have heard these hard words that our father's uttered.
Before the gods, I beg you both: if his curses
are fulfilled and you happen to
return home, don't treat me with dishonour.
Lay me in a grave with funeral gifts.   1410
The praise that is your due for all the work
you've done for our father will be made greater
still for service that you render me.
ANTIGONE: Polyneikes, please, listen to me.
POLYNEIKES: What is it, Antigone? Tell me.
ANTIGONE: Make your armies turn quickly back to Argos.
Don't destroy yourself along with Thebes.
POLYNEIKES: It's not possible. How could I lead the same
troops out again if I'm seen to be a complete coward?
ANTIGONE: Must you return to your anger, brother?
What   1420
profit is there in annihilating your fatherland?
POLYNEIKES: Exile is an indignity! I am the elder,
made a mockery by my younger brother.
ANTIGONE: Don't you see that you will make our father's
prophecies
come true? He's said that you'll kill each other.
POLYNEIKES: It's what he wants. Must I not concede?
ANTIGONE: This is terrible. Who will dare follow you, once
they've heard the predictions of Oidipous?
POLYNEIKES: I won't tell them. A great commander
reports good news and keeps bad news to himself.   1430
ANTIGONE: And you think that strategy is a good one?
POLYNEIKES: Yes. Don't hold me back. This is the path
that I must take, doomed though it is and luckless
because of my father and his Furies.
May Zeus bless you if you do what I ask.   1435
Let go of me. Farewell. You'll never lay eyes

on me alive again.
ANTIGONE: No. No.
POLYNEIKES: Don't lament me.
ANTIGONE: How could anyone
not weep for you, my brother? You are going to die.   1440
POLYNEIKES: If I must, I must.
ANTIGONE: Not if you listen to me.
POLYNEIKES: Don't urge what can't be done.
ANTIGONE: It's me who suffers
in losing you.
POLYNEIKES: What happens and what doesn't
are in the hands of the daimon. I pray
the gods that you both avoid all disasters – always.
Everyone knows, you don't deserve to suffer.

[*Exit* POLYNEIKES, *right*]

CHOROS 5

ELDERS (A1):   New troubles, new burdens, I see
            caused right now by this blind visitor –
            unless some destiny's at work.   1450
            I cannot call decrees
            of daimons vain.
            Time watches, always watches
            everything, each day turning some
            things aside, raising others up on high.

(*Thunder*)

            The sky thunders! Oh Zeus!

OIDIPOUS: Children! Children! Is there anyone here
to go and bring the great man Theseus?
ANTIGONE: Why do you ask to call him, father?
OIDIPOUS: The winged thunder of Zeus will lead me
      now   1460
to Haides. So send someone quickly.

(*Thunder*)

ELDERS (A2):   Watch out! The mighty, awesome thunderbolt
of Zeus comes crashing down. Fear
makes my hair stand on end.
I shake with fear. Again the
lightning flashes in the sky.
Why? Will it strike?
I am afraid. It never breaks out
without reason, without purpose.   1470

(*Thunder*)

Oh mighty sky! Oh Zeus!

OIDIPOUS: My girls, my life has now come to an end.
It is the Gods' decree. There's no turning back.
ANTIGONE: How do you know? How can you be sure?
OIDIPOUS·   I know well enough. Let someone go quickly
to the lord of Athens so that he'll come.

(*Thunder*)

ELDERS (B1)·   Ah! Ah! Again watch
out! The piercing thunder-crash!
Mercy, daimon, mercy! Maybe you intend   1480
to plunge the motherland into darkness?
Please be propitious!
Don't make me share in any way
some misfortune for seeing this extraordinary man.
Oh Zeus above, I call you.

OIDIPOUS: Is he near yet? Will he get here, children,
while I'm still alive and thinking straight?
ANTIGONE: What promise do you want for your peace of
mind?
OIDIPOUS: I will do him a great favour in return
for what he's done – just as I promised.   1490

ELDERS (B2):   Oh, oh, my son, come, come.
Even if you're deep inside the grove

of Poseidon, the sea-god, about to
make a sacrifice, hurry here.
For this stranger deems you,
your city and your people worthy
of a just return for what you've done.
Hurry, quickly, lord Theseus!

SCENE 6

(*Enter* THESEUS, *left, with an* ATTENDANT)

THESEUS: What's this commotion you've raised again –   1500
   Oidipous, and you people here as well?
   Is it because of the thunder of Zeus or a
   pelting hailstorm? When there's a storm like this,
   it seems that any divine portent is possible.
OIDIPOUS: Theseus, you are here and welcome. A
   god has made your journey one of great benefit.
THESEUS: What is it, son of Laios – this new revelation?
OIDIPOUS: My life turns in the balance and I do not want to
   die
   without being true to what I promised you about Athens.
THESEUS: What sign of death are you relying on?   1510
OIDIPOUS: The gods themselves are messengers to me.
   They have not made lies of signs which were foretold.
THESEUS: How can you prove that? Tell me, Oidipous.
OIDIPOUS: Heaven's thunder never ends and lightning
   bolts are flung from the unconquerable hand of Zeus.
THESEUS: I believe you. I'm certain that what you
   foretell is true. So tell me what to do.
OIDIPOUS: I'll tell you, son of Aigeus, of the
   incorruptible treasures laid up for Athens.
   Any moment now, I'll take myself   1520
   to a place to die – and I will need no guide.
   You must never show this place to any man
   or say where it is hidden, where it lies,
   so it may always stand as your defence
   instead of many shields or neighbouring ally's spears.
   When you go there by yourself, you'll learn
   mysteries which can never be spoken.

I'd not reveal them to these citizens
or to my children, though I love them too.
Guard them throughout your life, and when you come   1530
to die, reveal them to one special elder
who then should show the next, and so on.
That way you'll live in Athens unmolested by
the Thebans. Many cities treat others
who wish to live in peace with wanton violence.
The gods take note, after some time perhaps,
when any man spurns them and turns to madness.
Theseus, don't ever entertain the thought.
Ah, but I preach to one who knows already.
And now the place. God's spirit drives me on.   1540
Let's walk there now. Let us delay no more.
Daughters, follow me. I've now become
your new leader, as you were mine before.
Come. But don't touch me. Allow me to find
the hallowed grave myself where I will reach
my lot in life and lie covered in this earth.
This way. Here. Walk this way. This way Hermes, the
   Guide,
himself leads me – and she, goddess below.
Oh light, no light – though once before, my light –
my body feels you now . . . this last time.   1550
I creep towards my consummation, life
hidden below. But you, dearest of friends,
may you be ever happy, and your land,
your people. And in your prosperity,
commemorate my dying and you will fare well.

[*Exit* OIDIPOUS *into the* skene, *followed by* THESEUS,
ANTIGONE, ISMENE *and an* ATTENDANT]

CHOROS 6

ELDERS (AI):   If I may worship with my prayers
            the unseen goddess and you,
            oh lord of night, Aïdoneus,
            Aïdoneus, I beg you grant   1560
            that this stranger achieve his lot in life and reach

without pain or groans
the fields of the dead hidden below
and his Stygian home.
For no reason, many
troubles came his way.
May a just daimon raise him up again.

ELDERS (A2):   Oh earth's goddesses, oh the beast that can't be
        conquered,
     who, as legend has it, lies before
     the gates of hell,   1570
     the gates that draw so many,
     and growls from in the caverns – the untamed
     guardian of Haides –
     you, child of earth
     and Tartaros, to you
     I pray most earnestly
     to make the pathway clear when this
     man comes into death's realm.
     I implore you, who makes all mortals sleep forever.

                        SCENE 7

(*Enter the* ATTENDANT *from the* skene)

ATTENDANT: People of Kolonos. To be as brief as possible,
     I tell you that Oidipous is gone.   1580
     What has taken place took time and I
     will need time to tell you of it.
I ELDER: The poor man has died?
ATTENDANT: You can be sure
     that he's passed on to the life that lasts forever.
I ELDER: How? Without pain? By a miracle?
ATTENDANT: This precisely is what is most amazing.
     You were here and you know how he went
     away, not needing to be led in any way,
     but, before us all, he became his own guide.
     When he reached the steep way down,   1590
     dug into the earth with steps made of bronze,
     he stood still in one of the paths branching in all directions,

right near the hollow crater where the eternal
pacts between Perithous and Theseus are kept.
He stood midway between this and the rock of Thorikos,
between the hollow pear-tree and the marble grave.
Then he sat down and loosened his grimy clothing.
He called out to his daughters and told them to bring
him water from a stream, to wash and pour libations.
They went to the hill of Demeter with its new   1600
plantings in full view and carried out
their father's commands with speed. Then they washed him
and dressed him as the rites for the dead require.
When he was happy with his arrangements
and wanted no more to be done,
the thunder of Zeus shook the earth. When they
heard this, the girls shuddered and fell down
weeping at their father's knees. They began
beating their breasts and sobbing their eyes out.
When he heard this sudden outburst,   1610
Oidipous embraced them. 'Children,' he said,
'from today, you do not have a father.
All that I am or have has gone, and you
are free from your burden of care for me.
It has been hard, I know, my girls. But
one single sentence wipes out all the pain;
you never have been loved as much as I
have loved you. I will no longer be with you
while you live out the rest of your lives.'
They held on to each other tightly and   1620
they wept. They sobbed, all of them. When
the crying ended and the sobbing ceased,
it was quiet. And suddenly, some voice
called him. And everyone was terrified.
Our hair stood on end at once with fear.
The god called him, many times, in different ways.
'Oidipous, Oidipous, what are we waiting
for? Why are you delaying so long?'
Once Oidipous had felt the call from god,
he asked our lord Theseus to come to him.   1630
When he did, he said, 'Oh my dear friend,
give my children your hand – the time-honoured pledge –
and, girls, give him yours. Now promise me

you'll never, of your own choice, abandon them, but always
do whatever you think seems best for them.'
And like the noble man he is, Theseus concealed his grief
and promised him that he would fulfil this oath.
As soon as this was done, Oidipous laid his
blind hands on his girls and said to them,
'Children, be brave and noble. You   1640
must leave this place. It is not right that you should
see what you shouldn't see or hear what you shouldn't hear.
Go now quickly. But as for you, Theseus,
stay to learn what you must do.'
All of us present heard him say
this much. Then we went with the girls, in floods
of tears, moaning. And when we'd gone away
a little while, we turned around to look
And Oidipous was not there to be seen.
Only Theseus with his hand before   1650
his face, shading his eyes, as if in terror
of something no one could bear to look at.
Then shortly we saw him kneel without
a word and worship the earth and the Olympos
of the gods together at the same time.
By what fate Oidipous passed on no mortal
can explain except for Theseus.
It's certain that no fiery thunderbolt
of god or storm erupting from the sea
right then caused his disappearance.   1660
Someone sent from the gods perhaps. Or earth's
dark underworld kindly opened for him.
The way he went – no pain, no sickness – gives
no cause to grieve. Of all deaths in the world,
his was wondrous. Perhaps I don't make sense.
I won't apologize to those who think so.

1 ELDER: Where are his daughters and the people who went
    with them?

ATTENDANT: Not far. The unmistakable sounds of
    grieving indicate they're on their way.

[*Exit* ATTENDANT, *left*]

FINALE

(*Enter* ANTIGONE *and* ISMENE *from the* skene)

ANTIGONE (A1):   Oh! It's for us now, cursed sisters.   1670
    to lament without restraint the unnatural
    blood inherited from our father.
    While he lived, we bore
    his intense pain without relief.
    Now, in the end, we'll tell what can't be understood,
    what we saw and endured.
1 ELDER: What is it?
ANTIGONE: We can only guess, friends.
1 ELDER: He's passed away?
ANTIGONE: Yes, just as you'd wish.
    And why? No war,
    no shipwreck struck.   1680
    The dark lands embraced him
    and bore him to an unseen fate.
    Ah, night like death
    closes our eyes.
    Where will we wander –
    to what land or
    sea – to live out
    our bitter lives?
ISMENE: I don't know. May destructive
    Haides snatch me away   1690
    to join my dear father.
    Oh! My future
    life's no life.
1 ELDER: Dear, excellent children,
    put up with what God sends
    and don't inflame your passion. There's
    nothing to complain about.

ANTIGONE (A2):   Somehow I long for the old agonies.
    What was distressful was bearable
    when I held my father in my arms.
    Oh father, father,   1700
    torn away forever to the dark.
    Even there you will not lose

our love – both mine and Ismene's.

I ELDER: He got what –

ANTIGONE: – he got what he wanted.

I ELDER: And that was?

ANTIGONE: He wanted to die away
from home. Now he's made his bed
below forever in the shadows.
He has not gone unmourned.
My eyes, dear father, stream
with tears. I cannot   1710
quell the mighty sorrow
which I feel for you.
Oh, you wanted to die
away from home, but
why die without me there?

ISMENE: Dear Antigone, what does
the future hold for us
without a father?
[How can we survive
without him?]

I ELDER: But he let go of life   1720
quite happily, my girls,
so stop your grief. Everyone
bears sorrow at some point.

ANTIGONE (B1): Let's go back, Ismene.

ISMENE: What for?

ANTIGONE: I have a longing to . . .

ISMENE: [. . . to what?]

ANTIGONE: . . . to see his grave.

ISMENE: Whose grave?

ANTIGONE: Our father's grave, unhappily.

ISMENE: But how can that be lawful for us? Don't
you understand?

ANTIGONE: Why scold me?   1730

ISMENE: For this reason: because . . .

ANTIGONE: What reason?

ISMENE: . . . he was laid to rest without a grave, without us
present.

ANTIGONE: Take me back and kill me on that spot.

ISMENE: [Do you want to die?

ANTIGONE: What can I live for?]
ISMENE: Oh the misery of it all.
Where on earth will I endure a life?
I am alone. I have nothing.

I ELDER (B2): Don't be frightened, dear girls.
ANTIGONE: But where can I escape?
I ELDER: You've escaped before.
ANTIGONE: [From what]?
I ELDER: From falling into disaster. 1740
ANTIGONE: I think . . .
I ELDER: Now what's on your mind?
ANTIGONE: I've no idea how we'll get back
to Thebes.
I ELDER: Then don't seek to go.
ANTIGONE: So much trouble.
I ELDER: There was trouble before.
ANTIGONE: I was destitute then; now it's worse.
I ELDER: Yes, you're beset by a sea of troubles.
ANTIGONE: Yes, Yes.
I ELDER: I must agree.
ANTIGONE: Oh! Where can we go,
oh Zeus? To what remaining hope
does the daimon now drive me? 1750

(*Enter* THESEUS *from the* skene)

THESEUS: Stop lamenting, girls. Now that
a benefit lies stored in the earth's dark night,
we must not grieve. For divine anger would follow.
ANTIGONE: Son of Aigeus, we ask you one thing.
THESEUS: What do you want, girls?
ANTIGONE: We both want to look
on our father's grave.
THESEUS: But it's not right for you to go there.
ANTIGONE: Lord, Master of Athens, how can you say that to
us?
THESEUS: Girls, your father forbade me 1760
to go near that place
or tell any living person
of that holy grave where he lies.

He said that, if I obeyed this, then
our land would be free from disasters.
The daimon heard me promise
and the all-knowing god of oaths, servant of Zeus.

ANTIGONE: If this was his intention,
then it must suffice. Send us back
to ancient Thebes so that perhaps   1770
we can prevent the bloodshed threatening
our brothers.

THESEUS: I will do this now, and anything in the
future which is for your good, and
respects him under the earth who has just
gone from us. I am bound not to relax in this.

I ELDER: So put a stop to grief. Stir up
no more lament.
No matter what, these promises stand.

[*Exeunt* ANTIGONE *and* ISMENE, *right, and* THESEUS
and ELDERS, *left*]

TRACKERS

Translated by Michael Ewans

THE ACTORS AND THEIR ROLES

APOLLO	Actor 1
SILENOS	Actor 2
SATYRS	Choros
KYLLENE, nymph of the mountain	Actor 3
HERMES	Actor 3?

The skene *represents a cave*

(*Enter* APOLLO, *right, with a golden wreath*)

APOLLO: (*remains of six lines*) . . .
　　To all the gods and all mankind I, Loxias,
　　proclaim that I will give a fine reward
　　to anyone who's seen my cattle near or far;
　　it's terrible, it wounds my soul   10
　　that someone has abducted all my cows
　　and calves and herds of heifers.
　　All are lost. I'm following their tracks
　　in vain; they've simply vanished from my stables, just
　　as if a god had taken them! I never would have thought
　　that any of the gods or mortal men
　　would even dare to try to do this deed.
　　As soon as I found out, distracted by my care
　　I go, I search, and broadcast out aloud
　　to gods and mortal men so all may know;   20
　　. . . I hunt in mad pursuit.
　　I visited the tribe of Thrakia, to see which
　　soldier could . . .
　　　　(*six lines missing*)
　　. . . of the Thessalians   30
　　. . . and of Boiotian land . . .
　　. . . the Dorian . . .
　　　　(*two lines unintelligible*)
　　. . . I've come . . . allies . . .
　　. . . of Kyllene . . .
　　. . . to this place, and to a wood . . .

If there's a shepherd or a farmer
or a charcoal-burner here to listen to my words,   40
or any of the satyrs, children
of the mountain nymphs, I here proclaim to all:
the person who can catch the cattle stolen from
the god of healing gets this reward which I have here.

(*Enter* SILENOS, *left*)

SILENOS: The very moment that I heard a god's pure voice
raised up to make a public proclamation, I
came hastily, quick as an old man could,
Phoibos Apollo. I would like to be
your friend and benefactor; somehow I
will hunt this mystery down.   50
This prize, this golden crown is waiting here for me,
and I would really like to put it on my hair.
I'm going to send my sons out; they can use their eyes to
      search,
if you will truly do what you are promising.
APOLLO: Be well assured, I will – if you make good your
      word.
SILENOS: I'll bring you back your cows – if you make good
      your gift.
APOLLO: The finder gets the prize, whoever he may be; it's
      waiting here.
            (*four lines missing*)
SILENOS: What's this? How . . .?   62
APOLLO: Freedom for you and all your sons.

(*Enter* SATYRS, *left*)

CHOROS I

      (*fragments of twelve lines; Apollo has left when the
text resumes*)
SATYRS: . . . May the god who is our friend   76
            fulfil our labour, since he's shown
            us glittering bits of gold!

SCENE 2

SILENOS: Goddess Success, and god who guides us all,
    grant me success in what I plan to do,   80
    to hunt the plunder – spoils – the loot –
    the cattle stolen from Phoibos.
    If anyone has seen them or has heard
    he'd be my dearest friend if he tells us,
    and lord Apollo's greatest benefactor.
        (*fragments of two more lines by Silenos, then three by* 1
        Satyr)
SILENOS: Does someone say he knows this? Or does no one
    know?   91
    It's time for me to set to work.
    Come, everyone . . .
    sniff out the scent . . .
    perhaps, somewhere, some wind . . .
    squat double . . .
    follow the scent close . . .
    search, and . . .
    all will be well, and we will do this deed.
        (*The* SATYRS *are searching in two groups*)
1 SATYR: A god! A god! A god! A god! Hey! Hey!   100
    I think we've got them! Stop!
1 SATYR: Yes! Here are the cattle-prints.
1 SATYR: Quiet! Some god is leading us upon our way.
1 SATYR: My friend, what should we do? Have we been
    doing right?
    Well, what do you think over there?
                1 SATYR: We think you're right;
    this clearly shows they're definitely here.
1 SATYR: Look, look!
    Here is the imprint of their hooves again!
1 SATYR: Look closely!
    Here is a mark of the right size.   110
1 SATYR: Run hard, and . . .
    . . .
    if your ear catches any of those cattle's noise.
1 SATYR: I cannot hear their voices clearly, but here are
    the tracks and traces of the cattle,
    plainly visible; just come and see.

1 SATYR: Hey, look!
By god, the footprints are reversed.
They point straight backwards; look at them!
What is this? What on earth is the idea?   120
The ones in front have changed back to the rear, while these
are all entangled, facing different ways;
their driver must have been quite terribly confused.
SILENOS: What is this new technique of yours? What's this,
this new idea; do you hunt flattened
on the ground? What is your method? I don't understand.
You're lying flat like hedgehogs in a bush,
or like a monkey bending for a fart.
What's this? Where did you learn it? Where?
Tell me; I've never heard of anything like this.   130
SATYRS: Uh, uh, uh, uh.
SILENOS: Why are you howling? Who is scaring you? Whom
can you see?
What is disturbing you? Why carry on like madmen?
Are you looking underground for stores of grain?
Why so silent, chatterboxes?
1 SATYR: No, be quiet.
SILENOS: What's there that makes you move away?
1 SATYR: Listen.
SILENOS: How can I listen when I can't hear anyone?
1 SATYR: Do what I ask.   140
SILENOS: You're not exactly helping with my quest.
1 SATYR: Listen yourself, father, for just a moment,
to this noise that hurts us here and drives
us mad; no mortal ever heard this sound before.
SILENOS: Why does a noise make you so fearful and so
scared?
You're waxwork dummies, you are worthless
bits of wild beast shit; you see terror
in a shadow, you are scared of everything.
As helpers you are spineless, slovenly;
you've no minds of your own! Just bodies,   150
noisy tongues and pricks! When you're needed,
you are true in words, but run away from action.
Worthless beasts, your father was so great
that there are many trophies to his manly youth
set up in shrines of Nymphs;

he never was inclined to flight, he never lost his guts;
he did not quiver when he heard the noise of cows
grazing the hills; his spear was used for feats
of glory whose great lustre you defile,
scared by some shepherd's newest wheedling call.   160
You're terrified like babies of something you can't even see;
you throw away the golden treasure which
Phoibos promised and pledged to you –
also the freedom which he guaranteed
to you and me; you give it up and go to sleep.
Come back and search out where the cattle went
and find the cowman, or your cowardice
will make you sorry; you will shit yourselves!
I SATYR: Father, come here and help to guide me;
then you'll see if this is cowardice!   170
If you come, you'll find you're talking bullshit.
SILENOS: I will come, and show you I am right;
I'll round you up like hunters calling hounds!
Come on, stand where the three paths meet;
I'll be right where the action is and set you straight.
SATYRS: U! U! U! Ps! Ps! Ps! A! A!
                         I SATYR: What's your problem?
I SATYR: What is the point of shrieking, screeching,
    dirty looks?
                         I SATYR: Who is this, caught
    at the first turn?
I SATYR: Got him!
                         I SATYR: Here he is, here he is;   180
    you're mine! You're nicked!
I SATYR: Who is this at the second ...
         (*fragments of twenty lines*)
I SATYR: Father, why are you silent? Didn't we tell you
    truth?   203
Can you not hear the noise? Or are you deaf?
SILENOS: Ah!
         I SATYR: What is it?
                 SILENOS: I'm off!
                         I SATYR: Please stay.
SILENOS: No way! You're welcome, if you want
    to search and track and get rich quick by finding
    both the cattle and the gold; I think

I won't stay here and spend more time.

1 SATYR: I won't let you abandon me   210
and sneak away from work, before we clearly
know who's underneath this roof.
          (*fragments of four lines*)
. . . and he'll enjoy this. Now I'm going
to leap and jump and kick and force
the ground to ring with noise,
so he will hear me even if he's deaf.   220

(*They do this. Enter* KYLLENE *from the* skene)

KYLLENE: You wild beasts, why have you attacked
this green and wooded place with all this noise?
What's the idea? Why have you changed the work
with which you used to bring your master joy?
Always a little drunk, wearing the skins of fawns,
and carrying the gentle thyrsos in your hands,
you used to follow him chanting the ritual cry, together with
your families – the nymphs, and crowds of children.
Now I do not understand! Where are these newest twists
and turns of madness heading? It is very strange. I heard   230
some clarion calls like those of hunters
coming near a wild beast's cubs inside its lair,
and at the same time . . . thief . . .
you talked about a stolen . . . and also . . .
     . . .
. . . a proclamation . . .
then you stopped all that, and stamped your feet
all together here, beside my house.
     . . .
I heard this crazy . . .   240
                    . . . something's wrong with you.
You wouldn't hurt an innocent wood-nymph?

1 SATYR: Beautiful nymph, do not be angry!
          I don't come to bring the strife
          of enemies and war to you, nor will a hostile,
          foolish word from us hurt you.
          Do not assault us with reproaches, but
          please kindly tell us what is happening here;
          who sung that sound under the earth, which

was so wonderful, almost divine? 250

KYLLENE: This behaviour is much nicer than before;
hunting like this you will learn more
than by a deed of violence or harassment of
a frightened nymph; I do not like to see
loud quarrels started by an argument.
So please be calm, and tell me
just exactly what you want.

1 SATYR: Queen of this place, Kyllene,
I will tell you later why I came.
But tell me all about this sounding voice,
and who on earth is setting us on edge with it.

KYLLENE: Well, first you must know clearly that
if you don't keep my story to yourselves,
there'll be a penalty for you!
This deed is hidden in the palaces of gods,
so Hera does not come to know of it.
Zeus came in secret to this house of Maia, Atlas'
daughter, and took her virginity

. . .

forgetting all about his beautiful goddess
wife. 270
In this cave he created Maia's son,
and I nurse him in my own arms,
because his mother's strength is wracked by illness.
I remain beside his cradle, and provide
his infant needs – food, drink and all –
both night and day.
And he gets bigger every day – unnaturally, quite
astonishingly large; I am amazed, and scared.
He's only six days old, but he
is thrusting forward to the peak of boyhood. 280
He's a sprout which shoots straight up without delay;
such is the child our storage room conceals.
His name is Hermes, given by his father.
As for this sound you asked about, which rang out by
a strange device, he invented it himself
in just one day, out of an upturned shell.
That is the thing which he discovered – pleasure from a
creature
which has died . . .

(fragments of seven lines)

1 SATYR: . . . to make
a dead creature sing like that.

KYLLENE: Don't disbelieve; a goddess' words are true, and
smile on you.

1 SATYR: How could I believe so loud a voice comes from a
corpse?

KYLLENE: Believe. In death it got a voice it never had
alive.   300

1 SATYR: What shape was it? Long, humped or short?

KYLLENE: Short, pot-shaped, spotted skin, all creased.

1 SATYR: Perhaps a bit like a cat or a panther?

KYLLENE: Not at all; it's round, and has short legs.

1 SATYR: Then it's more like a weasel or a crab?

KYLLENE: No, not that either; have another guess.

1 SATYR: Well then, perhaps it's like a horned Aitnaian
beetle?

KYLLENE: Yes; you've very nearly guessed what it's most like.

1 SATYR: Which bit of it makes sound; inside or out?

KYLLENE: Its shell makes different sounds, just like an
oyster.   310

1 SATYR: What name d'you call it? Tell me, if you know.

KYLLENE: The boy calls the animal a tortoise and the
instrument a lyre.

*(fragments of twelve lines. Kyllene explains that Hermes
made his lyre by stretching ox-hide across the tortoise
shell)*

. . . It is the only thing he has to cure and comfort him when
he's unhappy; then he loves to go all wild and sing in
harmony with it; playing the lyre gives him a high.
That's how the boy contrived to make a dead beast sing.

SATYRS: The voice rings loud across the land;
the hand-plucked strings make clear, fantastic
sounds   330
scatter like flowers all around.
But here's what I am getting at:
know that the god (whoever he may be)
who made this, and nobody else
– lady, know this – can be our thief.
Please don't be difficult
with me, or take this hard.

KYLLENE: You must be mad! What theft do you allege?
I SATYR: Lady, I really do not want to stir you up.
KYLLENE: Are you calling Zeus' son a thief?   340
I SATYR: Yes; I would gladly catch him with the goods.
KYLLENE: And fair enough, if you are right.
I SATYR: You're right; I am.
KYLLENE: But are you sure he stole the cows?
I SATYR: I am quite certain that he did,
  because he fixed the hide onto the shell,
  after he cut . . .
            (*fragments of four lines*)
KYLLENE: . . . now at last I realize,   352
  you wretch, you're grinning at me as if I were stupid.
  You good-for-nothings! Everything's a joke to you.
  Well, for the future, it is fine by me –
  if it will make you happy or you think you'll gain –
  for you to laugh at me until your heart's content;
  but do not slander someone who is clearly Zeus' son
  by stirring up new charges levelled at a new-born boy.
  He's not a thief's son on his father's side,   360
  and there's no theft among his mother's relatives.
  Go somewhere else to find your thief (if there
  is really one) – and look in vain; Olympos up above
  will show who this boy is. Just pin this crime
  where it belongs; he has nothing to do with it.
  You've always been quite childish; you're a full-grown
  man, but fool round with your yellow beard just like a goat.
  Stop making your smooth prick swell up with joy!
  The gods will make you weep out loud for all
  your silly jokes, and I will laugh at you.   370
SATYRS: Twist and turn your words! Create
            whatever sharp ideas you can;
            you never will persuade me
            that the boy who made this thing
            by patching hides together stole the skins
            from any other cows than Loxias'.
            Don't try to put me off the track.   377
                (*three or four lines missing*)
  . . . madness . . .   380
KYLLENE: You utter wretch . . .
  . . . quick . . . anger . . .

I SATYR: The truth . . .
KYLLENE: . . .
I SATYR: The boy's a thief . . .
KYLLENE: Wretched behaviour . . .
I SATYR: Slander . . .
KYLLENE: But if it's true . . .
I SATYR: You must not . . .   389
        (fragments of seven lines)
KYLLENE: Many cattle graze . . .   397
I SATYR: But even more were . . .
KYLLENE: Outrageous! Who has got them?
I SATYR: That boy whom you've got shut up in there.   400
KYLLENE: Stop slandering the son of Zeus.
I SATYR: I'll stop when someone brings the cattle.
KYLLENE: You and your cows are making me quite sick.
I SATYR: If they are doing that, drive them out here at once.
        . . .

*The remaining fragments are too small to be translated; but it
is clear from one part of the next surviving column of the
papyrus that Apollo re-entered at line 452; he probably admit-
ted that the satyrs have earned the golden crown. It is likely
that Hermes emerged from the cave soon afterwards, and gave
the lyre to Apollo in compensation for the stolen cattle.*

SELECTED FRAGMENTS

Translated by Michael Ewans

PART ONE: TRAGEDY

---

1 Aias the Lokrian

During the sack of Troy, Aias the Lokrian raped Kassandra in the temple of Athena, pulling down the statue of Athena as well. He took refuge at her altar to escape punishment for sacrilege. Very little is known about the drama, but it is plain that there was a debate among the Greeks as to what to do with Aias; Athena herself appeared to the Greeks and rebuked them.

ATHENA: Men of Greece! Was there a second Dryas, whose offspring
came here to fight the Trojans? Who was he,
who dared to do these things against the gods?
Has Salmoneus, who made thunder-sounds from hides,
returned from Haides' inner depths to challenge Zeus again?
What kind of man can I imagine did such deeds,
who pulled my image from the base on which it stood,
and dragged the virgin prophetess away . . .

2 Aleus' Sons

Wealth finds men friends, and privileges,
and then finally the throne on high
of royal power, the nearest to the gods.
No one was ever born an enemy
to wealth – or if they are, they will not say.
For riches have a terrifying power to creep
in everywhere, even to sacred sites, and places where
a poor man, even if inside, could not obtain what he desires.
Wealth makes an ugly person beautiful,
an incoherent speaker clever with his tongue;
alone, wealth knows how to find joy even in
a sick-bed, and conceal its miseries.

10

3   *Eurypylos*

*We know little about the action, but clearly in this fragment a
Messenger is describing the death of Eurypylos and that of a
friend (probably Helikaon) to Astyoche and a female choros.*
        (small fragments of six lines)

MESSENGER: in between the armies . . .   7
    facing each other without boasts, without abuse,
    they struck the circles of their brazen shields.

    . . .   10

                        . . . without the spear
                        . . . with wrestling throws
                        . . .
                        . . . to the heavens;
                        . . . he was lamented
                        . . . they lacked instruments
                        . . . brandishes of the arm
                        . . . escaping
                        . . . the spear
                        . . . the middle   20
                        . . . far off
                        . . . below
                        . . . light
                        . . . [spear] of Achilleus
                        . . . healing
                        . . . I mean Telephos;
                        . . . healed . . .
                        . . . swiftly
    . . . destroyed his innards.

ASTYOCHE: Oioi! Oioi!   30
    I cry out twice.
I WOMAN: . . . of his father . . .
                        . . . he saw his children's fate.
ASTYOCHE: And a third onto me.
I WOMAN: Yes; he's brought . . .
                        . . . you are drenching . . .
                        you have lost your senses.
ASTYOCHE: Oh daimon, hateful daimon, you've destroyed
    me.
I WOMAN: You speak to one who's near; he stands inside
    and drags you around in confusion.

ASTYOCHE: He will be right to do that.
1 WOMAN: Yes.   40
ASTYOCHE: Quickest is best!
WOMEN: Ah!
        What shall we say?
ASTYOCHE: Will someone do what's right – cut off my
    head?
1 WOMAN: The daimon has destroyed you; was that not
    right?
ASTYOCHE: On top of all this horror, did the Greeks laugh
    terribly,
and trample violently on those two dead men?
MESSENGER: They did not manage to insult them,
since the two who'd fought together   50
lay in death not far apart,
one lacerated, and the other . . .
Many of the Greeks died there as well.
        (*small remains of eleven lines*)
. . . the south wind shattered'.
Words like these sounded from many mouths.
Then someone took many linen robes,
and hempen ones from Thrakia, and threw them as
a gift upon a corpse to which they gave no help.
Then Priam lay embracing the dead body;   70
he was not the father, but he spoke as if he was,
as he bewailed this kinsman of his sons,
a boy, an elder and a youth.
He did not call him 'Mysian', or 'son of Telephos',
but cried out to him as if to his own:
'My son, I have betrayed you, though you were
the last and greatest hope for Troy.
You did not stay with us for very long,
but you will leave us memory of many horrors.
Memnon and Sarpedon did not make us suffer   80
so much grief, although they were the best of spearsmen . . .'

4   Kreousa

My lord, don't be surprised if I hang on
to what I've gained like this. For even those who have
great wealth grasp at the chance of gaining more,

and for all human beings everything else
comes second after money. There are some who praise
the man who's free of sickness; but I think no one
who's poor lives without sickness; they are always sick.

5   Laokoon

MESSENGER: And now Aineas stands, son of a goddess,
in the gates; he has his father on his shoulders, with
his linen robe moist from the lightning-flash;
around him a whole mass of people from his house.
And he's accompanied by a huge crowd
of Phrygians who want to leave this land with him.

6   Nauplios

[Palamedes] showed the Argive army how to build a wall;
he invented weights, numbers and measures,
how to marshal armies and to read the signs in heaven.
And he discovered how to count
to ten, to fifty, and right to a thousand;
he showed how an army could light beacons;
and revealed things no one else yet knew.
He found out when the stars appear and when they turn,
trustworthy signs for those who guard while others sleep.
And for the men who shepherd ships at sea, he found   10
the turnings of the Bear and chilly moment when the Dogstar
sets.

7, 8   Men of Skyros

7

Sailors must be the most unhappy of all men,
since neither god nor mortal man could ever give
them their due share of wealth;
they risk long voyages, and take slim chances,
often suffer tragedy, and sometimes lose,
and only sometimes keep their profits.
I wonder at and praise these men

who constantly are brave enough to earn a scant
and painful living with long-suffering hands.

8

NEOPTOLEMOS: If it were possible to cure your troubles
or to raise the dead by weeping,
gold would be less valuable than tears!
But as things are, old man, it is impossible
to bring back to the light one hidden in his grave.
If tears could do it, why, my own father would now
have come back to the light!

9, 10, 11   *Niobe*

*Fragments of an ancient synopsis of the drama show that Apollo
killed Niobe's seven sons while they were out hunting; their
father Amphion tried to challenge Apollo, and was himself
killed. The fragments of the drama itself begin after Artemis has
killed six of the daughters.*

9

*This sequence is the only one in the surviving fragments which
raises interesting questions of stagecraft. It has been conjectured
that Apollo and Artemis are on the roof of the skene building
during this sequence; but it is far more likely that Apollo is now
in the* orchêstra, *and that Artemis is inside the* skene *(see
discussion of* Aias, Scene 1 *in Ewans 1999, 177–8). It is
possible, though less likely, that Artemis or even both gods were
suspended on the* mechane *(it is known to have been capable of
flying two actors from the appearance of Kastor and Pollux at
the end of Euripides'* Elektra*).*

(*fragments of three lines*)

APOLLO: D'you see that girl inside, who's terrified,
and trying to cower down inside the cellar, there,
beside the bins? Will you not aim an arrow
at her fast, before she hides out of our sight?
WOMEN: Aaah! Ah! Soon the fate of the girls

will be no different than the boys'.   10
This disaster overflows.

10

Niobe now enters, but is wandering distracted, and so does not talk to the Women. Against their expectations, Chloris is still alive; her voice is heard from inside.

WOMEN: . . .
          . . . she's gone mad . . .
NIOBE: Phoibos and his sister have destroyed me!
    Why drive me from my home? Why don't you aim
    your cruel arrows straight at me!
I WOMAN: . . . woman of many sorrows.
    Should I try to waft her steps this way?
NIOBE: I am destroyed. My children have all gone
    to the caverns of Tartaros. Where shall I hide?
CHLORIS: (*inside the* skene)
    I beg you, lady Artemis, don't shoot at me; don't kill me.   10
I WOMAN: . . . unhappy girl . . .

11

In the last fragment to survive from this exciting sequence Chloris appears, running for her life. Unless she was restrained by Niobe or the Women in subsequent lost lines, the fragment implies that Chloris simply ran out one of the parodoi *without taking any notice of them.*

I WOMAN: D'you hear? She's wandering, made distraught by
    her suffering.

(*Enter* CHLORIS *from the* skene, *running*)

    This is unbelievable, beyond all words!
    She's running from the palace, like a colt set free from
       harness –
    and we feared she'd died together with her sisters.
    Where are you going? What d'you fear now, poor girl? Stay
       here!

12   Polyxena

AGAMEMNON: No one who has to be the helmsman of the
   troops
could yield to everyone and give favours to all.
Not even Zeus, who's far more powerful than me,
is always popular when he sends rain or drought;
if humans could arraign him he would lose the case.
So how can I, a mortal woman's mortal son,
be cleverer than him?

13   Root-Cutters

In this fragment the choros *narrate Medeia's preparation of a
herb for magic – either the herb which she gave to Iason to
protect him during his ordeal, or that which she used to restore
the youth of his aged father Iason, by cutting him up and
boiling him with certain herbs; or even possibly the magic which
she falsely offered to give to the daughters of Pelias, when she
induced them to try the same process on him.*

CHOROS: Turning her eyes away from her hand,
   she caught the foaming juice from the cut
   in vessels of bronze . . .
   . . . and the hidden
   boxes conceal the cuttings of the roots,
   which she, naked, and crying out
   a ritual cry, cut off with bronze sickles.

14, 15, 16   Tereus

14

PROKNE: But now I'm nothing on my own. I often think
   like this about being a woman – that we are
   nothing. We are perhaps the happiest of all
   humanity when we are young and in our father's house;
   for innocence makes children grow in happiness.
   But when we are young women and can think,
   we're pushed aside and sold, deprived
   of both our parents and ancestral gods,

some to a foreign husband, some to a barbarian,
some to a house bereft of joy, and some into abuse.   10
One night yokes us to this fate, and then we must
praise it, pretending this is happiness.

15

CHOROS: Mankind is one race, and one day in our
          father and mother's lives gave birth to all of us;
          no one was born superior to anybody else.
          But a fate of misfortune nurtures some of us,
          others, prosperity; others, Necessity
          holds down in slavery.

16 (*the closing lines of the drama?*)

CHOROS: You are human, and you must think
          human thoughts; recognize that there's
          no other guardian of what will happen,
          of our destiny but Zeus.

17, 18   *Teukros*

17

TELAMON: So, my son, that joy
          was empty which I felt when I heard praise of you
          as if you were alive; in the darkness, all unknown to me,
          the Fury fawned on me, deceiving me with false pleasure.

18 *Oileus tried to comfort Telamon after he learned about Aias' suicide.*

You might well see the greatest and the wisest men
being just like Oileus is now, attempting to
bring comfort to someone who's suffering.
But when the daimon of a man who once was fortunate
swings back the balance of his life, most of
their sayings, good though they may be, just disappear.

19, 20   *Thyestes*

19

No one is wise except the man who pays due honour to the
gods.
You must look to the gods, and even if they tell you you
must go
outside the bounds of justice, you must go that way;
nothing is shameful if the gods have counselled it.

20

. . . There is a land surrounded by
the sea, Euboia; there a vine of Bakchos grows
in just one day. First in the light of dawn
the green vine-shoot puts out its twigs;
then midday makes the unripe grape grow large –
the fruit becomes sweet, and looks dark.
By evening it's grown to ripeness, and
is harvested; the drink is mixed.

21   *Tyro*

TYRO: I grieve for my lost hair, just like a foal,
whom herdsmen with rough hands
have seized inside the stable, and
have cropped the yellow mane off from her neck.
When she comes to the water-meadows for a drink
she sees herself reflected in the water,
with her mane of hair most shamefully cut off.
Even a person with no pity might well pity her,
as she goes mad, cowers with shame, and grieves
and weeps for what was once luxuriant and glorious.   10

PART TWO:

FRAGMENTS FROM UNKNOWN TRAGEDIES

22

MENELAOS: My fate always revolves on Fortune's
swiftly circling wheel, and changes shape,
just as the moon's appearance cannot stay
two nights in the same form.
First it emerges from invisible to new,
then makes its face more beautiful and full,
and then – as soon as it has reached its loveliest –
it flows away again and goes to nothingness.

23

Children, the love-goddess is not just the
goddess of love; no, she's called many names.
She is Haides, she's everlasting life,
she's raving madness, she is pure desire,
and she is grief. In her is all activity,
all peace, and all that leads to violence.
She seizes on the vital parts of all that
live, who is not greedy for this goddess?
She enters into every swimming fish,
and every four-legged beast on land;   10
her wing stretches out over every bird.
      . . . [She lives]
in animals, in men, and in the gods above.
Which god does she not wrestle with, and win three times?
If I may dare – and I may dare – to speak the truth,
she rules over the life of Zeus without recourse to spear
or sword; all the plans of men and gods
are cut short by the love-goddess.

24 Achilleus' Lovers

Since this was a satyr-drama, presumably the Satyrs were the choros, and aspired to be Achilleus' lovers. We know nothing about the drama except that Peleus and Phoinix were characters, and that there was a change of scene.

This disease is attractive, but bad;
I've got a pretty good comparison.
When ice appears outdoors, boys take
the solid crystal in their hands;
at first they get new pleasures from it
Later on, they're proud and will not let it go,
although then it is bad for them to keep it in their hands.
That's how the same desire often makes
a lover first take action, and then not.

25, 26 Inachos

25

Zeus, disguised as a dark-coloured stranger from Aigypt, has helped Argos by rescuing the city from a drought, imposed by Poseidon in anger because Inachos chose Hera as patron of the city rather than himself. However, Zeus fell in love with Inachos' daughter Io; in an attempt to shield Io from the jealousy of Hera, Zeus transformed her into a cow.

    (illegible fragments of twenty lines)
INACHOS: . . . than here.
        . . . one hated by the gods . . .
        I know who the stranger was
        . . . through the doors, all the pollution.
Before this he was praised, for he had done much good;   25

but now I've found he's done me ghastly harm.
And now he's gone; he's vanished from out here,
escaping from the guards; he has deluded me.
I SATYR: Yes, he had done. He darkened your eyes,
and he is free again. But all these things he did to you –   30
I'm not yet sure if we should call them terrible.
INACHOS: If they are terrible? They must be! He had dared to shame
the sacred table in a house which welcomes guests.
He laid his hand upon my daughter Io
and has gone; he hurried through the house.
And then the girl's nostrils . . .
took on cow shape . . .
she grew the head of a bull . . .
the neck on her shoulders . . .
cloven feet . . .   40
strike the floorboards . . .
a woman-lioness . . .
sits, worked in linen . . .
such . . .
the stranger . . .
I SATYR: I am speechless!
Ah! Ah!
    . . .
the stranger . . .
unbelievable . . .   50
SATYRS: Oh Earth, mother of the gods!
        unknowing . . .
        this man with many drugs . . .

I SATYR: the sooty-coloured foreigner . . .
    . . .
    the one with flashing eyes . . .

26

*We know from smaller fragments that Argos, the hundred-eyed
herdsman, was a character in this drama; he guarded the cow
for Hera, and was eventually killed by Hermes, who charmed
him to sleep by playing his pipe. In this fragment Hermes is
wearing Haides' cap of invisibility, and terrifying the satyrs.*

(Later, in a very fragmentary scrap of papyrus, he appeared, and quarrelled with Inachos.)

(unrestorable fragments of fifteen lines, then)

SATYRS: Very, very knowing was
    the man who once
    called you by your right name –
    beneath the immortal darkness
    given by the cap of Haides! –   20
1 SATYR: the messenger of Zeus' love-affairs, the great runner
    of errands; from your sounds we guess it's Hermes.
1 SATYR: Yes, Hermes himself; he's turned back towards me.
1 SATYR: You'll suffer once again for nothing before you can
    blink!
SATYRS: Ha! D'you see?
    It's best to stay away!
    It's madness to hear this.
    Zeus, this really shows
    no one should trust you!
    ... cursed ...   30
    ... with a clasp ...
1 SATYR: ever-changing quiet whispery sounds ...
    Like the sons of Sisyphos
    the sons of Zeus use every trick.
SATYRS: Is it really Zeus',
    truly Zeus' servant here?
    He's coming at me
      . . .
    this sound makes me terrified!!
1 SATYR: The fear of enemies ...   40
1 SATYR: The spider of Haides ...
1 SATYR: Make sure he does not come near the house ...
1 SATYR: Where should we stand? ...
1 SATYR: Watch out for sudden death ...

(fragments of four more lines)

27   Oineus

1 SATYR: ...
    ... to explain what he was doing. He who caused

this conflict should be made a prisoner!

OINEUS: I will tell you; but first I want to know
just who you are, why you are here, and from
what family you spring; I don't yet know.

1 SATYR: You will know all. We come as suitors,
we're the sons of nymphs, and Bakchos' servants, and
we live quite near the gods. We have trained
in every kind of skill: spear-fighting,
wrestling-contests, riding, running,   10
boxing, biting, twisting testicles –
and we can sing, and we know oracles
(not forgeries!) which are not yet disclosed;
we can do healing and astronomy,
and we can dance; even our farts
speak volumes. Our knowledge is excellent!
And you can use whichever of our skills
you want, if you give me your daughter.

OINEUS: I cannot fault your origins. But first
I want to look at this man who is coming here.   20

Elektra

MICHAEL EWANS

The Actors and their Roles

Actor 1, playing Elektra, speaks or sings 589 out of 1510 lines. This is the largest single role in the surviving Greek tragedies. Her almost constant presence after Scene 1, and the extremes of emotion to which the character is subjected, make this role even more dominant and demanding than the nearest parallel, Euripides' Medeia. Elektra required (and still requires) an actor-dancer of the highest calibre. Actor 2 took the parts of Elektra's three relatives: Orestes, Chrysothemis and Klytaimestra; these are a young male and two female roles, and so required a light- to medium-voiced actor. This leaves the two mature men – the Old Man and Aigisthos – for a deeper-voiced third actor. Neither the second nor the third actor was required to dance.

Date

Elektra is generally agreed on stylistic grounds to be a drama from Sophokles' late period, after 420 BC.[1] It is therefore almost certainly later than Euripides' Elektra, which used to be dated to 413 because of a supposed reference to the Sikilian expedition, but is now generally accepted as belonging to before 418.[2]

In the light of the ethical and political tendencies echoed by the portrayal of Orestes, the relationship between the Chrysothemis scenes and the moral issues which became explicit in the dialogue at Melos in 416,[3] and the close affinity with the dramatization of deception and

[1] Jebb 1894, lvi–lviii.
[2] Dale 1969, 227–8.
[3] This dialogue was recreated by Thoukydides at Histories 5.84–113.

expediency in *Philoktetes* (409), I am fairly certain that *Elektra* was created after the sack of Melos, and not long before or after the coup and counter-coup of 411. Dale notes a probable echo of lines 56ff. in Euripides, *Helene* 1050ff., and suggests 413 – the year before the first performance of *Helene*.[4]

The Production

This translation was first performed at King Edward Park, Newcastle, Australia in March 1998. The venue was a natural amphitheatre facing east, with sea views in the background. A sixteen-metre *orchêstra* circle was marked out, surrounded on two thirds of its circumference by an audience of up to 400 seated on sloping grass. Masks were not used; the actors, and the *choros* of seven, wore expressionistic modern dress. Behind the circle the *skene* was formed by three canvas panels painted as a triptych, evoking the horrors in the past of the royal household. A low structure, used by Klytaimestra and later Elektra as the altar of Apollo, was positioned at FC.

Scene 1

Elektra uses the opening pattern of a first scene whose action generates the rest of the drama, but is unknown to the *choros* and the individual characters who appear in Scene 2;[5] as in *Antigone*, Sophokles marks off Scene 1 by a sharp gender opposition. Two speakers of one sex initiate action in the first scene, and this action later disrupts the expectations of the *choros* and Scene 2 characters, who in *Elektra* are female in contrast to the male domination of Scene 1.[6]

The audience first sees the arrival of three determined, morally untroubled male conspirators;[7] they have reached Mykenai at the *kairos*, the 'right time' (22, 75) for action. The Old Man, the slave who has acted as Orestes' guardian and tutor during his boyhood, is a sinister figure; he has indoctrinated the boy that he must avenge his

---

[4] Dale 1969, 227–8.

[5] Cf. e.g. Aischylos, *Agamemnon*; Sophokles, *Ai* and *Ant*; Euripides, *Hippolytos*.

[6] At 20 the Old Man imagines that 'some man' might come out; Sophokles is preparing by contrast for the sudden intrusion of a female, when Elektra cries out at 77.

[7] Cf. Waldock 1951, 174.

father's murder (13–14).[8] Now he is almost a Svengali, leading Orestes and Pylades on from behind (27–8). Two free and well-born young men, fit and ready for action, are visually contrasted with this old slave; but Orestes turns out to be just like him.[9] Both the Old Man and Orestes delight in the creative use of words – and the Old Man will in Scene 3 reveal the ability to create a speech of extraordinary power over others, in response to Orestes' request now.

In the opening lines the Old Man should leave Pylades near the *parodos*, BR, and circle through the playing space via FC to L; he points out the sights to Orestes, who follows him, tentatively returning from exile and entering the centre of his kingdom, which the *orchêstra* represents.[10] The action is located in front of the palace at Mykenai, which in real geography is located above and fourteen kilometres away from the city of Argos; so the plain of Argos, grove of Io, *agora* and temple of Hera are all to be imagined in performance as being located to the left of the playing space. There is then a severe contrast at line 10 between the beauties of the distant *polis* and the horror behind the *skene* façade: 'this is the house of many deaths – the home of Pelops' family.' To establish this contrast, the Old Man must suddenly turn to approach the *skene*, BC, by 8 or 10; if Orestes has been drawn further into the *orchêstra*, e.g. to CL, to follow the Old Man's description as he points out the sights,[11] he can then end up at C for 10ff.: pupil to master.

The second beat of the speech requires a conspiratorial huddle, while the Old Man gathers together and energizes the two young men. The evocation of nature 'occurs in a paragaph which is carefully constructed, beginning and ending as it does with an exhortation to immediate action. Now dawn, in Greek poetry, proverbially awakes the birds to song and men to work. The picturesque description of the morning, therefore, is not merely suggestive of a cheerful and a hopeful atmosphere but also of the strenuous call to action.'[12] Indeed, the light

[8] Cf. Sheppard 1927, 4; *contra* Waldock 1951, 172–4.

[9] Cf. Reinhardt 1979, 137.

[10] Both the opening moves for this beat, and the conclusion with a close focus on the *skene* façade, are remarkably similar to the strategy required by Sophokles' text at the opening of *Phil*; cf. Ley's Notes, below, p. 227–8.

[11] A staff for the Old Man (which in our production became a magic wand) is a valuable prop both for this opening sequence and for illustrating the narrative of 'Orestes' death' in Scene 3.

[12] Sheppard 1918, 81–2.

of day itself is almost an enemy to these conspirators; and Elektra will soon align herself with an ominous bird, the nightingale.[13]

Orestes begins his response by repeating the emphasis on masculinity from line 20.[14] Then the close trio needs to be dissolved, with expansive movements for Orestes during the opening section of his speech, as he takes the initiative and launches the action for which the Old Man has called.

Lines 31ff. are crucial. The narrative of the oracle and its implications are short, but must be delivered from the centre. Like Sheppard and Kells, I find the distinctive form of Orestes' enquiry significant. In Aischylos' *Libation Bearers* (269ff.), Apollo ordered the son, under threat of the most strenuous penalties, that he must take vengeance on his mother; Sophokles' Orestes was under no such presssure; he simply assumed that he should, and felt the need only to ask Apollo how he should proceed.[15] From the *datum* of the oracle, Orestes then passes to the unknown future of the deception (44ff.). Here again, as at 25ff., the actor must move freely, to illuminate the improvisatory feel of the great lie that the Old Man has to create.[16]

But words have power, and Orestes is calmly proposing to create what will turn out to be a dangerous fiction. Orestes is certain that it can do him no harm (56ff.); and Sophokles aligns him carefully with one of the most questionable (and questioned) beliefs of contemporary amoralists by the wording of 61.[17] So Orestes needs a predominant

[13] Segal 1966, 492.

[14] 23. Kells 1973, 81 notes the use of military terminology in Orestes' speech: 'Orestes is primarily a soldier, trained in the Spartan fashion of strict discipline and obedience to orders.'

[15] Sheppard 1927, 3–4. Kells 1973, 4–6; cf. Reinhardt 1979, 137–8. But Kells is wrong to argue that Orestes does not act on the god's advice. Blundell rightly warns that 'we cannot assume that the playwright's approval [of Orestes' deed] is coextensive with that of Apollo' (1989, 189). This assumption is often made, especially by critics who believe that because Apollo was vindicated on a point of fact in *OKing*, he must also be morally right about the ethics of matricide in *El*.

[16] In the Greek text of 47, I conjecture *ogkon* (padding) for the manuscript's *[h]orkon* (oath). I have never understood why Orestes should ask the Old Man to 'swear an oath' (a dangerous procedure for a liar, as Sheppard correctly notes: 1927, 5); and in fact in Scene 3 he does not do so. But there are good reasons why the Old Man should 'add some padding' to Orestes' outline of the death story (Greek *ogkos* like its English equivalent was a theatrical term both for costume and for language) – and he does this, spectacularly, in Scene 3.

[17] Introduction pp. xviii–xix, above.

position – perhaps at the altar, FC – to emphasize the importance of 59ff. It is one thing to embrace deception because Apollo himself ordained it, as the appropriate means of vengeance on people who had used treachery themselves (Aischylos, *Libation Bearers* 555ff.); it is quite another to embrace it sophistically, because it has been profitable to other returning exiles.

Sophokles builds Orestes' vision to rhetorical heights, ending at 66. In the last phase Orestes should start circling towards the back through the left sector (since Pylades and the Old Man are still FR or R); he must be at least as far back as L by 68, in a good position to invoke the house directly, from enough distance away to make the prayer effective, in 69–72.

Orestes' move towards departure is interrupted by the outcry at 77, and he starts back towards the *skene* (BC) when he hears Elektra's voice. But the Old Man moves firmly towards Orestes, overrides his instinctive desire to stay, and leads him towards the R *parodos*.[18]

Choros 1

Sophokles replaces the customary choral entrance-song with a solo monody for Elektra, followed by a *kommos*.[19] This enables him to proceed with what by now was almost a standard pattern for the opening of dramas centred around an isolated female: an interactive Choros 1 is followed by a long speech of apology, which generates a brief dialogue with the *choros* members; then the entry of a new solo character moves the action from exposition into development.[20] Here the decision to use monody and *kommos*, together with the gender contrast from the characters in Scene 1, creates a striking contrast: the men of the opening scene were ready for action, and conscious (indeed, excessively conscious) that today is 'the Day';[21] by contrast Elektra is lost in a misery in which Time is endless.[22] This is perfectly dramatized

[18] On the implications of this crucial sequence see Introduction p. xxxii, above. Against Nauck's attribution of 80–81 to the Old Man and 82–5 to Orestes see Lloyd-Jones and Wilson 1990, 44.

[19] Cf. Euripides' *Elektra, Hekabe, Helene, Trojan Women*.

[20] Euripides, *Medeia, Hipplytos, Helene*; cf. also his *Iphigeneia among the Taurians* and Sophokles, *YWT*. NB also *Ai* (Tekmessa); also *Ant*, which follows this pattern exactly although the protagonist and the *choros* character are both male.

[21] Shepherd 1927, 4.

[22] Kells 1973, 87.

by the transition from spoken dialogue, which in Greek tragedy
proceeds at realistic clock time, to lyric and dance, in which the sense
of time is suspended.

Elektra's opening self-presentation is extraordinary in its range and
intensity. She is a creature of the dark; her costume must be black,
ragged (191); her face is 'etched by many sufferings' (1187) and perhaps
even her body is bruised (1196; there is no reason to suppose that the
Athenians could not use body make-up); all this expresses the abuse that
Elektra suffers daily for her defiance.[23] Effectively, she looks like a slave,
in visual contrast with the Women, and even more so with Chrysothemis
and Klytaimestra, both of whom should evidence the luxurious life of
the palace in their costumes. She also wears the mask of female mourning, with a sad expression (1309ff.) and close-cropped hair.[24]

Elektra emerges to greet the Sun and the Air; and this moment, when
she faces the light and describes her self-beating, and her ironically
titled 'all-night festivals' of grief for Agamemnon, must be a daily act
of lamentation which ritually discovers the light as if for the first time.

Elektra's monody deploys in order the three aspects of her extreme
situation: her lamentation (88ff.), her isolation (100ff.) and her determination to continue (104ff.). Then the song, which began with cries
extended to the heavens, ends with a long prayer to the gods of the
underworld (110ff.). The actress must dance a gradual possession of
the orchêstra. Elektra begins with an invocation to the powers above;
then she needs to enact vivid mime both of her own self-mutilation
(connecting back to the skene at 92) and of the murder, followed by
an address to Agamemnon (below the earth), and an evocation of the
stars and sunlight above (105–6). Finally, after she has mimed the
sorrows of Prokne, the dance must again focus on the ground, for the
address to the powers below before Elektra's collapse.

The Women's role is not a monolithic unity; this choros provides a
set of individual voices, and different perspectives on the action, as the
drama unfolds.[25] Right from the start they challenge Elektra's deter-

---

[23] It is ironic that Aristophanes (especially in Acharnians) pilloried Euripides
for insisting on presenting noble heroes in rags, when the one extant example
(apart from Menelaos in the relatively light drama Helene) occurs in a tragedy
by Sophokles.

[24] Expression: Winnington-Ingram 1980, 230 n. 44. Hair: Seale 1982, 59; cf.
ibid. 60 for the contrast with Chrysothemis, whose mask will have had the
unbound long hair of an unmarried young woman.

[25] Pace March 1996, 68. Against the assumption that all lyric stanzas must
have been sung by the whole chorus in unison cf. Ewans 1995, xxiv–xxv.

mined fixity in grief; and this *kommos* demands a complex choreographic response to the ebb and flow of the lyric debate, since the soloists in their seven stanzas display seven different responses to Elektra: in order severe and authoritative; bright and firm; tough and energetic; almost naïvely optimistic; knowledgeable and sympathetic; passionately challenging; and concerned. These seven danced interventions create a balance; by the end, Elektra retains the Women's sympathy, while they have still made clear that her position is extreme – and, to some of them, untenable.

The keynote is struck at once. The Women are Elektra's friends – and the choreography needs to establish this at once, by close physical contact. The first Woman makes it clear that she is on Elektra's side; but she does not understand why Elektra continues her lamentations far beyond their due period. It is not rational or reasonable (this must be conveyed by the other *choros* members supporting her in this dance); and Elektra has to concede this at once (136), interacting with the Women. They should take up her mood, and echo it in their steps during her response, which links A1 to A2. When the singer of A2 develops this attack (NB especially 140ff.), Elektra must retreat before dancing a powerful defence, choosing her two heroines from mythology – Prokne and Niobe – both of whom are fixed for evermore in their utterance of grief; but she does not convince the Women at all. The next Woman continues to object, naming Elektra's siblings.[26] Elektra ignores the mention of her sisters, but the optimistic description of Orestes leads her to exhibit her anger and her loss of hope.

The second B stanza is even more optimistic than the first: the singer has faith in Zeus, and in Time – the one *daimôn* in whom Elektra has none, since a seemingly endless period of defiance and suffering has not brought Orestes back. The singer should dance forward to a commanding postion, e.g. FC, and attempt to involve Elektra in a dance of happiness; but Elektra rejects this, and becomes isolated; 185ff. are the fullest declaration of her hopelessness. This turns the Women (C1) to a vigorous, evocative mime of the death of Agamemnon, and for a few moments Elektra could perhaps seem to dance in harmony with

[26] Sophokles is preparing the audience subconscioulsy for Chrysothemis to become a character in the drama, without making this explicit. (He obviously expected his Athenian audience to know their Homer, and not be puzzled by the similarity of sound, and meaning, between the name of the youngest sister, Iphianassa, and the name of the elder sister sacrificed at Aulis, Iphigeneia, which he avoids using in *Elektra*. *Contra* Winnington-Ingram 1980, 224 n. 26 and 336.)

them; but this is bitterly dissolved by her next stanza, which in turn evokes a firm response: the singer of C2 rebukes Elektra directly, reminding her that her suffering is her own choice. This forces a more expansive admission, which will become crucial to the understanding of the action: Elektra should dance in isolation, rejecting all the Women, as she sings that she is 'almost crazy', committed to act destructively, and her problems are incurable. One dancer responds to this with a declaration of sympathy, creating for a few brief moments an echo of the initial moments of closeness between Elektra and the Women; but the pathos is all the greater when Elektra in her final stanza rejects this attempt to reach her. At the end she is left at the centre in a mood of defiance and determination, isolated from the Women by her misery.

Scene 2

Elektra and the Women   After music and emotion come spoken words and reason. Sophokles uses a long solo speech to expound Elektra's motivation, and build up his picture of her suffering.

Focusing on an individual's position through a long speech, followed by a short dialogue with the *choros* and then an intervention by a new character, was a standard procedure for the second scene of a Greek tragedy; the best way to play these scenes is for the *choros* to retreat at the end of Choros 1 to a semicircular formation, spaced around the perimeter of the front half of the *orchêstra*, so the protagonist has a 'stage audience' at his or her disposal to start the scene. If Elektra begins at C she can come forward to interact with the *choros* member who spoke 251ff. (that speaker herself needs to have moved a few paces into the circle as she delivers those three lines); this gives Elektra space to range around in the front segment as she builds the first beat of the speech, and also allows the Women to show that she has stirred up their sympathy, if all the others move a little inwards as well (in our production, at 261).

Elektra claims that any princess would act like her in this situation; and she should advance vigorously towards the Women with this, as it is her main challenge to them. It is a logical development from her feelings in Choros 1; Sophokles displays her extended argument for this position because he is about to introduce Chrysothemis, who will show that it is not true. So the section to 260 expounds her claim; then, starting the new beat firmly at 261 and becoming more rhetorical and explicit in her word-painting after 266, Elektra presents her central motivations: her anger at seeing Aigisthos on her father's throne, her explicitly sexual anger at the thought of Aigisthos in her father's bed;[27] and then the behaviour of Klytaimestra, in particular the outrageous celebrations each month on Agamemnon's death-day.[28] In performance this sequence suggests first a movement by Elektra back towards the *skene* (to e.g. BR to begin 267), then a movement forward again from EBC at 270 to C by 274, followed perhaps by sideways pacing in 275–9 – always focused on persuading the Women of the reality of her suffering.

A new beat begins at 282: Elektra elaborates on her responses to the situation. In this section Elektra makes her mother's regular abuse real to the audience; after a possible preliminary move to C to gain dominance for the opening, this passage is most effective if Elektra, when impersonating Klytaimestra, twice chooses a *choros* member to be 'Elektra', overbearing the first one and making her retreat, then rushing at the second one – on the opposite side of the *orchêstra*, if possible, for maximum effect – and forcing her to the ground delivering Klytaimestra's 'screech' (299) standing over this young woman and browbeating her.

In 303ff. Elektra brings out 'the poignant kernel of her tragedy',[29] as it was foreshadowed in the dance at 222; here is her first sober admission of the central fact that the waiting for Orestes is destroying her. The importance of this beat is brought out, and the ring-composition of the speech is reflected, if Elektra moves back to C and stability returns to the blocking. She remains there to the end, when her defence of her inability to maintain the traditional Greek female excellences of *sophrosyne* and reverence is complete. Meanwhile the Women's fundamental sympathy can be expressed by moving them all a little towards her in response to the direct appeal at 307.

In the following dialogue individual Women should move in a few more steps towards Elektra as they deliver their speeches; if one or two others move in each time as well, the whole *choros* can end up in a tighter U around her. As well as developing the issue of Orestes' return, this dialogue adds a piece of important information: Aigisthos is away, and this fact both makes the conspiracy prosper more easily, and

[27] This is perhaps the most startling and explicit difference between Sophokles' version and the two other ancient ones: Jones 1962, 149–53. Strauss seized on it in his opera based on von Hofmannsthal's *Elektra*: Evans 1984, 142–5.

[28] On this and other perversions of ritual in *El* see Seaford 1985.

[29] Burton 1980, 194.

prepares for his return in the Finale. Chrysothemis' entrance is constructed to seem as if it interrupts the dialogue; but in reality there is nothing more that either Elektra or the Women could say about Orestes, so the drama moves seamlessly into its next phase.[30]

Elektra and Chrysothemis Sophokles now introduces a sister to play very much the same role as Ismene in *Antigone*. The similarities between the two secondary characters highlights the differences between the principals: Antigone's determination to bury her brother elicits Ismene's admiration and love, while Elektra's devotion to vengeance elicits neither of these emotions from Chrysothemis.

Chrysothemis has often been regarded as a weak and cowardly sister to a heroic and admirable Elektra.[31] But the Athenian audience would have appreciated at once the cogency of the three points that Chrysothemis makes in her first speech, since she accepts realistically the true nature of the sisters' situation, faced as they are with the superior power of their enemies. This can be seen by comparing her ideas with Thoukydides' analysis in the 'Melian Dialogue'.[32]

(1) Elektra continues to indulge in empty words, and express her emotions openly; this is futile (cf. *Histories* 5.89 *init.*).

(2) Since Chrysothemis and Elektra do not have the strength to overcome Aigisthos, there is no point in pretending to be able to do something; Elektra ought to admit this, as Chrysothemis does, and face the realities of the situation (cf. *Histories* 5.87).

(3) What Chrysothemis herself says is 'wrong', and what Elektra says is 'right'. But questions of right and wrong must yield to the power of the stronger, if a person wants to live with any freedom at all (cf. *Histories* 5.89 *fin.*, 97, 111).

Elektra's devotion to Agamemnon's memory does, of course, rest on another fundamental feature of Greek morality: the need to help one's own *philoi*; but her extreme interpretation of this duty has already been undermined by the concessions she had to make earlier, when defending her stance to the Women; and she is about to discover that her behaviour has led Aigisthos and Klytaimestra to resolve to kill her.

Since the original audience would have perceived Chrysothemis' position as strong, she must be played as a character almost as strong in her own way as her sister. In performance, therefore, Chrysothemis

---

[30] On seamless transitions inside scenes in Sophokles cf. Kells 1973, 111 (on 405ff.).

[31] Above, Introduction pp. xxxi–xxxii.

[32] Thoukydides, *Histories* 5.84–113. Cf. above, Introduction p. xviii.

needs to achieve a position of power for the climax of her speech; this can be done by having her circle away from Elektra to FC by 336, then advance towards her during 336–9, finishing at C. The speech is particularly effective if she turns away from Elektra at the very end, and addresses the last one and a half lines to the audience, presenting her last remark as thoughtful and strong, rather than weak and subservient.

Scenes 2 and 4 must portray a conflict between the powerful wills of two sisters who still have a bond between them, remembered and retained from before they drew apart. The actresses should work in rehearsal towards playing them as two women attached to each other against their will, as if by an invisible elastic. This can be conveyed right at the outset. Chrysothemis is striding firmly from the *skene* doors to the R *parodos* with her basket of offerings – which will become an important prop later in the scene, but is now strikingly ignored by both characters; but when she sees Elektra (just behind C), she feels compelled to turn back into the circle (to e.g. near BC) to address her.

The Women need to be at the perimeter of the *orchêstra*, since their two interjections are simply markers in the dialogue between Chrysothemis and Elektra, and both sisters almost totally ignore them. In our production they retreated to sit at ELC throughout the scene, with the exception of the two speakers who intervene; they rose, and advanced towards the principals to deliver their lines.

Chrysothemis is at C when she finishes her speech at 340. Her strong central position is now converted into relative weakness when Elektra takes over.[33] Elektra's long, dismissive speech is agitated and hostile; its opening calls for Elektra to circle around Chrysothemis, pinning her sister to the centre. This circling should be complete by 350, since Elektra then needs a strong position (e.g. BC) for her first effective point: that she *is* helping Agamemnon by annoying his murderers.[34] The rest of the speech is anger and sarcasm, in which Elektra attempts to appropriate the word 'wise' for her own conduct.[35] It demands in performance restless irregular movements to and away from Chrysothemis; if 367–8 are a furious final turn away from her sister, Elektra

[33] Elektra even prevents Chrysothemis from speaking, after apparently inviting her to do so (351).

[34] However, she is helping him only to a very limited extent, and – as she concedes at 355 – only if the dead can feel pleasure. This was debatable: cf. e.g. Theognis 973ff.; Aischylos, *Libation Bearers* 313–21; Aristotle, *Nikomachean Ethics* 1101a22–b9.

[35] Sophokles returns to this issue in Scene 4 and Choros 4.

ends with an appeal to the Women, which motivates one Woman's
attempt to pacify the sisters. (Modern spectators and readers tend not
to be impressed by balanced comments like 370–1; but the ancient
Greeks paid great attention to the 'mean', the course poised between
two extremes;[36] and of course this Woman is absolutely right.)

The *agôn* has been lopsided, since Elektra countered Chrysothemis'
succinct opening statement with a much longer and more emotional
speech.[37] Instead of rebalancing the *agôn* by replying in kind, Chrysothemis introduces a new element, the imminent escalation of Elektra's
torment, and the drama again moves seamlessly into a new phase.[38]

Chrysothemis deliberately responds not to Elektra but to the Woman
who intervened. This forces Elektra to drop her stance of petulant
defiance; she has to move to regain Chrysothemis' attention. Elektra is
at first incredulous, and then (outrageously, since imprisonment and
death are totally against her interests)[39] delighted by the news; the
sisters become enmeshed in an intense 1–1 *stichomythia*. Elektra's
responses are flamboyant: downright rude at 391, bitterly ironic at
393; although Chrysothemis is the questioner, Elektra is the leader,
and the whole section plays very well if Elektra turns away and makes
Chrysothemis follow her (in our production, she moved in an extended
half-circle from L to FR); this conveys how Elektra keeps voicing self-
destructive, literally careless thoughts while Chrysothemis, who cares
about her sister and is confident that she herself is right,[40] tries without
success to make Elektra see sense. The exchange needs to become quite
violent in vocal tone before it reaches the direct insult of 403, which
Chrysothemis, now BR, should counter by bluntly announcing her
departure (404), and then turning to leave. This forces Elektra to run

[36] Four conspicuous examples are Apollo's motto at Delphi, 'nothing in
excess'; Athena's advice to her citizens to avoid extremes of both tyranny and
anarchy in Aischylos, *Eumenides* 681ff.; *OKol* Choros 4; and Aristotle's
decision to frame his ethical philosophy around the concept of 'the mean',
Nikomachean Ethics 1106a23 ff.

[37] If Chrysothemis is played by a strong actress, it is possible to convey to a
modern audience the Greek dislike of inappropriately protracted emotion, which
would incline the audience against Elektra's recent performance; Chrysothemis
can make her own distaste explicit when she refers at 375 to her sister's 'long
drawn-out laments'.

[38] On the tyrants' proposal to bury Elektra alive like Antigone, cf. Seaford
1985, 318–9 and 1990, 78–80.

[39] Cf. Blundell 1981, 186.

[40] NB esp. 398.

from wherever she is (in our production, FR) and physically block the *parodos* so she can ask her question at 405.

Sophokles has now accomplished a third and final seamless transition in this scene. And the prop that Chrysothemis has been carrying throughout the scene comes into focus at last. Sophokles is about to reuse and reinflect two of the principal features of Aischylos' version in *Libation Bearers*: the moment where the *choros* of foreign slave women persuade Aischylos' Elektra to 'turn' the offerings that Klytaimestra sent her to pour at Agamemnon's grave, and the dream that Klytaimestra dreamed on the night before Orestes' return.[41] Elektra's interest successfully lures Chrysothemis back into the circle; indeed, Chrysothemis needs to be at the centre for full symbolic effect before 421, when she narrates and mimes the planting of the sceptre at the house's central hearth.

When Chrysothemis has told the dream, Elektra embarks on a passionate speech, which does persuade Chrysothemis. From here to the end of the scene, properties are highly significant. Though the text does not demand this, our Elektra attempted to seize Chrysothemis' basket from her at 434; our tough Chrysothemis (characteristically) prevented her from taking it. Next Elektra must draw her knife, perhaps even to mime the mutilation of Agamemnon at 443ff., and certainly to cut off her lock of hair (450).

Then she removes her belt (452); this is a striking moment, which must be emphasized in performance. For a Greek *parthenos* the belt around the waist is the token of her virginity, normally only loosed in the presence of another when her husband takes her on the wedding night. It is as if Sophokles' Elektra is giving herself to Agamemnon – and her dress hangs immodestly loose for the rest of the drama, signifying her wild, abandoned state.

Chrysothemis then places both the lock and the belt in her basket. Given the physicality of all this action, we found it appropriate for Elektra to seize a half-willing Chrysothemis at 453, and drag her so both are on their knees to make the prayer to Agamemnon below the

[41] Aischylos, *Libation Bearers* 84ff., 527ff. The dream in Sophokles' version is highly sexualized (cf. Winnington-Ingram 1980, 232 n. 52). Agamemnon plants the sceptre at the hearth, and so renews the royal house (which will bloom after Orestes' return); but he only plants this obvious phallic symbol of male fertility after penetrating Klytaimestra's body with his penis, as Orestes will with his sword. In Stesichoros' earlier poem *Oresteia* Klytaimestra dreamed that a snake covered in gore turned into Agamemnon. Aischylos developed the first half of this dream (*Libation Bearers* 126ff., 928), and Sophokles the second.

earth in 453–8. Our Chrysothemis now surrendered the basket to Elektra to symbolize that she relented from her hostility.

Elektra stands up for 459, followed by Chrysothemis. When one of the Women urges Chrysothemis to do as Elektra has asked, she has no reservations; as she explicitly says (466), this action is right, and it will not be harmful to her, as long as Klytaimestra does not hear. Therefore, 'it simply must be done'; here as at the outset Chrysothemis' stance and behaviour are fully in accordance with contemporary Athenian morality.

Chrysothemis could be imagined as agreeing to make her own offering when she gets to the grave. But we thought it useful to give visual force to her statement of resolve at 466, and to the new harmony between the sisters; our Chrysothemis determinedly cut off her own lock with Elektra's knife, and then exchanged the knife for the basket. Placing this lock beside Elektra's lock and belt, she turns and leaves.

Choros 2

A short celebration of the new hope which Klytaimestra's dream has – as the audience knows, correctly – given to Elektra. The first stanza requires extremely upbeat choreography; if sung by an individual, it should be assigned to the most optimistic of the Women (we chose the actress who had delivered B2 in Choros 1). Sophokles then explores the power of strophic responsion by setting to the same Greek metrical form – and probably to the same choreography[42] – a matching *antistrophe* of a much more sombre texture, in which not Justice but the Fury is pictured as coming to the house, and the dream is seen not from Elektra's perspective as sweet but from the murderers' as monstrous. The moods converge at the end of the two parallel stanzas, with the avenging memory of Agamemnon and the axe in A1 matched in A2 by a solemn assertion of the power of oracles.[43]

The *epode* closes the song on an even darker note; the choreography must become more animated to match the change of metre for A3,[44] as

[42] Cf. Ewans 1995, 133–4; also Wiles 1997, 87ff. *Contra* Pickard-Cambridge 1968, 252.

[43] Sophokles here glances briefly at one of the central issues of his earlier *OKing*; cf. esp. *OKing* 893 ff., with the discussions by Ewans and McCart at Ewans 1999, lxxvi–viii.

[44] In the original Greek, from choriambics and iambic dimeters to the more emotionally violent metre of syncopated iambo-dochmiacs interspersed with dochmiacs and cretics.

the *choros* evokes the first crime which began the chain of suffering and violence in the house of Atreus – a marriage after murder, just like that of Aigisthos and Klytaimestra.[45] Sophokles wants the whole sequence of crimes to be in the audience's minds when he brings on for Scene 3 the perpetrator of Agamemnon's death, which was the subject of A1 and A2. Klytaimestra's entry could hardly be preceded by a Choros less favourable to her.[46]

Scene 3

Elektra and Klytaimestra This long two-part scene, together with Choros 4 in which Elektra and the Women internalize its consequences, occupies the entire middle third of the running time.[47] The first part is a confrontation between Klytaimestra and Elektra, in which they argue the rights and wrongs of the murder of Agamemnon.

There is no such scene in Aischylos: *Libation Bearers* reaches its climax in a confrontation between Orestes and Klytaimestra, in which Klytaimestra pleads for her life with a son who is resolved to kill her, and the moral issues are aired in a short but intense *stichomythia*. But Euripides had already explored the possibility of a scene with an *agôn* in the late fifth-century style between mother and daughter, and Sophokles was plainly determined to match and outdo him.[48] Euripides' Orestes has already killed Aigisthos, and is waiting inside for Elektra to lure their mother in; so the debate is underlaid by the knowledge that Elektra is on the point of victory, and is toying with her mother. Sophokles places the *agôn* long before Elektra recognizes Orestes, and injects at the conclusion the news of 'Orestes' death', which makes a violent and different impact on the two women, driving them even further apart than they were at the end of the *agôn*.

Klytaimestra has resolved this day to tolerate Elektra's behaviour no

---

[45] Sophokles goes back one generation further than Aischylos, in whose *Oresteia* the Thyestean banquet is the first crime.

[46] I argued above (Introduction p. xxxiv) that the *skene* panels for this drama might not have presented the standard neutral palace façade; if the visual backdrop evokes the 'house of many deaths', it will begin to make its full impact now, as Choros 2 and Scene 3 make the audience focus on the past.

[47] Although 870 lies before the two-thirds point in line numbering (1007), the last scenes of the drama have a cumulative momentum, which virtually ensures that 870–1510 occupy less than one third of the drama's time in performance.

[48] Aischylos, *Libation Bearers* 892ff.; Euripides, *Elektra* 998ff.

longer; Elektra knows this but Klytaimestra does not know that she knows it. An element of hypocrisy – or determination, or simply exhausted malice – therefore underlines the range of moods in Klytaimestra's first beat (to 533): anger, maudlin grumbling, anger again, rueful acknowledgement of her crime, and pathos.

For many traditional interpreters, Sophokles' Klytaimestra is an almost totally unsympathetic character, and Elektra's arguments against her are compelling;[49] for Kells, by contrast, her moment of ambiguous feeling about Orestes' death at 766–71 is crucial, and Klytaimestra is 'a commanding and tragic figure'.[50] This goes too far, and damages what is in other respects a fine interpretation of Elektra. Von Hofmannsthal displayed great insight into Scene 3 when he created the play that became the text for Strauss's opera Elektra: in his 'tragedy after Sophokles' both Elektra and Klytaimestra have become degraded, their inner life soured by the hatred that has festered between them since the murder of Agamemnon.[51] In Sophokles also we should perhaps be prepared to find weaknesses in them both. His Klytaimestra has conducted monthly festivals in memory of Agamemnon's death, attempted to murder Orestes as well as Elektra, and treats Elektra savagely, even beating her herself.[52]

If Elektra is bound to Chrysothemis by an invisible cord of sisterhood, her bond with Klytaimestra is the volatile relationship of enemies who are still bound together by their blood-relationship. Klytaimestra's first beat is addressed to Elektra, and at times can be played as issuing in physical contact (e.g. in our production at 525 she poked Elektra with her staff, and pushed her shoulders); but it oscillates between passages that need close interaction with Elektra, long sections that can be played regally 'at large', turning away from Elektra, and a few brief moments where she makes an aside to the Women and/or the audience (e.g. 526–7). Klytaimestra's volatility is best illuminated by a sequence of irregular moves circling round Elektra, whom in our production we left at BC; Klytaimestra reaches the centre only at 528.[53]

Even when she begins to argue her case, Klytaimestra's rhetoric is still volatile. The reason for this is Elektra's refusal to answer her

[49] E.g. Bowra 1944, 239; Waldock 1951, 179–83.

[50] 1973, 7 (his italics).

[51] Cf. Ewans 1985, 145–6 and ff.

[52] As Stevens notes (1968, 114), the contrast with Euripides' Klytaimestra, who is a sympathetic character, is very marked.

[53] Klytaimestra pushed her to BR at 525–6. The Women had already scattered in two groups to EFL and EFR in fear when Klytaimestra first appeared.

questions. So our Elektra simply circled away from her mother in silence (anticlockwise, from BC round to FL by 551) each time Klytaimestra completes a question (535, 537, 543, 545); Elektra did not even respond to 545, which is a direct insult to Agamemnon's memory. This forced Klytaimestra to follow her; she also needs to lunge directly towards Elektra at 538, 542–3, and 546 – where in our production she actually seized hold of her daughter (FC). She only relaxes at the end of the speech, in the sequence leading to Elektra's being granted right of reply – at which point Klytaimestra must of course yield the centre area to her, since Elektra needs to start 558ff. at C. (Now it is Klytaimestra's turn to move around silently, suspiciously – in the front segment, since her position is the weaker.)

Elektra's speech is designed as a specimen of forensic eloquence: she states that Agamemnon had good reason to kill Iphigeneia, and then that even if he had done it for a weaker reason, to help Menelaos, this did not justify Klytaimestra's vengeance-killing. Although Klytaimestra's rhetorical questions sidestep or beg the important issues,[54] both parts of Elektra's response would also have been problematic for a late fifth-century audience. Elektra tells the standard version of Agamemnon's reasons for the sacrifice of Iphigeneia, in which he paid her life for a rash and arrogant boast;[55] but, after Aischylos' complex reinflection of the motivation, which made Agamemnon's dilemma at Aulis tragic, it unavoidably diminishes the force of her rhetoric.[56]

Klytaimestra ended by giving Elektra a warning (550–51). Elektra's own counter-warning to Klytaimestra at 580–84 makes a statement that could well be applied to Elektra and Orestes themselves. But as yet there has been no hint at the shock of the Finale, in which a ruthless and remorseless Orestes and Elektra quite literally get away with murder. Sophokles' spectators would at this point feel that they are hearing Elektra 'condemn herself out of her own mouth',[57] and she will herself incur suffering in turn.

Elektra begins powerfully, advancing towards Klytaimestra (who in our production was near the perimeter until 587) on 561–4, and then

[54] Blundell 1987, 164–5.
[55] Apollodoros, *Library, Epit.* 3.21.
[56] Aischylos, *Agamemnon* 183ff. (cf. Ewans 1995, 132–5). Kells 1973, 126 compares and contrasts Sophokles' presentation of Aias with Elektra's account here of Agamemnon, and writes: 'this was the popular belief . . . but did Sophokles expect an intelligent person to believe it?' Cf. Segal 1966, 536 n. 84 and 1981, 271; Winnington-Ingram 1980, 220; and Blundell 1989, 167.
[57] Kells 1973, 128.

ranging round the rear half of the *orchêstra* in 565ff;[58] 580ff. found her advancing with menace towards Klytaimestra, forcing her back to the perimeter.

At 585 Elektra begins a new and more emotional appeal; we found that this change of tone needed motivation. Klytaimestra in our production reacted with cold fury to the hectoring tone of 580–84, decided to leave, and moved determinedly towards the *skene* – only to be blocked at R by a rapid move from Elektra on 585.

From here on the speech needs to be constructed at least as much with an eye to Klytaimestra's movements as to Elektra's; the Queen's disposition changes gradually from the cold fury after 584 to the hot fury after 609, and this must be shown in movement and gesture, or 610ff. will not be intelligible. In our production Elektra first enraged Klytaimestra at 587–90, and her mother charged towards her (both BR). Klytaimestra then turned away towards the *skene* on 595, while Elektra retreated to BC, only returning to C over the next three lines. When Elektra focuses on Orestes at 601ff., this precipitated further agitated movement from Klytaimestra, which climaxed in an open rush at her, staff once again raised to strike, on 609. A hapless Woman of Argos attempts to stem the aggression at 609a, and only succeeds in bringing Klytaimestra's venom down on herself (612ff.; in our production Klytaimestra chased the Woman back to join the other Women at the edge (EFR), before the slightly calmer appeal to them at 614–15).

From 614 onwards the action needs to ease back gradually towards stability, because Elektra's confession at 616ff. needs both peace and a dominant position for Elektra – C or FC; this will also create a firm visual contrast when she allows Klytaimestra to make her offerings, by physically moving away from the area near the altar.

Elektra admits (616) that she has incurred shame; and the avoidance of shame was the main motivation for *agathoi* of both genders. The genuine pathos of this speech is not undermined by the sophistry of 619–21, where Elektra calls on the 'new thought' of the period to excuse herself from responsibility;[59] in Sophokles' vision of her tragedy it is in fact true that Elektra has been destroyed – compelled to act both crazily and self-demeaningly, i.e. against her own best interests – by the murder of her father.

The *stichomythia* should flare mainly in words, not in too much movement – except for Klytaimestra's threat at 626–7 – before Elektra

---

[58] She went briefly to the altar at FC for 576.
[59] Above, Introduction pp. xviiff.

releases the tension by yielding at 632 (in our production, with a mock-obeisance to the Queen) and moving away to the back half of the *orchêstra*; she allows Klytaimestra to pray, but 'upstages' her by her watchful presence.

Klytaimestra and Apollo Now once again, as in Scene 2, a prop that has long been visible, but totally ignored, suddenly comes into prominence. When she came in, Klytaimestra was followed by a Maidservant, who has remained EB in front of or beside the *skene* doors ever since, holding a bowl or tray of fruit. As the Queen moves to FC behind the altar for her prayer, this Maidservant will obey Klytaimestra's orders, bring the fruit forward, place it on the altar, and then retreat inconspicuously, which ensures that the focus is fully on the altar now, as it is used for the first time.

The central section of the prayer is a more intimate address to the god. This is easily expressed through movement, e.g. if Klytaimestra looks anxiously around at Elektra and the Women at 637ff., then kneels behind the altar at 643. (If the Women are EFR and EFL, and Elektra is moving around e.g. BL, Klytaimestra is truly surrounded by her enemies during this prayer.)

Then, after the central section is completed at 654, she should rise again, stepping back a few paces from the altar to give distance for the last few lines.

'Orestes' death' Klytaimestra has just prayed for the death of Orestes. Now for the first time since Scene 1 a man appears, and disrupts the world of *Elektra*, which has been exclusively female since Elektra's entrance.[60] Just as in the parallel scene in *Oidipous the King*, he is a messenger who comes to bring an answer to a queen's prayers – in both dramas, an answer that proves to be the Queen's undoing.[61] Rather than seeing in this an intervention by the gods, as did some earlier commentators,[62] we should recognize that in Sophokles the gods stand back, remote, while human actions fulfil their predictions.[63] Apollo told Orestes he would succeed if he used treachery; and so the Old Man's treachery does succeed. But – just as Apollo did not tell

[60] Gellie 1972, 117.

[61] On Iokaste's use of an altar FC in *OKing* Scene 4, cf. McCart's Notes in Ewans 1999, 290.

[62] Cf. esp. Kitto 1950, 133: 'We must see in it, as the original audience must have seen, the hand of the god. Apollo has heard the terrible prayer, and swiftly sends the fitting answer . . .' Also Seale 1982, 64.

[63] Cf. Ewans 1999, lxvi–xviii.

Oidipous *who* his parents were – he did not tell Orestes of the effect that his 'great story' would wreak on Elektra. Orestes will find out in Scene 5.[64]

Interpretation of the scene will vary, according to the extent to which a production overtly acknowledges the probability that the Old Man would recognize Elektra.[65] Our Old Man deliberately used Elektra's suffering at his 'news' to assist with the deception of Klytaimestra; if Scene 1 does characterize Orestes and his former tutor as examples of the new ruthless amoralists of the late fifth century, then the Old Man will use anything to achieve his ends. So, for example, our Old Man directed the gory climax of the depiction of 'Orestes' death' at her, standing over Elektra to deliver 752–6.

The Old Man delivers one of the finest 'messenger-speeches' in surviving Greek tragedy.[66] It is however unique, because the whole audience knows that it is a lie from start to finish. They will therefore focus on the reactions of Klytaimestra and Elektra to his falsehoods; so from the outset the Old Man should reinforce for the audience the fact that he is play-acting. We found that a steady, measured approach by the actor in the opening lines achieved this effect, and allowed the reactions of the two women to become the focus. Our Klytaimestra allowed a submerged desperation to surface at the start of 671, and again in 675, followed by a vicious snarl at Elektra in 678 (prefiguring the end of the scene); Elektra fell to her knees on 674, and collapsed by the end of 677, prompting two of the Women to run to her and comfort her.

The speech itself is a virtuoso performance, in every sense. We felt that the actor playing the Old Man must pause occasionally, to give the audience the feeling that the character is improvising to add the right kind of 'padding' (47) to the very short outline provided by Orestes in Scene 1.[67] Indeed, this speech requires some kind of theatricalist preparation at 680, while Klytaimestra yields the area near c,

[64] There are several stories that show how imprecise questions to the oracle yield a prophecy that is true, but leads the questioners to actions that harm them. Cf. Sheppard 1927, 3–4 citing Kroisos (Herodotos, *Histories* 1.91) and Xenophon (*Anabasis* 3.1.6).

[65] This possibility is flatly denied by Seale 1982, 65. But it transforms the dynamics of the scene in performance.

[66] On messenger-speeches in Sophokles cf. Ewans 1999, xxxi ff.

[67] For more elaborate uses of improvised fiction see *Phil* Scene 2, with Ley's Notes, below, p. 239. Cf. also Lichas' deception of Deianeira in *YWT*.

and the Old Man takes over that position.[68] We also found that the speech is helped by having a number of in-*orchêstra* audiences, since adequate enactment requires the Old Man to range freely around the playing space, and address different parts of the narrative to different groups. So Klytaimestra retreated to FL, while the Women were now divided into three groups: one EFR, one diagonally opposite them at EBL, and two individuals supporting Elektra at R. This enabled the Old Man to establish that he controls the circle; he could range round, engaging and disengaging from individuals and from the theatre audience. Lines 690ff. provide a good example: the actor obviously begins by addressing Klytaimestra, but in our production turned to the R group of the *choros* as he built towards the proclamation at 693 4. For these two lines he faced forward to address the centre of the audience; then he directed the generalization of 695–6 at Elektra, before turning back to Klytaimestra to resume his narrative in 697ff.

More controversially, we developed the idea of using the properties already present in the *orchêstra*: at 728ff. our Old Man seized some of the fruit which Klytaimestra had offered to Apollo, pulled it off the altar, smashed pieces together and then threw them away to illustrate the wreckage of the chariots. This business alarmed the Maidservant, who ran to cower behind Klytaimestra, and it disconcerted the Queen, who started a couple of paces towards the Old Man. So it increased the effect on his audience of the Old Man's narrative, by allowing him to illustrate it graphically; at the same time the Old Man destroyed the offerings with which Klytaimestra had prayed for the death of Orestes, perfectly symbolizing the destruction of that hope.

When the Old Man has finished, Klytaimestra circles, brooding, for a moment, as she reflects that her son's death is hurting her, as well as freeing her from fear (766–71, cf. 780–82).[69] For Kells this revelation of maternal feeling, and of suffering, is the central moment in *Elektra*,

---

[68] Our Old Man divested himself of his long travelling coat and sinister/ comical top hat, and handed these to two of the Women to mind before he began the narrative. This left him in black shirt and trousers, red braces and white bow tie, with a magic wand to use as a prop during the speech, to express his role here as a conjuror.

[69] 767–8 are a moment of what we would call introversion, or an aside; in the masked Greek theatre such lines must be addressed to part of the audience, not facing any of the other players.

and he is particularly severe on critics who complain that her remorse is short-lived;[70] but in performance it *is* only a passing feeling.[71] The Old Man's careful responses (with a feint at departure on 772) soon precipitate Klytaimestra's last substantial speech (773ff.), in which she reveals just how much and how long she has lain in fear, desperately waiting for this deliverance.[72] This is a speech of great power – note the build-up over nine lines from 774 to 782, before the tremendous release on 'And now! . . .' (783). Klytaimestra must therefore take the centre position back from the Old Man (at latest by 777), and will move away from it only a few paces (for a short advance towards Elektra on 784), before turning back to complete the speech with an address to the Old Man or to some of the Women.

It is very hard to see how this speech can be 'poetry of so intense and tragic a quality that . . . in this scene [Sophokles] subtly transfers our sympathy to her'.[73] Elektra may (depending on the production) be literally wrong when she says at 807 that Klytaimestra 'went in laughing'; but she is psychologically right. That is a fair summation of everything the Queen has said from 783 to her exit – note especially the brutality of her responses to Elektra's outburst of grief.[74]

The Old Man has now succeeded in deceiving Klytaimestra; so he makes a second feint at departure in 799, hoping to be invited inside the house for refreshment as a reward for his good news – and obtains the response that he needs. Klytaimestra makes a grand exit – with a parting shot at Elektra, 802–3 – and retires into the *skene*.

Elektra alone   Klytaimestra has finally silenced Elektra (note the constant wordplay on the word 'stop' in 795ff.). Against the knowledge that now Orestes will not come, all that Elektra can summon up is the hope that fortune might turn in her favour again (794). But this rapidly vanishes, after the exit of her tormentor.

[70] 1973, 7.

[71] So rightly Waldock 1951, 183: 'It is only a passing pang, a reaction of some nerve of motherhood, not quite atrophied even in her. She smothers it with no trouble. The feeling that floods her being is one of vast relief.' Cf. Stevens 1978, 115 and Winnington-Ingram 1980, 232.

[72] Again, von Hoffmannsthal seized on and magnified the central element in the scene, when he depicts his Klytaimestra as desperate for *Erlösung, Lindrung* – release from and healing of her inner torments.

[73] Kells 1973, 7.

[74] The Greeks often expressed triumph in terms of laughter. Cf. e.g. Athena at *Ai* 79: 'The sweetest of all laughter is to laugh at enemies.' And Elektra at 1153.

Elektra addresses her friends, circling in her agony, but reaching the central area on 807 or 808, ready for her brief elegy to the dead Orestes.[75] Brooding, she may pace around briefly on 814–6, before suddenly reaching her decision to die right beside the door. This is followed by a rapid cross up-*orchêstra*, to reach EBL beside the *skene* doors before the start of 819, where she obviously collapses to the ground during the rest of the line.

Choros 3

Instead of following the news of 'Orestes' death' with a conventional choral ode, Sophokles created this *kommos* – an extraordinary, expressionist interaction between Elektra and the Women, united in their outpouring of grief, during which Elektra totally takes into herself the emotional certainty that Orestes is dead.[76] One Woman's passionate appeal to Zeus and the sun-god provokes Elektra's outcries, which themselves precipitate an extremely close interaction, in which a line is twice divided into four between Elektra and two *choros* members (830, 845). (In our production the A stanzas were delivered with the Women moving in unison, in a curved line from BR to FR facing Elektra at BL.) The mood is extremely intense from the outset, and becomes even more so in the B stanzas. Here the *choros* – now reformed in a more prominent position, nearer Elektra (i.e. BC) – should perhaps gather Elektra in among themselves, as all the women are for a few moments bound together by their grief, but each B stanza ends with three lines that need separation, dissolving the pattern, as Elektra expresses her despair.

Scene 4

This climactic scene begins with a total contrast between the two sisters: Chrysothemis, who is of course still beautiful, enters happy, dynamic and excited – so excited that she forgets the modesty appropriate to an unmarried woman of noble birth, and has pulled her skirt above her knees so she can run back to bring her news (872);[77] Elektra

[75] Perhaps she falls to her knees BC on 808/9, in which case she should rise again halfway through 812.

[76] As Burton notes (1980, 206), this prepares the audience for her rejection of Chrysothemis' news in Scene 4.

[77] She has of course abandoned her basket, as Elektra suggested (448ff.).

is sunk in misery, no longer beautiful (1178), motionless and depressed. In performance, Chrysothemis is strong throughout the scene – except of course when she is grieving for 'Orestes' death'.

Scene 4 is in two parts; it is constructed in six beats.

(1) *The opening exchange.* Sophokles establishes a total polarity between the sisters, with Elektra slumped in despair at C at the end of Choros 3, while Chrysothemis runs in. Chrysothemis must go straight to Elektra, as she needs to be close, indeed touching Elektra with the dynamic energy of 877–8; Elektra can then physically rebuff her, pushing her away on 879–80. Chrysothemis rises to her feet, and then, as the girls (e.g.) circle each other during the following dialogue, she must gravitate towards the centre to tell her story.

(2) *Chrysothemis' narrative.* This solemn, beautiful speech should naturally be begun at C, to command attention to the speaker. But it is irresistible for Chrysothemis to enact her approach to the tomb of Agamemnon at 899ff., creeping towards the altar of Apollo at FC and miming her own actions during the rest of the story to 906. Then she reasons with Elektra, turning towards her at 907, engaging more closely with her by moving towards her at 909ff., then perhaps turning away for a few lines from 911 so she can turn back towards her with the radiant certainty of 915. Then she must return to the centre for the confident expression of hope in the closing pair of lines.

(3) *Elektra disillusions Chrysothemis.* Using a pattern already employed in the first Chrysothemis scene, Sophokles now converts Chrysothemis' position of strength into weakness. Elektra begins the *stichomythia* at a distance (e.g. L), to show her detachment from the 'deceived' Chrysothemis; Sophokles then inserts two lines for Elektra into what is otherwise a 1–1 *stichomythia*, to give her time to rush towards Chrysothemis at C, when she expresses her absolute conviction that Orestes is dead.[78] Elektra then needs to disengage herself again at some point during the following lines,[79] so Chrysothemis is momen-

[78] Earlier tragedy tended to favour a regular pattern of unbroken 1–1, or more rarely 2–2 *stichomythia* (usually with a two-line close); but even in the freer style of this late fifth-century *stichomythia* there are small-scale structural symmetries. The first subsection is palindromic or arch-shaped, with 4x1–1 on each side of Elektra's two lines at 924–5; then a pair of 2–2 (four lines), followed symmetrically by Chrysothemis' short outburst (also four lines). Elektra caps this with a two-line speech (938–9), to signal a new beginning (the second half of the scene starts here); this precipitates a 1–1 dialogue which occupies the rest of the beat, and 'launches' Elektra's big speech.

[79] We chose to move her towards the house (i.e. to BC) on 929.

tarily isolated for the short but moving speech at 934ff., in which she crumples in on herself.

Elektra's response to Chrysothemis' despair initiates the second part of the scene.[80] Elektra once again goes back to Chrysothemis at C during the two-line speech. In our production she knelt beside her sister until 943. Chrysothemis got up at 944, and responded strongly to Elektra's quite aggressive challenge in the rest of the dialogue.

(4) *The plan*. Elektra embarks on a massive attempt at persuasive rhetoric. It requires extensive, free-ranging moves to and away from Chrysothemis, who is C or BC – first turning away round to ERC on 950ff., then returning to Chrysothemis on 955–6. At 958ff. the rhetoric once again demands a rhetorical move – in our production Elektra circled to EFR at 958ff., then round to L by 966, ready to cross back on 967 and seize Chrysothemis on 968–9. After that Elektra needs to gain distance (Chrysothemis needs to have been moved away from C/ BC during this action), so that Elektra has a dominant position (e.g. BC) to begin the imagined 'citizens' proclamation' at 977ff. Chrysothemis' moves are few but important, as she will when this speech is over find the power to rebut Elektra's plan in a far shorter speech of her own, and the production must signal her reactions to the audience. We chose to make her turn away in disapproval at 957 and 962, forcing Elektra to restart her appeal.

Elektra's performance becomes outrageously overconfident when she imagines a speech of thanks, which the grateful citizens will deliver to the two young murderesses (977ff.).[81] Much of this speech will be played out to the sky and to the audience, so that in the closing six lines Elektra can gradually return back to Chrysothemis for a close, personal appeal – perhaps even, as in our production, kneeling in front of her sister to give full power to 986–8, then standing up again for the reminder in the last one and a half lines.[82]

(5) *Chrysothemis' rebuttal*. Taking revenge on your enemies and avoiding the shame of leaving them unpunished was in Greek values a

[80] Note how the transition, at 938–9, is once again seamless, and takes place inside a beat; cf. Kells 1973, 166.

[81] Cf. Kells 1973, 172. He correctly notes (168–9) that at 957 Elektra has evaded the issue of matricide; 956 is constructed in the original Greek, as in this English version, so that both Chrysothemis and the audience are shocked when the first word of 957 is not Klytaimestra but Aigisthos.

[82] Our feisty Chrysothemis angrily pulled her hand back out of Elektra's clasp at the end of 987.

basic goal of *male arete*.[83] Chrysothemis' statement that females are less strong with their hands than men (997–8) was for the original audience a simple, undeniable fact of life. In her world there were no handguns or other sophisticated weapons to compensate for the fact that men possessed, and had been trained to use, the dagger, sword and spear. And the Greeks saw no nobility in suicide, and no eternal bliss to be acquired by martyrdom.[84] Hence the great power of Chrysothemis' sarcasm in 1005–6: 'It's not exactly going to help us to escape, if we acquire great fame, while being tortured till we die.' Indeed, the speech is powerful throughout, starting with the first moments in which Chrysothemis ignores Elektra for three lines; she shows her disdain for her sister by responding to the Woman who spoke 991–2. Only then does she round on Elektra (who is now near BC), with the intense, stabbing questions of 995–7. In the rest of the speech Chrysothemis needs to range freely around the *orchêstra* (but without the recklessness with which Elektra moved); Chrysothemis' moves should probably include grabbing Elektra's hand at 997–8, going away from her to a dominant position by 1005–6, and turning back towards Elektra at 1009.

Elektra has, in Chrysothemis' opinion, lost her *sophrosyne* – her wisdom, caution, sense and insight (1013) – the chief component of *arete* for women.[85] Now one of the Women of Argos abandons the (qualified) support for Elektra, which as a group they have maintained until this point, and unequivocally supports what Chrysothemis has said (1015–16). It is as remarkable a turning-point as the moment when the Elders come out in open opposition to Kreon at *Antigone* 1098; and the Women will develop their new position almost immediately, in Choros 4.

(6) *The bonds of sisterhood are dissolved.* Elektra's dismissive response (1017ff.), and Chrysothemis' awe at her sister's stubborn determination (1021ff.), precipitate an angry 1–1 *stichomythia* which drives the scene to its conclusion. There will be moments where Elektra goes close to Chrysothemis: in anger (1031), and sarcasm (1033); and moments where Chrysothemis reaches out to Elektra (e.g. 1036); but

[83] Elektra is made to imply this when she has the 'proclamation' speak at 983 of their 'manly courage'. It also explains Chrysothemis' use of two military metaphors in 995–6.

[84] Cf. Ewans 1999, 204ff, on Ismene's similar position in *Ant* Scene 1. On the necessity to accept the power of those stronger than yourself, cf. Notes on Scene 2 above, p. 190.

[85] E.g. Plato, *Meno* 71e–73b. Cf. Adkins 1960, 161–2, 228 and 246–9.

overall this is a *stichomythia* of disengagement, in which the two participants go further apart both metaphorically and literally – e.g. in Elektra's moves during her responses at 1037 and 1039, which in our production took her around EFR to EFC to EFR by 1041, while Chrysothemis remained at or near C, to keep the dominance needed to support 1040.

Elektra has to admit (1027) that Chrysothemis is correct in denying that she, Elektra, is sensible. But she will not concede that Chrysothemis is 'right' (1037). For her part, Chrysothemis is prepared to concede for a moment that perhaps Elektra's extreme filial piety is 'right' (1042), but she opposes to that, in the rest of the dialogue, the certainty that Elektra's attempt to avenge Agamemnon by herself will end in suffering. And no one – not even Plato – could prove to any ancient Athenian's satisfaction (except perhaps his own and his students') that it would be better to suffer harm, even for a cause you believed to be just.[86] So Chrysothemis needs to disengage from Elektra, and from the argument, with the utmost force on 'Enough!' (1055), and leave in anger. Perhaps she can even walk away after 'go on' (1056), then turn round when she reaches the dominant position at BC to deliver the rest of the last two lines as an exasperated 'last word', before her rapid exit.

Choros 4

The Women are disturbed by the breakdown of the relationship between the two sisters; they first call to Agamemnon's spirit to help, and then reflect on Elektra's situation.

This fairly straightforward ode has suffered badly at the hands even of experienced interpreters, because most readers have been fixated on the belief that Elektra is an admirable example of heroic endurance, and the Women must therefore praise her without reservation. It has even been claimed that Chrysothemis is being criticized in the opening lines (and presumably therefore threatened with Zeus' thunderbolts at 1063–5!) for not nurturing her father, Agamemnon, as much as

---

[86] In Plato's *Republic* (357bff.), Sokrates' friend Glaukon challenges him to prove that a person is better off in this world to behave justly, even if he has to suffer torture himself and see his family suffering atrocious torments (361e–362). During the remaining nine books of the *Republic* Sokrates fails, since in the final analysis he has to appeal, with the Myth of Er (614ff.), to the minority belief in *post-mortem* rewards for wisdom and virtuous behaviour.

Elektra.[87] This is impossible; most modern scholars recognize that (as this translation makes explicit) the nurturing referred to in the first three lines is given by adult birds both to their aged parents and to their offspring; the Women call for all human beings to show more of the reciprocal help which is central to being *philoi*.[88]

The A stanzas are both in three parts, whose parallelism needs to be brought out in the choreography. The first four lines reflect in A1 on the dysfunctional family, and in A2 more specifically on the new, irreconcilable quarrel between the sisters. Then the middle section of A1 asserts that punishment will come (for Aigisthos and Klytaimestra, who have treated *philoi* like enemies), while A2 contrasts that hope for the future with the now total isolation of Elektra from her family. The last four lines focus on Agamemnon: in A1 the Women call to his spirit,[89] and in A2 they reflect on Elektra's loyalty to him.

The B stanzas, in which the Women focus more closely on Elektra, are also designed to be danced in three sections. In each matching stanza the first three lines expound Elektra's situation, and the present is again contrasted with a hope for the future; the middle section evokes her suffering, and in the last three lines the Women present their judgement upon her.

The transmitted Greek text is corrupt in line 1087. Most editors and translators reconstruct the passage so that it praises Elektra unequivocally; the Women end the stanza by singing words to the effect: 'you will be hailed as wise,/and called the very best of children.' However, this is simply impossible in the light of 1015–16, where one of the Women told Elektra that she should pay heed to Chrysothemis, and not attempt to assassinate Aigisthos; she will show 'true insight' by doing so. The Women cannot now contradict their recent agreement with Chrysothemis that Elektra's suicidal devotion to Agamemnon lacks sense. Any reconstruction of the Greek text must therefore include a negative; just as the Women describe Elektra's choice in 1085–6 as both full of glory and of everlasting tears, so too in 1087–9 it is both unwise and a unique exemplar of filial piety.[90]

[87] Jebb 1894, 144–5; Burton 1980, 209; Gardiner 1987, 154.

[88] Winnington-Ingram 1980, 244 n. 89; Blundell 1989, 150.

[89] Cf. Aischylos, *Libation Bearers* 315–519.

[90] So rightly Kells 1973, 183–4, 240–42; he changes two letters from the MS text to read '*ta me kal'ou kathoplisasa*' – 'you have not given arms to what you don't believe is right'. For an attempt at counter-argument, cf. Winnington-Ingram 242 n. 82. Kells' position – on an issue crucial to our entire understanding of *El*! – is loftily ignored e.g. by Lloyd-Jones and Wilson 1990, 64–5. Their

The last stanza presents no problems; the Athenian audience would have felt no tension when Elektra's behaviour is presented as unwise (i.e. not in her own best interests) and also as being in accordance with 'the greatest laws of all', presumably the unwritten laws of devotion to *philoi*.[91] Showing piety to Zeus through such devotion is not necessarily sensible, or in the interests of the person who shows it, when she lives under an authoritarian regime – as Antigone realized when she was about to be executed.[92]

The Women only involve Elektra in their dance when they turn towards her in the B stanzas. But the mood of the four stanzas is seamless – the sense even runs over from A1 to A2, which is rare in tragic lyrics; so there should be a continuous development in the music and the dancing from the opening anxiety to the closing tribute to Elektra.

Scene 5

The Recognition Elektra first grieves for Orestes over the urn, and then has the living Orestes revealed to her. The emotional stress that this charade inflicts on her, added to what she has already suffered, drives her insane. As she herself says, in a moment of terrible self-awareness after the recognition, 'You've wounded me in ways I cannot understand' (1315). But Orestes – unlike the Old Man in Scene 3 – does not inflict this torment on her deliberately. It is impossible to play the scene on the assumption that he knows from the outset that this woman is his sister. On the contrary, the ending of Scene 1 ensured that he does not; and the opening moves of this scene are carefully written to imply the same.[93] Indeed, much of its power arises because Orestes has no idea that this ragged, beaten woman, dressed like a slave and 'etched by many sufferings',[94] could possibly be his sister. As Elektra's speech over the urn unfolds, he gradually comes to realize that she is.[95]

Oxford Classical Text prints an earlier conjecture of Lloyd-Jones', which means literally 'you have given arms to a cure for what you do not believe is right'.

[91] These were underwritten by Zeus himself; cf. *Ant* 450ff., and Ewans 1999, 220 n. 53 on *Ant* 487.

[92] See *Ant* 921ff.

[93] NB esp. the phrasing of 1105 and 1125. Cf. Reinhardt 1979, 263–4 (n. 24) and Kells 1973, 187, *pace* Knox as reported by Downs 1996, 124–5.

[94] 1187. Perhaps this bold metaphor was depicted in Elektra's mask?

[95] This is quite easy to achieve in masked performance. To make his through-

From the R *parodos* two young men enter whom the audience recognize, but whom neither the Women nor Elektra have seen before. Pylades carries the urn, but at first he conceals it from all the women, and only brings it into Elektra's sight when Orestes gestures to him at 1113.[96]

Orestes is acting a part, and his mode of address is distant and formal;[97] he and his companion should therefore not advance very far into the *orchêstra* (in our production, they stopped at R). By contrast, after one of the Women has pointed him out to her at 1105, Elektra comes closer to them in three stages, at 1108–9, 1112–15, and 1119ff.; and perhaps the fact that she needs two more lines, after she has directly asked for the urn at 1120, implies that Pylades holds it back when Elektra advances towards him, and does not give it to her until 1125, after Orestes has told him to.

Elektra's lament is a virtuoso exercise in the literal act of make-believe which is at the heart of all theatre. The performer must here make real for the audience something that is at two removes from reality. Audiences and performers always know that they conspire together in the theatre to pretend (for example) that a prop funerary urn contains the ashes of a dead character; but here there is a second level of pretence, since the two male characters are aware that even inside the drama there are no ashes. 'Made of solid bronze but empty of the true Orestes, the stage prop for an elaborate fiction capable of eliciting Elektra's most intense emotions, the urn symbolizes the emptiness of language, its power to distort and manipulate, as well as to represent, reality.'[98] When Elektra pours out her grief for her brother, Sophokles provides his protagonist with an extraordinary opportunity to make Elektra's emotions so intense that for a few moments they overcome the audience's grip on not one, but two levels at which the scene is a fiction.

line credible, an unmasked Orestes would require double-takes, puzzled looks to Pylades and then back to Elektra and other business, which would all pull focus from Elektra as she performs 1126–70. A masked Orestes does not need to react at all until late in the speech – in our production, on 1164; of course he reacts very vividly after one of the Women addresses Elektra by name at 1171.

[96] Many commentators supply Orestes with one or more attendants (e.g. Reinhardt 1979, 135; Seale 1981, 69). This is totally inappropriate to what Waldock (1951, 170) well characterized as 'the private adventure of a little band of three'.

[97] Kells 1973, 186–7 on 1113ff. and 1117.

[98] Segal 1981, 282.

The speech is of course performed to the urn; but like (for example) Aias' speech with the sword as 'fatal' property,[99] it works better in performance if the actress at some point moves away from the urn, so that she can address it more effectively, gesture to it and move around it. In our production Elektra first took the urn to BC by the end of 1128, and then brought it down to C, and knelt, at the start of the apostrophe which begins at 1131. But she lowered the urn to the ground on 1136, ready for the increasingly intense section from 1138, where Elektra's suffering and growing desperation were expressed by ranging around the back left quadrant; she collapsed for a few moments at 1142, but then built the flow of her rhetoric to 1153-5 and knelt down again only at the end, closely facing the urn at 1157-9.

Then, 'carried away by her emotion, she bursts into short cries in lyric *anapaests*';[100] music is heard, Elektra stands, and she begins for a few steps to dance. But the burden of grief weighs her down; extraordinarily – given that Greek tragic characters normally rise to full lyric and danced expression of their suffering when they suffer loss – Elektra's attempt to dance collapses after three lines, and she returns to spoken words. From 1165 to the end Elektra returns to the impulse of 1158-9, she folds herself in onto the urn, as if she could now be put into it as she desires.

The actual recognition needs care and gradual pacing, since the brother and sister are initally contrasted in both stance and dynamic. Elektra remains brooding in one place on the ground, tightly embracing the urn at C while Orestes, after his expression of amazement (which can be played either to Pylades or to the audience), focuses ever more intently and closely upon her. But in a large performance area it is a mistake to bring them too quickly together. Clearly Orestes will move closer towards Elektra on almost all of his lines in the *stichomythia*; but 1181 is best played as an aside to Pylades, and indeed in our production Elektra rose to her feet at 1188, carrying the urn, and moved away from him towards the *skene* on 1190; although Orestes came slightly nearer to her during parts of the next sequence, he did not get really close to Elektra until 1205ff.[101]

[99] *Ai* Scene 3; cf. Ewans 1999, 187.

[100] Kells 1973, 191; he compares *YWT* 1081ff. – but there Herakles only has two lines of outcry, and he is unable to move.

[101] Sophokles first overcomes in two lines (1203–4) the problem of playing a private scene in the presence of the *choros*. This is perhaps rather artificial; but Sophokles has deliberately deprived himself of Aischylos' neat solution, which was also adopted by Euripides. In their dramas Orestes already knows that the

Becauses the urn symbolizes a dead Orestes, both psychology and theatrical practicality demand that Elektra cannot embrace the living Orestes until she has put it down. Sophokles makes a virtue out of this necessity; his Orestes begins to disclose himself to Elektra by making her realize that it does not contain her brother's ashes. The crucial moment is when Orestes, coming closer to her from 1209, persuades Elektra to abandon the urn;[102] in our production she put it down (on the altar, FC) at 1218, because from 1220 onwards Elektra, excited by the news that Orestes is alive, takes the lead.[103] She forces up the emotional temperature, as the dialogue is written from here to the climax in *antilabe*, and she advances towards him; Orestes should only reciprocate on 1222–3. Elektra then grasps Orestes' hand to take the signet ring at 1224, embraces him for 1226, and turns forward on 1227 to lead Orestes towards a group of the Women. One of them moves briefly towards Elektra in a joyful response.

And now Elektra, who could not dance her grief, dances her joy fearlessly, while Orestes pleads with her to show restraint. He is aware that they have no time, while Elektra needs the whole of Time for her rejoicing (1253–5).[104] The contrast between them is perfectly drama-tized in a lyric scene, since in the convention of Athenian tragedy music and dance suspend the sense of time. Orestes remains in spoken dialogue throughout to symbolize that he remains anchored to a firm sense of the real time that is elapsing, and the caution that they need to show. He remains virtually immobile at or near C, while Elektra recklessly uses the whole *orchêstra*, even including the rear sector near the doors of the hostile palace at 1241–2, to express her rejoicing. Significantly, the Women are not inspired to join her in this outburst.

Elektra is gradually calmed (starting after her second spoken line,

women of the *choros* are well-disposed, because he has overheard their conver-sation with Elektra before revealing himself; but Sophokles has avoided this, because he wants his Orestes to be ignorant of Elektra's identity when he inflicts the urn on her.

[102] Similarly, the crucial moment in Aischylos is where Elektra casts aside the lock of hair – *Libation Bearers* 165ff.; cf. Ewans 1995, 169–70. In both scenes Elektra must abandon the token of her brother before she can embrace the man himself (Euripides follows an entirely different route, since in his version the Old Man who once looked after Elektra and Orestes has stayed behind in Argos; he recognizes Orestes before Elektra, and overcomes her scepticism.)

[103] It is not practical for Orestes to take it from her during 1217, *pace* Jebb 1894, 165.

[104] Cf. Kells 1973, 206.

1256); but she only subsides at the end of the A3 *epode*, when she has expressed to the full her joy that Orestes has returned. The subscene ends when Elektra finally comes close to him, and caresses his face, at the end of the dance (1285–7; we discovered in rehearsal that it is a mistake if this is done at 1280, because it is then impossible to play the final stanza of dance effectively).

Just as in Aischylos and Euripides, the recognition is followed by plotting. The two speeches at 1288ff. begin with Orestes and Elektra close to each other, C/BC. Orestes can take her hands on 1298–1300; now that Elektra has been calmed to the discipline of speech, that closeness can be achieved which did not transpire immediately after the recognition, because Elektra was so excited. Very little movement is needed until after 1306, where Elektra perhaps moves towards the *skene* as she talks about affairs inside the palace. Then after 1311 she circles, brooding on what has happened to her. As she alludes to the damage that Orestes' 'death' and living return have done to her (1315), she can pick up the urn to reinforce this crucial point; then she tells us, almost incredibly, that the barriers between life and death are now so dissolved for her that if Agamemnon came back alive, she would believe it (in a few minutes, 1361–2, she will actually believe he has). But finally she becomes submissive (1318ff.; perhaps she should even kneel to Orestes at the end).

A noise is heard from the *skene* after 1321.[105] Elektra must immediately start to act the part of a graceful receptionist.[106] But she is not able to do this convincingly; 1324–5 would not conceal her glee, if one of Klytaimestra's cronies overheard the lines. Elektra here shows the first sign that 1315 is deeply true: her psyche has indeed been mortally wounded by the events, and the audience will soon fully realize this.

The Old Man Returns   Orestes has attempted to give Elektra some sense that the *kairos*, the moment for the deed, is now (1292); but he has failed, even though he secured her acquiescence (1318–19). Having sent the Old Man inside to spy out the situation (40–41), Sophokles is

---

[105] In our production, this was a loud cough from the Old Man. (The cries from indoors in e.g. *Ai* and Euripides' *Medeia* show that noises from inside the wooden *skene* were easily heard outside.) Alternatively he can simply start to open the *skene* doors slowly and noisily.

[106] Kells 1973, 210: 'Like many mad people, she is hard-headed and cunning about achieving her ends.' We solved the practical problem of the urn by having Elektra hastily hand it to Pylades during 1323, before moving swiftly towards the back to escort the young men inside.

ready to inject him back into this scene whenever he wants to; but he holds him in reserve until now, to allow the recognition scene to explore Elektra's emotions to the full; and so the Old Man can recall Orestes, abruptly and decisively, to the fact that now is a critical time – they are in the greatest danger (1330); but also, right now is the moment for the deed (1337–8). So his intervention must be as forceful as possible, driving down the centre line to BC or C; his delivery must be clipped and aggressive, in total contrast to the languor and emotional indulgence of Elektra's 1301ff., as well as to her artificial attempt to play hostess. The Old Man's lines are primarily addressed to Orestes and Pylades, in keeping with his male orientation throughout the drama, and he only explicitly glances at Elektra with 1336, before returning to Orestes for 1337–8 and the sinister *stichomythia* to 1345.

Then Elektra, who has been left at some distance from this dialogue after moving R or L for 1323ff., suddenly crosses to Orestes and the Old Man and intervenes. When she finds out who the Old Man is, she once again ignores a request for restraint (1353), and launches into an extraordinary speech. After circling in rapture around the Old Man, she first fondles his hands and then abases herself to kiss his feet (1358). 'The picture is grotesque, were it not for the sinister delusion that it embodies.'[107] In our production the pragmatic Old Man was clearly discomfited, and disengaged from her during 1358. Elektra remained on her knees for 1359–61, as she expresses the gruesome truth that his words in Scene 3 have destroyed her. Then she stood for the final peroration; now she actually believes that in this old slave she sees Agamemnon himself returned (cf. 1316–17).

These are the signs of growing madness.[108] The Old Man first attempts to control Elektra. Then, turning abruptly to Orestes and Pylades, he returns to the moment. It is the *kairos* – for matricide, since the Old Man confirms at 1368ff. that Aigisthos is away. Klytaimestra is alone. Orestes and Pylades make a brief obeisance to the gods of the household, whose sacred place lies right in front of the doors, and then go inside.

Left alone with the Women, Elektra regains command of the *orchêstra*, and goes straight to the centre. Sophokles creates a parallel with the prayer which Klytaimestra made to Apollo in Scene 3, since both

---

[107] Kells 1973, 214.
[108] So rightly Kells 1973, 213.

women pray for the death of a *philos*.[109] So like Klytaimestra she should advance from C towards the altar, then kneel at the end of 1379 or during 1380; after her prayer she rises, and goes rapidly up the centre line to enter the *skene* for the first time in the drama, as soon as she has finished delivering 1383.[110]

Choros 5

A short but intense Choros, in which the Women express their extreme excitement in the moments before the deed.[111] The certainty that they expressed in Choros 2 returns even more strongly, now that Orestes is home;[112] so they no longer criticize Elektra for lack of wisdom, as in Choros 4; but still, both now and in the Finale, they stress the horror of the deed.

We danced this ode as a menacing movement from the periphery (at EFR and EFL) towards the palace, which ended with the *choros* fanned out just in front of C, facing the *skene* and waiting for the death-cry.

This Choros almost deliberately echoes the style and content of Choros 6 in Aischylos' *Libation Bearers*, sung after Aigisthos has gone into the house, in which Orestes and Pylades are waiting for him. In both dramas the *choros*' role is to whip up the tension, and make the audience expect that the deed will happen at once.

Finale

The Death of Klytaimestra The last words of the Choros were 'there is no more delay'. But there is. In Aischylos, Aigisthos' death-cry was heard as soon as the Choros ended. Here it is not: Elektra reappears, so that Sophokles can create his uniquely revolting vision of Klytaimes-

[109] Segal 1966, 525; Blundell 1978, 175. The Greek word for a prayer literally signified a boast. Petitioners needed to establish that they had either formerly benefited the god with material offerings, or were about to do so now, in return for the favours requested. Elektra has to remind Apollo that she has previously made many offerings because – having given her belt and lock of hair to Agamemnon in Scene 2 – she now has nothing but the rags she stands up in.

[110] Cf. Ley's Notes on the long-delayed and decisive entry into the *skene* in *Phil*, p. 241 below.

[111] The metre in the original Greek was predominantly dochmiac, the most agitated of lyric metres.

[112] If AI is sung by a soloist, she should be the same Woman who sang AI in Choros 2, once again anticipating fulfilment of a dream.

tra's death; a half-demented daughter, outside, shouts out her fury against her slaughtered mother and calls to her brother: 'if you can, strike twice as hard' (1415). Inside the palace, Orestes obliges.[113]

Sophokles counterbalanced the sheer emotional horror of this sequence by imposing a complex, controlling musical form.[114] Lines 1397–421 and 1422–41 are matching stanzas, strophe and antistrophe; but there are only six lines of lyrics in each. Twice Women of the choros break into song: for two lines in A1 after Klytaimestra's first cry, and in A2 when one of them sees Aigisthos coming in the distance; and then for four lines to close off each of the two sections. (We froze all the choros except the Woman who delivered the two two-line sections, but the whole choros danced during the two four-line conclusions.)

These stanzas consist predominantly of extremely excited and rapidly delivered spoken dialogue. The structure of the sentences is exactly the same in each stanza;[115] but the speakers do not respond exactly: Orestes begins by taking over Elektra's parts in A1, but then, at and after 1429a, he takes Klytaimestra's. This is because up to 1406/1427c Elektra in the A1 stanza, and Orestes in the A2 stanza, is the 'leader', describing what has happened inside; but then comes the Women's interjection of two sung lines, reacting to Klytaimestra's death and Aigisthos' arrival respectively; after that in A1 Klytaimestra, dying, leads the dialogue and Elektra responds, while in A2 Orestes, reacting to Aigisthos' appearance in the distance, leads both Elektra and the Women.

The dialogue pattern is the same, and the music and dance of the Women's two lyric contributions need to be the same; but it is not

---

[113] Cf. Seale 1982, 75: 'Elektra appears mentally, if not physically, to appropriate the act by the violence with which she wills it. It is her play and this horror is her affair . . .' (Contra Rehm 1996, 57: 'Elektra finds herself playing a role no bigger than that of bloodthirsty cheerleader' (!!).)
The contrast between Elektra's interjections and the climax in Aischylos, where a reluctant and morally articulate Orestes concludes 'you killed, and it was wrong; now suffer wrong' (Libation Bearers 930) before leading his mother in to her death, is absolute.

[114] This is the second radical experiment with lyric form in El; cf. Choros 3. Gardiner (1987, 138) interestingly suggests that background music might have been played during the spoken sections of these two stanzas, to signal that it is not just ordinary spoken dialogue, but part of a complex responding section including choral lyric.

[115] It is therefore clear that some lines have been lost after 1427 and 1429; I offer supplements for performance in square brackets.

possible to block the two stanzas identically. They open similarly, with first Elektra and then the bloodstained Orestes emerging from the *skene* and advancing to engage the Women in dialogue; but the second halves of the stanzas are skewed in two different directions. In A1, the focus on the skene increases as Elektra turns to make her savage ripostes to Klytaimestra's voice from inside it; but in A2 the dynamics have to change because Orestes is in the *orchêstra* (though there is neither time nor space for him to advance very far into it, so not past BC); and because the Woman's sighting of Aigisthos coming down the L *parodos* at 1428 turns the attention of both Elektra and Orestes in that direction. Then another Woman, she who in A1 faced outwards to express her grief for the city and the family in two lines of spoken dialogue (1413–14), turns to Orestes to tell him to go inside again (1433–4). Finally, the Women's four-line lyric advice to Elektra spurs the action relentlessly onward to Aigisthos' arrival, just as their first stanza at the end of A1, evoking how blood flows from blood, sped the action forward from the murder to Orestes' emergence with a blood-stained weapon.

Aigisthos   Aigisthos is characterized at the outset as the typical tyrant of tragedy: arrogant, gloating over Elektra at 1145–7, and using for his regime the same metaphor of horse and bridle which his namesake in Aischylos imposed on the Elders of Argos.[116] But he is lured to his death with a sadism worthy of Jacobean revenge tragedy. When he singles out Elektra at 1445, she approaches deferentially, and toys with him. Almost her every word has double meaning, and her irony becomes hideous in 1452, in the riddling wordplay on 'pleasant' and cognates (1455ff.), and above all in the last two lines (1464–5), which are delivered as or after Elektra crosses up-*orchêstra* to open the *skene* doors. Here Elektra gladly embraces both Chrysothemis' acceptance of the wisdom of yielding to the stronger, and Aigisthos' implication that 'might is right' – now that she knows that she and her side have superior might. The challenge for the actress here is to show Elektra's joy and fierce exultance in her impending triumph to the audience, while also showing that she can (just) hold these emotions in check (Aigisthos only once – and only partially – detects something unusual in her behaviour: 1456).

However, this Aigisthos is not a cardboard villain.[117] Only a very

---

[116] 1462–3; cf. Aischylos, *Agamemnon* 1639–41.

[117] Contrast the unmitigatedly arrogant and complacent Aigisthos in Aischylos, *Agamemnon* Scene 8 and *Libation Bearers* Scene 5.

few minutes remain before Sophokles' sudden, shocking and abrupt
ending; and in those minutes, from the moment at which the shrouded
corpse is brought out on the *ekkyklēma*, the audience's moral responses
are violently dislocated. Aigisthos greets what he believes to be the
corpse of his greatest enemy with reverence and respect (1466–9); he
does not gloat, as any Greek would have been entitled to.[118] Orestes
meanwhile matches his sister's brutal ironies (1474). When his enemies
have revealed themselves, Aigisthos asks to speak a few last words
(1482–3). Elektra, who has been standing at a distance from the three
men beside the *ekkyklēma*, suddenly crosses to her brother. In her final
speech (1483ff.), she vehemently implores Orestes not to allow Aigisthos this right, and also demands that he receive 'the kind of burial a
man like him deserves/out of our sight' – to my mind a clear allusion
to the tradition that the corpses of Klytaimestra and Aigisthos were
cast into the valley below Mykenai.[119] Orestes agrees, so the avengers
deny Aigisthos both a few last words, one of the few rudimentary
'human rights' recognized by the Greeks,[120] and also a decent burial, a
right – even for enemies – whose violation Sophokles had passionately
condemned in two surviving earlier tragedies.[121] Aigisthos then gets the
better of Orestes right through the *stichomythia*, from the splendid
challenge of 1493–4 through to the irony of 1503. And at the end
Orestes displays a sadistic vindictiveness (1504–5), and an even greater
degree of self-righteousness about the 'punishment' that he is imposing
than that of Elektra earlier (1506–8; cf. 580–84 and 1381–3).

The action reinforces the revolting character of the words. Two
silent men bring out a shrouded corpse, and refuse to uncover it;
Aigisthos is made first to expose for himself the body of his wife, and
then to confront his executioners – since Orestes and Pylades must
draw their daggers or swords during 1475. Aigisthos is now herded
towards the *skene*, coralled between the two men and the venomous,
Fury-like Elektra.[122] Then, as or after Pylades pushes Aigisthos inside,
Orestes should take up a dominant position, c or FC, to deliver his

[118] Kells 1973, 226–7 against Jebb 1894, 196.
[119] Pausanias 2.16.5. Already in Homer (*Odyssey* 3.259ff.) Aigisthos was left
to the dogs and the birds; cf. also Euripides, *Elektra* 896–8. *Contra* e.g. Bowra
1944, 254–5 and Segal 1966, 521.
[120] Kells 1973, citing e.g. Thoukydides, *Histories* 2.67.
[121] *Ai* and *Ant*.
[122] Elektra has a concealed knife, since she needed one to cut off her lock of
hair in Scene 2. In our production she produced it now, and menaced Aigisthos.

closing 'moral' to the audience, before following in complacent triumph.

The last three lines deliver a final shock to the audience; in this version of the legend, and this version alone, there is no hint that any future suffering lies in store for the matricides.[123] But Elektra has become progressively more demented, more insatiable in her revenge ever since Scene 5; and 'the abrupt concluding statement that the chain of revenge and suffering is at an end hardly dispels the inherent evil of the final situation.'[124] Here, as often in drama of all periods, the spoken words alone do not express the whole situation;[125] a performance must therefore bring out the ironic disjunction between the triumph in the text and the other, unspoken aspects of the situation. In our production, as the Woman danced optimistically towards Elektra, the protagonist – now BC beside the *ekkyklêma* – turned towards her, smearing herself with her mother's blood and laughing hysterically; the Woman backed away in horror as the performance ended. I do not claim that this is necessarily how Sophokles ended his own production, but I do assert that our final image brought out, expressionistically, the situation implied at the end of *Elektra*. And Sophokles certainly intended something of the kind, since he left the *ekkyklêma* outside the *skene* until after the last lines; then the *choros* departed in silence.[126]

[123] In 1509 the Woman literally begins 'O offspring of Atreus'; since Orestes has already departed, and never lost his liberty, my translation makes explicit the clear implication (cf. Segal 1966, 530) that Elektra is being addressed.

[124] Seale 1982, 78; cf. Segal 1966, 523–4 and 530–31. Again here at the end von Hofmannsthal expressed what Sophokles implied. In Strauss's opera Elektra (who is now barely sane, as in Sophokles) dances like a mainad to celebrate her victory – and dies at the climax of her dance. There is nothing more for her to live for, now that her revenge is complete.

[125] *Pace* esp. March 1996, 78–81.

[126] The Woman's deictic reference to 'this violence' at 1509 virtually guarantees that the *ekkyklêma* is still in place to the end (and when could it have been withdrawn, during the successive exits of Aigisthos, Pylades and Orestes?). For the similar end of Aischylos' *Agamemnon* cf. Ewans 1995, 153 and 159.

Philoktetes

GRAHAM LEY

Philoktetes offers us the first certain date (409 BC) for a surviving tragedy by Sophokles, but the impact of his presentation as a whole on that occasion cannot be clearly judged, because the titles of the tragedies and *satyr-drama* produced with it are unknown. The playwright was in his eighties, and died three years later, after writing *Oidipous at Kolonos*.[1]

Three Versions of the Myth

The critical response to *Philoktetes* has an unusually long history, and it is one which, in its earliest manifestation, goes at least some way to providing us with a dramaturgical context for the tragedy. The Greek sophist Dio Chrysostom, writing at the end of the first century of the Roman Empire, made a comparison (*synkrisis*) of the tragedies on Philoktetes by Aischylos, Sophokles and Euripides.[2] Euripides' *Philoktetes* is known to have been produced in 431 BC, along with his surviving *Medeia* and another, lost tragedy, *Diktys*: this confirms that Sophokles wrote last.

The comparison by Dio offers an impression of the version by Aischylos. Odysseus came to Philoktetes in person, and was unrecognized by him. Odysseus himself convinced Philoktetes that Agamemnon was dead and the Greek army was destroyed, and he included in this extended fiction his own supposed execution for a crime. Since Dio adds that Philoktetes told his own story and described his misery

---

[1] The fact that nothing is known about the companion-pieces to any of Sophokles' surviving tragedies removes any sense of what Sophokles might have intended with a full presentation, and coincidentally renders the fragments less interesting than they might have been. For the fragments, see the recent edition by Lloyd-Jones (1996), which includes the sparse and unrevealing remnants (about six lines in total) of *Philoktetes at Troy*. There is no particular reason to suppose that this tragedy was presented with *Philoktetes*; in this connection, it should be remembered that *Antigone* was quite certainly written long before *Oidipous at Kolonos*. The lapse of the connected trilogy after the death of Aischylos made this non-sequential use of aspects of a myth by playwrights unexceptional.

[2] There is a full translation of Dio's comparison in Russell and Winterbottom 1972, 504-7.

directly to a *choros* of Lemnians, it is not difficult to imagine a tragedy composed by Aischylos for two actors, and so one that may date to the period before the introduction of the *skene*.[3]

In addition to what he says in his comparison of the three tragedians, Dio also wrote what appears to be a prose paraphrase of the opening of Euripides' *Philoktetes*.[4] In Euripides' version, it seems that Odysseus came to Lemnos with Diomedes, and was disguised by Athena (his voice and appearance were changed) for his confrontation with Philoktetes. Dio's paraphrase includes some interesting details: Odysseus was frightened by Philoktetes' appearance as he approached, 'moving along in pain and with difficulty', was threatened by Philoktetes with the bow, and was invited into Philoktetes' lodging, which contained 'bandages soaked in seepage from the wound'. There is also a warning about the dire company that Philoktetes provides when the disease afflicts him, and all these elements are found, redisposed, in Sophokles' version. Euripides also introduced a Lemnian who was sympathetic to Philoktetes, alongside a *choros* of Lemnians, and made the plot hinge on the arrival of a Trojan embassy seeking Philoktetes' aid in winning the war.[5]

For Euripides, in his presentation in 431 BC, *Philoktetes* may have picked up the theme of injustice, isolation and desertion so prominent in *Medeia*, herself a figure capable of delivering pain or salvation by means of superhuman powers. What is known of the other tragedy, *Diktys*, confirms that it contained an oppressive ruler and a stateless woman, who is at least supported by a kindly local inhabitant, which offers thematic connections from *Diktys* to *Medeia* and *Philoktetes* respectively.[6] The disguising of Odysseus by Athena, and Odysseus'

---

[3] Calder (1970) reviewed the evidence for the version by Aischylos. For the performance of tragedies by Aischylos before and after the introduction of the *skene*, see the introductions by Ewans (1996, xxiii–xxv; and 1995, xxv–xxvii) in earlier volumes of this series.

[4] Dio Chrysostom, *Discourse 59*; a literal translation, alongside the Greek text, is available in Lamar Crosby 1946.

[5] Dio's comparison is considered by Jebb 1898, xiii–xx. Webster's tentative reconstruction of Euripides' *Philoktetes* (1967, 57–61) will be reviewed in a new evaluation of the evidence, in the second volume of an edition and translation of the texts of the more substantial fragments of Euripides (the sequel to Collard, Cropp and Lee 1995).

[6] Appropriate speculation on the plot of *Diktys* is provided by Webster 1967, 61–4. Further links are apparent: for example, the ambition of Odysseus, openly expressed in Dio's prose version, is strongly suggestive of the ambitious aspirations revealed by and of Iason in *Medeia*. There is, as one might expect within

apprehensions that he may none the less be recognized by the 'wild' and possibly deranged man he is about to confront, strongly recall the opening of Sophokles' *Aias*.

Dio's comparison enhances our understanding of Sophokles' tragedy, because it emphasizes Sophokles' compositional choices in the context of previous dramas based on the same myth. The friendly Lemnian of Euripides is remarkably developed into the ambivalent figure of Neoptolemos, who faces both ways; astonishingly, Sophokles substitutes Achilleus' young son for the hardened Diomedes of the established myth.[7] The decisive intervention of a Trojan embassy in Euripides is transformed into the deceptive appearance of the 'Merchant', supposedly bringing news of the threatening 'embassies' despatched against both Neoptolemos and Philoktetes. Sophokles also increases the acute sense of betrayal and isolation, which undoubtedly characterized Euripides' complete presentation of 431 BC, by changing the identity of the *choros* characters, who are now Greek sailors; this highlights their cautious sympathy, by determining a clear alienation of their loyalty from Philoktetes.

Critical Views

Dio commended all three tragedies, while praising Sophokles for 'combining great charm with sublimity and dignity'.[8] But the loss of the versions by Aischylos and Euripides later in antiquity left Sophokles' drama to survive in isolation, and for the German enlightenment his *Philoktetes* became important for its presentation of pain. The art historian Winckelmann contended that classicism showed restraint in both its fine arts and its theatre; Lessing contested this strongly in his *Laocoon* (1766). For Lessing, Sophokles' tragedy was not ashamed to

the presentation, a contrast: while Iason is crudely unaware of the potential backlash, Odysseus self-consciously laments the dangers and difficulties in which ambition lands him.

[7] The Lemnian of Euripides' *Philoktetes* is significant because he is the first supportive individual in any version. Homer's *Iliad* offers a brief reference to the marooning of Philoktetes on Lemnos (*Iliad* 2.721ff.), and suggests that the Greeks will soon miss him. The later epics, the *Cypria* and the *Little Iliad* (particularly the latter) provided the substance of the myth, including the prophecy of Helenos, but with Diomedes on his own bringing Philoktetes to Troy, while Odysseus fetched Neoptolemos from Skyros. For a convenient summary of these sources, see Webster 1970, 2–3.

[8] Russell and Winterbottom 1972, 507.

reveal extreme pain finding its voice, and he insisted that the theatricality of the tragedy contained moments where its expression was dominant. The visual and physical quality of Philoktetes' appalling wound,
when combined with his social isolation, produced a particularly
intense form of sympathy in the audience, one which contemporary
theories of a decorous classicism falsely eliminated.[9]

Lessing's belief that the Greeks were not ashamed to express pain
and sorrow was alert to literary qualities apparent as early as the *Iliad*,
and indeed, Homer's short reference to Philoktetes (*Iliad* 2.718-25)
lays a great emphasis on this aspect of his condition. Whatever their
views, the eighteenth-century critics were aware that the theatricality
of *Philoktetes* was, in this respect, comparable to *Young Women of
Trachis*; and Lessing's insight might be extended by modern commentators to Kreon at the close of *Antigone*, Oidipous in *Oidipous the
King*, and Elektra in *Elektra*. In his strictures against tragedy, Plato
had established a philosophical emphasis on composure, which was
confirmed by Stoicism in particular; this required critical insistence
before it was displaced by an acknowledgement of the subtleties and
power of theatrical sympathy.

In the twentieth century *Philoktetes* has again played a significant
role in the evolution of the critical appreciation of tragedy. *The Wound
and the Bow* was the title-essay of a collection by the important
American critic Edmund Wilson, in which he promoted *Philoktetes* to
modern attention. For Wilson, 'the people of the *Philoctetes* seem to us
more familiar than they do in most of the other Greek tragedies', and
he explicitly followed the implications of Lessing's argument in rejecting the academic tradition that interpreted Sophokles as 'a model . . .
of coolness and restraint'.[10] Instead, Wilson acknowledged that Sophokles 'shows himself particularly successful with people whose natures
have been poisoned by narrow and fanatical hatreds', and in regard to
Philoktetes he detected a 'general and fundamental idea: the conception
of superior strength as inseparable from disability'. So the human
sympathy felt by Neoptolemos ends by linking the fateful weapon
inseparably to the man himself. Sophokles, according to Wilson, had a
'special insight into morbid psychology', an attitude that was 'clinical'

[9] Lessing had in mind here *The Theory of Moral Sentiments* by Adam Smith
as well as Winckelmann. His own, radical contentions were later opposed by
Herder and Schlegel; the controversy is partly represented in Dawe 1996, 81-99.

[10] Wilson 1941, 275 and 293 respectively.

in comparison to Aischylos and Euripides, and a 'cool observation of the behavior of psychological derangements'.[11]

Much of the criticism after the Second World War followed lines established or suggested by Wilson; the nature of 'heroism' and individualism in Sophokles became a consistent subject for study, alongside the playwright's 'humanism'.[12] There were also studies of technique, which interpreted Sophokles as a craftsman for the theatre, and dismissed literary readings which failed to take account of the imperatives of successful performance.[13] But *Philoktetes* figured prominently again in a further adjustment of approaches by the French critic, Vidal-Naquet, who with Vernant initiated perhaps the most influential tendency in tragic criticism in recent years. In his essay 'Sophocles' *Philoktetes* and the Ephebeia', Vidal-Naquet presented a structuralist view of the drama which aligned the 'mutation of its heroes' (he also uses the term 'transformation') with the Athenian institution of the *ephebeia*, which 'transformed' a boy into a man.[14] So Vidal-Naquet interpreted the *eremia* – signifying 'wild and distant countryside', and 'uncultivated land' – as distinctively that space in which the *ephebes* were expected to undergo duty, on the borders of the Athenian state. This 'wild world' exists between two others in the tragedy, the world of battle and that of the family home, and a choice must be made in the *eremia* between these two destinations.[15] In this interpretation, by its close the tragic action has accomplished two objectives: 'the wild man has been reintegrated in the city; the ephebe has become a hoplite' – the armed and patriotic soldier that a boy should become.[16] Contemporary concerns have added attention to the place of the tragedy in the Greek value system of 'helping friends and harming enemies', and to the literary precedent of the embassy to Achilleus in Homer's *Iliad* (Book 9), in which Aias, Odysseus and Phoinix attempt to induce an

[11] *Ibid.*, 287 and 290 respectively.

[12] Notably Whitman 1951 and Knox 1964. In his definition of the 'Sophoclean hero', Knox laid particular emphasis on alienation, and on the projection of that desolation into the situation of Philoktetes on Lemnos.

[13] Waldock 1951 and Kitto 1956; they continued a strain of criticism initiated by Wilamowitz (1917).

[14] Vernant and Vidal-Naquet 1981. Vidal-Naquet's essay had first appeared in French in 1971, and his initial work on the *ephebeia* was published in both French and English in 1968.

[15] *Ibid.*, 179.

[16] *Ibid.*, 187.

intransigent Achilleus to return his decisive strength to the battle against Troy.[17]

One neglected aspect of this drama is the extraordinary impression conveyed by Sophokles that Philoktetes is like a man who has died, in his ignorance of what has happened to the living. So his questions about the fate of warriors at Troy recall in some part the questions posed by and to Odysseus in Haides in Homer's *Odyssey* (Book 11), with a particular irony, since in the 'Nekuia' the dead Achilleus asks after and is informed by Odysseus about the exploits of his son Neoptolemos, who answers the questions in *Philoktetes*.[18]

In this drama Odysseus displays extraordinary theatrical abilities. The motif of disguise, which was given in Euripides' *Philoktetes* the form it takes in Sophokles' *Aias*, is brilliantly elaborated by Odysseus in the surviving *Philoktetes*. Odysseus is a playmaker, a contriver of a scenario, of action and plot to a dramatic purpose, like the kind of 'hero' (Dikaiopolis in *Acharnians*, Trygaios in *Peace*, and Lysistrate) that Aristophanes shaped for comedy. Sophokles had himself set partial precedents in Aias, Deianeira, and indeed Oidipous; but the technique is greatly developed, with a subtlety that is not evident and not required in the relatively simple 'play-acting' and revelation of Orestes in *Elektra*.[19] Neoptolemos is primed for his part, and left to improvise, and the only other character, the 'Merchant', is introduced to the scene to contribute to a fiction, costumed and taught his lines by the playwright-director Odysseus.[20] The fact that Odysseus then intervenes in his own play, apparently to no useful effect, and the action has to be resolved by a former tragic character made divine, suggests in Sophokles a complex of perceptions about his own artistry.

[17] Respectively, Blundell 1989, and the criticism offered by Rabel 1997 and Beye 1970.

[18] Others have drawn attention to different aspects of a close relationship with Homer's *Odyssey*: Fuqua 1976, Garner 1990, Davidson 1995, and Segal, who explores (1981, 297ff.) the link between Philoktetes and the Cyclops, Polyphemos.

[19] But see Ewans (above, p. 200) on the Old Man's 'messenger-speech'.

[20] Knox (1964, 190 n. 23) was scornful of Waldock's view that Sophokles himself was 'improvising' as he created/wrote this drama (Waldock 1951, ch. x 'Sophocles Improvises: the *Philoctetes*', 196–217). But the theatricalism sensed by Waldock deserves some redirected attention; we see Odysseus rehearsing performers into their parts, giving one (Neoptolemos) only a scenario and a story, and the other (the 'Merchant') a costume and a fairly complete script.

The Actors and their Roles

The demands on performers in *Philoktetes* are unusual in several respects. First, the tragedy has no female characters. Second, both the leading and the second actors maintain a single role throughout the drama, which depends almost totally on their interaction. This formal structure is not, substantially, similar to the early two-actor form of tragedy, which as far as we can see had no propensity to keep its two performers together in the acting area.[21] So, although thematically Neoptolemos is the type of an *ephebos* and warrior-in-learning, the role is intensely demanding, and not one for an apprentice. Third, the remaining actor is faced not only by all the demands for changes in costume and character, playing Odysseus, the 'Merchant', and Herakles, but also by two unusually abrupt and short interventions as Odysseus (see below).

The role of Philoktetes requires the ability to sing, and to give a formidably expressive representation of a man in physical agony, which is clearly related to that of Herakles in *Young Women of Trachis*. The Lookout who accompanies Odysseus and Neoptolemos in the opening scene has almost the status of a silent mask, but one that later speaks, as the 'Merchant'; yet the requirements of performance mean that the silent Lookout was played by an extra, and his mask was taken by the third actor later, to play the 'Merchant'. Two extras at least are required at another point, to arrive with Odysseus and pinion Philoktetes when he threatens suicide, and one earlier acts as a guide to the 'Merchant'. Calling any of these figures, or the *choros* character, 'sailors' perhaps creates an artificial distinction in the minds of a modern audience, since these are soldiers of the Greek army at Troy.[22] But it is perhaps preferable, because it constantly recalls to us the presence of a ship, which is plainly essential to the tension of the tragedy.

Scene 1

The opening of *Philoktetes* provides an immediate definition of the acting area within a generic setting, that of a cave and its environs.

[21] The deployment of the Scout in *Seven against Thebes* and Pelasgos in *Suppliants* by Aischylos reveals no interest in keeping either character uninterruptedly in front of the audience.

[22] I agree with Gardiner (1987, 16ff.) here rather than Burton (1980, 6 and 226).

This setting is exploited for tragedy, *satyr-drama* and comedy, and it seems plausible to assume it was created by scene-painting, and perhaps by minimal construction, notably around the central door in the *skene*.[23] One of three actors identifies the acting area as Lemnos and one of his companions as Neoptolemos, the son of Achilleus. Gradually, through his initial account, and decisively when Neoptolemos replies to him, we gather that he is Odysseus; it is possible that his costume may have provided some suggestions, since Odysseus is often pictured wearing a felt cap.

It is clear from the script that Odysseus invites Neoptolemos to look around for a cave, and that Neoptolemos then quickly finds it, away from Odysseus. Neoptolemos also looks inside the cave, and then is told to send his follower, the third figure, to keep a lookout on the track. In our workshop we developed the suggestions I had earlier made in print,[24] and made Odysseus and Neoptolemos arrive in the *orchêstra* from the L *parodos*, looking out towards the audience; Odysseus remained at LC, while Neoptolemos ranged round to ERC during Odysseus' introduction. This then permitted Neoptolemos suddenly to observe the cave to his left, on the façade of the *skene*, and to approach it swiftly while Odysseus withdrew in apprehension to EFL. However the cave was actually represented or constructed, it presumably made use of the opening in the façade provided by the main doors, and Neoptolemos may peer into this. As soon as it is plain that the cave is empty, at 31, we had Odysseus draw a little closer to the *skene* at BL, and we made Neoptolemos come away from the cave after he has inspected it (by 39), to BR. It seemed to us that the Lookout would have waited by the L *parodos*, where his mask would be visible, and we felt that the 'track' (48) he is sent to guard was the one by which all three had entered; towards the close of the scene, Odysseus says he will go back to the ship and send the Lookout back too, which suggests that he will pass him (124–5).

For the exchange between Odysseus and Neoptolemos, we felt that

[23] On scene-painting, see Ley 1989, and the references to sources there. Caves appear regularly in illustrations of dramatic scenes on vases: for example, plate 6 in Ley 1991 (Euripides' *Antiope*), with the brief discussion attached at 96–7.

[24] In Ley 1988 I gave what I called a 'scenic plot' of the script of *Philoktetes*, looking at how the drama may have been performed: the opening was discussed in the introduction at 87, and later, in the commentary, at 95–6. Seale 1982 also concludes in favour of a setting indicated by scene-painting (27), but suggests that Odysseus 'leads the way' and then 'lurks in the background' (28); these instructions are hard to interpret in terms of the Greek acting area.

Odysseus would not confront the younger man directly, and so we brought Odysseus forward to C, which allows him a strong position from which to communicate the (literal as well as metaphorical) plot to the audience. Yet, with Neoptolemos behind him, his position is not as secure as it might seem, so we brought Neoptolemos across from BR to BL by the middle of the speech; by the end he was facing out at BL. His reply was delivered as he moved forward to FL. As the *stichomythia* gathered intensity, Neoptolemos finally came towards Odysseus at C, perhaps at 106, but Odysseus withdrew to FR, leaving Neoptolemos 'on the spot' at C. We brought the two together at C, climactically, for the crucial announcements at 114–15, when Neoptolemos faces the fact that his *kleos* – the glory of taking Troy – will totally depend on having the bow. By the end of the scene, Neoptolemos is left in the empty space, with an uncomfortable commitment to lie, rather than persuade or use force.

It could not be clear to the audience from the exchanges in this scene whether Philoktetes' presence at Troy or the possession of his bow was more important.[25] The implication is that Neoptolemos will gain Philoktetes' sympathy, and take him with him supposedly on a journey 'home' to Greece and away from Troy. The plan is not fully spelled out, but the point of the deception – that Neoptolemos has quarrelled with the Greek leaders and is sailing home – must be that Philoktetes will want to seize the chance to go with him. Odysseus is to be kept away from Philoktetes, but how he would be later is not remotely clear; is there more than one ship?[26] The audience might well be a little confused by this opening, not least because in the epic story Odysseus fetched Neoptolemos to Troy separately from Philoktetes, while Aischylos and Euripides had included Odysseus in the embassy to Philok-

[25] There is, of course, no explicit reference to a prophecy at this point. But the firm assertions that the Greeks will suffer without the bow (66–7), and that Troy will not be taken without the bow (68–9) or the bow and Philoktetes (112–15) would undoubtedly sound to Greek ears like the conditional results established in oracular or prophetic utterances. It would be natural to assume, as an audience member, that Odysseus was in command of information of which Neoptolemos was ignorant.

[26] Odysseus refers to 'the ship' at 132, which suggests that he shares one with Neoptolemos and the crew, of whom part from the *choros*. The fact that Sophokles has not troubled to make this circumstantial detail clear suggests we should beware of a critical literalism in interpretations of the drama. In other words, we might need to adjust our impression of the questions that a majority of the Athenian audience would be inclined to ask during their experience of a tragedy.

tetes, exploiting the contrast between their characters and values.[27] Modern commentators generally assume that the element of deception is confined to the idea of a quarrel between Neoptolemos and the generals. But one challenging and subversive interpretation suggests that Neoptolemos has not yet even been to Troy, and so has not received his father's armour from Odysseus; in this interpretation, the whole of the story is a fiction.[28]

Choros 1

The system of this entry-song, alternating song (from the *choros*) and chant (from Neoptolemos), is one that Sophokles used in the first Choros of *Antigone* and of *Elektra*, except that in *Antigone* the *choros* performs both song and chant. Whether we should think of an alternating pattern of dance (with the song) and measured movement (with the chant) is a difficult question. Sophokles used a similar system again in the entry-song in *Oidipous at Kolonos*, and there it is plain that eventually Oidipous does move (192ff.), but apparently only step by step, helped by Antigone;[29] for sequences of this kind, conclusions on performance drawn from the text and metre are extremely difficult.

The *choros* either comes into the *orchêstra* and sings, or comes in singing, and they will come either from the *parodos* used so far, or from both.[30] It is interesting to speculate how they were costumed, particularly whether they were armed, which would certainly be plausible. It is tempting to place Neoptolemos at C, and have the *choros* positioned in an arc behind him, or in two groups to either side of him. The one strong indication in the script is the direct reference to the *skene* from 159ff., and it is hard to imagine a *choros* that did not look

---

[27] The surviving ancient summary of the epic poem *Little Iliad* provides the early version.

[28] Calder 1971: he is impatient with the criticism that sees Neoptolemos as a decent young man who just tells a few little lies.

[29] See the commentary by McCart below, p. 259–61.

[30] A modern sense of plausibility would argue that they all should arrive from the same direction as the actors, from the ship, and so from the same *parodos*; but cf. McCart on *OKing* Choros 2, in Ewans 1999, 273 n. 25. It is tempting to leave Neoptolemos briefly alone in the space before they arrive, to confirm his sole responsibility for the task of deception that lies ahead. Some have felt that the *choros* might be present from the beginning of the tragedy (e.g. Webster 1970, 66 and 79): the weak case for this is discussed at length and dismissed by Gardiner 1987, 14–16.

towards the *skene* at that point. That would give a basic scheme: the Sailors' first focus would be on Neoptolemos (A1), then on the wider *orchêstra* as the immediate environs ('For now, look around without fear . . .', 144–6), with the questioning about the actual abode in A2 followed by its identification, in a sequence somewhat reminiscent of the opening scene. The pair of *strophe* and *antistrophe* B1 and B2 is not separated by any interjection from Neoptolemos, and has no local focus, since the speculation is on the absent Philoktetes and his way of life, effectively in the wild.

The concluding part of the *parodos* then responds to the stimulus of sound, and agitation and uncertainty are explicit (C1 and C2).[31] The dance for C1 should surely reflect these qualities, in a futile search for the source of the sound 'in the distance' (208). In our workshop we felt that the obvious final position for the Sailors would be away from the *skene* and both *parodoi*, in groups at FL and FR, with Neoptolemos at FC, all facing towards the back. Both C1 and C2 are clearly bound up with the entry of Philoktetes, and I shall discuss them in connection with Scene 2.

Scene 2

The entry of Philoktetes himself brings together a number of questions about presentation, at the same time as it establishes some essential thematic qualities of the tragedy. Philoktetes has been deprived of human society, and the physical embodiment of that is the poverty of his material resources, his divorce from the fruits of agriculture, his juxtaposition to the life of wild animals, and the symbolic as well as literal limitation of his disability and its repugnance for other men. His location on the margins, in the equivalent of a beast's lair rather than a constructed home, in what is specifically a non-cultivated and unin-habited landscape, emphasize that the direction of the tragedy will be concerned with the possibilities of his reintegration. His position is not that of the exile, who will welcome a call to return home to civic rights; he might himself now be 'wild', and irredeemably so. As such, he may be infused with some of the characteristics of Polyphemos, the

---

[31] Burton (1980, 229) notes what he calls a 'circular or ABA construction' in the entry-songs of both *Philoktetes* and *Oidipous at Kolonos*, describing the changes more closely in this case as being 'from absorption in the plot to contemplation and then back again to alert suspense'. I find the attentiveness of the Sailors rather more vivid than that description generally suggests.

anthropoid monster of the *Odyssey*, and be just as dangerous and intractable.[32]

The nearest surviving Sophoklean precedent is Aias, who sought the margins after insult had led him to confuse the worlds of men and beasts. The difference is that the pleading for Aias' reintegration came after his resolute suicide, whereas Philoktetes must be faced alive, because he is enduring, fortified by insult and exclusion, but not demoralized by shame. Dramatically, this is the compelling force of his myth; a culture rarely faces up directly to its own powers of marginalization. This dramatic subject is at the heart of tragedy's concern with language as significant social action, and, in the circumstances, the vital instrument of persuasion is inevitably drawn into the mode of deceit.[33] Yet with such a confrontation, it is perfectly possible that neither force, nor persuasion, nor deceit will be adequate to the task. The society may simply not possess the means to encompass what it has defined as being outside its own limits.

It would be immensely helpful to be sure of how Philoktetes was introduced to the acting area, but unfortunately Sophokles has not made this explicit in his script.[34] We can be sure of the cave, and analogies with Aristophanes' *Birds* and Euripides' *Kyklops* at least show that the symbolism of the cave as the wild place at the cultural margin was familiar to comedy and satyr-drama as well as tragedy.[35] Similarly, the costume of Philoktetes, which will be so manifestly contrasted to the ordered, military clothing of the Sailors and of Neoptolemos, indicates rejection and marginalization in a mode quite familiar to tragedy; Aristophanes' parody of the Euripidean 'anti-hero'

[32] Some of the most expansive thematic criticism comes from Segal 1981; he compares Philoktetes and Polyphemos at 297 and 300.

[33] Persuasion is specifically studied by Buxton 1982, and has been a leading problem in criticism since Kitto 1956, who notes usefully in this context that 'the essential meaning of the verb peithein is not "to persuade" but to "win over"' (97). Most recent contributions concentrate on the final role of Herakles (p. 253–4 below, with references).

[34] It is worth noting here that a similar uncertainty attends the intervention of Herakles at the close of the drama: Sophokles' script does not include any description of the visual event, which is unusual. Cf. Euripides, *Orestes* 1625ff. but contrast e.g. *Andromache* 1226ff., *Ion* 1549ff., *Elektra* 1233ff.

[35] Detailed discussion at Ley 1988, 111–15. Craik 1990 mentions the context briefly before (eccentrically) advocating the use of the roof of the *skene* in *Phil* and Aristophanes' *Birds*.

in rags in *Acharnians* leaves that in no doubt.[36] But there are two issues that pose problems for theatrical realization: that of movement and immobility in the portrayal of Philoktetes and the action of the tragedy; and (of lesser importance) the use of the *skene* to represent both the cave and a cliff-face.

The lesser problem concerns the reference to the double (or twin) mouth of the cave, which Dale suggested allowed for a front and back entrance, one visible in the façade of the *skene*, and one imagined to exist at its rear.[37] This suggestion has been combined with an interpretation of the references to sound only in the final section of the entry-song of the *choros* to create a partial consensus, about a supposed *coup de théâtre* by which Philoktetes first appears at the *skene* doors.[38] The text and sense of 146–9 do not help to settle this, since they contain a word that refers to his 'wandering' on a path, and also a reference to his abode, and the text has justifiably provoked discussion.[39] Similarly, a Sailor's idea (156) that 'he may surprise me, appearing suddenly from somewhere' must be reconciled with what follows almost immediately, namely Neoptolemos' conviction that 'he is ploughing his way/along somewhere near to this spot in search of food' (162–3).

The problem with a *coup de théâtre* of the supposed kind is that it seems to lack a clear function; it also removes the possibility of the audience appreciating Philoktetes' pain and disability in the sheer difficulty of moving, in favour of his making a sudden, pathos-laden appearance. The *coups de théâtre* that are achieved by revelation at the central doors of the *skene* seem to me to be shocking in a different way: the revelation of havoc (Euripides' *Herakles* and Sophokles' *Aias*) or of triumphant and vindictive murder (twice in Aischylos' *Oresteia*).

[36] Of course, the ultimate precedent for the hero in rags was Odysseus himself, in the *Odyssey*.

[37] Dale 1969, 119–29, esp. 127–9.

[38] Those accepting Dale's suggestion of an initial appearance from the cave include Kamerbeek 1980, 9–10; Taplin 1987 (after some earlier doubts); and Seale 1982, 31. The germ of the idea goes back to Woodhouse 1912, 243–4, who also has Herakles appear from the cave (248).

[39] Jebb (1989, 33–4) and Lloyd-Jones and Wilson (1990, 182) offer the most sober discussions. As Lloyd-Jones and Wilson remark, in contradicting the idea that Philoktetes appears from the cave, 'the word used to describe him reminds the audience that he will be coming from a distance' (182): the Greek word is *hodites* (literally 'wayfarer' or 'traveller'), and is Homeric. I have used 'wanderer' in the translation, because the important idea is that Philoktetes is out on the track away from home, rather than that he is making a journey.

Of course, not all theatrical effects are related, but I cannot see the value of him popping up simply to surprise the Sailors; it seems like the resource of a different kind of theatre.

I therefore suggest that Philoktetes arrived very slowly down the R *parodos*.[40] This is how the feared Polyphemos arrives in Euripides' *Kyklops* to Odysseus, Silenos and the Satyrs, and in Dio Chrysostom's paraphrase of Euripides' *Philoktetes* Odysseus remarks that Philoktetes is approaching, 'moving along in pain and with difficulty'. In Sophokles' script there is no such commentary, yet the sound of Philoktetes approaching is 'just like/the voice of a man who has to force/his way along . . .' (205–7). The cave has been repeatedly declared empty, and the R *parodos* has not been used; indeed, it would not be used at all in this drama, if Philoktetes did not use it now. If the L *parodos* is associated plainly with the ship and the shore, the R might readily be associated with the hinterland, the wild, and Philoktetes' isolated life on Lemnos.[41] The calls from Philoktetes are heard first, and I suspect that there is then silence, as Philoktetes drags himself towards the *orchêstra*. In our workshop, Philoktetes used his first lines intermittently as he approached, with pauses for taking breath, but also knowing that he would not risk drawing near to the group. So even by the close of his first speech, the actor had not moved beyond the edge of the *orchêstra* at BR.

[40] Those who have shared this view include Jebb 1898, 45 (his stage direction for Philoktetes' entry), Robinson 1969, Davidson 1990, and – by implication – Lloyd-Jones and Wilson 1990. Criticizing the idea of an entry from the mouth of the cave, Davidson comments that 'such an arrangement would not facilitate the portrayal of Philoktetes' lameness at his first appearance' (308). Davidson also convincingly notes (30) a Homeric precedent for the cave with two mouths and a spring, in the Naiads' cave on Ithake, in *Odyssey* 13.109–11; this parallel was adduced earlier by Segal (1981, 359–60). Since this is the exact point of Odysseus' landfall in Ithake, after ten years of wandering, the connotations are thoroughly appropriate to a drama of traumatic reintegration, for which the climax will also be the triumphant use of a great bow.

[41] Despite determining that in *Philoktetes* one side indicates 'wilderness' and the other 'civilization', in accordance with his strict structuralist scheme for the lateral axis in the Athenian theatre, Wiles perversely assumes that the wilderness side is not used for the entry of Philoktetes (Wiles 1997, 153–4, with n. 73). This side is either used, momentously, for the arrival of Philoktetes, or it is not used in the performance at all, since characters otherwise all arrive or leave by the path leading to the ship. I can think of no plausible reason why Sophokles should have decided not to use arrivals from one side of his theatre throughout this drama, especially if that side carries the relevant and potent significance that Wiles would ascribe to it.

Neoptolemos and the Sailors may withdraw to the front perimeter of the *orchêstra* while Philoktetes approaches, or may show further signs of apprehension during his greeting to them. There can be little doubt that the speech is punctuated, not merely by the approach I have suggested, but by the failure of the visitors to respond, which prompts Philoktetes to increasingly pitiable pleas for human communication. So it is to Neoptolemos' credit, whatever we may feel about his motives, that he breaks ranks to speak.[42] Theatre semiologists might well enjoy the distinct activity of the signifying systems of costume and language at this moment in communicating 'Greekness'. The costumes exchange their dialogue immediately, but Philoktetes has to wait for the answering sound to his own; conversely, Philoktetes looks like a wild man, but his speech contradicts that visual impression or prejudice immediately.

In fact, the ease and simplicity of Sophokles' control of immensely powerful feelings in this scene is remarkable. The word for 'stranger', *xenos*, carries all the appropriate ambivalence; probably Greek and unknown, but perhaps not Greek, and containing within that fluctuation of possibility the reciprocity of 'guest' and 'host', another familiar function of the term. The facility of the change to 'my son' is a superb illustration of the shift in feelings that occurs once a common ethnicity is established, and Neoptolemos' required statement of paternity registers a further escalation of warmth and emotion. In return, Philoktetes' declaration of his own identity leads not just to the revelation of the source of intense physical pain, but to a fraught relationship with 'Greekness', in his own conditions of life and in his inevitable response to those Greeks who have imposed them on him. The result of all this is 'pity', as expressed by the Sailors (317–18), and sympathy in the supposed experience or harsh treatment of Neoptolemos by the Greeks, as he recounts and invents it. Aristotle understood pity as a significant component of the emotional appeal of tragedy, and both Plato and Aristotle knew that sympathy was dependent on a sense of similarity, a disturbance to which democratic feeling was perhaps all the more

---

[42] '. . . that Philoktetes includes them all in his first address . . . could suggest that at the end of the final antistrophe they are grouped around Neoptolemos, who only steps forward from them at line 232': Gardiner 1987, 21. Seale 1982, 32 mentions the 'physical recoil of both Neoptolemos and the Chorus' (225–6), although Philoktetes may be acknowledging the position they have previously taken up, rather than their reaction at that moment.

prone.[43] The mark of genius in this deceptively simple yet intricate composition is that the pity and the sympathy are in one sense feigned, subject to a motive by which Philoktetes is made once again a victim. Properly understood, it is a scene that might lead anyone to despair.

The physical tension in the scene is not imported by performance to a verbal art of feeling and expression, but is explicit in what we know and are given to see. Philoktetes will limp, or drag his foot, and it is plain – if only from the later parts of the drama, to those who are frightened of physicality – that these features as well as his appearance make him a pariah. Sophokles repeatedly emphasizes the idea of stench, and the thought that it might be unbearable; revulsion would not have seemed as intolerable to the Athenians as it does to the liberal and safely sanitized conscience of the modern west.[44] If Philoktetes is aware of revulsion, and its dangers to this occasion of humane exchange, as his opening remarks must indicate, then he will be seen by the audience to be wary of approaching too closely to the Sailors or to Neoptolemos. For his part, if he is to gain the bow, or Philoktetes' confidence, Neoptolemos knows he must at some point come close to Philoktetes, and this the audience must also know or expect. The Sailors are under no such imperative, since their presence alone is indicative of support for their general.

If Neoptolemos detaches himself from the *choros* on his first response to Philoktetes, both he and Philoktetes are theoretically free to approach each other, as familiarity is established through patronymics. Yet although 'son of Achilleus' (241) is immediately meaningful to Philoktetes, Philoktetes himself remains, supposedly, unfamiliar to Neoptolemos. So in our workshop we had Neoptolemos move to the side at ELC as he responds to Philoktetes, while Philoktetes despite his increasing excitement remained at EBR. During the first part of his self-introduction (from 254 to 284) he might gradually approach C, facing Neoptolemos, but then withdraw, either on a lateral to FR, or back towards EBR. We found that by the close of this first section he should have returned to

[43] I am referring, of course, to Plato's fear of the effects of sympathy in Book 10 of *Republic* (605cff.), and Aristotle's commentaries on pity and related issues in *Poetics* (49b27, 52a2–53b22) and in *Rhetoric* (b85b11ff.). I have discussed these issues at some length in the first part of Ley 1999.

[44] Stephens 1995 offers a salutary reminder that the action of the Greeks in expelling Philoktetes would hardly have seemed so unacceptable to an Athenian audience: Philoktetes' cries were monstrous, and his incurable wound stank unbearably. Stephens emphasizes that this proved to be a religious as well as a public problem, as Odysseus remarks in the opening scene (8–11).

near c, keeping the address to Neoptolemos direct. He is then well placed, at just R of c, to use one hand to gesture towards the *skene* at 286, and then to raise the bow in his other hand at 288. This whole central section of his autobiography, from 285 to 299, is surely mimetic, with the Sailors as an immediate audience, and it opens and concludes (298–9) with a reference to the *skene*. If this is the case, then the concluding section (300–316) would be more directly addressed to Neoptolemos and the Sailors, inviting attention for the spectacle which Philoktetes offers in the Lemnian environment of the *orchêstra*.

For the exchange that follows, we found that Neoptolemos was drawn towards Philoktetes initially, as he asserts a common experience in 'witnessing' the hostile acts of the Atreidai and Odysseus (319–21), but then withdrew towards FL as he began to elaborate his fiction (329–31). When invited to give his story in full, he began to work the lateral from FL to FR, leaving Philoktetes at c as the innocent audience of his narrative, and keeping the *choros* close at hand to corroborate what for him is a new and dubious stratagem.[45] Plainly the feelings of the listening character must be a focus of attention, and in this case the antics of Philoktetes will express a kind of joyous indignation. The inclusion of direct quotation in the script is a clear invitation to a degree of mimetic vitality from Neoptolemos: a lively lie is a good lie, and this is surely a performance. This quality is enhanced by the intervention of Choros 2, which adds music and dance to the depth of conviction achieved by acting, and draws the Sailors unequivocally into the deception. The deity supposedly invoked lends local colour to the conviction, and the appeal to the god is cleverly interlaced with the fiction, occurring not just in an elaborate opening but also near the end of the song.[46]

The song undoubtedly marks a subtle advance in the relationship

---

[45] For Calder 1971 the whole of this narrative is a lie, while Hamilton 1975 compares the mixed truth and falsehood of what Lichas tells Deianeira in *YWT*. Sophokles exploited the pathos of a complete fiction inflicted on a credulous leading character in *El*, as Orestes makes the most of the urn; but that misery is to be reversed, and is intended to be so. See Ewans' Notes above, pp. 210–3.

[46] Burton (1980, 232–3) gives a good discussion of the song, noting that Sophokles substitutes it for the usual, two-line spoken contribution from the *choros*. Gardiner (1987, 23–5) concludes that 'the Athenian audience would not have been offended at hearing Greeks . . . call an essentially foreign divinity to witness a lie'; but Haldane (1963, 56) remarks that the cult of Kybele was established at Athens about 430 BC. Ussher 1990, 124 suggests that the Sailors' intervention may follow a signal from Neoptolemos, as had been arranged previously in the opening exchange between them (147–9).

between Philoktetes and the visiting Greeks, because Philoktetes is now convinced that they have a grudge similar to his own (403–6). This conviction gains strength from the sharing of 'friends and enemies' that follows. As Neoptolemos started the process of sympathy by 'bearing witness' (319) to the oppression of the Atreidai, so Philoktetes here is drawn into 'bearing witness' to the assertion that war never takes the bad men but only the good (436–8). Like the invocation by the *choros*, witnessing could have a place in a process of validation, and the sequence leads to a firm declaration by Neoptolemos, which falls significantly short of being an oath of vengeance or a pact. None the less, Neoptolemos is apparently pledging himself to a life of marginalization and isolation in a similarly barren environment ('rocky Skyros', 459), even if that is his home. It is a clever moment, achieved with considerable care; what appears to be a balance in fate and situation, a kind of sympathy, is bound to leave Philoktetes feeling none the less deprived, because Lemnos cannot be to him what Skyros is to Neoptolemos. The concluding word (in the Greek, as in the translation) is 'home' (460), and it carries the full force of the deceit and contrivance from the opening of the scene, and indeed nearly from the opening of the drama, until this point. If Neoptolemos is an unpractised liar, Sophokles certainly makes him an expert deceiver, because at just this moment he turns to leave. In our workshop we followed the hint in Choros 1, and had Neoptolemos gesture to the Sailors to follow him, and collect behind him at FL. He had himself moved little during the previous exchanges, but the lateral from FL to FR and back was exploited as he responded to Philoktetes' questions. A movement from Neoptolemos towards EBL would be enough, with the choral movement, to prompt Philoktetes to his despairing supplication. If Neoptolemos was left at FR, he would have to pass across Philoktetes to leave by the L *parodos*; if he was left at FL, he would have to stop. We felt that the Sailors would fan back to the perimeter of the *orchêstra* at EFR and EFL once Philoktetes makes his appeal.

Touch is a standard feature of supplication where an individual is involved; in other kinds of appeal, taking refuge at an altar or within a temple, or binding oneself to it, provides the equivalent connection in the case of seeking sanctuary or pleading for support. [47] Here touch is not involved initially, as it seems, although it may be later in the

---

[47] The leading study of supplication (*hikesia*) a significant, ritualized act which offers great opportunities for dramatic and theatrical exploitation, is Gould 1973.

sequence (485), as Philoktetes increases the pressure on Neoptolemos.[48]
As Philoktetes appeals to Neoptolemos' noble birth, conjoining that to
a reference to himself as a 'cargo' to be 'stowed in the hold', we had
Neoptolemos simply turn his face and body away at FR. We know
from the script that he remained silent, but in performance Philoktetes
may pause at the end of 483, awaiting a reply. Philoktetes might then
make an additional move towards him, upright, as he appeals to him
to 'nod' in agreement (484–5), and then fall to his knees at 485.[49] The
language in itself unfortunately does not help us to determine whether
Philoktetes grasped the knees of Neoptolemos, or refers to his own,
because it is open to either interpretation.[50] Practical considerations are
valuable here. If Philoktetes holds Neoptolemos, when does he let go
and when does he get up? Neoptolemos might break away from him
almost immediately, prompting the emotive references to his home and
his father, and Philoktetes could then get up after the song at 507–18.
But this would create a harsh movement of repugnance and rejection,
to which one might expect some reference from Philoktetes. We found
it was better to have Neoptolemos turn away from the spectacle of this
pitiable figure on his knees, leaving him to add a further plea and to be
left isolated close to C, while the *choros* sings in apparent support.
Neoptolemos then turns back to face the Sailors, and gestures towards
Philoktetes at 519–21. With the help of his bow, Philoktetes would

[48] Kaimio (1988, 54–5) rightly includes this moment in her section on the
lack of physical contact, while noting the possibility of contact later at 485. But
the difficulty of moving is only one consideration; Philoktetes knows, and the
audience must also sense, that he risks everything if he engages repugnance
(473–4) by coming too close too soon to his potential means of salvation.

[49] Taplin (1978, 113–14) has a good if short section on Neoptolemos'
silences, and his use of silence as a ploy; he adds, quite plausibly, a pause at the
end of 479 and in the middle of 486. In performance, the speaking actor's
invitation to reply, or his expectation of receiving a reply, will be as significant
as the silence from his partner. In this section, as in Philoktetes' opening speech
as he approaches the *orchêstra*, the profound desire for a response on the part
of someone who rarely hears another voice offers an opportunity to the actor
for great interpretative subtlety and tonal control.

[50] For the record, those in favour of a lack of physical contact are Jebb 1898,
85; Webster 1970, 101 (on 486); Kaimio 1988, 54–5; Ussher 1990, 127. Seale
(1982, 33–4) has Philoktetes come 'right up to Neoptolemos'. Kamerbeek
(1980, 85, on 484) is in favour of contact, because grasping the knees is 'the
most characteristic feature of *hikesia*', a comment which fails to allow this
moment to be theatrically distinctive. In contrast, the varieties of theatrical
supplication, realized or unrealized, are well reviewed by Kaimio.

then labour to his feet, preparing to go, at 530–32, sufficiently animated to begin moving towards the *skene* at 533–5, inviting Neoptolemos to follow him.

If we understand deceit as the dominant motive, Neoptolemos has achieved his objective; he has persuaded Philoktetes to want to leave with him, even to plead to do so. In this case, the second short song from the *choros* at 507–18, which proves to be in responsion to the first at 391–402, is consistent in carrying forward the deception; the only potential complication is the alleged presence of pity, mentioned once more in the song.[51] The gullibility of Philoktetes at this moment is appalling, because he is helpless, and has no choice but to believe in the deception. From our vantage point, the most constructive comparison is with the gullibility of Othello, which is (by contrast) terrifying, because he is inclined to be deceived, and in a position to take a vicious course of action as a consequence.

Strictly speaking, for Odysseus to despatch the sham 'Merchant' at this juncture is a mistake, although we might, as an audience, imagine that he does not know that. Philoktetes is ready to leave, and the arrival of this mask, which we may recognize, takes us back to the state of things at the planning of the deception in the opening scene. Plainly, what the 'Merchant' has to say is rehearsed, because it answers to a situation in which Philoktetes is reluctant to leave by suggesting urgency and coercion, and introducing through the prophecy of Helenos a manner in which Philoktetes might be compelled to aid the Greeks. Odysseus must have designed this to send Philoktetes headlong in the opposite direction, and it is consistent with the stratagem outlined in the opening scene, and subsequently followed by Neoptolemos, which was to rely on the idea that Neoptolemos was sailing away from Troy to the east, to Skyros and towards the Greek mainland.

The prophecy is, of course, crucial to the myth and the motives of the Greeks at Troy, and will be crucial in offering Philoktetes the *kleos* and *time* of being a decisive figure in the capture of Troy.[52] Critics

[51] Gardiner (1987, 22–30) has a long and at times rather involved commentary on these two short songs, and on comparable examples in Aischylos and Euripides.

[52] I have found Gill 1980 most helpful on the prophecy, which has occupied almost every modern critic from Bowra 1944 forwards, not always to great purpose. Gill rightly notes (139–40) that the prophecy presumably took the form of a 'riddle', or an enigma, and I would suspect that the manifest critical confusion partly stems from the fact that it does not appear in that form in the drama.

have wondered that Odysseus seems to be fixated on the bow alone in the opening scene, and that Neoptolemos seems to be unaware of how much he depends on Philoktetes or on the bow for his own role in the prospective victory. Scene 1 establishes that Neoptolemos apparently needs to have these matters emphasized to him to be convinced that he must act in his own self-interest; it is not an issue whether he has previously been aware of them or not. It can hardly be contested that Sophokles is willing to show Odysseus as confused in his attitudes, and the only useful explanation would seem to be that Sophokles is portraying the urgency of pragmatism; 'get the bow first, and then . . .' is the picture of his mentality that we are shown by the playwright, and that is perhaps all we are meant to see. Sophokles has displaced Odysseus from his role in the earlier tragic versions, in which a preoccupation with his motives must have provided some of the substance of the tragedy; it does not do that here.

If Philoktetes has withdrawn some way towards the *skene*, perhaps to BC, then the 'Merchant' can approach Neoptolemos (at ER) directly from the L *parodos*, while apparently ignoring Philoktetes, leaving his 'guide' at EBL. Neoptolemos would come forward to RC to answer him, and to play the game that he knows will follow, even if he does not know the script. The actor playing the 'Merchant' is playing a character acting a scripted deceit, unlike Neoptolemos, who is improvising a deception of which very little has been scripted. This rehearsed script is reasonably secure; whatever the situation, the man will speak first to Neoptolemos, then acknowledge Philoktetes, then deliver the report of the prophecy of Helenos, and then go, without becoming involved in any further complications. It is almost a parody of the use of a third actor, or a 'messenger', whose information alters the course of the action by changing the other characters' knowledge of the situation. This was almost certainly one of the earliest mechanisms of tragedy, in the two-actor period before 458 BC; it is interesting that here it has almost reached its demise by being transformed into a redundant exercise, deployed by an absent character who cannot witness what is actually happening in the action he hopes to control.

In our workshop, we found that it increased Philoktetes' interest in what the 'Merchant' was saying to have the 'Merchant' draw forward a little to FC at 561, as if speaking to the Sailors as well as Neoptole-mos. Philoktetes then might himself draw forward and aside, to BR, from which position he can make his interjection at 578. This triangle allows for the deceitful performance from 580 to 590 to be most impressive, with Neoptolemos and the 'Merchant' working together to get Philoktetes excited. The 'Merchant's' narrative can then be delivered in a series of movements that exploit his relationship in the space to Philoktetes, Neoptolemos and the Sailors. It is noticeable that it does not include direct quotation, and so may be less mimetic than Neoptolemos' earlier story. The 'Merchant' gestures at Philoktetes at 612, and the effect of the speech as a whole would be obviously greater if it was not delivered directly to Philoktetes. We had the 'Merchant' conclude at c, which increased the impression that Philoktetes was not being addressed. He would then turn as Philoktetes exclaimed at 622, and with a dismissive lack of interest turn on his heel to leave by the L parodos, perhaps stopping and briefly turning back to face them both to wish them luck at 627.

The concluding part of the scene brings Neoptolemos with Philoktetes into the cave together, and, as I have argued before, this is all the more impressive if it is the climax of achievement for both, as well as the first use of the central entry to the *skene* in *Philoktetes*.[53] It is not in itself a surprising moment; the resolution to go had been reached just before the arrival of the 'Merchant', and it might well have been followed by collecting belongings.[54] It may be that Philoktetes demonstrates a desire to leave immediately, following the 'Merchant', and if so he is held briefly by Neoptolemos' comments about the winds. The action is redirected towards the cave by Neoptolemos, but Sophokles pauses to reinstate the bow in our experience; it is as if Neoptolemos is momentarily subject to the fixation of Odysseus in the opening scene, and he is promised the opportunity to hold it. In fact, he has the right – 'it is lawful' – and that is because the bow is a symbol of what is gained by the extremes of friendship; Neoptolemos has granted Philoktetes the possibility of release and restoration, and Philoktetes granted Herakles a release from a tortured life on Mount Oita. As Gill interprets it, the bow is an 'instrument of . . . heroic achievement', which is 'inseparable from genuine friendship', and the significance of the bow is that 'heroic achievement depends on authentic friendship'.[55]

[53] Cf. Ley 1988, 97.

[54] Seale 1982, 35–6 would read an increasing sense of hesitation into Neoptolemos' comments about the adverse winds and his suggestion that the belongings are collected.

[55] Gill 1980, 138–9. Taplin (1978, 89–93) has something similar in mind when he writes of the bow as 'a sacred symbol of trust' in his discussion of its significance as a stage property. See also Harsh 1960, 414 ('the ideals symbolized by the bow'); Segal 1980, 131–3; and Seale 1982, 36–7 ('an instrument of good

Philoktetes' explanation (662–70) of why and when it is 'lawful' (*themis*) to handle the bow expresses this.

Choros 3

This is the only *choros* in the drama which is independent of the actors, and the conclusion must be that it was danced in the full *orchêstra* and out to the audience. When an actor is involved with a choral song, he provides a focus or point of reference to some extent by being addressed, and Sophokles has made it quite clear that the actors have left the playing space before this song begins.

The structure of the song is typical of the formal balance and correspondence found in a sequence of *strophe* and *antistrophe*. The opening (of A1) contrasts Philoktetes to the impious Ixion, but it is itself counterbalanced at the end of the second *antistrophe* (B2) by the introduction of Herakles. Ixion invaded heaven, and was cast down to Haides for an act of extreme impiety; Herakles, after his great labours on earth, was taken up to heaven. Each suffered torment, but that of Ixion continued as a punishment, while that of Herakles was a transforming fire, putting an end to the torment of his body. The contrast of Ixion with Philoktetes is of two figures who suffer constantly and terribly, but whose sufferings are distinguished – respectively – by the presence and lack of an ethical and religious justification for that suffering. The role of Herakles in the song is to provide a suitable and convincing parable of liberation and restoration for Philoktetes after terrible suffering. Between Haides and the Olympian heavens – the extremes of punishment and reward – lies the earth, and Philoktetes' reward will be on the human scale, to return 'home', to Malis and the 'banks of the Spercheios'. Philoktetes is linked to Herakles by the act of friendship, conducted by one who has *arete*; meeting another man with hereditary *arete* will guarantee Philoktetes that vital, transforming journey across the sea.

The problem with this intricate and powerful set of contrasting and balancing themes is that until this point the Sailors have been a willing participant in deceit, in their loyalty to Neoptolemos. The pretence of conveying Philoktetes home is probably the core of that deception, as I have said, granted that the story that Odysseus outlines to Neoptolemos has Neoptolemos sailing away from Troy to his home. Yet here,

works'). Kaimio (1988, 84) believes that Neoptolemos may actually touch the bow here, 'but does not take it into his possession'.

the Sailors sing – apparently without the constraint of the presence of Philoktetes – of this return, as if they believed in it. This has prompted the suggestion that Philoktetes and Neoptolemos reappear from the cave at the end of B1, requiring the *choros* to sing the final *antistrophe* as a form of deceit.[56] If this was the case, then it is an interesting example of a script written for a specific form of production, which must presumably have relied for its realization on the involvement of the playwright as director, or on exact instructions conveyed by him to the director. The alternative interpretation has to understand choral song in a different manner, as a mode of generating, developing or encouraging expectation, or even hope, in the audience.[57] Both the expression of sympathy for a character, often in the context of comparisons with the fate of others, and the sympathetic expression of what a character may hope are familiar qualities of Sophoklean choral songs.[58] We may call this the generation of false expectations in the audience, or we may allow it to be a particular extension of sympathy which is not simply manipulative; so, through the means of the Choros, we are travelling sympathetically with the character rather than simply being fooled by the playwright.

If Athenian choreography is mimetic, as Wiles has plausibly suggested, then there is ample scope in this song for mimetic dance and movement, which would identify the *choros* as a body of dancers with the suffering character who is the subject of their dance.[59] The isolation, and the divorce from the civilized arts of agriculture which produce bread and wine (B1), could then be contrasted impressively with the meeting of two men (B2) which will lead to reintegration.

Scene 3

Neoptolemos and Philoktetes reappear at the mouth of the cave – i.e., the central entrance to the *skene*. If the opening of the scene is to be effective, then both must progress some way into the *orchêstra* before

[56] There is an extensive review of the various proposals in Gardiner 1987, 30–36; the proposal that Philoktetes and Neoptolemos reappear was made by Jebb 1989, 119 (on 718ff.).

[57] Burton (1980, 237–9) has a good summary of these possibilities.

[58] *Ibid.*, 238 writes of 'Sophocles' habit of using his choruses as an instrument with which to guide the mind and emotions of his audiences in any direction required by the immediate dramatic context'. I would regard this as a rather too mechanical and 'instrumental' description of the phenomenon.

[59] Wiles 1997, 87–113.

Philoktetes stops in the full view of the audience; Neoptolemos leads on, presumably towards the L *parodos*, before turning round to face him. The sense of B2 in the previous song may have drawn the *choros* into a formation, perhaps divided at ECR and ECL, suitable for marching out behind them both. In our workshop we felt that the *choros* would, almost immediately, begin to withdraw and spread out in apprehension (at EFL and EFR), recalling their position and attitude at the first approach of Philoktetes. If Philoktetes is left behind, then it is relatively easy for him to have taken a position centrally, probably at BC, between the *skene* and C. He will, presumably, stretch out his foot at 747–9 in the appeal to Neoptolemos to strike it off with his sword, and at 761 Neoptolemos significantly offers to take hold of him and help him. His movement towards Philoktetes is a major gesture towards physical contact, and it is followed by the handover of the bow, which Sophokles scripts at some length. At 813 Philoktetes asks Neoptolemos to pledge with a hand-clasp that he will stay by him when he is asleep. But the physical contact apparently drives Philoktetes over the edge of rational consciousness, and what follows must be a struggle of some sort, until Neoptolemos declares that he is letting go of Philoktetes' hand because he is now coming to his senses (818).[60] Philoktetes then collapses at 819–20, and gradually falls asleep, his head drooping.

The playwright scripted a fairly precise series of movements here, which we can follow with some conviction, but the quality of the scene is unquestionably dominated by the extraordinary demands on the performer playing Philoktetes. The Greek includes its own sequence of 'ah' and 'oh', with imprecations and invocations, and the pain is charted from apprehension and onset through agony to delirium and collapse. The extraordinary fury and terrifying sequential logic of this trauma resonate throughout the theatre, while two acts of immense significance take place during it, almost as incidents. Neoptolemos is fitted by his *arete* to handle the bow, but his *arete* is in the service of deception; the achievement of Odysseus' original aim in Scene 1 leaves him unavoidably with a problem, which he himself had indeed sensed then (86ff.). The problem is compounded by the pledge he offers to Philoktetes, which confirms their friendship at the moment that it establishes physical contact. Philoktetes cannot bear physical contact, and it traumatizes him, which confirms the certainty of his isolation

---

[60] Kaimio (1988, 24) in a discussion of the scene notes that a helping or restraining hand causing pain is a convention of tragic theatre: it occurs e.g. with Herakles and the Old Man in *YWT* (1007ff.).

and embodies his profound alienation: his attempt to establish trust is suffused with agony and temporary madness.[61] No one can be sure of anything after this scene, although what the two characters might have hoped for is plain enough.

Some aspects of this scene recall Herakles and Hyllos in *Young Women of Trachis*, in particular the agony and the pledge of hands. Yet the *mise-en-scène* is distinctly different, and the location of the scenes in their respective plays ensures a different dynamic. In this drama, Philoktetes is not alone, and the *choros* does not remain silent.

Choros 4

An invocation to Sleep, which resembles in part a *paian* to Apollo, because both are healers, sung with Neoptolemos standing over the body of Philoktetes, or at least begun and ended with him in that position.[62] It is probably best if the bow is not moved away from Philoktetes, since although the Sailors urge theft and desertion, there is no real sign of temptation in the words of Neoptolemos. The song could see Neoptolemos draw briefly away from the sleeping body towards the Sailors, in hesitation, and then return to link bow with body as the force of his own words registers. But I suspect the simpler interpretation is true, that the song has Neoptolemos standing by Philoktetes at BC marvelling at the bow, and the *choros* to either side of the pair, perhaps divided into two groups at RC and LC, or spread in a horseshoe around the *orchêstra*, with the two points converging at BC. The lyric exchange contrasts readily with Choros 3, because the two actors now provide a focus, and the song is substantially addressed to them.

The Sailors ask Sleep to 'come to us' and to 'come to me' gently; this is a curious version of the prayer to a god to visit the subject benignly, because they are clearly not in need of a nap at this moment, nor is Sleep easily understood as a rampaging *daimōn*.[63] The relative

---

[61] As Taplin expresses it (1978, 112), 'it is . . . as though the contamination of his deceit aggravates Philoktetes' anguish.'

[62] On the invocation as a *paian*, see Haldane 1963. Sleep was also associated with the cult of Asklepios, the son of Apollo, and anecdotal evidence gives Sophokles a considerable involvement with healing cults at Athens.

[63] This kind of prayer is found in a thoroughly explicit form in Euripides' *Medeia*, when the *choros* prays (627–41) for love not to fall with intense force on them, after witnessing the bitter quarrel between Iason and Medeia. The subjective intrusion of a *choros* is part of the sympathetic range in their lyric contribution.

ease of sympathy in the lyric role of the *choros* is at work here, as it sings on behalf of Philoktetes, but just as readily associates sleep self-interestedly with the 'moment' or 'opportunity' of complete deception. Neoptolemos responds (in the original Greek) in dactylic hexameters, the metre of epic and its heroes, and one that also carries religious connotations, including those of oracle and prophecy.[64] There is no other conclusion to draw about Neoptolemos' response than that the intense experience of proximity to Philoktetes has allowed him to understand what he knew already, that Philoktetes has a role to fulfil in the victory at Troy.[65]

The Sailors' dance is relatively agitated and excited (despite their apparently calm appeal to Sleep), as the original Greek metre establishes and their sense of urgency confirms. For them, 'opportunity' rather than Philoktetes the man offers the victory (conclusion to A1), and the rest – if it is truly destined, as Neoptolemos in prophetic mode suggests – will be brought to fulfilment by the divine powers (opening of A2). The wind, like the opportunity, is favourable, but the song itself has the quality of something momentary and inconclusive, since it is – unusually – curtailed by a character suddenly stirring and awakening rather than by one appearing.

Scene 4

The drama continues with the same characters in front of the audience and without the introduction of any new stimulus in the form of a change in situation, or a challenge posed by something learned or by an arrival. The action is seamless, and it permits pain and disability to assume prominence. The principal action is here that of getting up, the debate about whether it may be better to do so on one's own, with the help of a single person, or of several.[66] The Sailors have been vigilant (867), while Neoptolemos has stayed by Philoktetes's side, and Philoktetes' choice of Neoptolemos as his helper confirms this disposition.

---

[64] See Burton 1980, 242–3, and Gardiner 1987, 38 (citing Winnington-Ingram 1969 and 1980) for discussions of the implications of these hexameters, including the overtone of competitive achievement.

[65] Gill (1980, 141) sets out this conclusion calmly and persuasively.

[66] Kaimío (1988, 83–5) comments on the innovative status accorded to physical contact in Philoktetes: 'Sophocles has used physical contact only after emphasizing to the utmost the lack of all human contact suffered by Philoktetes and his caution, in spite of his eagerness for contact, in imposing his physical presence on others' (84).

This second moment of contact produces a loss of control by Neopto-lemos, just as the first had thrown Philoktetes into spasms. The fact that Philoktetes interprets this as revulsion at the wound (900–901) indicates that Neoptolemos has broken away from him, and in our workshop we held Neoptolemos between Philoktetes and the L *parodos* which would lead him to the ship, perhaps at BLC. The appeal by Neoptolemos to Zeus (908–9) indicates a further gesture of invocation or a movement, possibly forward to LC or ELC, and the relative distance allows Philoktetes to refer to Neoptolemos as 'this man here' (910). At this point, Neoptolemos is drawn to address Philoktetes directly, and he may not only 'face' him but also move up towards him. In revealing the direction of their voyage Neoptolemos is leaving himself with persuasion in place of deception, and the distance between him and Philoktetes remains sufficient for the bow to be out of arm's reach (924). In our workshop we placed him finally at LC, with the opportunity to back away towards ELC.

Persuading Philoktetes is like coercing Antigone or mollifying Aias, or advising Oidipous not to bother about the problem of his parentage. In ruling out persuasion and relying on deceit, Odysseus had identified the nature of the central character in his scenario with unhesitating certainty, much as an older spectator might know Sophoklean characters. Neoptolemos' naïve declaration prompts a cataclysmic reaction, and Sophokles can explore the extraordinary and furious temper of desolation that lies in Philoktetes. It is a magnificent speech for the actor, with appeals to Neoptolemos and to the environment of Lemnos, both unanswered, and a final reference to the desolate image of the *skene*. Philoktetes is centrally placed, at BC, and may approach Neop-tolemos a little when he begs for his weapons, to find Neoptolemos turning away from him at LC, perhaps to ELC. Then comes the appeal to Lemnos, taking in the expanse of the *orchêstra* and *theatron*, and the mimetic bitterness of the gestures with his betrayed hand. That he is empty-handed is, of course, visually and theatrically crucial, because it leads into the reference to the *skene*, which will be for him, a disarmed man, a tomb of rock like that decreed for Antigone. He concludes with an imprecation against Neoptolemos, but one which he then modifies; this gives us – only at the end of the speech – the sense of a histrionic quality aimed at effect. Ultimately, there is something tractable here, or manipulative, which is rooted in Philoktetes' aristo-cratic instinct for friendship and 'nobility', qualities that may somehow deny the otherwise uniform harshness of reality. The ensuing dialogue proves Philoktetes to be manipulative; he has sensed the working of that pity, which a desperation born of previous failures has managed to evoke in his guests.[67]

For Odysseus' intervention modern commentary offers a variety of staging solutions, which do not seem to me to be particularly helpful.[68] The concerns are that Odysseus seems to appear suddenly in the acting area, and then that Philoktetes seems to threaten to jump off a precipice. As Odysseus arrives, Philoktetes is looking to Neoptolemos, and Neoptolemos is addressing the Sailors. The *orchêstra* is large; if Philoktetes has come slightly forward to C in pleading with Neoptolemos, who continues to face the *choros*, then Odysseus can be introduced from the L *parodos*, followed at a little distance by at least two Sailors. It is clear from the dialogue that he does not, initially, intervene physically. That Philoktetes recognizes Odysseus' voice (976) rather than his clothing or appearance is hardly surprising, and is all the more convincing if Philoktetes is in front of Odysseus, and cannot turn easily. Odysseus for his part is armed, and would keep clear of Philoktetes, and Neoptolemos is silent (at ELC) holding the bow, not offering it to either. The two Sailors come from behind Odysseus to embody his threat of force, and Philoktetes withdraws to the *skene*. The script asks us to envisage a height sufficient to kill someone with suicidal intent, but it does not determine that Philoktetes has climbed it; the intention is declared, but the action and progress of a man in his state could be imagined to be feeble.[69] Philoktetes turns towards the

[67] It hardly needs noting that there is a strong sense of class in this tragedy, but it may need emphasizing that the contrast between the landfall of the son of Achilleus and those of occasional traders (like the 'Merchant') is crucially important to Philoktetes' own sense of opportunity. On aristocratic values in Sophokles, see Winnington-Ingram 1980, 307ff., who asks appropriate questions about political ideology but is not noticeably keen to answer them; and briefly, on this drama, Segal 1981, 304–5.

[68] Taplin (1971, 28–9), with a rare show of enthusiasm for scene-painting, suggested that Odysseus has slid along behind the panels carrying the set-painting; Seale (1982, 49) partly echoed this proposal, but noted (53 n. 38) that Webster (1970, 128, on 974) had been in favour of arrival from a *parodos*. As Webster calmly observes, 'Philoktetes and Neoptolemos and the chorus are so deeply engaged that Odysseus can come up the *parodos* unnoticed.' Jebb (1898, 157) has Odysseus appear 'from behind the cave'. Craik (1990, 82–3) develops this idea to fit with her (highly unlikely) scheme for a cave with one entrance on the roof of the *skene*: in this *mise-en-scène*, Philoktetes first enters on the roof, and so does Odysseus here, with Philoktetes making a bid for the same heights soon after.

[69] The spectators are perhaps expected to imagine, as at 28–9, that the rear

skene with resolution at 999, but is easily caught and pinioned by the Sailors a few lines later.

If Philoktetes is brought away from the cave, and forward, this leaves him in a good position to hold forth against the two men, and in our workshop we had Odysseus now cross to RC, in a show of confidence. Philoktetes can now turn his mask first to one side and then to the other, since movement of any other kind – apart from a demonstrative pulling on his captors – is denied to the actor. Odysseus begins to speak in reply at RC, but clearly refuses to argue directly with Philoktetes. So we had him cross back to LC, perhaps BL, turning round to give the command to release Philoktetes at 1054. His men would then come to stand behind him again, and his taunt that others may use the great bow is timed to coincide with the release; that, with the threat to leave, is surely a challenge to Philoktetes, and an attempt to draw him out. At least, that is what an audience would conclude from the reaction of Philoktetes (1063–4), and Odysseus follows it immediately with a show of movement.[70] Philoktetes then appeals to Neoptolemos, who has remained motionless at EL, probably facing away from Philoktetes, and Odysseus speaks rapidly and sharply in warning to him (1068–9). Philoktetes then appeals to the Sailors, spread in two groups at EFR and EFL, and Neoptolemos obediently chooses to follow Odysseus, leaving them to fill the vacant space around Philoktetes. If Odysseus is allowed to leave before Neoptolemos has spoken, it would demonstrate an almost complete confidence in his military authority over the young man, which was established in the opening scene.[71]

Choros 5

This Choros is a *kommos*, a lyric exchange between the Sailors and Philoktetes; in A1, A2, and B1, B2 it is characterized by a lack of

segment of the *orchêstra* for a few moments represents an area higher than the centre and front, as at Aischylos, *Suppliants* 713ff. If painted panels on the *skene* façade represent rocks, the impression given by intention and movement is considerable.

[70] Since a clear pattern of explicit motivation is dear to modern critics, opinions are divided on whether Odysseus is bluffing, or resigned to Philoktetes' intransigence. Kitto (1956, 124) is in favour of bluffing, and Knox (1964, 192 n. 38) in favour of resignation; Winnington-Ingram (1980, 293) even believes that it is 'probable' that Odysseus was 'happy for the sailors to remain', and so, I presume, must be imagining more than one ship, or some very hard rowing.

[71] Seale (1982, 42) may be envisaging something of this sort, but his description of this sequence is unusually hard to follow.

communication, the *choros* contributing in each case a coda to a song
from Philoktetes: in A1 and A2 Philoktetes also punctuates his song
with cries, which I have represented as stage directions.[72]

The isolation that surrounds so many Sophoklean characters can
leave them as outcasts, with their final resting-place provided by a bare
landscape. So the *eremia*, the deserted shore not occupied by humans,
receives Aias, the rock tomb Antigone, and both Herakles and Oidipous are finally blessed by finding a sacred place, which is closer to the
gods than to humans. The cave is for Philoktetes a living tomb, which
is the experience decreed for Antigone, and the theft of the bow leaves
Philoktetes' hands free to express his desolation. The Sailors must
surely face him during this song, although the most radical choreography would have Philoktetes finally free to move slowly about the
orchêstra, and the *choros* moving to provide a frame for him in each
position. Philoktetes' repeated references to the bow and its use, to the
arrows, and to birds would permit mimetic gesture; but it is difficult to
see that full mimetic dance would be convincing, given that his
disability is so plainly established in the rest of the drama.

By the close of B2 the choreography must in some way embody the
Sailors' dramatic insistence that Philoktetes should break from his
sense of desolation and 'come closer to one who approaches you in all
goodwill' (1164). Certainly this conclusion to B2 prompts Philoktetes
to address them directly, acknowledging their presence for the first
time, and a more vigorous and combative exchange follows with C1,
an extraordinary lyric dialogue which must have demanded innovative
and striking choreography.

The possibilities from this outline seem to be either to hold Philoktetes near C for A1, A2, and B1, B2, with the *choros* towards the
perimeter throughout, but closing and appealing at the end of B2; or
to have the Sailors remain at EFL and EFR for A1 and A2, when
Philoktetes is referring to the *skene*, and then for him to come forward
across C to FC for B1 and B2, while they give him room, and yet keep
in contact, by moving back along the perimeter to positions at LC and
RC.

The latter scheme is attractive, because the threat to leave early in

---

[72] As Gardiner (1987, 43) observes, this part of the *kommos* shows 'a
complete absence of communication between chorus and character'. Segal
(1981, 333) draws attention to the significance of Philoktetes' cries: 'the stricken
hero's intensity of suffering places him at the border between human speech and
animal cry.'

CI would be effective if the *choros* was towards the rear of the *orchêstra*; but if Philoktetes is conceived to be as immobile in the *kommos* as he has been in the action of the drama, a threat to wheel past him and out would be consistent with the more static scheme, with Philoktetes marooned at C.

At 1196 the pressure on Philoktetes to move ('Take a step forward . . .') is repeated, and the manner in which this is countered by reference to the wound and the foot must have had some reflection in the choreography. It seems an inevitable conclusion that Philoktetes remains at C, isolated and obdurate; towards the close of CI he may begin to retire towards the *skene* (in contrast to approaching the choral groups, or leaving by a *parodos*). As he withdraws into the cave, the Sailors must take up positions at EFL and EFR, their movement confirming that contact has not been established even by the end of the *kommos*.[73]

Finale

Odysseus and Neoptolemos arrive, arguing, at L, and Neoptolemos is still holding the bow.[74] In our workshop we had Neoptolemos continuing across the *orchêstra* to RC, leaving Odysseus at BL. By the middle of their *stichomythia* they close in on each other at C, with Neoptolemos indicating by this movement his intention to return the bow. The confrontation at C is the first of its kind, open and combative, in *Philoktetes* and as Neoptolemos turns to make towards the *skene* Odysseus threatens to draw his sword (1254–5). I should like to see Neoptolemos move the bow from his right hand to his left, to make his answering threat more demonstrative; Odysseus must turn as Neoptolemos continues towards the *skene*, and then leave, with Neoptolemos' final words delivered loudly as he leaves. Neoptolemos keeps

[73] Burton (1980, 248) writes of an 'apparently hopeless ending' to the exchange between the *choros* and Philoktetes. The Sailors make no further intervention in the Finale, and the impression given, as in *YWT*, is that the *choros* character cannot confront this traumatized figure. This 'failure' of the *choros* is worth noting in relation to the need for the final appearance of Herakles in this tragedy.

[74] Calder (1971) believes that the script reveals that the argument is part of a continuing pretence: as Neoptolemos and Odysseus enter, 'the effect is that Neoptolemos has been rehearsed and is being prompted' (164), and they do not know that Philoktetes 'does not hear them' (166).

to this volume, summoning Philoktetes from the cave. In our work-shop, the Sailors drew nearer, leaving EFL and EFR for EL and ER.

It seems clear that Philoktetes remains by the entrance to the cave for the first part of this exchange. His view is resigned and cynical, and he has committed himself to the cave resolutely; the visual message that he may retire into it at any moment is undoubtedly helpful here. The offering of the bow is best made to pull Philoktetes from this position into one of restored friendship, and Philoktetes should be drawn from the entrance towards Neoptolemos, at EBC, in front of the *skene*.[75] As Odysseus arrives in haste at the L *parodos*, Philoktetes has received the bow, and the script reveals that he attempts to string an arrow. Odysseus cannot be near Philoktetes – a bow is not a revolver – and Neoptolemos holds Philoktetes, while Odysseus escapes back down the L *parodos*. The moment is easy to visualize, and Philoktetes lowers the bow as he speaks contemptuously of Odysseus' ignominious retreat (1305–7).

The bow has returned to Philoktetes, and Neoptolemos is exonerated of any blame; what is more, he is confirmed as his father's son. The way is left open for persuasion, and Neoptolemos can call on Zeus to witness his oath that what he says is true. Yet he also criticizes Philoktetes for becoming 'savage', divorced from the concerns of men, and deaf to proper advice. In our workshop, we felt that Neoptolemos should use the *orchêstra*, initially moving away from Philoktetes to RC as he criticizes him, and turning to him at RC when he calls on Zeus at 1324. We then allowed Neoptolemos to use the lateral to LC as he explained that healing would be the result of going to Troy. He turned at LC, as he confirmed his confident statement by reference to the prophecy of Helenos, and directed his strong conclusion to Philoktetes from that position.[76] We also found that, in reply, Philoktetes initially

[75] For Taplin (1978, 131–3) (cf. 1971) the passage of the bow from one to another is a 'mirror scene', here recalling a similar gesture at 971f. My difficulty with this is that, on the first occasion, Neoptolemos is still in doubt, asking the Sailors what he should do, when Odysseus intervenes. Here the act is premedi-tated and willed, and about to take place. Dramatically, the one moment plainly recalls the other; but visually I suspect they may have been different and distinct, because the action has developed, and with it our sense of motivation.

[76] This is, of course, the fullest and most persuasive version of the prophecy and of the future that the audience has heard. It is released when it may be most useful, and, incidentally, when it puts the greatest pressure on both Philoktetes and the dramaturgy: if this is the future, how will Philoktetes avoid it, or Sophokles allow him to be persuaded, granted his obstinate resentment? Gill

wrestled with himself on the spot, at BC, but that he was drawn forward to C, so that when he addresses Neoptolemos at 1362 he can turn to the side, without confronting him. The ensuing dialogue, in which Neoptolemos makes no attempt to revise his story of the theft of his father's armour, is strong but inconclusive, and neither man has much reason to shift his ground, until Philoktetes demonstrates his final refusal by moving back towards BC (1392). When Neoptolemos declares his awareness of the impasse, released from the dialogue by Philoktetes' movement, he might be seen to move towards the path at the L *parodos*; our inclination was to make him move just a little further towards the Sailors, at FLC, as if about to take them with him. From there he can abruptly turn, and come towards Philoktetes, as he agrees to take him with him, and offers to lend him the physical support he needs. The two may either progress some way towards the L *parodos*, and finally halt at EBL, as Philoktetes prepares to kiss the ground in farewell; or they may be preparing to leave during this exchange, with Neoptolemos supporting Philoktetes, and Philoktetes raising the bow defiantly, without progressing far.[77]

They are interrupted by Herakles, who has come from 'the heavens' (1413–14), as they seem about to depart from the constraints of the myth, of the prophecy which grants it inevitability, and from the full achievement of their own *arete* (1420, linked explicitly to 1425). Modern critics have been rather vexed by Herakles, uncertain about where to place him and apologetic about his intrusion. It has been suggested that he comes from the cave, appears on the *skene* roof, or on the *mechane*.[78] If he is suspended on the *mechane*, like a god, then

(1980, 141) suggests that Neoptolemos has by now demonstrated his understanding of the worth of Philoktetes, and of 'genuine friendship': 'Sophocles does not allow Neoptolemos to state the terms of the oracle until he responds, in action as well as feeling, to its spirit.'

[77] Seale (1982, 45) following Robinson (1969, 42) reasonably envisages a slow departure, but fails to take account of the final gesture of farewell, kissing the ground. Webster (1970, 155, on 1402) believes the change of metre indicates 'moving off', but does not comment on the final gesture. Taplin (1978, 134) is aware that the script suggests punctuated movement, suggesting halts at 1404 and 1407, although he erases the physicality of the final gesture by translating 'Make your farewell to the land, and come.'

[78] Woodhouse (1912, 248) had Herakles appearing from the cave; Webster (1970, 8) is followed by Seale (1982, 45) in opting for the roof, but without explanation; Wiles (1997, 181) states that 'we need only envisage the crane where separation from the earth is at issue', but despite the crucial importance of Herakles' apotheosis perversely places him on the roof. Rabel (1997, 300)

we do not need to explain his own reference to his visible immortality (1420) by imagining a process of rejuvenation: after all, Philoktetes has not seen any sign of Herakles since he burned his body on the pyre on Mount Oita.[79] Herakles offers Philoktetes both healing and fame, and warns against impiety, an ominous note that points beyond the immediate concerns of this tragedy to the future impiety, when Neoptolemos kills Priam at an altar.[80] Herakles is the embodiment of heroic achievement and friendship for Philoktetes, perhaps the only person Philoktetes would trust apart from his own father, and he recommends achievement and friendship (with Neoptolemos) to Philoktetes. The bow is, of course, the symbol as well as the instrument of that achievement, and it must be used.[81]

Human obstinacy, resentment, and alienation are replaced by fulfilment through action, with its rewards in healing and fame. Herakles removes himself from the scene, and Philoktetes is left to address the *theatron* expansively, as the now more benign landscape of Lemnos. The *anapaestic* metre, used from 1445 to the end, is associated with movement, and perhaps Philoktetes does move as he addresses the features of the island, particularly from 1461 as he declares that he is leaving it. As the Sailors also leave behind the two main characters, it cannot now be far from the audience's mind that the restoration and satisfaction that await Philoktetes were not promised to everyone in the glorious sack of Troy.

prefers the *mechane*. (Craik 1990, 83 seems to compromise, by having Herakles arrive on the *mechane* and land on the roof.)

Mastronarde (1990), in the most thorough study of the use of the *mechane* and the roof, may have put his finger on the reason for this range of interpretation: 'the crane is perfectly possible, and we should not consider it less likely simply because of some prejudice about the dignity of Sophocles' dramaturgy' (271).

[79] Webster (1970, 157, on 1420) believes that Herakles 'appears young and beautiful' in explanation of his visible immortality, rather than trusting to the *mechane* to make the point.

[80] Segal (1995) takes this warning as the key to unlocking the religious concerns of the tragedy, which began with Philoktetes' trespass at the shrine of Chryse.

[81] Rabel (1997, 298) argues that Herakles succeeds in persuasion because he 'uses the details of his own life in order to provide a paradigm for heroic emulation', one which Philoktetes could have no difficulty in accepting; this contrasts, for Rabel, with the failure of the embassy to Achilleus in the *Iliad* as well as the failure of the human agents in this drama.

Oidipous at Kolonos

GREGORY MCCART

The Actors and their Roles

It is not necessary to presume that, contrary to convention, this drama needs four rather than three speaking actors.[1] Oidipous and Antigone are in the playing space for most of the drama and are the major roles which would have been taken by the first and second actors respectively. The Stranger, Ismene and Theseus in Scene 2 can be allocated to the third actor. In Scene 3, during which the third actor plays Kreon, Antigone is abducted. The second actor then returns to this scene, after sufficient time to change mask and costume, as Theseus. In Scene 4 Theseus returns with Antigone and Ismene, so we can presume that the second actor has resumed the role of Antigone and the third actor the role of Theseus. This means that Ismene must be played by a silent actor; that is why Sophokles has assigned no lines to her in Scenes 4, 5 and 6, at the end of which the character exits.[2] All three speaking actors are off the playing space during the Attendant's speech in Scene 7. However, since Antigone and Ismene return immediately the Attendant finishes speaking and in the subsequent scene they both sing, we can assume that the role of Ismene has been resumed by the third actor. That leaves only the first actor to play the Attendant. In the Finale, both second and third actors, as Antigone and Ismene, are on the playing space when the character of Theseus, now played by the first actor, makes an appearance.[3]

In summary, therefore, we can say that the first actor would have played Oidipous, the Attendant and Theseus in the Finale, the second

---

[1] The debate on this has been longstanding. See, for example, Campbell (1871, 243) and Ceadel (1941, 139–47) who opt for four and Pickard-Cambridge (1968, 142–4) who opts for three.

[2] This silent performance poses a problem for modern, unmasked acting (as Taylor 1986, xxii discovered), because it constrains the actor playing Ismene to respond only through facial expression and physical gesture for three entire scenes. It is challenging for an unmasked actor to sustain credibility in these circumstances. Masked acting, which is more demonstrative, presents no such problem.

[3] Pavlovskis (1977, 120) argues, unconvincingly in my view, that the role of Theseus, for patriotic reasons, could not be played by more than one actor.

actor Antigone and Theseus in Scene 3 and the third actor the Stranger, Ismene, Kreon, Polyneikes and Theseus in Scenes 2, 4 and 6.[4] Juggling the roles and masks in this fashion in composing the tragedy was a radical, virtuoso achievement for the octogenarian playwright.

The Productions

This revised translation of the drama was first workshopped in October and November 1997 in the Arts Theatre at the University of Southern Queensland. The workshopped production featured masks, and the performance took place on a circular performing area ten metres in diameter. A production of an earlier version of the translation took place in the same theatre in 1989 That production did not use masks. These notes draw on my experience as director of both productions, but refer specifically to the 1997 workshopped production.

Scene 1

The first and second actors in the roles of Oidipous and Antigone, respectively, enter the orchêstra down the R parodos. This action signals that they are arriving from outside the locale in which the action of the drama is set. It is reversed when Antigone and Ismene leave at the end of the drama, in one of several mirror-scenes that occur in Oidipous at Kolonos. The commencing sequence is concerned primarily with identifying the place that Oidipous and Antigone have reached.

Before either of the actors speaks, it is clear to spectators from their masks or make-up and motion that the older male character is blind and is led by a young girl. In our production, Oidipous clutched a staff in the right hand,[5] and rested his left arm on Antigone's right shoulder.[6] The appearance of Oidipous is often referred to, and it is very easy to create an image of him from these descriptions in the text. He is blind

[4] Flickinger (1918, 180) made this same allocation.

[5] The staff became a significant property in our production. Segal (1980, 125–42) examines how the sword in Ai, the robe in YWT, the urn in El and the bow in Phil are endowed with significance. See also Ewans and Ley's notes on these properties: 1999, 187–8 and 194 and above, pp. 241–2. For additional comment on the use of properties in tragedy, see Taplin 1978, 77–100; Segal 1980, 139; Ewans 1982, 2–4; and Easterling 1989, 62–3.

[6] In an action which amounts to a total renunciation of the 'heroic temper', as Knox (1964, 145–6) observed.

(1 and *passim*), old (20 and *passim*), fatigued (11, 19–20), terrible to see and hear (141) but, for all that, obviously a man of some dignity (8, 76, 1640). He has journeyed painfully (205), is disfigured (286, 552) and stricken (327). He cannot carry out a ritual of purification without help (495–6) and, left to himself, barely has the strength to crawl along (501–2).[7] Physically wretched (576), he is a sorry sight (745) and has no apparent means of support (747). He is covered in dirt (1258), his ribs are wasted (1260) and his hair is dishevelled and wind-blown (1261). He carries precious little food (1263) in a wallet attached to a cord around his neck.[8] He is clothed in rags (1357), and grimy ones at that (1598). These descriptions are of invaluable assistance to the mask-maker or make-up artist, the costume designer and the director in developing the visual dimension of the principal character, and this dimension comes into the drama even before a word is spoken.[9]

The first thirty-two lines of the drama are expository and initiate the plot. The spectators learn the names of the two characters (1 and 14),[10] their relationship as father and daughter, and the fact that they are homeless, wandering but, in spite of all, content.[11] Antigone describes the setting, thus doing double service: for Oidipous within the fictive action and for the spectators observing it. The place is a sacred grove with lush vegetation and prolific bird-life, and this was probably depicted by *skenographia*.[12] It also contains a place for the tired

---

[7] There is no reference to Oidipous limping, and this would suggest that he didn't. See McCart in Evans 1999, 292 n. 73 on *OKing*; also cf. Taplin 1983, 155–6 and 175.

[8] Jebb (1900, 199) recalls the description of the costume Athena creates for Odysseus in disguising him as a wandering beggar (Homer, *Odyssey* 13.437ff.); it includes a 'mean, much-tattered wallet'.

[9] Similarly, Antigone is small (148), barely out of childhood (346, 751), barefooted, hungry, and suffering from exposure (346–51), unhappy (559), degraded and impoverished (749–51). See Hammond (1984, 373–5) for a description of characters in Euripides' *Elektra*, also drawn from analysis of the text.

[10] Flickinger (1918, 212) cites this as an example of a clever introduction in 'part compensation for the lack of a handbill'.

[11] Jones 1962, 174: 'The bitterness of life is countered here by Sophocles in the thought that the aged are patient and satisfied with very little.'

[12] On *skenographia* cf. Ley 1989, and on its use in *El* and *Phil*, cf. Evans' and Ley's Notes above, pp. 183 and 226–7. Whitman 1983, 232 noted how the fearsome goddesses of Aischylos have here been so transformed by Sophokles that their appropriate sound-association is that of the music of nightingales,

Oidipous to be seated. It is apparent from subsequent action in this scene that this first resting-place is inside the grove, though visible to passers-by and close enough to an exit for Oidipous and Antigone to disappear from sight fairly quickly (113–16). Given the extensive use of the two *parodoi* throughout this drama, the only feasible place to set this seat is in the central opening of the *skene*.

The Stranger enters in a hurry, and impatiently interrupts Oidipous' formal greeting;[13] this begins a forty-eight-line exchange which includes more essential information for the spectators. In particular, they learn that the grove is dedicated to the goddess daughters of Earth and Darkness, named by the local inhabitants as the kind Eumenides but known by other names elsewhere.[14] One of those other names is the Erinyes or Furies, goddesses feared for the powerful vengeance they exact on mortals who offend them. Oidipous has unwittingly done so by entering their grove which, unlike other groves, is not to be used as a resting-place for travellers. Spectators also learn that the action takes place at Kolonos, a place near Athens and one regarded as a sacred site critical to the city's survival. The Stranger refers to a statue of the horseman, Kolonos, which presumably is visible and situated in the performing area (BL in our production).[15] Though scandalized by Oidipous' claim that he will never leave this grove, the Stranger is mollified by his apparent nobility and his 'heroic resolve',[16] and leaves to seek the advice of his fellow-citizens of Kolonos as to whether this blind wanderer who has offended the goddesses should be offered hospitality.

Oidipous' prayer to the goddesses of the grove explains the reasons for his refusal to leave the sacred site. He recalls prophecies of Apollo which implicated a grove dedicated to these goddesses who, like him, take no wine,[17] and the coincidence of a violent storm in signalling

which rounds off the sequence between Oidipous' arrival and his eventual acceptance where reference to them recurs at lines 668–80. But we cannot be sure whether the ancient Greeks used sound effects to create the ambience described or whether they relied solely on the words of the actor and the imaginations of the spectators – a view espoused by Arnott 1989, esp. 132–45.

[13] This interruption throws an effective emphasis on the sacredness of the ground on which Oidipous has trespassed; Mastronarde 1979, 64–5.

[14] For general discussion on the Euminides, see Linforth 1951, 92–7, and Knox 1964, 194; *contra* Brown 1984a, 260–81, esp. 276–81.

[15] Jebb (1900, 21) inclines towards the presence of a statue on the performing area, as do Walton 1987, 91 and Wiles 1997, 148.

[16] Knox 1964, 10–11.

[17] Henrichs (1983, 89–90) sees particular significance in this association.

the moment when he will, as he puts it in a metaphor drawn from a chariot-race, 'round the last bend in his life of pain' (91). He is confident that the time has come. It might appear as if this prayer, which in broad terms summarizes the action of the drama, deprives the subsequent action of dramatic interest but, as we shall see, Sophokles cleverly manipulates the action in order to create a sustained suspense.

The stage action in this scene is straightforward. Antigone leads Oidipous, who has one hand on her shoulder and another clutching his staff, down the R *parodos* onto the *orchêstra*. They stop at EBR soon after entering, when the weary Oidipous asks to be seated (9). Antigone leads him towards the rock at the mouth of the grove (EBC) while she describes what she sees. After 22, she seats Oidipous, and after 27 she is about to go off L to see if there are inhabitants nearby; but her movement is arrested when she catches sight of the Stranger entering along the L *parodos*. The Stranger arrives at 32 when he is announced by Antigone, and stops momentarily on entrance BL before challenging Oidipous. At 54, the Stranger moves to the visual and acoustic centre of the *orchêstra*, a position of prominence, in order to describe the region and its worship. He breaks back towards BL at 75 when he surmises Oidipous' noble origins, and agrees to consider his request to summon Theseus. He exits along the L *parodos*. Oidipous prays and at 113, after Antigone has announced the arrival of the Elders, he struggles to his feet, and is led into the grove out of sight after 116.

Choros 1[18]

The entrance of the Elders from Kolonos is exciting theatre.[19] The verse-form that Sophokles employed here is recognized as one which is intermediate between fully sung lyrics and spoken dialogue.[20] We can perhaps conclude from this that the entrance-song was energetic and

[18] There is a lacuna in the Greek text of this choral ode after 182. Four (bracketed) lines are surmised in the translation, following Lloyd-Jones and Wilson 1990, 223.

[19] Gardiner (1987, 109–16) describes the Elders as compassionate and honest, and explores the significant role they play in the action throughout the drama. See also Esposito (1996, 85–114, esp. 102–4) for comment on the increasing dramatic and interactive roles of Sophokles' *choroses*.

[20] See Jebb (1900, lvii–lxxxii) for a metrical analysis of the drama.

dramatic,[21] as the Elders danced their vigorous search for Oidipous. [22] In A1 the Elders reiterate the fearsomeness of the goddesses whom Oidipous has offended, before Oidipous makes an unexpected appearance at the mouth of the *skene* and announces that he is their quarry. The Elders' response in A2 is to sing and dance encouragement to Oidipous to leave the sacred area. The action in this first part of the entrance-song and dance suggests choreography is vigorous and agitated, even somewhat threatening; in keeping with the frantic search, the dancers in our production covered the expanse of the *orchêstra* during the *strophe*, excluding the area EBC, which was off-limits. The intense emotion of the *antistrophe* appears to require the same type of vigour and expansiveness of movement.

The short exchange between Oidipous and Antigone at lines 170–75 initiates a crucial action. It is important to understand the significance of this action for the staging of this sequence and a corresponding one later in the drama (Scene 6). Normally entrances from the *skene* are introduced by few lines or even none at all, while many entrances from either of the *parodoi* are accompanied by lengthier introductions (see, for a prime example, Antigone's description of Ismene's arrival at 310–21). Here we have an 'entrance', or at least a move from the centre of the *skene* onto the *orchêstra*, which occupies twelve lines of song and four lines of address (176–91). This is a clear indication of two things: first, Oidipous, old and blind, weary and frightened, moves slowly; and second, he covers considerable distance from his first sitting place to the second sitting place, which is away from the sacred area. For the remainder of the drama, Oidipous' disabilities largely prevent him from moving freely (at least until his exit);[23] and in the ancient theatre the primary focus, both visual and acoustic, is the centre of the *orchêstra*;[24] so it is a logical conclusion that a bench or rock has been

[21] Seale 1982, 119; Kirkwood 1958, 204. This sequence is a typical case of contextual and verbal parallelism reflected in the visual dimension, according to Taplin 1979, 122. For similar correspondences, see 1271–9 and 1541–52.

[22] On dancing *choroses* in tragedy, see Davidson 1986. Aylen (1985, 20–22) and Walton (1984, 62–6) also explore the importance of dance in the performance of tragedy. Lawler (1964) is the principal authority on dance in ancient Greece.

[23] This is hardly justification for having him static for the remainder of the drama, as some scholars suggest (e.g. Dale 1969, 125–6; Seale 1982, 137). We found in our production that there was ample scope and even demand for Oidipous to be mobile.

[24] Ley and Ewans 1985; cf. Rehm 1992, 34–6, Wiles 1997, 63ff.

preset as this second seat close to that spot, just upstage of centre, so that Oidipous is the focal point of attention. This is where Antigone leads him from EBC to C during the B1 stanza.[25] The painstaking nature of the journey also reflects and emphasizes the vulnerability and fragility of Oidipous as he has himself led – delivered up as it were – into the hands of people whom he does not yet know he can trust.[26]

The action in this scene is comparatively easy to imagine and to reproduce in performance, since so much detail is narrated or commanded in the text: 'come on away', 'Hold me then', 'I am moving away', 'Come forward still', 'Come this way, father', 'Don't step beyond that slab of rock', 'Can I sit down?' and so on.[27] These descriptive lines provide clear 'stage directions' which only need to be heeded by the actors. The length of time it takes to sing the entire passage clearly indicates a journey of some distance. The actual sitting down on the rocky step is similarly painstaking, occupying most of the B2 stanza (192–202). Oidipous' agonizingly slow journey from the mouth of the grove to taking his seat near the centre of the performing area is marvellously reversed later in the drama (see the commentary on Scene 6), in another example of a mirror-scene.

When Oidipous sits, the Elders calm him; in doing so they gather round him, drawing close to him for the first time in the performance. The *antistrophe* closes on the usual formal questions by prospective hosts of a stranger; but in this instance they instigate greater drama because Oidipous, against all custom, refuses to tell them who he is. Constrained however by the rigour of the custom and by Antigone's advice, Oidipous relents. The Elders' reaction is precisely as he had feared. Rumours of his parricide and marriage to his mother had spread far and wide and enhanced his unwelcome reputation as a man suffering from *miasma*, a man therefore to be avoided lest infection from the pollution spread to those who come into contact with him. Despite their earlier promise that they would not evict him from their land, the Elders' fear prompts them to argue that their act of unfaithfulness merely matches his earlier concealment of his identity, and that they are released from the bonds of their promise.

[25] This placement and blocking avoids all the staging problems imagined by Brown (1984b, 13).

[26] Walton (1984, 123) notes the strength of Sophokles' dramatic technique in generating sympathy for his characters.

[27] Reinhardt (1979, 200) comments that the abundance of opposing movement in this sequence is more than is usually found in earlier Choroses.

The Elders' horrified reaction to the gradual revelation of Oidipous' identity ('son of Laios ... 'race of Labdakos' ... 'miserable Oidipous' ... 'luckless Oidipous': 220–24) indicate a rapid reversal of their comforting move towards him and suggest a withdrawal as far away from him as possible – to the perimeter of the *orchêstra*.[28] Antigone's plea (237–54) is so impassioned that it drives her from Oidipous' side to dance an approach to the Elders each in turn – 'looking eye to eye' as she puts it (245–6) – and to encircle the entire *orchêstra* from, in our production, BR via FC to BL. This action brings the long entrance-song and dance to a close.

Scene 2

This scene is exceptionally long by the standards of tragedy; it comprises 413 lines, and amounts to nearly one quarter of the drama. A sequence featuring Oidipous is followed by one involving Ismene, after which an Elder instructs Oidipous in a ritual of purification; this is followed by a *kommos* shared by Oidipous and the Elders, at the close of which Theseus makes his long-awaited entrance.

Oidipous and the Elders (255–309) The scene opens with the Elders' rejection of Antigone's plea on the grounds that they fear the gods who have so afflicted Oidipous, whatever the reason. Oidipous' response to this is an interesting exercise in interpretation for performance. In essence, Oidipous argues that Athens is supposed to be renowned for its hospitality, that he has been passive rather than active in his misfortunes, that his disfigurement and the rumours about him are not good reasons for ejecting him, that the gods take note of impious behaviour which the Elders are initiating, and so they, in turn, should wait for Theseus' judgement. Up to this point in the drama, Oidipous' vulnerability and weakness have been prominent, although he displayed a determination in the face of the Stranger's insistence, and a resilience during the Elders' concerted efforts to dislodge him from the grove. It is also true that *thymos* or fiery temper is typical of the way

---

[28] Jebb (1900, 45) adds a stage direction which has the Elders half turning from him, holding their mantles before their eyes as they cry out. Seale (1982, 120) and Winnington-Ingram (1980, 268) applaud this suggestion. We preferred in our production a more vigorous recoil. See Burton (1980) for an excellent description of Sophokles' exploitation of sung dialogues in this drama.

his character is depicted in both of Sophokles' Oidipous tragedies.[29] This – along with the assertive use of language to begin the address – suggests an explosive outburst rather than a repeat of Antigone's empathic style of entreaty.

In our production, Oidipous rose from his seat, driven by passion, and gesticulated emphatically, using also his staff, in a severe rebuke of the Elders.[30] In so doing he asserted his dignity and his innate, though up till now repressed, heroic status while putting arguments which in the end persuade the Elders to wait for Theseus. The sequence ends in a downbeat fashion, with an exchange of pleasantries about Theseus as the Elders relent a little and relax, but keep their distance all the same. Antigone, whose concern for her father's well-being brought her to his left side during his outburst in her accustomed role as guide, is in a prime position to see and announce the next arrival, who is not the expected Theseus from the L *parodos*, but the unexpected Ismene from the R.

Oidipous and Ismene (310–460) Ismene enters on a horse, which Antigone recognizes as bred in Aitna.[31] Antigone's lengthy introduction to her entrance (310–21 including a half-line, excitable intervention by Oidipous) exploits the 'dramatic potential of the *parodos*',[32] and clearly indicates that the entrance takes some time. This is in keeping with an entrance on foot or one in which Ismene's servant (specifically referred to in 334) leads the horse onto the *orchêstra* and then to C, where Ismene dismounts after greeting Oidipous and Antigone. While the use of a horse in a modern indoor theatre is out of the question, the open

[29] Winnington-Ingram (1980, 257–60) is of the opinion that Oidipous' *thymos* was excessive when he stabbed out his eyes, and remains so in his dealings with his sons. Knox (1966, 20–24) saw Oidipous' actions in the drama as emanating from an imperious anger. Kitto (1973 [1939], 149) was inclined towards a more complex interpretation of the Sophoklean hero. Bushnell (1988, 101–2) reminds us that we must recognize the Oidipous of the Attendant's messenger-speech (Scene 7), who expresses a tenderness and pity for his daughters. The development of the character of Oidipous for performance needs to explore all these avenues to arrive at something that approaches the complexity of this extraordinary Sophoklean hero.

[30] For an impressive catalogue of actions actually described in the texts of tragedies as expressions of the emotions of grief, fear, desire, aversion and pleasure, see Shisler 1945, 12. Cf. also Stanford 1983.

[31] Wiles (1997, 149) finds significance in the fact that it is a female pony, promoting the male/female binary opposition in the drama.

[32] Gould 1989, 12–13.

space of the ancient theatre provided no such difficulty.[33] We need only to recall the entrance of a chariot carrying Agamemnon and Kassandra in Aischylos' *Agamemnon* and to note, in general, the equine expertise of the ancient Athenians, celebrated in this very drama (Choros 2: 668–70, 706–17), to realize that such an entrance is not only feasible but theatrically appealing. Ismene dismounts during the *antilabe*, prior to embracing Oidipous and Antigone at 329b. This image of the three characters embracing is repeated later in the drama (1112–14), in another example of a mirror-scene.

Ismene's revelation of the difficulties she has suffered in trying to find Oidipous, and to do so without opponents in Thebes knowing, prompts another outburst from her father in which he excoriates the Aigyptian behaviour of his sons, and compares it in most unfavourable terms with the nurturing role adopted by his daughters.[34] The personal references in the speech to Antigone (345ff.) and to Ismene (353ff.) prompt the actor playing Oidipous to reach out to each of them at the appropriate moments with gestures signifying love and dependence.

There is a painting on a kalyx-krater dated to pre-340 BC which represents three characters sitting on a bench.[35] The central character is an old white-haired, bearded man clothed in decrepit robes and holding underneath his cloak what appears to be a staff. On his left a similarly dressed, slight young girl is sitting, her feet not touching the ground. Her face is turned towards the central figure. On the right of this figure sits another female character, dressed elaborately in decorated robes and ornate headdress. Her left arm is raised under her cloak as if in emphatic gesture. Standing behind her and to her right is a male character holding a staff with left hand on his hip and an attentive gaze on his face. What appears to be a tambourine-type instrument lies on the floor in front of him. This scene probably represents the moment in *Oidipous at Kolonos* when Ismene, who comes with the one servant she can trust, straight from the palace and therefore dressed opulently, brings her news to the dishevelled Oidipous and Antigone. The bench on which they are sitting represents the rocky slab to which the Elders guided Oidipous during Choros 1. Our production recreated this disposition, with the Servant EBR and the three principal characters seated on the stone bench C. They moved

[33] Cf. Haigh 1907, 201. *Contra* Jebb 1900, 58.

[34] Sophokles' comments on the habits of Aigyptians reflect those of his contemporary and friend Herodotos (*Histories* 2.35).

[35] See the cover of this volume.

into these positions as Ismene began her reply to Oidipous at 361. The Elders remained at the perimeter of the *orchêstra* out of apparent respect for the intimacy between the three characters.

The information Ismene passes on in the subsequent speech and *stichomythia* confirms in part the oracle cited by Oidipous in his prayer to the goddesses in Scene 1, namely that the time has come when he will be an agent of reward to those who receive him and ruin to those who exiled him (92–3). It also informs Oidipous and the audience of the conflict that has initiated the dramatic events that soon follow. Both Thebes, ruled by Eteokles and Kreon, and Polyneikes with his Argive army now realize from the oracles that whoever has power over Oidipous will win the ensuing battle. This sequence therefore marks the point in the drama where Oidipous' personal plight – his need for hospitality and his conviction that somehow his life will come to a close in this place – escalates into (if we may use contemporary language) an international incident. Three *poleis* now have a stake in the issue: Thebes, Argos and Athens, although Athens is yet to realize the significance. Oidipous does, but it is not this that immediately occupies his thoughts. It is rather the response of his sons to the new oracle.

Instead of inviting Oidipous back to Thebes to reinstate him to the extent possible, Polyneikes and Eteokles choose to use him for their own purposes and continue to ignore his needs. All this becomes particularly clear later in the drama, with the appearance firstly of Kreon and secondly of Polyneikes. For the present, the important issue is that Oidipous, once – and still – ruined, will now be restored to a position of power. And this is what he can promise the Elders. Before he does that, however, his *thymos* wells once again, and he willingly and publicly embraces the role of arbitrator in his sons' conflict to their ultimate destruction. He claims for the first time that his self-blinding was an overreaction to the 'errors' of the past and that the subsequent exile imposed on him by the city was unjustified; his sons' refusal to prevent this exile was particularly unforgivable. Sophokles seems unconcerned about consistency in relation to who precisely was to blame for sending him into exile. Here it is 'the city'[36] (440) but in his

---

[36] The notion of city, applying to both Thebes and Athens, here and throughout the drama, is difficult to fix precisely. Easterling (1997, esp. 34–6) suggests Sophokles adopts 'heroic vagueness' which allows then and now for diverse political readings. See Slatkin (1986) on the drama as a political moral. Wiles (1997, 220–21) also comments on the play's political implications.

confrontations with Kreon and with Polyneikes later, he accuses both
of them individually of banishing him (770 and 1364–5). One gets the
impression of a cartel operating in Thebes which shared responsibility
for sending him into exile.

This address is a public declaration, arising from the information
received in private conversation with Ismene. When Oidipous rose to
address the Elders, they indicated their attention in our production by
moving a step or two towards him. His promise to them that he will
be their saviour (459) drew from one Elder advice as to what he should
do in order to purify himself, before he could fulfil any protective role
for Athens.

The Ritual of Purification (461–509)   In many of the surviving tragedies, religious ritual and cultic celebration feature intrinsically or
extrinsically. This drama is an example of both.[37] A cult in honour of
the *heros* Oidipous was established in Kolonos, and Sophokles' drama
can be read in one way as a fictive justification for the existence of the
cult. That is the extrinsic reference. The intrinsic reference to ritual
constitutes this sequence in Scene 2. The description of the rite is very
detailed and leads to speculation that it was recognizable to the
Athenian spectators in 401 BC. A singular feature of the ritual is one to
which Oidipous had previously referred in his prayer to the goddesses
in Scene 1: the libations are made with vessels filled with water, or
with water mixed with honey. The absence of wine is specific to
worship of the Erinyes or, in Kolonan terminology, the Eumenides.
The ritual is also dramatically important. As we shall see, when
Theseus arrives, events in the drama escalate and these events require
that Oidipous be accepted by Athens and the Elders. That cannot
happen until he has undertaken a purification rite to acquit him of the
punishment due for his earlier trespass into the grove. For this reason,
Sophokles has the Elders sufficiently swayed by Oidipous' promise of
protection that they offer him this advice – and thereby clear the decks,
as it were, for later plot development.[38]

[37] Reinhardt (1979, 193–4) interprets the action of the drama interestingly
as 'an enactment of cult-legend: the visible testimony and perception of a
mystery presented as narrative, celebrated in song and dance, and still potent.'
Lardinois (1992) argues that the drama represents Athenian appropriation of a
panhellenic figure. For more on ritual in tragedy, see Easterling 1993, 7–23 and
Seaford 1994.

[38] Gardiner (1987, 112–13) invests the Elders with too much authority in
asserting that they and not Theseus acquit Oidipous of his *miasma*. For a more
balanced view, see Gellie 1972, 167.

The allocation of lines in this sequence poses an interesting challenge. While the first Elder to speak does so in the singular (464), Oidipous twice uses the plural in seeking and acknowledging the advice (465 and 493). This might suggest an allocation of lines to more than one speaker. If this is done in performance, it creates a sense of a communal rather than individual softening of attitude towards the visitor. In our production, each Elder, on the assigned line, moved towards Oidipous, seated centre, and adopted prayerful poses mimetically derived from the specific liturgical instruction.

Oidipous' 'two disabilities' – frailty and blindness – prevent him from carrying out the rite. While this is a credible excuse, it also serves Sophokles well in his plot development. By having Ismene volunteer to perform the rite on her father's behalf (a concession foreshadowed by an Elder at 486), Sophokles achieves two important objectives, one in the fictive world of the drama, the other in the theatrical operation of the performance. Ismene exits along the R *parodos* to perform the ritual. We know that she must exit in this direction because Kreon, who appears in the next scene, comes from out of town and in the course of the scene announces that he has abducted Ismene.[39] This can only happen if her exit and his entrance spatially coincide. By having Ismene go to perform the ritual, followed by the servant leading the horse, Sophokles, in terms of the fictive world of the drama, removes her from the protection of the Elders and makes her subject to Kreon's action. In terms of its theatrical operation, Sophokles, by this device, also allowed the third actor to divest himself of the mask and costume of Ismene and to don those of Theseus, who will appear in the next scene. And Sophokles allows the actor sufficient time to do so; he now introduces a *kommos* into the action.

Kommos (510–48) A *kommos* indicates a heightening of the drama. The first actor and members of the *choros* now sing and dance a narrative; this dramatizes a vigorous interrogation, which returns to the Elders' understandable curiosity about the infamous individual who has appeared on their doorstep. The mood of the *kommos* is in stark contrast to the mood of the previous sequence, which was con-

[39] Knox (1966, 151) believes that the description of the ritual is spun out too long simply in order to get Ismene off. But in performance, the sequence intimates for the first time an acceptance of Oidipous and provides dramatic contrast with the previous and following sequences, as is typical of Sophoklean construction (cf. Winnington-Ingram 1980, 250; Burton 1980, 262; and Easterling 1989, 60).

ciliatory. Here the Elders' determination to seek confirmation of the rumours they have heard drives them to ignore Oidipous' discomfort and obvious unwillingness to discuss the matters they raise, namely his marriage to his mother and the killing of his father. The story itself of course would have been well known at the time of the play's première performance, but rehearsing the events once again allows Sophokles the opportunity to have Oidipous for a second time declare his innocence – an innovation in the story peculiar, as far as our sources reveal, to this drama. It is essential for Sophokles to reiterate Oidipous' conviction of his innocence in order to reverse the traditional view of him as guilty, and to prepare the way for transforming his *miasma* into a quality that elevates him by the end of the drama to the status of a *heros* celebrated in cult. The doggedness of the Elders' interrogation suits a choreography that has them hound the seated figure of Oidipous, centre. On the arrival of Theseus, in our production, the Elders retreated BRC to BLC and observed the subsequent exchange.

Oidipous and Theseus   Finally, 469 lines since the Stranger exited to alert the Elders and then Theseus of Oidipous' arrival, and 240 lines since he was last mentioned, Theseus arrives. The Athenian tragedians' fluid use of time and place refutes the strictures imposed by the neoclassical scholars through the so-called unities.

Theseus is a difficult character for a modern actor to portray.[40] So highly regarded was he in ancient Athens as the model leader that his depiction here and elsewhere borders on an adulation, which deprives the character of a range of human qualities that might be seen as less than heroic. The modern actor needs to appreciate that the character was created by an Athenian for Athenian consumption at a time when politically and militarily Athens was on its knees. Theseus in this drama is a reminder of the perfection desired in a ruler. He is, like the staircase made of bronze in this very grove (57 and 1592), a bulwark for Athens against its enemies; he needs to be portrayed as invincible, intelligent and generous. This portrayal can be abetted by the way in which the Elders defer to him on his entrance, and throughout his presence on the *orchêstra*. That way he can appear to be a mortal with a near-

---

[40] This is so even when we accept the comparison by Stanford (1983, 25) to the Theseus of Euripides' *Suppliant Women, Herakles* and *Children of Herakles*, who is also characterized by compassion, the source of which is personal suffering and survival.

divine aura, and a worthy recipient of the singular gift bestowed by Oidipous later in the drama.

His very first address is indicative of intelligence and generosity.[41] He has already come to his own (correct) conclusions about Oidipous and is proud to compare his own life's experiences with those of his visitor. This is against all expectations encouraged by the tentative aspirations of Oidipous himself at the commencement of the drama and the terrified and violent response of the Elders, once they had learned who he was. Theseus is exceptional: he understands, he is compassionate, and he leaves Oidipous with no need to mount the kind of apologia that the attitude of the Elders earlier required. So the scene can be devoted to advancing the plot, and having Theseus alerted to the fact that new oracles and Oidipous' arrival at the grove have implicated Athens in potential inter-city conflict. Such a conflict would be contrary to the existing political alliance between Athens and Thebes which is presumed in the fictive world of the drama, and it takes a prophetic and magisterial speech from Oidipous to convince Theseus that conflict is likely to erupt and that Athens' victory will rely on the talisman of Oidipous' buried corpse.

Up to this point in the scene, there is little need or justification for movement by the actors playing Oidipous and Theseus. It is appropriate that they share the focus close to the centre of the *orchêstra*, and turn to and away from each other as prompted by the flux of emotional responses suggested by their speeches and stichomythic exchanges. When Theseus announces his acceptance of Oidipous and his granting him citizenship, in our production he broke R, moved towards BC to face the Elders, and completed a circular movement by arriving L to make his offer to Oidipous to accompany him (638). In choosing to stay at the grove site out of respect for Apollo's oracles and expectation of his own restoration, Oidipous becomes agitated when he speaks of the violence he anticipates from his sons, expressed in *antilabe* (652–6), before Theseus concludes the scene with an authoritative assertion of his unassailable protection of Oidipous,[42] and departs along the L *parodos*.[43]

[41] Easterling (1973) argues that Sophokles' use of word repetition is often functional. She finds evidence in this sequence that repetition of particular words in the Greek builds up an impression of rapport between Oidipous and Theseus. See, for example, 590/1, 631/6, and 638/40.

[42] Three interpolated lines (658–60) have been excised from the translation: There are so many threats – mostly bellowed

Choros 2

A number of ancient sources record an ancedote relating to a supposed
court case involving Sophokles and his son, Iophon.[44] In order to refute
his son's charge that he was incapable of running his property because
of senility, Sophokles quoted this choral ode to the jurors to demonstrate his sanity and intelligence. He was acquitted of the charge, and
escorted from the court with applause. The authenticity of the story
cannot be determined, but perhaps its existence reflects the regard in
which the aged Sophokles was held with respect to his dramatic
composition and in particular to this particular ode. The ode celebrates
Athens for its breeding and training of horses, its legendary superiority
at sea, its soil which produces olives, fruits, flowers and abundant
vegetation, its prolific water supply and bird-life and the belief that the
gods choose to live there. It is an eloquent example of an extreme
patriotism more concerned with feeling good than with actuality.[45]
When it was first sung and danced in 401 BC, it must have been a
poignant moment for the spectators who had lived through the loss to
Sparta in the Peloponnesian War and the consequent political turmoil
and social unrest in Athens.[46] Still, nations proud of their past may be
defiant in the face of defeat. In terms of the drama, the ode marks a
major change in performative style after such a long scene, entirely
spoken apart from the brief *kommos* at 510–48. The logaoedic metre
in the Greek original, as in the entrance dance, allows for a vigorous
display in choreographing the narrative. The energy of the Elders
contrasts with the frailty of Oidipous. As well as celebrating Athens,
the ode signals the Elders' acceptance of Oidipous in obedience to
Theseus' instruction, and this brings the first phase of the action, which
was initiated when the Stranger challenged Oidipous to leave the grove,
to closure.[47] The question posed by Oidipous in his opening speech has
now been answered, and he has received the hospitality he sought.
However, the action initiated by Ismene's arrival is yet to be resolved.
During the singing and dancing of this ode, the third actor, inside the

out in anger to no purpose. When
common sense returns, the threats are gone.
[43] Bushnell (1988, 94–5) discusses Theseus' role in fulfilling Apollo's oracles
concerning Oidipous.
[44] Jebb 1900, xxxix–xlii.
[45] Cf. Whitman 1983, 232.
[46] Cf. Knox 1964, 154–5; Taylor 1986, xxx.
[47] A mood of tranquillity descends (Burton 1980, 274).

skene building, dons a new mask and costume, for the fourth time in the drama – this time those of Kreon.

Scene 3

Action on the *orchêstra* up to this point in the drama has been relatively restrained, governed principally by the entrances and exits of characters and the physical responses of the Elders. That restraint is abandoned in this scene in most decisive fashion: it calls for extensive use of gesture and movement throughout.[48] Kreon enters with at least two guards down the R *parodos*, having come, like Ismene, from Thebes. It is apparent from his opening lines to the citizens of the country that he has now entered that the Elders 'shrink away' from him. Effective use can be made of the open space of the *orchêstra* if the Elders group BL/ FL opposite to Kreon R and the guard ERC.

Kreon's speech is a masterpiece of hypocrisy.[49] His temerity can be embodied if the space of the *orchêstra* is used by the actor playing him as his auditors cower away from him. In our production, he assumed a prominent position BC before circling the seat via R and coming to Oidipous and Antigone L. This put him to the left of Antigone, to whose condition he then called attention. His demeanour towards her and his gestures were intimidatory. On the pretext of hiding the shame of having Antigone prey to all kinds of dangers, Kreon invites Oidipous to return home to Thebes; in concluding with this invitation, in our production, he divested Oidipous of his staff as a sign of disempowering him. The question of whether or not touching a polluted man was believed to be infectious arose at this point in rehearsal. It is clear that the Elders avoided contact with Oidipous, but Antigone of course does not. At the end of *Oidipous the King*, Oidipous asks Kreon to take his hand as a pledge, and it is apparent in the text that Kreon does so (1510). Later in this drama, Oidipous asks Theseus to take his hand, but then withdraws the request in view of the taint of evil which he says lives with him (1130ff.). It would appear therefore that while kin

---

[48] Pickard-Cambridge (1968) cites a number of passages in tragedy to support his contention that gesture and movement in performance were frequently mobile and rapid. Cf. also Ewans 1995, xix–xxvii. For an excellent discussion of gesture in tragedy, see Arnott 1989, 44–73, esp. 70–72. Gould (1989, 12) cites this passage with its interaction between actors and *choros* as clear textual evidence for the absence of any high stage in the classical Greek theatre.

[49] Cf. Reinhardt 1979, 211. Gellie (1972, 171) calls the speech 'graceful and gentle' (!).

are unaffected by touch, others might well be. It was felt that Kreon's close association with the family of Oidipous allowed him to come in contact with the polluted man.[50]

In our production, this touch galvanized Oidipous into sudden action as once again but more intensely than before his *thymos* welled, allowing him to overcome his frailty and weariness.[51] He crossed blindly, feeling his way, towards R away from Kreon in order to deliver the powerful and bitter attack on Kreon's duplicity. During the fierce stichomythic exchange that followed, the old warriors stood, toe to toe as it were, venting their spleen on each other.[52] On the line in which Kreon threatens that Oidipous will come to grief (816), he broke away from Oidipous to FC, in our production, in order to prepare for Antigone's abduction.

The action that erupts after this is the most dynamic – and perhaps the most violent[53] – in surviving tragedy, and a credit to the sustained innovativeness of the ageing playwright. There is a number of ways of blocking the action, but each must respect certain requirements. For a start, Oidipous is blind, and therefore his actions are unguided and even reckless and dangerous. Antigone seeks refuge, as she says (828ff.), presumably with the Elders, but in vain. Kreon himself snatches Antigone away as he says, 'I take what's mine' on the tripartite 831, and drags her towards the R *parodos* as the Elders attempt to free her. Oidipous gropes helplessly in the direction of her voice. On the command 'You! Get her out!' (847a), Kreon thrusts Antigone towards his guards who immediately drag her out along the R *parodos*. It is also important to note that a third of the lines are sung and danced in a *kommos* shared by Oidipous, Kreon and the Elders, consisting mainly of the exciting dochmiac metre in the Greek. The allocation of lines, both spoken and sung, to individual members of the *choros* is irresistible in creating the chaotic and threatening action demanded. In our production Kreon snatched Antigone, cowering behind the Elders BLC, and with his guards guided her around the perimeter of the *orchêstra* from BL via EFC to ERC. Meanwhile, the Elders grouped and confronted

---

[50] Taplin (1979, 65–6) is wary of actual physical contact in performance, but allows for the possibility that emotive pathos might override meticulous religiosity.

[51] 'The heroic fire is re-kindled': Knox 1964, 157.

[52] '[T]he two old men are striking blow for blow' (metaphorically at least); Winnington-Ingram 1954, 17. Cf. Euripides, *Children of Herakles* 50–79, 71, 127–9.

[53] Cf. Burton 1980, 65; Seale 1982, 129; Burian 1974, 420 n. 29.

the trio as they traversed the performing area. Oidipous' anguish and helplessness were signified by his inept attempts to reach out to and rescue his daughter.

This passage of vigorous action ends with the guard taking Antigone off, while Kreon, in his overweening arrogance, returns to confront Oidipous. It is apparent in the subsequent action that the Elders are now emboldened, given the absence of Kreon's armed guard. They prevent Kreon from leaving and themselves prepare to pursue the girls. In our production, Kreon moved from EBR to FC as he commenced his attack on Oidipous, who remained C. At the same time, the Elders grouped BR/BL. The second part of the *kommos* is also in dochmiacs in the Greek and is sung by Oidipous, Kreon and the Elders. The lines and half-lines are assigned in precise responsion to those of the *strophe*. The Elders encircled Kreon and Oidipous during the *kommos* dance and as they shouted out for help in the last three lines, one of them wrested Oidipous away from Kreon to FC while the others broke towards the R *parodos* to set off in search of the abductors. Theseus' sudden entrance froze all action.

The sequence that follows is another example of the tragedians' complete disinterest in verisimilitude. The visible action and particularly the imagined action off is temporarily suspended while Theseus, Kreon and Oidipous debate issues of hospitality, justification, and ethical matters relating to *miasma*, blame and innocence. It is a reminder that the ancient Greek theatre was more than a site for spectacle and story-telling. It was a forum for often passionate debate on matters that touched the very heart of that culture and society. The most significant aspect of the debates in this sequence is Oidipous' repetition for the third time of his innocence, and this time his justification is argued with the rigour of a barrister. He questions how he can be blamed for being born the way he was and for retaliating when attacked by another man. This speech is an emphatic declaration of Sophokles' major revision to the story of the house of Labdakos, and asserts personal responsibility as a principle that overrides inherited guilt.[54] The gravity of the three long speeches demands for each of the characters the prominence that the visual and acoustic centre of the *orchêstra* provides, and the blocking in our production

[54] Two interpolated lines (954–5) have been omitted from the translation:
There's no old age for a fighting spirit, only
death. Pain doesn't touch the dead.

allowed for this. The scene ends with suspense, as Theseus ushers Kreon off along the R *parodos* in search of the abducted women.

Sophokles has led his spectators a long way from what appeared to be a straightforward plot, articulated by Oidipous in his prayer to the goddesses in Scene 1.

Choros 3

The third Choros consists of two strophic pairs and achieves two things dramatically: it sustains and intensifies the suspense surrounding the rescue attempt; and it does away with the need for a later messenger-speech in that it creates the off-stage battle, imagined as happening simultaneously, in song and dance.[55] The sound effects of war and the flurry of activity in conflicting forces are features of this ode. The clash of armour and the careering horses and chariots are set against a geography well known to the original spectators. The battle is imagined as taking place within the region governed by Athens down along the Bay of Eleusis (south-west of Athens), near a place that housed a temple dedicated to Apollo, or further along where the Mysteries associated with the goddesses Demeter and Persephone were conducted annually by priests descended from the warrior Eumolpos.[56] A2 pursues this conjecture by suggesting the mountainous region further west as a possible site for the engagement. The confidence of the Elders in Theseus is unswerving and they sing in B1 of their wish to fly to the clouds to observe the battle down below. They complete their song and dance with a prayer to the powerful foursome: Zeus, Athene, Apollo and his unnamed sister, Artemis. Their confidence is not necessarily justified, and it leaves the outcome of Theseus' rescue efforts in suspense – but not for long. The vigour of the envisaged action suggests choreography of similar vigour. In our production, pairs of Elders in turn enacted the events of the narrative (FC), while the distraught figure of Oidipous lay collapsed on the ground in front of them.

Scene 4

This short scene closes one sequence in the plot development and initiates the next. It is in two halves. On the one hand, the reunion

[55] Kamerbeek 1984, 148. See Burton (1980, 281–2) for an inspired discussion of this ode.

[56] Cf. Jebb 1900, 166–8 for a discussion of the geography and religious rituals referred to here by the Elders.

between Oidipous and his daughters and the brief report of Theseus'
comprehensive victory over Kreon put an end to Thebes' attempt,
through Kreon's disingenuous entreaty and physical violence, to take
charge of Oidipous so that he would serve as a harbinger of success in
their impending battle against the Argives. On the other hand, Theseus'
news that some stranger has prostrated himself at Poseidon's altar and
begs audience with Oidipous initiates the attempt by Polyneikes, on his
own behalf and that of his Argive comrades, to persuade Oidipous to
join forces with him for the same reason.

As the battle-dance ends, an Elder announces the return of Antigone
and Ismene (who is now played by a silent actor), escorted by Theseus.
The *antilabe* between Oidipous and Antigone evokes the emotive
nature of the rescue and reunion. It also has the dramatic effect of
delaying the actual physical embrace, which allows the action to dwell
on the emotions of joy and excitement – emotions which are absent for
much of the time in this fraught drama. The use of *antilabe* here, and
the delay in completing the embrace, mirror almost exactly the arrival
and welcome of Ismene in Scene 2. There is no doubt that Sophokles
intended the stage action to recall that meeting, and in doing so to
recall Ismene's announcement of Apollo's most recent oracle concerning Oidipous, and the important role he is to play in the ensuing
conflict between Thebes and Argos. On that occasion, conversation
turned quickly to the matter of Oidipous' sons and how their behaviour
towards their father warranted censure. And now in this scene, the re-
enactment of the excited exchanges and the embrace, with Oidipous
again flanked by his daughters, leads immediately to concerns about
the reasons for Polyneikes' prostration at the altar of Apollo. Before
this occurs, however, there is time for some Athenian breast-beating as
Oidipous thanks Theseus and in doing so lauds the qualities of
righteousness, humaneness and honesty which are claimed to be
endemic to Athens. By Oidipous' aborted attempt to take Theseus by
the hand in gratitude – aborted as he recollects his *miasma*[57] –
spectators are reminded that, despite the successful rescue and the
reunion, Oidipous' new status as one who belongs in Athens (637) has
not completely restored him to the glory promised by Apollo as
reported by Ismene (394).

---

[57] Easterling (1977, 128): 'a touch of great psychological nicety; it is worth
considering the possibility that the whole sequence – Creon's kidnapping of
Antigone and Ismene, and their rescue by Theseus – is designed to lead up to
this dramatic moment.'

After a verbally excited but physically restrained entrance, Antigone and Ismene joined Oidipous (c) in our production – at his left and right side respectively. Theseus stopped R while the Elders grouped BR/ BC. The *stichomythia* between Theseus and Oidipous (1154–68) contains one-, two- and four-line exchanges, the import of which is to move the focus of attention gradually from the rescue of the girls to the arrival of Polyneikes.[58] But it is not until the mention of a relative in Argos that the identity of the figure at the altar is realized. The *stichomythia* breaks into *antilabe* at 1169 and 1170, signalling a quickening of the exchanges; in our production Oidipous, at this point, broke away from engagement with Theseus to FL. Oidipous' *thymos* again gets him into trouble with his host and with the gods. His refusal to recognize Polyneikes' supplication is an offence to Poseidon and puts Theseus in a very awkward situation.

At the close of his appeal to Oidipous to respect the gods, Theseus, in our production, moved towards the Elders (BR/BC) to enlist support, after which Antigone approached Oidipous with her own appeal. This is Antigone's longest speech, and its length is particularly significant in the light of Oidipous' earlier instruction to her that her age and sex compel her to speak briefly (1115–18).[59] This emphasizes the importance of what she has to say, and justifies a prominent position on the *orchêstra*, which in our production incorporated the area confined by C/FL/FR/C. Only after this, for his daughters' sake, does Oidipous relent. Fearful of a repeat of Kreon's violent attack, however, Oidipous implores Theseus to protect him. Theseus goes out L to grant Polyneikes his supplication, while Antigone and Ismene lead Oidipous to the seat at C, as weariness and anxiety overcome him.

[58] At this point in the drama there appears to be an inconsistency in Sophokles' imagining of spatial directions. The altar of Poseidon has already been established as lying beyond the L *parodos* (cf. Taplin 1983, 158–61), in Kolonos of which he is the patron-god. Theseus had gone in that direction towards his palace after 667 and he had returned from there before 887. It would seem unlikely then that Theseus would learn of the arrival of Polyneikes at this altar on his return from rescuing Antigone and Ismene (that is, from beyond the R *parodos*). This remains a puzzle for logicians, but does not become an issue in performance, as the narrative takes dramatic precedence over logical inconsistency. The other difficulty – how did Polyneikes, who has come from Argos, get into Kolonos? – is casually resolved by Theseus' report that the suppliant had got to the altar 'somehow' (1157).

[59] Winnington-Ingram 1980, 259.

Choros 4

All the choral odes in this drama evolve directly from the dramatic action of the preceding scenes except this one, where the connection is less specific.[60] The first choral ode enacted a search for Oidipous and an attempt to evict him. The second was a patriotic song and welcome to Oidipous as a compatriot. The third was a battle-hymn envisaging the conflict between Theseus and Kreon. And now we have a depressing meditation on the miseries of life, completely in accord with a strain of ancient Greek thought,[61] but only vaguely connected with Oidipous, to whom specific attention is eventually given in the last stanza. The unrelenting nature of their guest's sufferings can serve in performance as a prompt for the Elders' reflection. The strophic pair rehearses life's agonies in a litany of woes. Death is referred to as a 'companion' who does mortals a favour in leading them away. Then, in the *epode* A3, the Elders point to Oidipous, whose sufferings they describe in terms of a desolate cape battered by constant winds and storms from every direction. The ode is in sharp contrast to the joy of the reunion enacted in the previous scene, and articulates a motif that runs through the drama, from Oidipous' opening address and his prayer in Scene 1 to his eventual release. The life of Oidipous is the perfect narrative to illustrate the arbitrary nature of an existence subject to whims of the gods and accident, rather than to clear thinking and goodwill.

Scene 5

This scene features two magnificent set pieces: Polyneikes' declaration of war and appeal to Oidipous for support; and Oidipous' vitriolic response.[62] Each of the speeches is a gift to an actor, incorporating as they do an expansiveness and a dramatic power that make great demands on vocal and physical performance, and provide great rewards. The contest between father and son is grounded in the ancient Greek heroic tradition with its warrior-code based on honour, shame,

[60] Winnington-Ingram (1980, 252 n. 10) makes a case that it is about youth and age and refers to Polyneikes and Oidipous.

[61] Cf. Herodotos, *Histories* 1.31–3, where Solon advises Kroisos that only the dead can be called happy.

[62] Kitto (1961 [1939], 381) dismisses this scene as marginal to the plot but Gellie (1972, 167) recognizes its centrality.

righteous indignation and personal excellence.[63] Both characters assert these values in arguing their cases.

This centrepiece is bracketed by sequences involving Polyneikes and Antigone. After Antigone announces the entrance of Polyneikes and describes his mask or face – for the benefit of Oidipous within the fiction and the spectators observing it – as a weeping visage, Polyneikes laments the circumstances and condition of Oidipous.[64] He addresses his sisters before accusing himself of being a scoundrel for learning of his father's situation so late. It is tempting to read a wicked duplicity in this, since it is almost unbelievable that the parlous condition of his father had not occurred to him before. But Polyneikes is not a Kreon,[65] and his character as sketched in this scene allows for a different interpretation. The ancient tragedians were not concerned with depicting characters in all their psychological complexity. They tended to sketch them in broad strokes with a focus on the one or more of their principal characteristics that contributed to the narrative. In this drama, Oidipous is characterized as a person of dignity and fearsome temper, Theseus as gracious and generous, Antigone as caring,[66] Kreon as duplicitous and brutal.

The principal characteristics Polyneikes displays in this scene are a heroic, if foolhardy, determination and what can perhaps best be described as a blockheadedness.[67] His determination is evidenced in his successful strategy in getting an audience with Oidipous, his reported marriage/alliance in Argos in order to raise an army, and his insistence at the end of the scene on persevering with his attack on Thebes even though he believes that he will die in the attempt. His blockheadedness is apparent in his naïve expectation that his father might actually pardon him and join him in his attack against their joint mother-city. His drawing a parallel between his own homelessness and that of Oidipous, given what the spectators have already heard about his role in his father's exile, appears to be both presumptuous and insulting. However, in condemning his brother Eteokles for usurping the throne

[63] Adkins 1960, 30–60, 153–69; cf. Lloyd-Jones 1990 [1987], 253–80.

[64] The value of this description for costume design is discussed above in the notes to Scene 1.

[65] Cf. Taplin 1983, 160–62.

[66] She represents 'humanity and mercy' according to Burton 1980, 255.

[67] Reinhardt (1979, 218) notes the futility, vanity, deception and blind illusion that characterizes Polyneikes. Easterling (1967, 6) recognizes his 'extraordinary tactlessness and artificiality' and the 'tone of uneasiness in the speaker . . . a kind of awkward frigidity'.

through trickery ('he seduced the city', 1298), Polyneikes implies a cunning which his brother has but he does not. And so his sorrow over Oidipous' condition can be played as a sincere grief emanating from his own suffering in exile, which has led to a late appreciation of his father's circumstances.[68]

But such a display of grief, felt or engineered, only prompts Oidipous to remain silent (1271) and to turn away from his son (1272). In our production, Polyneikes' entrance brought him down the L *parodos* to L, while Antigone and Ismene withdrew to EBR/EBL with the Elders, who formed a silent and unsympathetic group of observers to what then unfolded. Oidipous stayed centre, sitting like a stone in 'malign sublimity'.[69] Polyneikes' deictic gestures during the description of his father's condition allowed him to move around Oidipous from L to BRC. On his plea to Mercy at 1267, he moved to the left of Oidipous to make his supplication. Oidipous' turn away from him in the middle of 1272 was abrupt and pronounced, although he remained seated.[70] Polyneikes crossed to Antigone and Ismene at BRC on 1275, and gestured also to Ismene when he appealed to them to intercede for him. At Antigone's urging, he ignored his father's silence and made his case.[71] During this long and powerful address, the actor in our production used BC as a place to assert Polyneikes' right to speak with gestures encompassing those present, before he stepped forward on 1291 to address Oidipous directly but from behind him. When he commenced his account of the strategies he adopted and the adventures he experienced in Argos, he broke towards L and turned back to Oidipous on 1308, when he directed his rhetorical question to him. In detailing the leaders of his cohorts, Polyneikes evokes passion and confidence; this prompted a blocking in which the actor claimed a place of major prominence between C and FC. When Polyneikes asserted his rights as Oidipous' son at 1323, the actor broke quickly to the right of Oidipous and again adopted the pose of a suppliant. Oidipous did not move. On Polyneikes' preposterous identification of his homeless situation with that of Oidipous at 1335b, the actor rose and sat beside Oidipous to his left, usurping Antigone's normal place and laying claim to an intimacy his character did not deserve.

[68] Cf. Bowra 1944, 325.
[69] Jebb 1900, xxiii.
[70] Cf. Arnott 1989, 65.
[71] One interpolated line (1300) has been deleted from the translation: 'It's what I have been told by soothsayers.'

Oidipous dismisses Polyneikes' grief over his condition, and rehearses once again the sufferings of exile and the nurture provided by his daughters. As he recounts his distress, the anger and the hurt well up in a passionate display, evocative of a deep-seated agony. His voice rises and falls and cracks as the memories of his pain return to haunt him. He invokes the *daimôn* and utters the prophecy of mutual destruction on his sons. He is justified in doing this because he must uphold the social imperative of care for parents, an imperative flaunted by his sons.[72] But to play this sequence as if Oidipous enjoyed his task misses the point. His continuing heartache is precisely that he suffers in having to speak such horrors. To allow an implacable anger to swamp the performance is neither theatrically satisfying nor dramatically appropriate.[73] After all, Oidipous too, along with his sons, suffers from the *daimôn* that afflicts the entire family.

The sequence of thought in this passage is a little erratic, suggesting a mind in conflict, reflected in physical actions might well appear erratic as well and apparently out of control in performance. Oidipous' *thymos* reaches a new intensity as he disowns his sons in a powerful invective. In particular, he details the failure of Polyneikes' strategy, and prays that he will never have a place to live – now or beyond the grave. The bitterness of these lines and the passion of the invocation to the 'pitch-black fathering dark', to the goddesses of the grove and to Ares, the god of war, suggest an equivalent vocal and physical intensity in the performance; vigorous gestures are required, for example, at 1383 and 1389ff.

At the close of the imprecatory address, the actor playing Oidipous broke left of centre in our production, allowing the actors playing Polyneikes, Antigone and Ismene to assume prominence C/RC. Then the bitter exchange between Antigone and Polyneikes ebbs and flows, with the latter's determination to proceed with his plans in the face of her

[72] In doing this he is fulfilling his duty in terms of loving friends and harming enemies. See Blundell 1989, 238–48; Hester 1977, 22–41; and Whitman 1951, 241.

[73] According to a reviewer, this happened with Taylor's version of the Theban dramas for BBC television: Murray 1986, 1033. London's National Theatre production of the two Oidipous tragedies resisted the temptation: *Theatre Record* 1996, 1169–78. Winnington-Ingram (1954, 19) rightly notes that Oidipous' anger arises from his pain. Easterling (1967, 13) perceives that his curse on his sons is 'just and psychologically plausible, and though appalling, not vindictive'. Vickers (1973, 474–5) makes the important point that no character, not even Antigone, condemns Oidipous for his behaviour.

entreaties to abandon them. At 1437 Polyneikes tears himself away; but Antigone prevents him, as the concluding *antilabe* reaches new heights of desperation – only to end with Polyneikes' gentle prayer for his sisters, and his departure along the R *parodos* towards his elected destiny in Thebes.

Choros 5

Choroses in tragedy are normally used as a means of reflection on the issues at stake or to celebrate them or to amplify them.[74] New information and developments in the plot are confined to scenes. During this Choros, however, a major event takes place which initiates the final action of the drama. This is the violent storm foretold by Apollo which, coinciding as it does with Oidipous' arrival at this particular grove, signals the completion of his life, as Oidipous himself announced in his prayer to the goddesses in Scene 1. The initiating action here is again announced by Oidipous in spoken exchanges with Antigone between the verses sung by the Elders. This is an unusual form, and the effect is one of dramatic urgency.[75] The choral song and dance is fragmented by the intervening spoken sequences and this fragmentation, together with the sound effects of the storm, creates a chaos that needs to be reflected in the choreography.

Throughout the Choros, the principal metre used in the Greek is the dochmiac, indicating great excitement. The first *strophe* however commences with the more measured iambic metre. It is a reflection by the Elders on what has just taken place. The Elders are astonished by the terrible curses Oidipous has invoked, which will lead to the deaths of his sons. In the face of these new disasters, they can only take refuge in resignation to the will of the *daimôn* and to the vagaries of arbitrary time. Immediately after the penultimate line of the *strophe*, a sound effect representing thunder is heard; this sound effect initiates the concluding action.[76] While the Elders react in consternation at the

---

[74] Arnott 1989, 27.

[75] Taplin (1971, 31–2) sees a mirror reflection in visual and aural correspondences between this ode and the sequence during which Antigone was abducted. In that scene, Oidipous was powerless and dependent on Theseus, whereas here and in the subsequent scene he assumes authority even over Theseus. This mirror imaging could well be reflected in the blocking, making the transition visually clear.

[76] There is no reliable source for the nature of the *bronteion*, but the sound

sudden storm, Oidipous on the contrary welcomes it.[77] He calls for someone to go and bring Theseus. In terms of the conventions of performance, there is actually no one on the performing area who can go: members of the *choros* do not leave the performing area as individuals, especially during a song and dance, and Antigone and Ismene are not inhabitants of the region. When Theseus does arrive at 1500, he does so of his own volition in response to the commotion raised by Oidipous and the Elders, and not because of some message. Oidipous' calls for someone to go therefore, unfulfilled as they must be, contribute to an urgency which must translate into action on the performing space.

In our production, an eager Oidipous occupied the front section of the *orchêstra* throughout the scene (pursued by Antigone and Ismene), as his sense of urgency propelled him blindly in different directions; the Elders possessed the central area, enacting gestural patterns that reflected their fear and panic. Thunderclaps sounded when the choral cries provided the cues. This Choros is highly theatrical, with the combination of disparate performative modes, sound effects, cries and shouts, upbeat melody, and frenetic movement. It dramatically heralds Theseus' return, and the final turn in the course of the drama.

Scene 6

This short scene of fifty-five lines includes a miraculous event, conveyed by ingenious stage action.[78] The miraculous event is the blind Oidipous assuming the role of guide for those who previously guided him, while the stage action is a mirror-reflection of action detailed and enacted in Choros 1.

The scene commences with Oidipous convincing Theseus that the storm is a sign from Zeus that his life is now to be consummated. Oidipous then fulfils his promise that the hospitality and generosity shown to him by Theseus will reap a great reward. This also fulfils Apollo's prophecy, related in the prayer to the goddesses in Scene 1,

effect of thunder was probably created by the use of pebbles and a bronze vessel.

[77] Linforth (1951, 99–100) points out that, throughout the drama, Oidipous principally wants his miserable life to end. There is no hint that he finds any conscious enjoyment even in the idea of heroization.

[78] '[G]rander and more imaginative than any in Greek tragedy': Kitto 1961 [1939], 383. In Jebb's view (1990, xx), 'a splendid opportunity . . . to an actor in the modern theatre no less than in the ancient'.

that this grove would prove to be the place where Oidipous would bring rewards to those who received him and ruin to those who shunned him. Oidipous' gift is, as he said earlier (576ff.), his 'poor body' which, buried in Athenian soil, will prove to be a spiritual strength to Athens of greater worth than regional alliances. Oidipous also promises to reveal to Theseus alone the precise place of his death, and certain mysteries which are not to be revealed except to one other at the time of Theseus' own death. This special privilege that Oidipous grants to Theseus would have served as another reinforcement of the singularity of Athens in its possession of potent wisdom. It may have sounded rather wistful when first heard in 401 BC, after the devastation of the Peloponnesian War.

The sixteen-line sequence from 1540 to 1555, during which Oidipous narrates his departure and goes on his way without a guide, is a theatrical demonstration of the famous inversion celebrated in Sophokles' previous drama on Oidipous: those who see are blind to the truth while those who cannot see, like Teiresias and now Oidipous, perceive the deeper truths. Oidipous now 'sees' what was hidden from him: not only the pathway that leads him to the place where he will die, but also the purpose of his living as he did. It is a stunning theatrical effect to watch the blind man, who up to this point had been led by another or lost by himself, guide the others.

The sixteen lines also indicate that it takes time for Oidipous to traverse the distance, and this reveals Sophokles' ingenious use of stage action. Usually a lengthy description of an arrival applies, as we saw in Scene 2, to entrances along a *parodos*. There is no example, however, in surviving tragedy of an exit along a *parodos* being described at similar length. It is also true that if Oidipous were to make this exit along a *parodos* (presumably the right one), as some scholars have argued, then the convention would clearly indicate that he was going away from the locale and, in terms of this drama, towards Thebes.[79] This would give a completely false signal. During Choros 1, we saw how Oidipous' departure from the grove, guided by Antigone, was painfully slow. It took sixteen lines of instruction and response for Oidipous to leave the rocky outcrop where he had first sat down inside the forbidden area, and to walk to the rocky bench outside it (176–91). The move was in effect from EBC to C. Oidipous, in the final sixteen lines of Scene 6, reverses the original journey: he goes from C to EBC as

[79] So e.g. Jebb 1900, 239; Winnington-Ingram 1980, 253; Walton 1984, 122–3; Brown 1984b, 13.

he speaks, and then exits into the *skene*, leading his daughters as he was once led by them (1452-3).[80] The reversal of action theatrically signals that Oidipous, who, like everyone else, had been forbidden to enter the grove dedicated to the goddesses, now enjoys a special relationship with this grove and these fearful goddesses.[81] He now repossesses, with total authority, the 'forbidden space' EBC which all the actors have avoided since Oidipous was directed out of it during Choros 1. His heroization is demonstrated and the cult celebrated at Kolonos in his honour is verified. His new authority extends to Antigone, Ismene and Theseus as they follow him into the grove – with, presumably, the Attendant on Theseus who will return in the next scene as a messenger.

Choros 6

This short *strophic* pair is a prayer to a number of *chthonic* gods and goddesses who administer to the dead. The Elders pray that Oidipous will make his way to his place beneath the earth without more sorrow and pain. Prayerful gestures of imploration to these gods suggest a choreography incorporates deictic motion towards the earth, and a solemn manner in the dance.

Scene 7

Choros 6 allows time for the actor playing Oidipous to change into the costume and mask of the Attendant. It must be this actor because Antigone (who has been played throughout by the second actor) and Ismene (who has been played by the third actor and by a supernumerary) enter immediately the Attendant's messenger-speech is done. It is also most appropriate theatrically for the first actor to play the role,

[80] So also Pickard-Cambridge 1946, 51; Whitman 1951, 231; Arnott 1975, 51 (stage direction): Seale 1982, 137; Taplin 1983, 183; Wiles 1997, 146, 165-6. Cf. Kassandra's final journey to death inside the *skene* in Aischylos, *Agamemnon* Scene 6.

[81] Ley (1988, 113) observes that Sophokles' dramas consistently reflect 'a profound awareness of the traumatic bond between character and *skene*'. This is nowhere more evident than in this tragedy. Winnington-Ingram (1980, 249) notes its strong sense of locality, and devotes an appendix to the matter (339-40). Dunn (1992) argues that the whole drama is a gradual process of learning the significance of the site. On lateral polarization in the use of spatial aspects, see Wiles 1997, 146-53.

and for the spectators to hear the same voice that they had heard as Oidipous relate the wondrous events of his passing, and quote his parting words to his daughters.

The locale described by the Attendant in specific references to landmarks such as the steps of bronze, the rock of Thorikos, the hollow pear-tree, the marble grave and the hill of Demeter, and in recalling Theseus' relationship with his famous comrade in arms, Perithoos, would appear to be a significant site in late fifth-century Athens. In terms of the drama, this serves to convey that the place Oidipous chose for his last rites was already particularly resonant for Athens. Oidipous, the Theban, is linking his passing and the protection of his buried corpse emphatically with Athenian heroic legend. The proper rites of the dead – washing, robing in white and lamentation – were accompanied by the continuing presence of Zeus' thunder and eventually his divine voice. This theophany gives additional significance both within the drama and beyond it to Oidipous' protective connection with Athens.

Oidipous' parting words to Antigone and Ismene are remarkable for their celebration of love as the only thing that can erase the effects of suffering. This is not a notion normally associated with ancient Greek thought, and suggests a new-found wisdom promoted by the playwright. The narrative details the action of Theseus taking the girls' hands in pledging his care for them, their departure with the Attendant and the vision of Theseus praying, contrary to custom to the gods of the earth and those on Olympos together with the same rubric. This reported action signifies that Oidipous' passing is an event that draws the reaches of the cosmos together, in an extended version of Oidipous' own claim that his arrival in this place is a sign that draws his own life together (46b). The Attendant ends this moving account with a rebuke to those who might entertain some scepticism about his report.

It is difficult to know how messenger-speeches might have been performed in ancient Greece. They derive, it would seem, from the tradition of the rhapsodist telling or chanting his story to the accompaniment of music. It has been suggested that the retention of messenger-speeches in tragedy merely reflects a conservatism.[82] However, this underrates the power of an actor's performance even in modern times, let alone in an oral culture.[83] Unlike the actor who personified a fictional character in the first person, the rhapsodist sang

[82] Bremer 1976, 29–48, esp. 42.
[83] See Havelock 1982, 185–8; Ewans 1999, xxxi–ii.

about characters and their exploits in the third person. Messengers tend to play a similar role. Their function in the drama is not to present a character, but to tell a story about other characters already known to the spectators. Whether, in telling this story, they used gesture and movement for emphasis and explication we do not know; but if they did, it would seem to be in keeping with the sort of physical performance that the mask demands. In any case, messenger-narratives are characterized by attention to precise detail, as we have seen above. This precision assists the spectator to imagine the reported events with clarity and to be appropriately moved by them. Messenger-speeches recount dramatic events, often of a violent nature although here of a wondrous one, and prepare for the revelation of the consequences. So for example, the Servant's messenger-speech in *Oidipous the King* recounts the events of Iokaste's death and Oidipous' blinding himself, and in doing so it prepares for Oidipous' horrific return. The Bodyguard's messenger-speech in *Antigone* recounts the events that took place at Polyneikes' burial site, and at the cave where Antigone had been entombed, in preparation for the arrival of Kreon bearing the dead body of his son. Here the speech prepares for the return of the distraught, orphaned daughters who are left alone to bear the burdens of a cursed line.

In our production, we chose an elaborate histrionic style for the Attendant's performance, with deictic and mimetic gestures supporting the narration.[84] The Elders sat or squatted in a semicircle around c, and formed an inner arc of spectators for the address.

Finale

The second and third actors return for a long duet of lamentation, which persists despite attempts by some of the Elders to point out that Oidipous passed away as he wished.[85] This thought does not console the sisters; nor does the memory of Theseus' promised protection. Antigone and Ismene are the orphaned remnant of a once-royal line, and are inconsolable. The desperation of their cries and pleas suggests a choreography embodies their anguish. At 1724 the pace of performance increases as the *antilabe* requires, and the rapid exchanges

[84] Cf. Arnott 1989, 69.
[85] See Easterling (1997) for an excellent discussion of the play's ending in 'a refusal of ritual'. For comment on the lament in ancient Greece, and particularly in *El*, see Seaford 1985, 315–23.

between Antigone and Ismene and between Antigone and the Elders generate high drama. The authoritative voice of Theseus on his return from the grove again puts a sudden stop to action.

Theseus grants the girls' wish to return to Thebes in an attempt to stop the bloodshed between their brothers – an attempt doomed, as those who know the story understand, to fail, with fatal consequences for Antigone. Then Antigone and Ismene, in our production, moved together towards the R *parodos*. As they did so, an Elder spoke the last comforting lines of the tragedy. Antigone and Ismene went out along the R *parodos*, in a mirror-image of the entrance of Oidipous and Antigone at the beginning of the play. When they had gone, Theseus, followed by the Elders, went out along the L *parodos*.

GLOSSARY OF PROPER NAMES

ACHAIA, literally, a region of the northern Peloponnese (as at *Elektra* 701); but like Homer, Sophokles often uses 'Achaians' as a synonym for 'Greeks', especially in *Philoktetes*, where the action takes place during the Trojan War.

ACHILLEUS, son of Peleus and the nymph Thetis; king of Phthia in Thessaly, lover of Patroklos; the central hero of Homer's *Iliad*.

ADRASTOS, king of Argos, father-in-law of Polyneikes, and leader of the expedition of the Seven against Thebes.

AGAMEMNON, son of Atreus, grandson of Pelops; king of Mykenai and Argos, brother of Menelaos and husband of Klytaimestra. Commander-in-chief of the Greek expedition against Troy.

AIAS (1), son of Telamon, the king of Salamis. Founder of Aiantis, one of the ten tribes of Athens, and worshipped in Attika as a *heros*.

AIAS (2), son of Oileus, king of Lokris. He raped Priam's daughter, the prophetess Kassandra, in Athena's temple during the sack of Troy, and was killed either by Athena herself or by Poseidon for this sacrilege during his homeward voyage.

AIDONEUS, an alternative name for Haides.

AIGEUS, king of Athens and father of Theseus. The Aigeian Sea is named after him because he leaped into it when he was led to believe that Theseus had been killed by the Minotaur.

AIGISTHOS, the only child of Thyestes to survive Atreus' massacre of Thyestes' children; he inherited the blood-feud with Atreus' son Agamemnon.

AIGYPT, country in north-east Africa; rather larger than modern Egypt, since it stretched west well into modern Libya.

AINEAS, Trojan hero, son by the goddess Aphrodite of Anchises (who foolishly boasted of his relationship with the goddess, and was struck by Zeus' thunderbolt in punishment). One of the principal heroes fighting for Troy in Homer's *Iliad*; after the capture of Troy, he retreated to Mount Ida with his friends and the images of the gods, and according to later mythology crossed into Europe and finally settled at Latium in Italy, and became the ancestral hero of Rome.

AINIANS,   tribe living around the upper River Spercheios in Thessaly.

AITNA,   modern Etna, town and volcano in north-east Sicily.

AITOLIA,   a region of western Greece, surrounding the River Acheloos.

ALEUS,   king of Tegea. Apollo prophesied that if his daughter had a son, that grandson would kill Aleus' sons. Aleus made his daughter Auge the priestess of Athena, but Herakles got drunk while visiting him, and made her pregnant with Telephos.

AMPHIARAOS,   son of Oikleus, one of the Seven against Thebes; a prophet as well as a warrior. He was persuaded to take part in the siege, although he knew it would kill him, by his wife Eriphyle, whom Polyneikes had bribed. After his death his son Alkmaion avenged him by killing his own mother.

ANTIGONE,   daughter of Oidipous, sister of Eteokles, Polyneikes and Ismene.

ANTILOCHOS,   son of Nestor, killed at some time during the Trojan War.

APHRODITE,   the goddess of love.

APIANS,   people of the Argive plain; named after Apis, a son of Apollo and a healer, who once cleansed this land from pollution.

APOLLO,   son of Zeus and Leto, and brother of Artemis; a major Greek god, worshipped especially at Delos and Delphi. God of archery (and so particularly able to protect his friends and send sudden death on his enemies); music and painting; purification from *miasma*; healing from disease; and prophecy.

AREOPAGOS,   'Place of Ares'; seat of Athens' oldest and most aristocratic court.

ARES,   the god of war, son of Zeus and Hera.

ARGOS (1),   one of the two most important cities in the Peloponnese, located in a level, fertile plain in the north-east, just west of the River Inachos.

(2),   the hundred-eyed, son of the Earth, appointed by Hera to guard Io from Zeus. Hermes killed him at the command of Zeus.

ARKADIA,   region of the central northern Peloponnese.

ARTEMIS,   sister of Apollo; a virgin goddess, imaged as a huntress. As a female counterpart to Apollo, she both inflicted and could cure diseases in women. She was also the protectress of the young, and the goddess who presided over childbirth.

ASKLEPIOS,   a miraculous healer, son of Apollo. His sons were the doctors accompanying the Greek expedition to Troy.

ASTYOCHE, sister of Priam, wife of Telephos and mother of Eurypylos.

ATALANTA, mother of Parthenopaios, one of the Seven against Thebes. She was nurtured in the wilds of Arkadia under the protection of Artemis. She evaded abduction by kentaurs, and took part in the hunt for the Kalydonian boar. She was the most swift-footed of mortals, and she only married after Milanion beat her by a stratagem, assisted by the goddess Aphrodite.

ATHENA, goddess of wisdom, and patron deity of Athens. The cult title Polias refers to her role as the guardian of the city of Athens.

ATHENS, the largest and most important city in mainland Greece.

ATLAS, a Titan, brother of Prometheus; he was condemned by Zeus, in punishment for the war of the Titanes against the Olympians, to support the weight of the heavens on his shoulders and was transformed into the great mountain ridge in north-west Africa.

ATREUS, son of Pelops, and king of Mykenai. He avenged himself on Thyestes, who had seduced his wife and fraudulently claimed the kingship, by murdering Thyestes' children and serving their flesh and vitals to him at a banquet. Atreus' sons were Agamemnon and Menelaos, often referred to as the 'sons of Atreus' or 'Atreidai'.

AULIS, a port on the coast of Boiotia, where the Greeks were marooned, unable to sail to Troy until Agamemnon sacrificed his eldest daughter Iphigeneia to Artemis.

BACKHOS, see DIONYSOS.

BARKA, Greek city in north-west Africa.

BOIOTIA, plain in central Greece, north-west of Attika; the principal city was Thebes.

CHALKODON, a king of Euboia; his son Elphenor was among the Greek army at Troy.

CHLORIS, the only child of Niobe and Amphion to survive the massacre by Apollo and Artemis. She later became wife of Neleus and mother of Nestor.

CHRYSE, a small island near Lemnos; the Greeks put in there on the way to Troy, and Philoktetes was bitten by a snake near the precinct of the island's eponymous goddess.

CHRYSOTHEMIS, third daughter of Agamemnon and Klytaimestra, after Iphigeneia and Elektra.

DARDANOS,   the mythical founder of Troy and begetter of its royal line. His grandson Tros gave his name to the city.

DELPHI,   a town in Phokis, on the slopes of Mount Parnassos; site of Apollo's principal oracle.

DEMETER,   sister of Zeus, goddess of agriculture and of all the fruits of the earth. She had a particularly splendid temple at Eleusis, where the mystery cult initiated worshippers of Demeter and her daughter Persephone.

DIONYSOS,   son of Zeus and Semele; god of ecstatic possession, fertility and the life-force, both creative and destructive – especially as manifested through liquids, the sap of young trees, the blood of young animals and humans, and wine. His followers are called Bakchantes, after his alternate cult title Bakchos.

DORIANS,   the ancestors of the Peloponnesians; they originally came from a small region in central Greece, but conquered the indigenous Peloponnesians during legendary times.

DRYAS,   father of Lykourgos, the Thrakian king who dared to fight against the god Dionysos.

ELEKTRA,   second daughter of Agamemnon and Klytaimestra.

ETEOKLES,   son of Oidipous and brother of Polyneikes

ETEOKLOS,   an Argive, one of the Seven against Thebes.

EUBOIA,   a long island in the Aigeian, lying off the coasts of Attika, Boiotia and southern Thessaly.

EUMENIDES,   'The Kindly Ones' – a euphemistic name for the Furies.

EUMOLPOS,   the founder of the Eleusinian mysteries, and the first priest of Demeter and Dionysos; his descendants inherited the priesthood.

EURYPYLOS,   son of Telephos, and king of Mysia after his death. He fought for the Trojans against the Greeks towards the end of the war, and was killed in a duel with Neoptolemos.

FURIES,   female *daimones* of the underworld, who call for and work towards vengeance on murderers.

HAIDES,   brother of Zeus and Poseidon, husband of Persephone. Zeus' counterpart below the earth, the ruler of the underworld to which humans pass after death. His kingdom is often called 'Haides', abbreviated from 'Haides' halls'.

HELENOS,   a Trojan prophet, son of Priam.

HERA,   wife of Zeus and goddess of marriage.

HERAKLES,   son of Zeus by Alkmene, the wife of Amphitryon king of Thebes; the greatest Greek hero. He performed twelve Labours, superhuman feats, after he had been commanded by Apollo to serve Eurystheus for twelve years.

When Herakles was dying he commanded his son Hyllos to take him to Mount Oita and burn him on a pyre (see *YWT*). But the only person prepared to light the pyre was Philoktetes; in gratitude, Herakles gave him his famous bow. After his death Herakles was made immortal, and married the goddess Hebe.

HERMAION,   a mountain on Lemnos.

HERMES,   son of Zeus and Maia, herald and messenger of the gods. He was the god who escorts travellers, and conducts souls between the worlds of the living and the dead; also the guardian of paternal rights, and the god of deception and trickery.

HIPPOMEDON,   one of the Seven against Thebes.

ILION,   Troy.

INACHOS,   an Argive, father of Io. He gives his name to the main river of Argive territory.

IO,   daughter of Argos, founder of the first royal line of Argos. She was desired by Zeus, transformed into a cow by Hera, and made to undergo a tormented journey to Aigypt. There Zeus transformed her back into human shape, and made her pregnant with Epaphos, the founder of the line of Aigyptian kings. See Aischylos, *Suppliants* 538ff., and *Prometheus Bound* 846ff.

IPHIANASSA,   fourth and youngest daughter of Agamemnon and Klytaimestra.

ISMENE,   daughter of Oidipous, sister of Antigone, Eteokles and Polyneikes.

ITYS,   see PROKNE.

KAPANEUS,   one of the Seven against Thebes.

KEPHALLENIA,   island adjacent to Ithaka, and part of Odysseus' kingdom.

KEPHISSOS,   the largest stream in Attika, flowing from Mount Pentelikos through Kolonos and west of ancient Athens into the Saronic Gulf.

KLYTAIMESTRA,   daughter of Tyndareus and Leda; half-sister of Helene, and wife first of Agamemnon and then of Aigisthos.

KOLONOS,   a *deme* of Attika, north-west of Athens; Sophokles' birthplace.

KREON,   son of Menoikeus; brother of Iokaste, and therefore brother-in-law to Oidipous.

KREOUSA,   daughter of Erechtheus, king of Athens, wife of Xouthos and mother of Ion by Apollo. The story of how she rediscovered her son was dramatized in Euripides' surviving drama *Ion*.

KRISA,   small town south of Delphi, with a plain stretching to the Gulf of Korinth.

KRONOS,   the youngest of the Titanes, son of Ouranos and Ge (Heaven and Earth); he deprived Ouranos of the government of the world, and was himself dethroned by his own son, Zeus.

KYLLENE,   the highest mountain in the Peloponnese, marking the frontier between Arkadia and Achaia. The nymph of the mountain is a principal character in *Trackers*, which is set near her cave.

LABDAKOS,   son of Polydoros, himself the son of Kadmos, the founder of Thebes, and grandson of Agenor; father of Laios.

LAERTES,   former king of Ithaka and father of Odysseus.

LAIOS,   king of Thebes; son of Labdakos; first husband of Iokaste and father of Oidipous.

LAOKOON,   a Trojan, priest of Apollo. He tried to persuade the Trojans not to take the Trojan Horse into the city; but as he prepared to sacrifice to Poseidon, two gigantic serpents destroyed him. The Trojans took this as a portent that they must keep the horse.

LEMNOS,   a large island in the north-west Aigeian. Although it was inhabited from early in Greek history, Sophokles uniquely chooses to make it an uninhabited empty space in *Philoktetes*.

LIBYA,   country in north-west Africa, partly colonized by Greeks; its principal city was Kyrene.

LOXIAS,   probably 'the crooked one'; a cult title of Apollo, referring to the obscurity of many of his oracles.

LYKIOS,   a river on the island of Lemnos.

LYKOMEDES,   king of Skyros; grandfather of Neoptolemos on his mother's side.

MAGNESIA,   the southern coastal region of Thessaly.

MAIA,   the eldest and most beautiful of the Pleiades. Zeus made her pregnant with Hermes in a cave on Mount Kyllene.

MALIS,   a region to the south of Thessaly, on the northern side of Mount Oita; kingdom of Poias and Philoktetes.

MEDEIA,   daughter of Aietes, king of Kolchis. She used her magic to help Iason to win the Golden Fleece, and fled with him to his land of Iolkos in Thessaly. Later she restored Iason's father Aison to youth by cutting him up and boiling him in a pot together with certain herbs. She also helped Iason to avenge his father's murder, after Aeson had been killed by his half-brother Pelias, by pretending to Pelias' daughters that she could rejuvenate him as well – but broke her promise after they had cut him up. Pelias' son Akestes expelled Iason and Medeia from Iolkos, and they went to Korinth, where in Euripides' drama Iason deserted her for the king's daughter, and she avenged herself by killing their sons and fleeing to Athens.

MEMNON, the king of Aithiopia, who came late in the Trojan War to help Priam. Achilleus killed him in a long and bitter conflict.

MENELAOS, son of Atreus, king of Sparta and husband of Helene, whose abduction by Paris of Troy caused the Trojan War.

MYKENAI, the ancient city overlooking the plain of Argos, which was Agamemnon's capital.

MYRTILOS, the servant of King Oinamaos, whom Pelops bribed to remove the lynch-pins of the king's chariot so the king would fall to his death. Instead of rewarding Myrtilos, he cast him into the sea. Myrtilos cursed Pelops' family before he drowned.

MYSIA, the north-west corner of Asia Minor.

NAUPLIOS, son of Poseidon by Amymone, and king of Euboia; father of Palamedes. He avenged himself for Palamedes' death by persuading the wives of three Greek kings to become unfaithful, and by lighting a false beacon, which lured many of the returning fleet onto rocks.

NEOPTOLEMOS, son of Achilleus. He was too young to go on the Trojan expedition; but in the tenth year, after a prophecy that Troy could not be taken without his help, Odysseus and Phoinix went to Skyros to fetch him.

NESTOR, king of Pylos in the south-west Peloponnese. He was an old man when he took part in the Trojan expedition, and often gave lengthy advice to the other Greek commanders.

NIOBE, daughter of Tantalos, and wife of Amphion, king of Thebes. She boasted that she was a better mother than Leto. Apollo and Artemis killed all but one of her children in revenge. Niobe's grief was so great that she wasted away, and was transformed into an ever-weeping stone.

ODYSSEUS, son of Laertes and king of Ithaka, husband of Penelopeia and father of Telemachos; the most cunning of the heroes who joined the expedition against Troy. His adventures after the war, and his return home, are the subject of Homer's epic poem *The Odyssey*. Because of his ingenuity, he was especially favoured by Athena. In some derogatory accounts he was the illegitimate son of the trickster king Sisyphos.

OIA,   a district of Attika between Athens and Eleusis.

OIDIPOUS,   son of Laios and Iokaste; ruler of Thebes after he rid the city of the Sphinx, until he discovered that his wife was his own mother.

OILEUS,   king of Lokris; father of Aias the Lokrian.

OINEOS,   king of Kalydon in Aitolia; father of Tydeus.

OITA,   mountain in Malis in southern Thessaly, near Olympos and overlooking Trachis; site of Herakles' funeral pyre.

OLYMPOS,   a mountain in the north-east of mainland Greece, the dwelling-place of the gods.

ORESTES,   only son of Agamemnon and Klytaimestra.

PAKTOLOS,   a stream flowing through Sardis in Lydia (in the central west of Asia Minor), believed to bear gold dust.

PALAMEDES,   son of Nauplios and Klymene. He detected the ruse that Odysseus used to try to get out of sailing to Troy, and in revenge Odysseus falsely accused him of treachery after planting under his bed a forged letter from Priam. The Greeks stoned him to death. He became known as a wise man and an inventor.

PALLAS,   a cult-title of Athena, of unknown origin and meaning.

PARIS,   a son of Priam and Hekabe. His abduction of Menelaos' wife Helene caused the Trojan War.

PARTHENOPAIOS,   'The maiden-faced'; son of Atalanta from Arkadia.

PELEUS,   king of Phthia, husband of Thetis and father of Achilleus.

PELOPS,   son of Tantalos and father of Atreus; grandfather of Agamemnon and Menelaos. In *Elektra* his murder of Myrtilos is the first crime in 'the house of many deaths', the house of Atreus. The Peloponnese is named after him.

PEPARETHOS,   island off the coast of Magnesia, north-east of Euboia and north-west of Skyros.

PERITHOOS,   Theseus' friend, who accompanied him on his visit to the underworld and was revered as a *heros* at Athens.

PERSEPHONE,   daughter of Demeter and wife of Haides.

PHANOTEUS,   a Phokian, brother of Strophios' father, but an enemy of him and his family; friendly to Klytaimestra and Aigisthos.

PHILOKTETES,   the son of Poias, king of Malis; the only man brave enough to set fire to the pyre of Herakles, and deliver him from his agony. He earned Herakles' unconquerable bow and arrows as his reward. On the way to Troy, when the Greeks had put in at a small island called Chryse, Philoktetes was bitten on the foot by the snake that guarded the precinct of the local goddess Chryse. The other Greeks abandoned Philoktetes on Lemnos, unable to bear his outcries and the stench of the festering wound.

PHOIBOS,   cult title of Apollo, meaning 'bright' or 'pure'.

PHOINIX,   friend of Peleus, who looked after Achilleus as a child and later accompanied him to Troy.

PHOKIS,   the region of central Greece surrounding Mount Parnassos.

PHRYGIA,   the region directly surrounding Troy in north-west Asia Minor.

POIAS,   king of Malis in west central Greece; father of Philoktetes.

POLYNEIKES,   son of Oidipous, and brother of Eteokles. When Eteokles kept the throne, he persuaded the Argives, under his father-in-law Adrastos, to march against Thebes so he could reclaim it as his inheritance.

POLYXENA,   daughter of Priam and Hekabe, sacrificed by the Greeks to the ghost of Achilleus to appease him before they sailed home.

POSEIDON,   brother of Zeus, god of the sea.

PRIAM,   king of Troy.

PROKNE,   daughter of Pandion, king of Athens, and wife of Tereus, king of Thrakia. Prokne killed her son Itys, and served him as a meal to her husband in revenge for Tereus' rape of her sister Philomela. When she prayed to be turned into a bird to escape from Tereus' pursuit, the gods changed her into a nightingale. The sad song of the nightingale is her lament for Itys' death. Philomela became a swallow, and Tereus a hoopoe.

PROMETHEUS,   a Titan, the benefactor of mankind who stole fire from the gods. His name means 'forethought'.

PYLADES,   son of Strophios the Phokian; companion of Orestes since childhood.

PYLOS,   city and kingdom in the south-west Peloponnese, ruled by Nestor at the time of the Trojan War.

SALMONEUS,   son of Aiolos and brother of Sisyphos. He declared himself equal to Zeus, and even imitated Zeus' thunder and lightning; but Zeus killed him with the thunderbolt, destroyed his town of Salmone in Elis, and punished him in Haides.

SARPEDON, a prince of Lykia, who came to Troy as an ally of the Trojans; he was killed by Patroklos.

SIGEION, a town on the coast near Troy; the site where Achilleus was buried.

SILENOS, the father of the satyrs; a selfish, alcoholic and lecherous old man who was also the tutor of Dionysos, and an inspired prophet.

SISYPHOS, king of Korinth, notorious for his tricks. There was a rumour that he was Odysseus' real father, not Laertes.

SKYROS, an island east of Euboia; ruled by Lykomedes, and foster-home of Neoptolemos.

SPARTA, principal city and most powerful military force in the Peloponnese.

SPERCHEIOS, river in southern Thessaly, flowing into the Gulf of Malis.

STROPHIOS, king of Phokis; Orestes grew up in his home.

STYX (adjective stygian), the principal river of the underworld; its name means 'hateful'.

TALAOS, an Argive; father of Hippomedon.

TARTAROS, river and region in the deepest part of the underworld.

TELAMON, brother of Peleus, who became king of Salamis. Father of Aias by Eriboia, and later of Teukros by the Trojan woman Hesione.

TELEPHOS, son of Herakles by Auge, daughter of King Aleus of Tegea. He found his mother at the court of Teuthras, king of Mysia, and succeeded to his throne. He married Priam's sister Astyoche, and opposed the Greeks when they landed in Mysia on the way to Troy, being wounded by Achilleus. However, an oracle foretold that he would guide the Greeks to Troy, and he did this after being cured by Achilleus' spear of the wound that he had inflicted. His son Eurypylos later fought against the Greeks, and was killed by Achilleus' son Neoptolemos.

TEREUS, see PROKNE.

TEUKROS, son of Telamon by the captive Trojan princess Hesione.

THEBES, the principal city of Boiotia, in central Greece.

THERSITES, a notoriously impudent and ugly common soldier on the Trojan expedition; in *Iliad* 2 he abused Agamemnon, and was beaten by Odysseus to general approval by the commanders (although his advice was sensible).

THESEUS, son of Aigeus and king of Athens. Sophokles alludes only by implication to his visit to the underworld with Perithoos, in an outrageous attempt to abduct Persephone; he does not allude at all to his battle against his cousins the Pallantids, his defeat of an invasion by the Amazons, his son Hippolytos by the Amazon queen or his marriage to Phaidra. *Oidipous at Kolonos* presents him patriotically as a strong and intensely honourable king, embodying all the virtues which the Athenians liked to believe they possessed.

THESSALY,   the plain surrounding Larisa in north-west Greece.

THORIKOS,   the reason why the rock mentioned at *Oidipous at Kolonos* 1595 was given this name is unknown.

THRAKIA,   the relatively uncivilized tribal lands north of the part of the Aigeian coastline between the River Strymon and the Hellespont.

THYESTES,   brother of Atreus, king of Argos, who served him a banquet of his own children's flesh after he had committed adultery with Atreus' wife. He secretly raped his own daughter Pelopia in revenge; she later married Atreus, who brought up Aigisthos as his own son. Aigisthos took revenge in the next generation by seducing Klytaimestra and helping her to murder Atreus' son Agamemnon.

TRACHIS,   city in Malis in central Greece; near Thermopylai, and below Mount Oita.

TROY,   a city in Phrygia in modern Turkey; sacked after a ten-year siege by the Greek expedition commanded by Agamemnon and Menelaos.

TYDEUS,   son of Oineus, father of Diomedes. He fled from his native Kalydon to Argos after murdering a kinsman, married one of Adrastos' daughters, and became one of the Seven against Thebes.

TYRO,   daughter of Salmoneus, wife of Kretheus, mother by Poseidon of the twins Pelias and Neleus. She was blamed by her father for her pregnancy, and brutally ill-treated by her stepmother. But her sons rescued her.

ZEUS,   the most powerful god; son of Kronos and Rhea. Husband of the goddess Hera; father by Almene of Herakles. Originally a sky and weather god, his weapon was the thunderbolt. He punished oath-breaking, and some other kinds of wrongdoing; in particular, the table of hospitality was sacred to him as the protector of the rights of guests and hosts. However, Zeus did not make the world, and he was not omnipotent or omniscient. Despite his great and wide-ranging powers, other gods as well as human beings could defy him (at their own risk).

GLOSSARY OF GREEK WORDS

agathos, a good or noble man – head of an *oikos* by virtue of a combination of birth, wealth and military ability. Plural *agathoi.*

agôn, a contest, in athletics or warfare; in tragedy, a formally structured scene in which one speaker puts a case, and is answered (usually after a two-line interjection from the *choros*) by another speaker with a speech of approximately the same length. Plural *agones.*

agora, the market-place or city square; the centre of political, legal and social life in the city-states of ancient Greece.

anapaests, the metre of the chanted sections of a Greek tragedy, midway in intensity between speech and lyric song. Often used as the accompaniment for the entrance-march of the *chorus.*

antilabe, the division of single spoken lines between different speakers.

antistrophe, see *strophe.*

arete, excellence; the qualities of the *agathos* – good birth, wealth and military ability. Female excellence consisted in good birth and *sophrosyne,* q.v.

bakchantes, dancing, female worshippers of the god Dionysos. When in a state of Dionysiac ecstasy they could perform extraordinary physical feats.

bronteion, the machine for producing the special effect of the sound of thunder. Later tradition suggests that stagehands rattled a copper vase of small stones.

choros, literally song (and dance) – denotes either the group of fifteen *choros* members or the odes (songs) that they perform.

chthonic, from the earth or the underworld.

daimôn, a god or god-like power; *daimones* are often what we, like later, more rationalist Greeks, would call personifications of abstract forces – e.g. Madness, Fear, Persuasion.

deme,   the local areas or village communities into which Athenian citizens' places of residence were divided, and by which they were known (e.g. Sophokles' full name was Sophokles son of Sophilos from Kolonos).

dike,   often translated 'justice', it usually means a recompense or fair requital rather than any more sophisticated concept of justice.

ekkyklêma,   the 'rolling-out machine', used in tragedy when the pressure of events inside the building represented by the *skene* has such implications for the public world outside that they must be seen (as they could not, if simply displayed in the entrance, because of shadows).

ephebos,   a young man who has just reached military age (eighteen). Plural *ephebes*; abstract noun *epehebeia*.

epode,   a third stanza, sometimes added as a tailpiece after a pair of *strophe* and *antistrophe*; in the same metres but not responding exactly in its structure to those stanzas.

eremia,   an empty place which has not been touched by civilization.

eusebeia,   piety – observance of the gods' wishes and due reverence to them.

heros,   a legendary figure, who was considered to have divine powers, and was therefore worshipped in a cult, especially by his descendants and by residents of the local territory near his place of burial.

hikesia,   the act of supplication, seeking the protection of others.

hoplite,   a heavily armed footsoldier, clad in bronze armour with sword and round shield. Hoplites rated midway between the aristocracy, who could afford to be cavalrymen, and the lower ranks, who on land could only be light-armed slingshot-throwers, but became increasingly powerful during the late fifth century because they were at the oars during sea battles.

kairos,   the right time or appropriate moment for action.

kleos,   glory, fame or renown.

kommos,   a lyric lamentation, sung by the *choros* and one or more solo actors. Plural *kommoi*.

mechane,   the crane used in and after the late fifth century to swing into view gods and other characters who are to be imagined as flying into the playing area. (Hence Latin *deus ex machina*, 'god from the machine'.)

miasma, pollution; the word embraces both literal dirt and what we would call psychic pollution automatically incurred by breaches of taboo, e.g. bloodshed.

moira, a person's share or lot in life; the 'destiny' which is not a predetermined fate, but gradually takes shape as a human life unfolds.

oikos, the great household, consisting of an *agathos'* family and the dependants who work for him, which was the basic unit of Greek society.

orchêstra, the circular dance-floor on which tragedies were performed.

paian, hymn to the god Apollo as a saviour.

parabasis, the choral ode towards the middle of an Aristophanic comedy, in which the *choros* steps out of the plot of the drama (but not out of character) to address the audience on matters of current political and social concern, in a mixture of seriousness and caricature.

parodos, one of the two entrance-ways, one on each side of the *orchêstra.* By a convention which reflected the reality of the theatre's location, the *skene* left *parodos* was imagined as leading to 'downtown' from the place where the action was set, and the *skene* right *parodos* to the countryside and to other *poleis.* Plural *parodoi.* (Some scholars, following the interpolated ch. 12 of Aristotle's *Poetics,* use this term to indicate the entry-song, the first choral ode of a tragedy or comedy. They favour the synonym *eisodos* for the side entrance-ways.)

parthenos, a young woman who has begun to menstruate but is not yet married.

philia, a friendship or alliance, bound by loyalty or blood-relationship; it especially included relatives and other members of your own household. A person so bound to you was your *philos*; plural, *philoi.*

polis, a city which, with its surrounding territory, was also an independent state; the largest social unit in ancient Greece after their formation in the eighth to sixth centuries.

satyr-drama, the farcical and ribald afterpiece to each competitor's offering of three tragedies. The *choros* played the role of the half-animal, half-human satyrs, and their father Silenos was normally one of the characters.

skene,   literally and until *c.* 460 a tent in which the actors changed masks and costumes. After that it was a wooden building behind the *orchêstra*, with a pair of double doors and a practicable roof.

skenographia,   the use of changeable painted panels on the front of the *skene*, on which features of the relevant façade could be painted, to indicate the kind of place in front of which the action was set – e.g. a palace, house, temple, cave, grove or tent.

sophrosyne,   self-restraint and mental balance. An excellence, especially in women, for whom it included chastity and fidelity.

stichomythia,   literally 'step-speech'; a dialogue sequence of rapid cut and thrust, in which normally the speaker changes every line.

strophe, antistrophe; literally 'turn' and 'counter-turn'; the metrically responding stanzas (A1, A2; B1, B2 etc.) in solo and choral lyrics.

theatron,   the 'seeing-place' – the part of the theatre in which the audience sat.

thiasos,   a company of worshippers singing and dancing in praise of Dionysos.

thymos,   spirit (as in 'high-spirited') or temper.

time,   honour or status; always in terms of concrete possessions and/or privileges.

tragoidia,   the Greek name for the genre, of wider application than the modern word 'tragedy', since it includes some dramas in which catastrophe is survived, or avoided altogether, and some dramas which modern critics would regard as nearer to melodrama.

tychê,   fortune or chance.

SUGGESTIONS FOR FURTHER READING

Arnott, P. (1989): *Public and Performance in the Greek Theatre*, London. The best book on this subject, covering a wide range of features of the Greek theatre.

Blundell, M. W. (1989): *Helping Friends and Harming Enemies*, Cambridge. A study of the ways in which decisions are reached and choices made in five Sophoklean tragedies, with special reference to the fundamental code of Greek values described by the title.

Burton, R. W. B. (1980): *The Chorus in Sophocles' Tragedies*, Oxford. A thorough, comprehensive analysis of the choral odes.

Easterling, P. E. (ed.) (1982) *Sophocles, Trachiniae*, Cambridge. This is an edition of the Greek text; but its Introduction presents, in a form accessible to the Greekless reader, Prof. Easterling's pioneering interpretation, which inaugurated modern appreciation of *Young Women of Trachis*.

Ewans, M. (ed.and tr.) (1995); *Aeschylus: The Oresteia*, London.

Ewans, M. (ed. and tr.) (1996a): *Aeschylus: Suppliants and Other Dramas*, London. Two companion volumes to this book, containing the work of the first surviving Greek dramatist. The introductions deal in detail with the theatre space and performance style of Athenian tragedy.

Ewans, M. (ed.) (1999): *Sophocles: Four Dramas of Maturity*, London. A companion volume to this book, containing Sophokles' earlier four surviving dramas.

Gardiner, C. P. (1987): *The Sophoclean Chorus: A Study of Character and Function*, Iowa City. An examination of the extent to which the chorus should be perceived as a character in the drama. Less comprehensive than Burton, but containing many valuable insights.

Jones, J. (1962): *On Aristotle and Greek Tragedy*, London and New York. A pioneering book; the chapters on Sophocles are particularly strong on the concept of mutability.

Ley, G. (1991): *A Short Introduction to the Ancient Greek Theater*, Chicago. The best introduction for students and readers new to the subject.

Rehm, R. (1992): *The Greek Tragic Theatre*, London. The most recent introduction to the nature and context of Greek tragic performance, with a particularly good chapter on *Oidipous the King*.

Seale, D. (1982): *Vision and Stagecraft in Sophocles*, London. This book is limited by its concentration on the theme of vision and on words for seeing; the suggestions for theatre practice were not tested in performance, and are often undermined by the author's belief in a raised stage. However, there are stimulating chapters on all seven dramas, with many worthwhile ideas.

Segal, C. (1981): *Tragedy and Civilization: An Interpretation of Sophocles*, Cambridge Mass. This book is extremely detailed, and has little sense of the scripts as texts for performance; but it is very important as the first reading to develop a sense of the bleakness of Sophokles' tragic vision, and to apply structuralist insights, in particular the antithesis between civilization and barbarism.

Taplin, O. (1978): *Greek Tragedy in Action*, London. This book, which is accessible to the Greekless reader, provides good discussion of gestures, props, tableaux and other important topics.

Walcot, P. (1976): *Greek Drama in its Theatrical and Social Context*, Cardiff. A short and excellent book.

Winnington-Ingram, R. P. (1980): *Sophocles: An Interpretation*, Cambridge. Very good literary interpretations of the dramas.

Other References Cited in the Introduction and Notes

Adkins, A. W. H. (1960): *Merit and Responsibility: a Study in Greek Values*, Oxford.

Arnott, P. D. (1962): *Greek Scenic Conventions*, Westport, Conn.

Arnott, P. D. (tr.) (1975): *Oedipus at Colonus and Elektra*, Northbrook, Ill.

Arrowsmith, W. (1958): 'Introduction to *Orestes*' in *Euripides IV: Four Tragedies* (ed. D. Grene and R. Lattimore), Chicago, pp. 106–11.

Aylen, L. (1985): *The Greek Theater*, London.

Bain, D. (1977): *Actors and Audience: a Study of Asides and Related Conventions in Greek Drama*, Oxford.

Beye, C. R. (1970): 'Sophocles' Philoctetes and the Homeric Embassy', *Transactions of the American Philological Association*, 101, 63–75.

Bieber, M. (1954): 'The Entrances and Exits of Actors and Chorus in Greek Plays', *American Journal of Archeology*, 58, 277–84.

Bowra, C. M. (1944): *Sophoclean Tragedy*, Oxford.

Bremer, J. M. (1976): 'Why Messenger Speeches?', *Miscellanea Tragica in Honorem J. C. Kamerbeek*, Amsterdam, 29–48.

Brown, A. L. (1984a): 'Eumenides in Greek Tragedy', *Classical Quarterly*, n.s. 34. 2, 260–81.

Brown, A. L. (1984b): 'Three and Scene-Painting Sophocles', *Proceedings of the Cambridge Philological Society*, 210, 1–17.

Burian, P. (1974): 'Suppliant and Saviour: Oedipus at Colonus', *Phoenix*, 28, 4, 408–29.

Burnett, A. P. (1971): *Catastrophe Survived: Euripides' Tragedies of Mixed Reversal*, Oxford.

Bushnell, R. B. (1988): *Prophesying Tragedy: Sign and Voice in Sophocles' Theban Plays*, Ithaca and London.

Buxton, R. G. A. (1982): *Persuasion in Greek Tragedy. A Study of Peitho*, Cambridge.

Calder, W. M. (1970): 'Aeschylus' *Philoctetes*', *Greek, Roman and Byzantine Studies*, 11, 171–9.

Calder, W. M. (1971): 'Sophoclean Apologia: *Philoctetes*', *Greek, Roman and Byzantine Studies*, 12, 153–74.

Campbell, L. (ed.) (1871): *Sophocles: The Plays and Fragments*, Oxford.

Ceadel, E. B. (1941): 'The Division of Parts among Actors in Sophocles' Oedipus Coloneus', *Classical Quarterly*, 35, 139–47.

Collard, C., Cropp, M. J., and Lee, K. H. (eds) (1995): *Euripides: Selected Fragmentary Plays*, Vol. 1, Warminster.

Craik, E. (1990): 'The Staging of Sophocles' *Philoktetes* and Aristophanes' *Birds*', in *Owls to Athens* (ed. E. Craik), Oxford) 81–6.

Cropp, M. et al. (1986): *Greek Tragedy and its Legacy: Essays Presented to K. J. Conacher*, Calgary.

Dale, A. M. (1969): *Collected Papers*, Cambridge.

Dale, A. M. (1983): *The Lyric Metres of Greek Drama*, Ann Arbor, Mich.

Davidson, J. F. (1986): 'The Circle and the Tragic Chorus', *Greece and Rome* 33.1, 38–46.

Davidson, J. F. (1990): 'The Cave of Philoctetes', *Mnemosyne*, 43, 307–15.

Davidson, J. F. (1995): 'Homer and Sophocles' *Philoctetes*', in *Stage Directions: Essays in Ancient Drama in Honour of E. W. Handley* (ed. A. Griffiths); BICS Suppl. 66, London, 25–35.

Dawe, R. (1996): *Sophocles: the Classical Heritage*, New York.

Downs, D. (1996): 'Directing Sophocles' *Electra*', in *Sophocles' 'Elektra' in Performance* (ed. F. Dunn), Stuttgart, 111–30.

Dunn, F. M. (1992): 'Introduction: Beginning at Colonus', *Yale Classical Studies*, xxix, 1–12.

Dunn, F. (ed.) (1966): *Sophocles' 'Elektra' in Performance*, Stuttgart.

Easterling, P. E. (1967): 'Oedipus and Polynices', *Proceedings of the Cambridge Philological Society*, n.s.13, 1–13.

Easterling, P. E. (1973); 'Repetition in Sophocles', *Hermes*, 101. Band. Heft 1, 1. Quartel, 14–34.

Easterling, P. E. (1977): 'Character in Sophocles', *Greece and Rome*, 24, 121–9.

Easterling, P. E. (1978): '*Philoctetes* and Modern Criticism', *Illinois Classical Studies*, 3, 27–39.

Easterling, P. E. (1989): 'Sophocles', *The Cambridge History of Classical Literature* Vol. 1 Part 2: Greek Drama (eds. P. E. Easterling and B. M. W. Knox), Cambridge, 43–64.

Easterling, P. E. (1993): 'Tragedy and Ritual', in *Theater and Society in the Classical World* (ed. R. Scodel), Ann Arbor, 7–23.

Easterling, P. E. (1996): 'Weeping, Witnessing, and the Tragic Audience', *Tragedy and the Tragic: Greek Theatre and Beyond*, Oxford, 175–81.

Easterling, P. E. (1997): 'Constructing the Heroic', in *Greek Tragedy and the Historian*, Oxford, 21–37.

Esposito, S. (1996): 'The Changing Roles of the Sophoclean Chorus', *Arion*, 3rd series, 4.1, 85–114.

Ewans, M. (1982): 'The Dramatic Structure of *Agamemnon*', *Ramus* 11.1, 1–15.

Ewans, M. (1984): 'Elektra: Sophokles, Von Hofmannsthal, Strauss', *Ramus*, 13.2, 135–54.

Ewans, M. (1996b): 'Patterns of Tragedy in Sophokles and Shakespeare', in *Tragedy and the Tragic: Greek Theatre and Beyond* (ed. M. Silk), Oxford, 438–57.

Flickinger, R. C. (1936): *The Greek Theater and its Drama*, 4th edn., Chicago.

Fuqua, C. (1976): 'Studies in the Use of Myth in Sophocles' *Philoctetes* and the *Orestes* of Euripides', *Traditio*, 32, 29–95.

Garner, R. (1990): *From Homer to Tragedy*, London.

Gellie, G. H. (1972): *Sophocles: A Reading*, Melbourne.

Gill, C. (1980): 'Bow, Oracle and Epiphany in Sophocles' Philoctetes', *Greece and Rome*, 27, 137–46.

Gould, J. (1973): 'Hiketeia', *Journal of Hellenic Studies*, 93, 74–103.

Gould, J. (1989): 'Tragedy in Performance', *The Cambridge History of*

Classical Literature, Vol. 1 Part 2: Greek Drama (eds. P. E. Easterling and B. M. W. Knox), Cambridge, 6–29.

Green, J. R. and Handley, E. (1995): *Images of the Greek Theatre*, London.

Green, R. Lancelyn (tr.) (1957): Euripides, *Cylops* and Sophocles, *The Searching Satyrs*, Harmondsworth.

Grene, D. (1967): *Reality and the Heroic Pattern: Last Plays of Ibsen, Shakespeare and Sophocles*, Chicago.

Haigh, A. E. (1907): *The Attic Theatre: A Description of the Stage and Theatre of the Athenians and of the Dramatic Performances at Athens* (rev. by A. W. Pickard-Cambridge), Oxford.

Haldane, J. A. (1963): 'A Paean in the *Philoctetes*', *Classical Quarterly*, 13, 53–6.

Hamilton, R. (1975): 'Neoptolemos' Story in the Philoctetes', *American Journal of Philology*, 96, 131–7.

Harrison, T. (1991): *The Trackers of Oxyrhynchus* (2nd edn.), London.

Harsh, P. W. (1960): 'The Role of the Bow in the *Philoctetes* of Sophocles', *American Journal of Philology*, 81, 408–14.

Havelock, E. (1982): *The Literate Revolution in Greece and its Cultural Consequences*, Princeton.

Henrichs, A. (1983): 'The "Sobriety" of Oedipus: Sophocles OC 100 Misunderstood', *Harvard Studies in Classical Philology*, 87, 87–100.

Hester, D. A. (1977): 'To Help one's Friends and Harm one's Enemies: A Study in the *Oedipus at Colonus*', *Antichthon*, 11, 22–41.

Jebb, R. (ed. and tr.) (1894): *Sophocles: Electra*, Cambridge.

Jebb, R. (ed. and tr.) (1898): *Sophocles: Philoctetes*, Cambridge.

Jebb, R. (ed. and tr.) (1900): *Sophocles: Oedipus Coloneus*, 3rd edn., Cambridge.

Kaimio, M. (1988): *Physical Contact in Greek Tragedy*, Helsinki.

Kamerbeek, J. C. (comm.) (1980): *The Philoctetes*, Leiden.

Kamerbeek, J. C. (comm.) (1984): *The Oedipus Coloneus*, Leiden.

Kells, J. (ed.) (1973): *Sophocles: Electra*, Cambridge.

Kirkwood, G. M. (1954): 'The Dramatic Role of the Chorus in Sophocles', *Phoenix*, 8, 1, 1–22.

Kirkwood, G. M. (1958): *A Study of Sophoclean Drama*, New York.

Kiso, A. (1984): *The Lost Sophocles*, New York.

Kitto, H. D. F. (1950, 1961 [1939]): *Greek Tragedy: a Literary Study* (2nd and 3rd edns), London.

Kitto, H. D. F. (1956): *Form and Meaning in Drama*, London.

Knox, B. M. W. (1964): *The Heroic Temper: Studies in Sophoclean Tragedy*, Berkeley.

Lamar Crosby, H. (ed. and tr.) (1946): *Dio Chrysostom IV: Discourses 37–60*, Cambridge, Mass.

Lardinois, A. (1992): 'Greek Myths for Athenian Rituals: Religion and Politics in Aeschylus' Eumenides and Sophocles' Oedipus Coloneus', *Greek, Roman and Byzantine Studies*, 33, 4, 313–27.

Lawler, L. B.(1964): *The Dance in Ancient Greece*, Seattle and London.

Ley, G. and Ewans, M. (1985): 'The *Orchestra* as Acting Area in Greek Tragedy', *Ramus* 14.2, 75–84.

Ley, G. (1989): 'Agatharchos, Aeschylus and the Construction of a Skene', *Maia*, n.s. 1, 35–8

Ley, G. K. H. (1988): 'A Scenic Plot of Sophocles' *Ajax* and *Philoctetes*', *Eranos*, 86, 85–115.

Ley, G. K. H. (1999): *From Mimesir to Interculturalism: Readings of Theatrical Theory before and after Modernism*, Exeter.

Linforth, I. M. (1951): 'Religion and Drama in *Oedipus at Colonus*', *University of California Publications in Classical Philology*, 14, 75–191.

Lloyd-Jones, H. (1990 [1987]): 'Honour and Shame in Ancient Greek Culture', in *The Academic Papers of Hugh Lloyd-Jones; Greek Comedy, Hellenistic Literature, Greek Religion and Miscellanea*, Oxford, 253–80.

Lloyd-Jones, H. (ed. and tr.) (1996): *Sophocles III: Fragments*, Cambridge, Mass.

Lloyd-Jones, H. and Wilson, N. G. (1990): *Sophoclea: Studies on the Text of Sophocles*, Oxford.

March, J. (1996): 'The Chorus in Sophocles' *Electra*', in *Sophocles' 'Elektra' in Performance* (ed. F. Dunn), Stuttgart, 65–81.

Mastronarde, D. (1990): 'Actors on High: the Skene Roof, the Crane and the Gods in Attic Drama', *Classical Antiquity*, 9, 247–94.

Mastronarde, D. J. (1979): *Contact and Discontinuity: Some Conventions of Speech and Action on the Greek Tragic Stage*, Berkeley.

Murray, O. (1986): 'Beyond the Conventions', *Times Literary Supplement*, 19 Sept., 1033.

Pickard, J. (1893): 'The Relative Positions of Actors and Chorus in the Greek Theatre of the v Century BC', *American Journal of Philology*, 14, 68–89.

Pickard-Cambridge, A. W. (1946): *The Theater of Dionysus in Athens*, Oxford.

Pickard-Cambridge, A. W. (1968): *The Dramatic Festivals of Athens* (2nd edn.) (rev. by J. Gould and D. M. Lewis), Oxford.

Rabel, R. J. (1997): 'Sophocles' *Philoctetes* and the Interpretation of *Iliad* 9', *Arethusa*, 30, 297–307.

Radt, S. (1983): 'Sophokles in Seinen Fragmenten', in *Sophocle* (ed. J. Romilly), Geneva, 185–222.

Rehm, R. (1988): 'The Staging of Suppliant Plays', *Greek, Roman and Byzantine Studies*, 29.3, 263–307.

Rehm, R. (1996): 'Public Spaces, Private Voices: Euripides' *Suppliant Women* and Sophokles' *Elektra*', in *Sophocles' 'Elektra' in Performance* (ed. F. Dunn), Stuttgart, 49–59.

Reinhardt, K. (1979): *Sophocles* (trans. of 1933 book by H. and D. Harvey), Oxford.

Robinson, D. B. (1969): 'Topics in Sophocles' *Philoctetes*', *Classical Quarterly*, 19, 34–56.

Russell, D. A., and Winterbottom, M. (eds) (1972): *Ancient Literary Criticism: the Principal Texts in New Translations*, Oxford.

Schneidewin, F. W. (ed.) (1883): *Sophocles Drittes Bändchen: Oedipus auf Kolonos*, Berlin.

Scodel, R. (1984): *Sophocles*, Boston.

Seaford, R. (1980): 'Black Zeus in Sophocles' *Inachos*', *Classical Quarterly*, 30, 23–9.

Seaford, R. (ed.) (1984): *Euripides; Cyclops*, Oxford.

Seaford, R. (1985): 'The Destruction of Limits in Sophokles' *Elektra*', *Classical Quarterly*, 35, 2, 315–23.

Seaford, R. (1994): *Reciprocity and Ritual: Homer and Tragedy in the Developing City-State*, Oxford.

Segal, C.P. (1966): 'The *Electra* of Sophocles', *American Journal of Philology*, 97, 473–545.

Segal, C. P. (1980): 'Visual Symbolism and Visual Effects in Sophocles', *Classical World*, 74, 125–42.

Segal, C. (1995): 'Philoctetes and the Imperishable Piety' (1977), reprinted in C. Segal, *Sophocles' Tragic World*, Cambridge, Mass.

Segal, E. (ed.) (1983): *Oxford Readings in Greek Tragedy*, Oxford.

Sheppard, J. T. (1918): 'The Tragedy of Electra, According to Sophocles', *Classical Quarterly*, 12, 80–88.

Sheppard, J. T. (1927): '*Electra*: A Defence of Sophocles', *Classical Review*, 41, 2–9.

Shisler, F. L. (1945): 'The Use of Stage Business to Portray Emotions in Greek Tragedy', *American Journal of Philology*, 66, 377–97.

Slatkin, L. (1986): 'Oedipus at Colonus: Exile and Integration', in

Greek Tragedy and Political Theory (ed. J. P. Euben), Berkeley, Los Angeles and New York, 210–21.

Smith, J. L. (1973): *Melodrama*, London.

Stanford, W. B. (1968): *The Ulysses Theme*, Oxford.

Stanford, W. B. (1983): *Greek Tragedy and the Emotions: An Introductory Study*, London.

Stephens, J. C. (1995): 'The Wound of Philoctetes', *Mnemosyne*, 48, 153–68.

Stevens, P. T. (1978): 'Sophocles: *Electra*, Doom or Triumph?', *Greece and Rome*, 25, 111–20.

Sutton, Dana F. (1984): *The Lost Sophocles*, Lanham (Maryland).

Tanner, R. G. (1966): 'The Composition of the *Oedipus Coloneus*' in *For Service to Classical Studies* (ed. M. Kelly), Melbourne, 153–92.

Taplin, O. (1971): 'Significant Actions in Sophocles' *Philoctetes*', *Greek, Roman and Byzantine Studies*, 12, 25–44.

Taplin, O. (1977): *The Stagecraft of Aeschylus*, Oxford.

Taplin, O. (1983): 'Sophocles in his Theater', in *Sophocle* (ed. J. Romilly), Geneva, 155–83.

Taplin, O. (1987): 'The Mapping of Sophocles' *Philoctetes*', BICS 34, 69–77.

Taylor, D. (tr.) (1986): *Sophocles: The Theban Plays*, London.

Theatre Record (1996): Twickenham.

Trendall, A. D. (1989): *Red Figure Vases of South Italy and Sicily: A Handbook*, London.

Ussher, R. G. (ed.) (1990): *Sophocles' Philoctetes*, Warminster.

Vernant, J.-P., and Vidal-Naquet, P. (1981): *Tragedy and Myth in Ancient Greece*, Brighton.

Vickers, B. (1973): *Towards Greek Tragedy*, London and New York.

Waldock, A. J. A. (1951): *Sophocles the Dramatist*, Cambridge.

Wilson, E. (1941): *The Wound and the Bow*, Cambridge, Mass.

Walton, J. M. (1984): *The Greek Sense of Theatre*, London.

Walton, J. M. (1987): *Living Greek Theatre: A Handbook of Classical Performance and Modern Production*, Westport, Conn.

Webster, T. B. L. (1967): *The Tragedies of Euripides*, London.

Webster, T. B. L. (ed.) (1970): *Sophocles: Philoctetes*, Cambridge.

Whitman, C. (1951): *Sophocles: a Study in Heroic Humanism*, Cambridge, Mass.

Whitman, C. H. (1983 [1951]): 'Apocalypse: Oedipus at Colonus', in *Oxford Readings in Greek Tragedy*, (ed. E. Segal) Oxford, 229–43.

Wilamowitz, T. von (1917): *Die Dramatische Technik des Sophokles*, Berlin.

Wiles, D. (1997): *Tragedy in Athens: Performance Space and Theatrical Meaning*, Cambridge.

Wilson, E. (1941): *The Wound and the Bow*, London.

Winnington-Ingram, R. P. (1954): 'A Religious Function of Greek Tragedy', *Journal of Hellenic Studies*, 74, 16–24.

Winnington-Ingram, R. P. (1969): 'Tragica', *Bulletin of the Institute of Classical Studies*, 16, 44–54.

Woodhouse, W. J. (1912): 'The Scenic Arrangements of the Philoktetes of Sophocles', *Journal of Hellenic Studies*, 32, 239–49.

SOURCES FOR THE FRAGMENTS

Everyman	Loeb and Radt	Source
1	10c	P. Oxy., 3151.44
2	88	Stobaios, *Anthology*, 4.31.27
3	210	P. Oxy., 1175, 2081 (b)
4	354	Stobaios, *Anthology*, 4.31.28
5	373	Dionysios Halikarn. *Hist. of Early Rome*, 1.48.2
6	432	Achilleus, *Introduction to Aratos*, 1
7	555	Stobaios, *Anthology*, 4.17.3 + P. Oxy., 2077 fr.1
8	557	Stobaios, *Anthology*, 4.56.17
9	441a	P. Oxy., 37 (1971)
10	442	*New Classical Fragments* (1897)
11	444	*New Classical Fragments* (1897)
12	524	Stobaios, *Anthology*, 4.8.13
13	534	Macrobius, *Saturnalia*, 5.19.8
14	583	Stobaios, *Anthology*, 4.22.45
15	591	Stobaios, *Anthology*, 4.29.12
16	590	Stobaios, *Anthology*, 3.22.22
17	577	Stobaios, *Anthology*, 4.54.9
18	576	Stobaios, *Anthology*, 4.49.7
19	247	Orion, *Florilegium*, 5.10
20	255	Scholiast on Euripides, *Phoinissai*, 227
21	659	Aelian. *On the Nature of Animals*, 11.18
22	871	Plutarch, *Life of Demetrios*, 45.3
23	941	Stobaios, *Anthology*, 4.20.6
24	149	Stobaios *Anthology*, 4.20.46
25	269a	P. Oxy., 2369
26	269c	P. Oxy., 2369
27	1130	P. Oxy., 1063

Elektra

Orestes returns to Argos as a young man; he is accompanied by the Old Man who brought him up to avenge his father's death, and by Pylades, his friend since boyhood. They make a plan: the Old Man will tell Klytaimestra a story to convince her that Orestes is dead, and gain admission to the palace. Orestes and Pylades will go and make offerings on Agamemnon's grave.

They are just about to leave when a female voice is heard inside, crying out. Orestes thinks it might be Elektra and wants to stay, but the Old Man hurries him off.

Elektra comes out, and laments her slave-like existence. The Women of Argos enter, and ask her why she continues to mourn her father, and defy Aigisthos and Klytaimestra. She tells them how she is constantly wounded by Klytaimestra's celebrations of Agamemnon's death, and her sexual union with Aigisthos.

Chrysothemis appears; Klytaimestra has had an ominous dream, and has sent her to place offerings on Agamemnon's grave. Elektra persuades her to throw them away. Chrysothemis tells Elektra that Klytaimestra has resolved to have her buried alive, as soon as Aigisthos comes home. Elektra welcomes this news; it will put an end to her sufferings.

After Chrysothemis has gone, Klytaimestra appears. Mother and daughter engage in a sustained and at times vitriolic argument about the murder of Agamemnon. At the end, Klytaimestra approaches the altar of Apollo, and prays for her dream not to be fulfilled. She offers up a secret prayer – undoubtedly for the death of Orestes.

The Old Man now makes his appearance, and delivers a virtuoso account of a chariot-race at the Games at Delphi, in which Orestes' chariot crashed when he was on the verge of victory, and he was killed. Elektra is devastated; Klytaimestra is unable to conceal her relief. She invites the Old Man inside. Alone with the Women, Elektra pours out her grief.

Chrysothemis comes back, full of joy; she found offerings on

Agamemnon's grave, which she believes must be from Orestes. Elektra convinces her that Orestes is dead, and then tries to persuade Chrysothemis to help her in an attempt to murder Aigisthos. Chrysothemis refuses, and goes back into the palace.

Two young men now appear; one of them carries an urn. The audience recognizes Orestes and Pylades. When they tell her the urn contains Orestes' ashes, Elektra begs to be allowed to hold it, and pours out a moving elegy. Orestes gradually realizes who she is, and reveals himself to her. Elektra dances in ecstatic joy, while Orestes attempts to restrain her jubilation.

The Old Man comes out, and rebukes them. They have almost wrecked the plot by their loud rejoicing. He sends Orestes and Pylades into the house; Klytaimestra is alone, they will have no better opportunity.

Elektra prays briefly to Apollo, and goes inside. Soon she comes out again, to guard the doors in case Aigisthos comes; she waits passionately for the outcome. When Klytaimestra's first cry is heard, she screams, 'Strike twice as hard!'

Orestes comes out; but the Women see Aigisthos approaching. They hurry him back in. Aigisthos orders Elektra to open up the palace doors, so everyone can see the corpse of Orestes. She does so, and the two young men bring out a shrouded corpse. Orestes invites Aigisthos to remove the covering; he sees the bloodstained body of his wife, and recognizes who Orestes must be. He pleads to be allowed a few last words; but Elektra, insatiable in her vengeance, denies him. Orestes takes Aigisthos in to his death. Elektra remains, triumphant.

Philoktetes

In the tenth year of the Trojan War, Odysseus and Neoptolemos arrive in front of the cave of Philoktetes on the desert island of Lemnos. The Greeks abandóned him there on their way to Troy, because he had a festering wound from the bite of the snake which guarded the temple of Chryse, on an inhabited island nearby which they had visited.

The cave is empty, but shows signs of habitation. Odysseus tells Neoptolemos that he must deceive Philoktetes into believing that he is going to take him home; in reality the Greeks have been told by a prophet that only with Philoktetes' bow can they sack the city.

Odysseus leaves, and Neoptolemos discusses the situation with his Sailors. Then Philoktetes returns with his bow from foraging, and tells his story to Neoptolemos. Neoptolemos tells Philoktetes that Odysseus has deprived him of the armour of his dead father, Achilleus; he now hates the Greek leaders, and is on his way back home to mainland Greece. Philoktetes begs Neoptolemos to take him home. As they are about to leave, a 'Merchant' (in reality one of Odysseus' sailors in disguise) comes to tell Neoptolemos that the Greeks are pursuing him, and Odysseus is coming to take Philoktetes back to Troy. When he leaves, Philoktetes and Neoptolemos go into the cave to gather Philoktetes' few belongings.

When they come out, Philoktetes is attacked by stabbing pains in his foot. Neoptolemos looks after his bow for him, and Philoktetes, exhausted by his sufferings, falls asleep. When he wakes up, he praises Neoptolemos for his nobility. Now Neoptolemos, who feels pity for Philoktetes, hesitates to go through with the deception; he reveals his true mission. Odysseus enters with two sailors, who pinion Philoktetes. Philoktetes denounces him, but Odysseus states that they only need the bow, abandons Philoktetes, and takes Neoptolemos back to the ship.

Philoktetes is left for a short time with the Sailors. During their exchanges he bitterly bewails his fate; then he goes in.

Suddenly Neoptolemos returns, pursued by Odysseus. He has now decided to undo his former deceit, which he regards as shameful. Odysseus leaves, threatening to report his disobedience to the commanders.

Neoptolemos calls Philoktetes out, and tries to persuade him to come to Troy. When he fails, he gives the bow back to Philoktetes. Odysseus re-enters suddenly and tries to forbid this, but Philoktetes aims his bow at Odysseus. Neoptolemos prevents him from firing, but Odysseus runs away. Neoptolemos tries once more to persuade Philoktetes to come to Troy, telling him the whole of the prophecy given by the captive prophet Helenos. When Philoktetes remains obdurate, Neoptolemos agrees to take him home.

As they are about to leave, Herakles appears. He tells them that they must go to Troy, and will be amply rewarded. Philoktetes agrees, and after he has bidden farewell to Lemnos they leave.

Oidipous at Kolonos

Led by his daughter Antigone, the aged, blind beggar Oidipous arrives at Kolonos, a village near Athens. They rest in the mouth of a grove; but a local Scout arrives, and orders them to leave that place, since it is sacred to the terrifying goddesses of the underworld, the Eumenides. When he hears this Oidipous refuses to move; he has reached his resting-place. The Scout is unwilling to force him, so he leaves to tell the villagers about the stranger.

Oidipous pleads with the Eumenides to receive him. Then some Elders of Kolonos arrive, and insist that he move out of the sacred area before he speaks to them. Reluctantly, with Antigone's help, Oidipous comes forward and sits. When he tells the Elders who he is, they are horrified, and want to drive him away. Antigone pleads with them, and Oidipous argues powerfully that they are pledged to offer him sanctuary as a stranger, at least until their ruler comes.

Suddenly Ismene arrives on a pony. After the joyful reunion she brings Oidipous bad news from Thebes. Eteokles has deposed Polyneikes from the throne, and Polyneikes is raising a foreign army to attack his own homeland; meanwhile the Thebans have dispatched Kreon to bring Oidipous back – not to live or be buried in Thebes, but to the borders, since they have been told he will bring them prosperity. Oidipous furiously denounces his sons, and promises that he will be able to give the Athenians power, if they receive him.

Ismene is sent to perform an offering to the Eumenides for Oidipous, to make up for his earlier trespass in their grove. The Kolonians then question Oidipous about his parricide and incest.

Theseus arrives, and at once offers to help Oidipous. He offers to take Oidipous home with him; Oidipous declines, saying that he will master his opponents here. Theseus leaves.

Kreon arrives with some guards. He invites Oidipous to come home, on behalf of all the Thebans. Oidipous denounces him furiously. Kreon reveals that he has captured Ismene, and then, after a struggle, his guards abduct Antigone.

Theseus enters, summoned from a sacrifice by the noise. As soon as he hears what has happened, he despatches one of his servants to muster people to recapture the girls. He rebukes Kreon for presuming that the Athenians would allow him to do this. Kreon tries to defend his actions, but Oidipous delivers a masterly counter-plea. Then Theseus makes Kreon lead him to where the girls are held captive.

The Elders evoke the battle in song and dance; then Theseus returns with Oidipous' daughters. They are reunited. Theseus tells Oidipous something he has just learnrd: that a relative of Oidipous has taken refuge at the altar of Poseidon, and wants an audience with Oidipous. Oidipous guesses it is Polyneikes, and refuses. Antigone pleads passionately for her brother to be heard, and Oidipous relents.

The Elders sing a deeply pessimistic song. Then Polyneikes arrives. Oidipous refuses to answer him; prompted by Antigone, Polyneikes tries to plead for Oidipous to abandon his anger, and take Polyneikes' side in the coming dispute with Eteokles. Oidipous denounces him pitilessly, and disowns him. Antigone pleads with Polyneikes to abandon what he now knows will be a hopeless attack on Thebes, but he insists that he has no choice, and leaves her heartbroken.

As the Elders begin another song, thunder breaks out. Oidipous recognizes this as a sign that the gods are calling him, and asks for Theseus to be brought back. He comes, and Oidipous in his final speech prophesies great benefits to Athens for receiving him. Gifted in his last moments with supernatural vision, he walks unaided into the grove, leading Theseus, Antigone and Ismene.

Theseus' Attendant returns to tell the Elders what has happened. Oidipous made ritual preparations to die, then said farewell to his daughters. The god summoned him; Oidipous made Theseus promise to look after his daughters, and then sent the others away. When the Attendant looked round, Oidipous had disappeared, and Theseus stood shading his eyes, then knelt in prayer.

Antigone and Ismene return, grieving. For a few moments Antigone wants to go back to her father's grave; but Theseus, who now returns, reminds her that she cannot. So she begs him to send her and Ismene back to Thebes, to try to prevent their brothers from bloodshed. Theseus agrees.

Trackers

Apollo has lost his herd of cows; he offers a reward for finding them. Silenos enters and offers to search. He is followed by his sons, the satyrs; together they look around, and find cattle-prints – reversed, to put them off the scent. Then they hear a sound from underground, which scares them. Silenos ridicules them for cowardice – but then he hears the sound himself, and is just as terrified as they are. The satyrs leap up and down loudly to try to bring out whoever is causing it.

Kyllene enters from her cave, and rebukes them for making so much noise. She is frightened of them, but they reassure her, and she tells them about the sound. She is nursing the infant god Hermes, who is highly precocious, and has invented a musical instrument made from an upturned shell. The satyrs do not understand at first, but then she tells them he created the instrument by stretching ox-hide across the shell. At once the satyrs say Hermes must have stolen Apollo's cattle. Kyllene angrily denies this, and the papyrus ends during the heated argument that follows.

ACKNOWLEDGEMENTS

All three contributors would like to thank their respective universities – Newcastle, Exeter and Southern Queensland – for supporting grants towards the research on which these translations and notes are based.

The translation of *Elektra* was first performed in King Edward Park, Newcastle, Australia in March 1998. Michael Ewans would like to thank Shona Spence (co-director), Constance Colley (composer), Heidi Marosseky (choreographer) and the cast, in particular Alida Vanin (Elektra), Kellie Watson (Chrysothemis), Judy Knapp (Elektra), Garth Russell (Old Man) and Huw McKinnon (Orestes).

The translation of *Philoktetes* was workshopped in the Roborough Studio at the University of Exeter in September 1997. Graham Ley would like to thank Eileen Tapsell, Pauline Meredith-Yates, Jane Milling and Teresa Rodrigues for their participation. Roger Clegg also kindly participated in a later presentation of part of the work for the Centre for Mediterranean Studies at Exeter.

Gregory McCart would like to acknowledge the following people who made significant contributions to the production of *Oidipous at Kolonos* in 1989 and to the masked workshop in 1997, both in the Arts Theatre, University of Southern Queensland: Tony Smith, Angela Pearson, Samantha Rittson, Lynne Eisentrager, Linda Muirhead, Michelle Fornasier, Helen Thompson, Yvette Konig, Michael Gallaway, Joanne Knowles, David McCartney, Beth Armstrong, David Moran, Mark A. Ross, John Boyce, Dirk Hunter, William Dowd, Nicci Coggan, Brian Lucas, Bob Hartley, Helen Krsticevic, Joshua Parnell, Hannah Durack, Alexis Cornish, Nicholas Backstrom, Danni Bower, Tahnee McIlwraith, Sarah Kennedy, Michelle Coughran, Helen Shield, Hannah Waters, Victoria Taylor and Paul Dalglish.